Environmental Science

by
Judy Braus
and
Sara St. Antoine

PEARSON
AGS Globe

Shoreview, Minnesota

About the Authors

Judy Braus, M.A., is the Vice President of Education at the National Audubon Society. She has worked in the field of environmental education for more than 25 years. Before coming to Audubon, Ms. Braus was the Director of Education at World Wildlife Fund, the coordinator of environmental education at the U.S. Peace Corps, and the Director of School Programs at the National Wildlife Federation.

Sara St. Antoine, M.E.S., has written and edited books, articles, classroom activities, radio shows, and Web text for young people on a variety of environmental science topics. She has worked with the American Association for the Advancement of Science, Conservation International, the National Wildlife Federation, World Wildlife Fund, and many other organizations involved in environmental initiatives.

Photo credits for this textbook can be found on page 538.

The publisher wishes to thank the following consultants and educators for their helpful comments during the review process for *Environmental Science.* Their assistance has been invaluable.

Charmain Barker, Department Head of Science, St. Augustine Catholic High School, Markham, Ontario, Canada; **Monica Baker-Eady,** Science Teacher, Lakeside High School, Atlanta, GA; **Patricia M. Foy,** Science Department Co-Chair, Charter Oak High School, Covina, CA; **Kathie L. Haney,** English Teacher, Cass High School, Cartersville, GA; **Deborah Hartzell,** Lead Teacher for Special Education, Lakeside High School and Columbia High School, Stone Mountain, GA; **Shelly M. Holt,** Earth Science Teacher, Western High School, Las Vegas, NV; **Debby Houston,** Research Associate, Florida State University, Tallahassee, FL; **Carl C. Hughes,** Science Teacher, Gregory Portland Int., Portland, TX; **Denise M. King,** Instructional Coordinator, Leary School, Alexandria, VA; **Steven Lauterbach,** Science Teacher, Oldham County High School, Buckner, KY; **Susan Loving,** Transition Specialist, Utah State Office of Education, Salt Lake City, UT; **Jan Manchester,** Lead Resource, DCD, St. Paul Schools, St. Paul, MN; **Harriet F. Nicholson,** Science Teacher, West Bainbridge Middle School, Bainbridge, GA; **Katherine M. Pasquale,** Intervention Specialist, Euclid High School, Euclid, OH; **Keith Powell,** Transition Coordinator, School District of Greenville County, Greenville, SC; **Kristi Schertz,** Biology and Advanced Physical Science Teacher, Saugus High School, Saugus, CA; **Dr. Bradley F. Smith,** Dean, Huxley College of Environmental Studies, Western Washington University, Bellingham, WA; **Linda Kay Williams,** Teacher, Magnolia Elementary School, Magnolia, MS

Publisher's Project Staff

Vice President of Curriculum and Publisher: Sari Follansbee, Ed.D.; Director of Curriculum Development: Teri Mathews; Managing Editor: Julie Maas; Editor: Sarah Brandel; Development Assistant: Bev Johnson; Director of Creative Services: Nancy Condon; Senior Designer: Tony Perleberg; Production Artist: Marie Mattson; Senior Buyer: Mary Kaye Kuzma; Product Manager—Curriculum: Brian Holl

ISBN 0-7854-3944-7

12 13 14 V054 15 14

1-800-328-2560
www.agsglobe.com

Contents

How to Use This Book: A Study Guide

Welcome to *Environmental Science*. Science touches our lives every day, no matter where we are—at home, at school, or at work. This book covers the environmental sciences. It also focuses on skills that scientists use. These skills include asking questions, making predictions, designing experiments or procedures, collecting and organizing information, calculating data, making decisions, drawing conclusions, and exploring more options. You probably already use these skills every day. You ask questions to find answers. You gather information and organize it. You use that information to make all sorts of decisions. In this book, you will have opportunities to use and practice all of these skills.

As you read this book, notice how each lesson is organized. Information is presented in a straightforward manner. Tables, illustrations, and photos help clarify concepts. Read the information carefully. If you have trouble with a lesson, try reading it again.

It is important that you understand how to use this book before you start to read it. It is also important to know how to be successful in this course. Information in the first section of the book can help you achieve these things.

How to Study

These tips can help you study more effectively.

◆ Plan a regular time to study.

◆ Choose a desk in a quiet place where you will not be distracted. Find a spot that has good lighting.

◆ Gather all the books, pencils, paper, and other equipment you will need to complete your assignments.

◆ Decide on a goal. For example: "I will finishing reading and taking notes on Chapter 1, Lesson 1, by 8:00."

◆ Take a five- to ten-minute break every hour to stay alert.

◆ If you start to feel sleepy, take a break and get some fresh air.

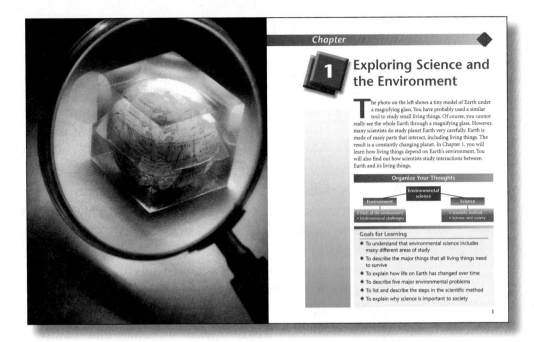

Before Beginning Each Chapter

◆ Read the chapter title and study the photograph.
   What does the photo tell you about the chapter title?

◆ Read the opening paragraph.

◆ Study the Goals for Learning. The Chapter Review and tests
   will ask questions related to these goals.

◆ Look at the Chapter Review. The questions cover the most
   important information in the chapter.

Note These Features

Notes
Points of interest or additional
information that relate to the lesson

Science Myth
Common science misconceptions
followed by the correct information

Science at Work
Careers in
environmental science

Science in Your Life

Examples of environmental science in real life with connections to technology and consumer choices

Science in Your Life

Achievements in Science

Historical scientific discoveries, events, and achievements

Achievements in Science

Technology and Society

Examples of science in real life with connections to environmental science, technology, and society

Technology and Society

Investigation

Experiments that give practice with chapter concepts

Discovery Investigation

Experiments with student input to give practice with chapter concepts

Environmental Issues in the World

Examples of real-life problems or issues affecting the United States or the world and their solutions

Map Skills

A map skills activity that relates to chapter content

Map Skills

Math Tip

Short math reminders or tips connected to a lesson

Math Tip

Express Lab

Short experiments that give practice with chapter concepts

Express Lab

Link to

A fact that connects environmental science to another subject area, such as biology, chemistry, physics, earth science, social studies, language arts, math, health, home and career, arts, and cultures

Link to ➤➤➤

Research and Write

Research a topic or question, then write about it

Research and Write

Before Beginning Each Lesson

Read the lesson title and restate it in the form of a question.

For example, write:
How does science work?

Look over the entire lesson, noting the following:

◆ bold words
◆ text organization
◆ notes in the margins
◆ photos and illustrations
◆ Lesson Review questions

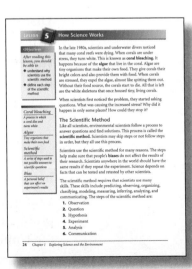

As You Read the Lesson

◆ Read the lesson title.
◆ Read the subheads and paragraphs that follow.
◆ Before moving on to the next lesson, see if you understand the concepts you read. If you do not understand the concepts, reread the lesson. If you are still unsure, ask for help.
◆ Practice what you have learned by completing the Lesson Review.

Bold type

Words seen for the first time will appear in bold type

Glossary

Words listed in this column are also found in the glossary

Using the Bold Words

Knowing the meaning of the boxed vocabulary words in the left column will help you understand what you read. These words are in **bold type** the first time they appear in the text. They are also defined in the paragraph.

> **Environmental science** is the study of how living things, including humans, interact with their environment.

All of the boxed vocabulary words are also defined in the **glossary.**

> **Environmental science** (en vī rən mən´ təl sī´ əns) the study of how living things, including humans, interact with their environment (p. 2)

Word Study Tips

◆ Start a vocabulary file with index cards to use for review.
◆ Write one term on the front of each card. Write the chapter number, lesson number, and definition on the back.
◆ You can use these cards as flash cards by yourself or with a study partner to test your knowledge.

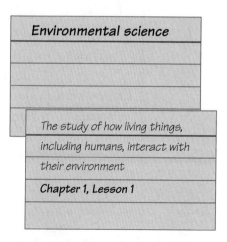

Environmental science

The study of how living things, including humans, interact with their environment

Chapter 1, Lesson 1

Taking Notes

It is helpful to take notes during class and as you read this book.

◆ Use headings to label the main sections of your notes. This organizes your notes.

◆ Summarize the important information, such as main ideas and supporting details.

◆ Do not try to write every word your teacher says or every detail in a chapter.

◆ Do not be concerned about writing in complete sentences. Use short phrases.

◆ Use your own words to describe, explain, or define things.

◆ Sometimes the best way to summarize information is with a graphic organizer. Use simple concept maps, charts, diagrams, and graphs in your notes.

◆ Try taking notes using a three-column format. Draw two lines to divide your notebook page into three columns. Make the middle column the widest. Use the first column to write headings or vocabulary words. Use the middle column to write the main information. Use the last column to draw diagrams, write shortcuts for remembering something, write questions about something you do not understand, record homework assignments, or for other purposes. An example of three-column note-taking is shown below.

◆ Right after taking notes, review them to fill in possible gaps.

◆ Study your notes to prepare for a test. Use a highlighter to mark what you need to know.

Vocabulary	Definition	Additional information
Environmental science	The study of how living things, including humans, interact with their environment	There are many areas of study that contribute to environmental science, such as earth science, biology, and anthropology.

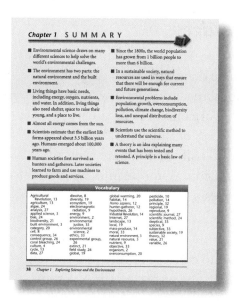

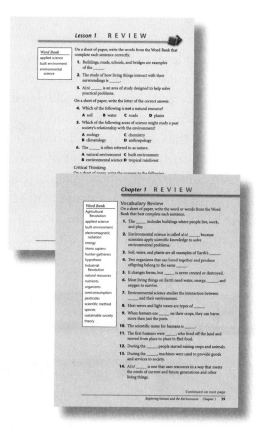

Using the Summaries

◆ Read each Chapter Summary to be sure you understand the chapter's main ideas.

◆ Make up a sample test of the items you think may be in the test. You may want to do this with a classmate and share your questions.

◆ Read the vocabulary words in the Vocabulary box.

◆ Review your notes and test yourself on vocabulary words and key ideas.

◆ Practice writing about some of the main ideas from the chapter.

Using the Reviews

◆ Answer the questions in each Lesson Review.

◆ In the Chapter Review, answer the questions about vocabulary under the Vocabulary Review. Study the words and definitions. Say them aloud to help you remember them.

◆ Answer the questions under the Concept Review and Critical Thinking sections of the Chapter Review.

◆ Read the Test-Taking Tip.

Preparing for Tests

◆ Complete the Lesson Reviews and Chapter Review(s).

◆ Complete the Investigations and Discovery Investigations.

◆ Review your answers to Lesson Reviews, Investigations, Discovery Investigations, and Chapter Reviews.

◆ Test yourself on vocabulary words and key ideas.

◆ Use graphic organizers as study tools.

Using Graphic Organizers

Graphic organizers are visual representations of information. Concept maps, flowcharts, circle diagrams, Venn diagrams, column charts, and graphs are some examples of graphic organizers. You can use graphic organizers to organize information, connect related ideas, or understand steps in a process. You can use them to classify or compare things, summarize complex topics, and communicate information. You can also use them to study for tests.

Concept Maps

A concept map consists of a main concept or idea and related concepts. Each concept—usually one or two words or a short phrase—is written in a circle or a box. The organization of concepts in the map shows how they are related.

In the concept map below, *Major threats to biodiversity* is the main concept. It appears on the first level of the map, shown by the color red. *Habitat loss and fragmentation, Introduced species, Pollution, Population growth,* and *Overconsumption* are all related to *Major threats to biodiversity.* They are part of the second level of the concept map, shown by the color blue. Each one is connected to *Major threats to biodiversity* with a straight line to show they are related. The main concept is the most general. The other concepts are more specific. You will find a concept map at the beginning of each chapter of the book. This simple concept map identifies the main concepts discussed in the chapter and shows how they are connected.

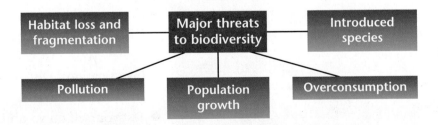

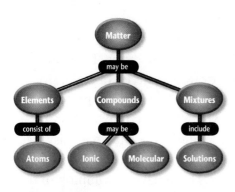

Prophase

The chromosomes in DNA have been copied and paired.

Metaphase

The nucleus disappears. Paired chromosomes line up in the center of the cell.

Anaphase

Paired chromosomes separate and move to opposite sides of the cell.

Telophase

Two nuclei form. The cell divides into two identical daughter cells.

Four Biomes

Tundra	Grassland	Tropical Rain Forest	Desert
cold, dry frozen below the surface	temperate humid	warm wet	very dry
lichens, low shrubs	grasses	palms, tree ferns, vines	cacti
polar bears, caribou, wolves	antelopes, bison, coyotes	bats, birds, monkeys	lizards, snakes, kangaroo rats

The graphic organizer at the left is another example of a concept map. This is an example from chemistry. To create this concept map, write the main concept. Draw a circle around it. Next, identify important ideas related to the main concept. Choose a word or a short phrase for each idea. Then add lines to link related ideas and concepts. The lines should not cross. You can label the lines to tell why the circles are linked.

Flowcharts

You can use a flowchart to diagram the steps in a process or procedure. The flowchart at the left shows the process of meiosis, an example from biology. Notice it is a vertical chart. Flowcharts can be vertical or horizontal. To make a flowchart, identify the steps to include. Write each step in the correct order, either in a vertical column or in a horizontal row. Draw a box around each step. Connect the boxes with arrows to show direction. You can label the arrows to tell what must happen to get from one step to the next.

Column Charts

You can use a chart or a table to record information and organize it into groups or categories for easy reference. A chart can be a table, a graph, or a diagram. A table is data systematically arranged in rows and columns. To create a column chart, determine the number of items, groups, or categories you want to use. Decide on the number of columns and rows. Draw a chart with that number of columns and rows. Write a heading at the top of each column. Fill in the chart and a title.

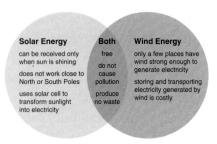

Venn Diagrams

A Venn diagram can help you compare and contrast two objects or processes. To create a Venn diagram, draw two circles of equal size that partially overlap. The circles represent the two things you want to compare. List the characteristics of one in the left circle. List the characteristics of the other in the right circle. List the characteristics both have in common in the area where the two circles intersect.

Circle Diagrams

A circle diagram shows a cycle that repeats. A circle diagram is similar to a flowchart except the last step is connected to the first step. To make a circle diagram, first identify the steps in the process or procedure. Then write the steps in a circle instead of a line. Use arrows to connect the steps. The circle diagram at the left shows the scientific method.

Graphs

You can use a graph to make comparisons and identify patterns among data. Graphs come in many forms such as line graphs, bar graphs, and circle graphs. To create a line or bar graph, draw two perpendicular axes. Label each axis to represent one variable. Add data. Each point or bar indicates a set of values for the two variables. Connect the points or compare the bars to see how the two variables relate. A circle graph shows the size of parts in a whole. To make one, draw a circle. Draw pie-shaped sections of the circle in proportion to the parts. For example, if lions make up one-quarter of a whole population, their section is one-quarter of the circle. Label each section and write its percentage of the whole.

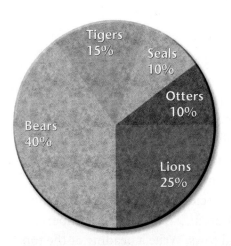

Safety Rules and Symbols

In this book, you will learn about environmental science through investigations and labs. During these activities, it is important to follow safety rules, procedures, and your teacher's directions. You can avoid accidents by following directions and handling materials carefully. Read and follow the safety rules below, and learn the safety symbols. To alert you to possible dangers, safety symbols will appear with each investigation or lab. Reread the rules below often and review what the symbols mean.

General Safety

◆ Read each Express Lab, Investigation, and Discovery Investigation before doing it. Review the materials list and follow the safety symbols and safety alerts.

◆ Ask questions if you do not understand something.

◆ Never perform an experiment, mix substances, or use equipment without permission.

◆ Keep your work area clean and free of clutter.

◆ Be aware of other students working near you.

◆ Do not play or run during a lab activity. Take your lab work seriously.

◆ Know where fire extinguishers, fire alarms, first aid kits, fire blankets, and the nearest telephone are located. Be familiar with the emergency exits and evacuation route from your room.

◆ Keep your hands away from your face.

◆ Immediately report all accidents to your teacher, including injuries, broken equipment, and spills.

Flame/Heat Safety

◆ Clear your work space of materials that could burn or melt.

◆ Before using a burner, know how to operate the burner and gas outlet.

◆ Be aware of all open flames. Never reach across a flame.

◆ Never leave a flame or operating hot plate unattended.

◆ Do not heat a liquid in a closed container.

◆ When heating a substance in a test tube or flask, point the container away from yourself and others.

◆ Do not touch hot glassware or the surface of an operating hot plate or lightbulb.

◆ In the event of a fire, tell your teacher and leave the room immediately.

◆ If your clothes catch on fire, stop, drop to the floor, and roll.

Electrical Safety

◆ Never use electrical equipment near water, on wet surfaces, or with wet hands or clothing.

◆ Alert your teacher to any frayed or damaged cords or plugs.

◆ Before plugging in equipment, be sure the power control is in the "off" position.

◆ Do not place electrical cords in walkways or let cords hang over table edges.

◆ Electricity flowing in wire causes the wire to become hot. Use caution.

◆ Turn off and unplug electrical equipment when you are finished using it.

Chemical Safety

◆ Check labels on containers to be sure you are using the right substance.

◆ Do not directly smell any substance. If you are instructed to smell a substance, gently fan your hand over the substance, waving its vapors toward you.

◆ When handling substances that give off gases or vapors, work in a fume hood or well-ventilated area.

◆ Do not taste any substance. Never eat, drink, or chew gum in your work area.

◆ Do not return unused substances to their original containers.

◆ Avoid skin contact with substances used in lab. Some can irritate or harm skin.

◆ If a substance spills on your clothing or skin, rinse the area immediately with plenty of water. Tell your teacher.

◆ When diluting an acid or base with water, always add the acid or base to the water. Do not add water to the acid or base.

◆ Wash your hands when you are finished with a lab activity.

Eye Protection

◆ Wear safety goggles at all times or as directed by your teacher.

◆ If a chemical gets in your eyes or on your face, use an eyewash station or flush your eyes and face with running water immediately. Tell your teacher.

Animal Safety

◆ Do not touch or approach an animal without your teacher's permission.

◆ Handle and care for animals only as your teacher directs.

◆ If you are bitten, stung, or scratched by an animal, tell your teacher.

◆ Do not expose animals to loud noises, overcrowding, or other stresses.

◆ Wash your hands after touching an animal.

Hand Safety

◆ Wear protective gloves when working with chemicals or solutions. Wear gloves for handling preserved specimens and plants.

◆ Do not touch an object that could be hot.

◆ Use tongs or utensils to hold a container over a heat source.

◆ Wash your hands when you are finished with a lab activity.

Plant Safety

◆ Do not place any part of a plant in your mouth. Do not rub plant parts or liquids on your skin.

◆ Wear gloves when handling plants or as directed by your teacher.

◆ Wash your hands after handling any part of a plant.

Glassware Safety

◆ Check glassware for cracks or chips before use. Give broken glassware to your teacher; do not use it.

◆ Keep glassware away from the edge of a work surface.

◆ If glassware breaks, tell your teacher. Dispose of glass according to your teacher's directions.

Clothing Protection

◆ Wear a lab coat or apron at all times or as directed by your teacher.

◆ Tie back long hair, remove dangling jewelry, and secure loose-fitting clothing.

◆ Do not wear open-toed shoes, sandals, or canvas shoes in the lab.

Sharp Object Safety

◆ Take care when using scissors, pins, scalpels, or pointed tools or blades.

◆ Cut objects on a suitable work surface. Cut away from yourself and others.

◆ If you cut yourself, notify your teacher.

Cleanup/Waste Disposal

◆ If a chemical spills, alert your teacher and ask for cleanup instructions.

◆ Follow your teacher's directions to dispose of and clean up substances.

◆ Turn off burners, water faucets, electrical equipment, and gas outlets.

◆ Clean equipment if needed and return it to its proper location.

◆ Clean your work area and work surface.

◆ Wash your hands when you are finished.

Exploring Science and the Environment

The photo on the left shows a tiny model of Earth under a magnifying glass. You have probably used a similar tool to study small living things. Of course, you cannot really see the whole Earth through a magnifying glass. However, many scientists do study planet Earth very carefully. Earth is made of many parts that interact, including living things. The result is a constantly changing planet. In Chapter 1, you will learn how living things depend on Earth's environment. You will also find out how scientists study interactions between Earth and its living things.

Organize Your Thoughts

Environmental science

Environment

- Parts of the environment
- Environmental challenges

Science

- Scientific method
- Science and society

Goals for Learning

- ◆ To understand that environmental science includes many different areas of study
- ◆ To describe the major things that all living things need to survive
- ◆ To explain how life on Earth has changed over time
- ◆ To describe five major environmental problems
- ◆ To list and describe the steps in the scientific method
- ◆ To explain why science is important to society

1

Think about some of the advances in science that have happened in the last decade. Scientists have developed new ways to track **organisms,** or living things, such as whales and butterflies. They have designed cars that run on both gas and electricity to save energy. They have even discovered new plants and animals that no one has ever seen before. These are just a few examples of what scientists are learning about the earth.

Science and the Environment

All of these discoveries show **environmental science** at work. Environmental science is the study of how living things, including humans, affect and interact with their **environment.** The environment is an organism's natural and human-made surroundings. Environmental scientists work to understand the environment in order to solve environmental problems. They also try to prevent new problems from happening in the future.

The environment has two major parts, the **natural environment** and the **built environment.** The natural environment is often called nature. The built environment includes what humans have made, such as roads and buildings. The environment also includes the relationships among living and nonliving things. Environmental scientists study both the natural environment and the built environment to understand how they affect each other.

Organism

A living thing; one of many different forms of life

Environmental science

The study of how living things, including humans, interact with their environment

Environment

An organism's natural and human-made surroundings

Link to ➤➤➤

Language Arts

The word *environment* comes from the French word *virer,* which means "to turn." The word *environ* means to encircle, or surround.

Environmental science builds on many other areas of science. These areas include biology, earth science, chemistry, physics, and the social sciences. It explores how people use **natural resources,** such as water, plants, coal, and soil. Unlike many other sciences, environmental science is an **applied science.** That means its goal is to provide practical solutions to environmental problems. Environmental scientists look for ways people can interact with the environment without harming it.

Natural environment

All living and nonliving things found in nature

Built environment

What humans have made, such as roads and buildings

Natural resource

A material found in nature that is useful to humans

Applied science

A field of study that uses scientific knowledge to solve practical problems

Map Skills: Physical Map of the United States

One way to learn about the physical environment is through maps. A physical map shows natural features, such as mountains and rivers. It also shows elevation, which is the height above sea level. The colors on the map represent different ranges of elevations. Notice that the units are in meters. Use the map and the legend to answer the questions below.

1. What natural resource is shown in blue?

2. What color represents the highest elevations?

3. Which mountains are taller: the Rocky Mountains or the Appalachian Mountains? How do you know?

4. What is the elevation range of most of the southeastern United States?

5. What body of water does the Mississippi River empty into?

There are many kinds of environmental scientists. They have different backgrounds and different points of view. Some are conservation biologists who study living things and how to protect the environment. Others are earth scientists who study air, water, and land systems. Some are social scientists, such as geographers and anthropologists. These scientists look at different **cultures,** among other things. Cultures are the languages, religions, customs, arts, and dress of a people. All of these things help determine how people relate to the environment.

Different areas of science within environmental science are listed in Table 1.1.1. They are followed by some real-life examples of environmental scientists.

Table 1.1.1 Different Areas of Science Within Environmental Science	
Area of science	Definition
Biology	The study of living things
Ecology	The study of interactions between living things and their environment
Zoology	The study of animals
Botany	The study of plants
Ethology	The study of animal behavior
Microbiology	The study of microorganisms
Earth science	The study of the planet over time
Geology	The study of the solid parts of the earth
Climatology	The study of climate
Hydrology	The study of the earth's water systems
Meteorology	The study of the earth's air and weather
Paleontology	The study of fossils and prehistoric life
Chemistry	The study of matter and how it changes
Biochemistry	The study of the chemistry of living things
Geochemistry	The study of the chemistry of the earth
Geography	The study of places, people, and cultures
Anthropology	The study of human cultures
Sociology	The study of human societies
Demography	The study of population dynamics

Link to >>>

Biology

Though Wangari Maathai is a biologist, she won the Nobel Prize for Peace. Nobel Prizes are also awarded for physics, chemistry, medicine, literature, and economic sciences.

Figure 1.1.2 *In 2004, Wangari Maathai received the Nobel Peace Prize for her work.*

Wangari Maathai is a biologist. She is the first African woman to win the Nobel Peace Prize. For more than 30 years, she has worked with communities throughout Africa to plant trees. The trees provide resources for communities and help prevent soil from washing away. Her work has also provided jobs for many poor people in Africa. She has shown firsthand how a healthy environment can improve the quality of life.

Jason Clay is an anthropologist who works to reduce the impact of food production. He is researching ways to grow shrimp and salmon that do not harm the environment. He is also working to protect the fish in oceans and rivers.

Eric Dinerstein is a conservation biologist. He is working to prevent rhinoceroses, tigers, pandas, and other large animals from disappearing. In the past 50 years, the numbers of these large animals have decreased. Dr. Dinerstein is trying to protect the land they need to survive.

Figure 1.1.3 *Eric Dinerstein traveled to China to study giant pandas and help preserve their habitat.*

All of these scientists ask questions and conduct research to learn how people and the environment interact. They share their findings with others, including other scientists and the public. Scientists build on what others have discovered before them to make new discoveries. In this textbook, you will read about how science helps people learn more about the environment.

Express Lab 1

Materials

◆ paper

◆ pencil

Procedure

1. Look around your classroom. Observe and write down the things that surround you.

2. Identify which natural resources might have been used to make these things.

3. List all the natural resources that you identified.

Analysis

1. Which natural resources are used to construct buildings?

2. Which natural resources on your list will be used up or eaten? One example is an apple someone brought for lunch.

3. Which natural resources do you share with other students? One example is the water in the drinking fountain.

Word Bank

applied science

built environment

environmental
science

On a sheet of paper, write the words from the Word Bank that complete each sentence correctly.

1. Buildings, roads, schools, and bridges are examples of the _____.

2. The study of how living things interact with their surroundings is _____.

3. A(n) _____ is an area of study designed to help solve practical problems.

On a sheet of paper, write the letter of the correct answer.

4. Which of the following is **not** a natural resource?

  A soil   **B** water   **C** roads   **D** plants

5. Which of the following areas of science might study a past society's relationship with the environment?

  A ecology   **C** chemistry
  B climatology   **D** anthropology

6. The _____ is often referred to as nature.

  A natural environment **C** built environment
  B environmental science **D** tropical rain forest

Critical Thinking

On a sheet of paper, write the answers to the following questions. Use complete sentences.

7. As an applied science, what is the main goal of environmental science?

8. Name a natural resource and one reason that it is important to people.

9. List three different areas of science that are part of environmental science. How do they each relate to the environment?

10. Give two examples of the types of work environmental scientists do.

Objectives

After reading this lesson, you should be able to

◆ list the things that organisms need to survive

◆ explain where most of Earth's energy comes from

◆ describe how water, oxygen, energy, and nutrients are important

Cell

The basic unit of life

Dissolve

To break apart

Research and Write

Use the Internet to research another planet. Write a report explaining how its conditions would make it difficult for humans to live there.

Earth is the only planet in the universe known to support life. It is home to gigantic blue whales and bumblebee bats the size of a dime. It is home to tiny mosses and giant redwood trees. All of these organisms need certain things to survive, including water, oxygen, and energy.

The Importance of Water

Sea jellies, often called jellyfish, have bodies that are more than 95 percent water. These creatures live in the ocean, pushed along by currents and wind. They have a bell-shaped body and thin, dangling arms. Unlike true fish, jellyfish do not have backbones. Instead, they are related to corals and sea anemones. Without water, sea jellies could not exist.

Water is important for people, too. Each person needs to drink about 1.9 liters of water every day to stay healthy. In the United States, each person uses about 379 liters each day. This water is used in many ways, such as for drinking, bathing, and flushing toilets. In other areas of the world, there is not enough water available. More than 2 billion people do not have enough water for drinking or cleaning.

Take a Breath

Another thing that organisms need to live is oxygen. When you take a breath, you bring oxygen and other gases into your lungs. The oxygen is picked up by chemicals in your blood. It travels to all of your body's more than seven trillion **cells.** Cells are the basic units of life that make up all living things. Oxygen helps the cells get the energy they need from food. When you breathe out, you give off carbon dioxide as a waste product.

Oxygen can **dissolve,** or break apart, in water. Many organisms that live in water, such as fish, use gills to absorb this oxygen. Gills are organs that allow fish to breathe underwater. Like people, fish need oxygen to get energy from food.

The Energy Connection

All life needs **energy,** which is the ability to do work. Without energy, organisms could not grow, move, think, or heal. Organisms also need energy to **reproduce,** which means to breed and produce offspring. Organisms get the energy they need from their environment. Where does the earth's energy come from? Almost all of Earth's energy comes from the sun. It travels from the sun in waves, such as heat waves and light waves. These waves are types of **electromagnetic radiation.**

When sunlight strikes the earth, most of it bounces back into space as heat waves. Enough makes it to Earth to provide the energy organisms need to live. Some sunlight is absorbed into the water and ground. Some is absorbed by animals in the form of heat. Plants use some to make food.

Energy is never created or destroyed. It just changes form as it moves through living systems. You will learn more about energy in Chapters 2 and 7.

What We Need to Survive

Living things need water, oxygen, energy, and **nutrients,** which are chemicals needed for growth. Each **species** has its own specific set of needs. A species is a group of organisms that can breed with each other. Each species also has different requirements for where it can live. Frogs and willow trees are examples of species that need a wet environment. Some species, such as parrots and orchids, thrive in environments that stay hot all year. Other species, such as tigers and eagles, need a lot of open space to find enough food. Some species, such as snow leopards and snowy owls, do best in cold, snowy weather.

Energy

The ability to do work; found in many different forms

Reproduce

To breed and produce offspring

Electromagnetic radiation

Radiation that is made up of electric and magnetic waves

Nutrient

A chemical organisms need to grow

Species

A group of organisms that can breed with each other

Liters, kilograms, and meters are metric measurements. Appendix A on pages 502 and 503 shows how these and other metric measurements can be converted to customary measurements, such as gallons, pounds, and feet.

Link to >>>

Physics

Electromagnetic radiation moves by electromagnetic waves. Electromagnetic waves are different than many other types of waves. They do not need a medium, such as air or water, to move through. This is how electromagnetic radiation can move through outer space.

Pesticide

Any chemical used to kill or control pests

Science Myth

Myth: Radiation is always dangerous.

Fact: Radiation is the release of energy. Some types of radiation, such as nuclear radiation, are strong enough to harm humans. Most types of radiation are harmless. For example, you are able to see thanks to light radiation. Heat radiation keeps you warm in winter. Radiation is also used to treat cancer.

Environmental scientists study what organisms need to survive. They explore how living things interact with their environment. They also study how organisms interact with the living and nonliving parts of their environment. For example, farmers use **pesticides** on their crops. These poisonous chemicals can harm more than just the pests. In many cases, pesticides have poisoned birds and even humans. It is difficult to know exactly how changes in the environment will affect different organisms. That is one of the reasons environmental science is so important.

★ ★

Achievements in Science

Silent Spring

At first, the development of the pesticide DDT was celebrated by the public. In fact, a Swiss chemist received a Nobel Prize in 1948 for his discovery of the pesticide properties of DDT. The chemical promised to greatly decrease the populations of disease-carrying mosquitoes. Few people imagined that this chemical could harm the environment.

A biologist named Rachel Carson became concerned about the effects of DDT and other pesticides. She and several other biologists noticed that birds were dying in areas where DDT was being used. These scientists eventually began their own research on the pesticide. In 1962, Carson published the research results in her book *Silent Spring*. The book revealed how DDT was killing many more organisms than anyone had thought. She also explained how destroying large numbers of animals would affect the environment.

Silent Spring made people realize that using chemicals could have negative effects on the environment. In response, the U.S. government investigated DDT and banned its use in 1972. This action helped start the environmental movement. You will learn more about DDT in Chapter 3.

Lesson 2   R E V I E W

Word Bank

energy

organisms

pesticides

On a sheet of paper, write the word from the Word Bank that completes each sentence correctly.

1. Birds, fish, and trees are all examples of _____.

2. Many different activities, such as dancing and talking, require _____.

3. Farmers use _____ to control unwanted organisms on crops.

Choose the term from Column B that best matches the phrase in Column A. Write the letter of your answer on a sheet of paper.

Column A	Column B
4. these organs help fish get oxygen from the water	**A** electromagnetic radiation
5. electric and magnetic waves	**B** gills
6. chemicals that help plants and animals grow	**C** nutrients

Critical Thinking

On a sheet of paper, write the answers to the following questions. Use complete sentences.

7. Describe what would happen if living things ran out of oxygen.

8. What is the relationship between oxygen and food in the human body?

9. Explain where most of Earth's energy comes from and how it travels to Earth.

10. Why is Earth the only planet in the universe with life?

A Short History of Life on Earth

Objectives

After reading this lesson, you should be able to

◆ discuss how life on Earth has changed over time

◆ describe the lifestyle of hunter-gatherers

◆ explain how the Agricultural Revolution changed the world

◆ describe how the Industrial Revolution has affected the environment and people's lives

Homo sapiens

The scientific name for modern humans

Hunter-gatherer

A person who hunts, gathers food, and moves from place to place to survive

Scientists estimate that the earliest life forms appeared on Earth about 3.5 billion years ago. It took another 3 billion years for human history to begin. Based on recent discoveries, scientists think the first humans emerged more than 100,000 years ago. These early humans, who were called Cro-Magnons, were the first *Homo sapiens.* They made and used tools, created art, and hunted to find food.

From the beginning, humans depended on the environment to survive. They also affected their environment in many ways, just as they do today. Over time, human societies have found three main ways to survive. One way was as hunters and gatherers. Another was by farming the land. A third was by using machines to produce what people need.

Living Off the Land

The first humans lived in small groups. As the seasons changed, they moved from one place to another to find food. They were called **hunter-gatherers.** This means they survived by hunting animals and collecting plants to eat. When one place ran out of food, they moved to another area.

People lived as hunter-gatherers for most of human history. Hunter-gatherers knew a lot about their environment. They knew which plants could be eaten and where to catch animals. This information was passed down from one generation to the next.

Many of the early hunter-gatherer tribes were very small in numbers. The effect they had on their environment was limited. As their numbers increased, so did their impact on the environment. Scientists believe that some tribes might have hunted certain species faster than they could reproduce. This could have helped to wipe out giant bison and other large animals.

Sidebar Definitions

Agriculture

Another word for farming

Agricultural Revolution

A period in history when hunter-gatherers learned to farm and raise animals for food

Cycle

A repeating pattern

Landscape

The characteristics of the land

Math Tip

To estimate means to make a close calculation of an amount.

Today, only a few hunter-gatherer societies exist. However, many people still hunt for food and collect berries and other plants.

The Agricultural Revolution

About 11,000 years ago, a huge change took place in hunter-gatherer societies. Some of the tribes started planting seeds and growing crops. They also started raising animals that could provide them with food and clothing. Instead of moving when the seasons changed, people started to stay in one place.

Agriculture, also called farming, allowed people to raise more food. Farming supports around 500 times more people than hunting and gathering, using the same space. With better crops and the invention of the plow, there was enough food to support even more people. The number of humans quickly increased.

Historians call this period of time the **Agricultural Revolution.** The Agricultural Revolution changed people's diets. People started eating grains, such as wheat, barley, rice, and corn. Beans were also an early crop. Many of the grains people eat today came from these early wild plants.

The Agricultural Revolution also changed how people lived. Farming communities began to thrive. People worked together to build cities. However, as more people lived in smaller areas, they faced new problems. For the first time, they had to deal with getting rid of waste and keeping water supplies clean. The Agricultural Revolution also started a **cycle,** or repeating pattern, of environmental change that continues today. Farming has completely changed the **landscape** in most parts of the world. Chapters 8, 10, and 11 will discuss more about the effects of farming on the environment.

The Industrial Revolution

In the mid-1700s, another revolution took place. This revolution was run by machines. Before that, agriculture and manufacturing were accomplished by people and animals. With the invention of the steam engine, factories could **mass-produce** clothes, building materials, and equipment. To mass-produce is to produce in large quantities using machines. Machines also helped make farming and transportation more efficient. With motorized farm equipment, more land could be farmed using fewer people.

The Industrial Revolution, as it was called, caused far-reaching changes. On the positive side, fewer people were needed to produce the goods that people needed. Goods are items people buy, like beds, cars, and televisions. These goods also cost less because many could be made at once. Many new inventions made people's lives easier. Electric lights, automobiles, and computers are just a few examples.

The Industrial Revolution also created new environmental problems. Large-scale farming led to a loss of **habitat,** or living space, for many wild animals. **Pollution** from farms and factories increased. Pollution is anything humans add to the environment that is harmful to living things. In cities, air and water pollution became serious problems. Machines required more and more energy and resources. All this has led to a number of environmental problems.

Mass-produce

To produce in large quantities using machines

Industrial Revolution

A period in history when humans started using machines to produce food and other products

Habitat

The place where an organism lives

Pollution

Anything added to the environment that is harmful to living things

Link to ➤➤➤

Social Studies

The steam engine is commonly believed to be the invention that started the Industrial Revolution. The first working steam engine was developed by Thomas Savery. This engine used coal to heat water into steam. The force of the steam moved the machine's different parts. This steam engine, the "Miner's Friend," was used to pump water out of coal mines.

One of the biggest side effects of the Industrial Revolution was the increase in population. Since the 1800s, the human population has climbed from 1 billion to more than 6 billion. This has put a number of different pressures on the environment. You will learn more about population problems and solutions in Chapter 6.

Environmental science focuses on solving the environmental problems that have increased since the Industrial Revolution. The timeline in Table 1.3.1 shows how much time has passed since the earth formed. By comparison, the changes humans have caused are recent events.

Table 1.3.1 Timeline	
4.6 billion years ago	Earth and planets formed
3.7 billion years ago	Earth's crust hardened
3.5 billion years ago	first life in the oceans; photosynthesis begins
650 million years ago	first multicellular organisms appear
500 million years ago	first land plants appear
250 million years ago	mass extinction (99 percent of life disappears)
245 million years ago	age of the reptiles begins
200 million years ago	continents drift apart
65 million years ago	age of dinosaurs ends with mass extinction (70 percent of life disappears)
3.5 million years ago	first prehumans appear
100,000 years ago	first *Homo sapiens* appear
10,000 years ago	first record of human history
4,500 years ago	pyramids were built
650 years ago	Black Death
270 years ago	beginning of the Industrial Revolution
230 years ago	birth of the United States

Lesson 3   R E V I E W

Word Bank

Agricultural
  Revolution

habitat

Industrial
  Revolution

On a sheet of paper, write the word or words from the Word Bank that complete each sentence correctly.

1. About 11,000 years ago, during the _____, people started planting crops and raising animals.

2. Many goods and services today are a result of the _____.

3. A(n) _____ is the place where an organism lives.

On a sheet of paper, write the letter of the correct answer.

4. Farming supports over 500 times as many people as _____.

   A hunting and gathering **C** searching and moving
   B industry   **D** raising cows

5. Which of the following did **not** happen as a result of the Industrial Revolution?

   A The world's population decreased.
   B The world's population increased.
   C More goods and services became available.
   D Pollution increased.

6. During the Agricultural Revolution, _____ provided power.

   A animals   **C** machines
   B computers   **D** plants

Critical Thinking

On a sheet of paper write the answers to the following questions. Use complete sentences.

7. How did hunter-gatherers survive when they ran out of food in one location?

8. Compare the Agricultural Revolution and the Industrial Revolution.

9. Describe one way that farmers affect the environment.

10. What are some ways the Industrial Revolution affected the environment?

Materials

- 460 pennies
- timeline on page 15
- 4 index cards
- marker

Understanding Earth's History

Earth was created approximately 4.6 billion years ago. However, life did not appear until over one billion years later. Even after the first basic signs of life, it took over three billion more years for the first pre-humans to appear. This lab will help you visualize periods of time during Earth's long history.

Procedure

1. Place the pennies in one large pile. These pennies represent Earth's history.

2. Mark the index cards A, B, C, and D.

3. Divide the pennies into two piles. Put 110 pennies in Pile A and 350 pennies in Pile B. Pile A represents the time period from Earth's creation to the appearance of life. Pile B represents the time period from the appearance of life to the present time.

4. Take 65 pennies from Pile B and place them in Pile C. This third pile shows how long organisms with more than one cell have existed.

5. Take one penny from Pile C and place it in Pile D. This represents the last 10 million years of Earth's history. The time period since *Homo sapiens* appeared would be one-hundredth of this penny.

Continued on next page

Cleanup/Disposal

Return the pennies to your teacher. Wash your hands with soap and warm water.

Analysis

1. How would you represent recorded human history using these pennies?

2. How would you represent the point when dinosaurs became extinct?

Conclusions

1. How many years does each penny represent?

2. What type of life has been present through most of Earth's history?

Explore Further

Create your own timeline by using a meter stick and a piece of tape. Measure out the amount of time for each event from left to right.

Table 1.3.1 Timeline	
4.6 billion years ago	Earth and planets formed
3.7 billion years ago	Earth's crust hardened
3.5 billion years ago	first life in the oceans; photosynthesis begins
650 million years ago	first multicellular organisms appear
500 million years ago	first land plants appear
250 million years ago	mass extinction (99 percent of life disappears)
245 million years ago	age of the reptiles begins
200 million years ago	continents drift apart
65 million years ago	age of dinosaurs ends with mass extinction (70 percent of life disappears)
3.5 million years ago	first prehumans appear
100,000 years ago	first *Homo sapiens* appear
10,000 years ago	first record of human history
4,500 years ago	pyramids were built
650 years ago	Black Death
270 years ago	beginning of the Industrial Revolution
230 years ago	birth of the United States

Objectives

After reading this lesson, you should be able to

◆ describe a sustainable society

◆ list five environmental challenges

◆ explain why values are important to solving environmental problems

Diversity

Variety

Ecosystem

All of the living and nonliving things found in an area

Sustainable society

A society where current needs are met while preserving natural resources and systems for future generations

Global

Affecting the entire world

Regional

Affecting part of the world, such as a country

Local

Affecting a certain place

For most of human history, people have believed the earth had unlimited natural resources. There were huge forests and oceans, as well as fertile soils where crops could grow. There was also an amazing **diversity,** or variety, of wildlife. Today, however, people are using many resources faster than they can be replaced. As a result, pollution and overuse are harming many of the world's **ecosystems.** An ecosystem is made up of all the living and nonliving things in an area. When part of an ecosystem is harmed, the entire system is affected.

Protecting ecosystems is only one goal of environmental science. One of the most important goals of environmental science is to create a more **sustainable society.** A society is a group of people who share a common culture. A sustainable society works to meet the needs of the current generation while preserving resources for future generations. The natural systems that support life on Earth are also protected. However, there are a number of environmental challenges that prevent societies from becoming sustainable.

Major Environmental Challenges

Some environmental challenges are **global** and affect the whole world, such as rising temperatures. Others are **regional,** such as an oil spill that affects the ocean near several countries. Environmental challenges can also be **local.** Examples would include chemicals polluting a local lake or trash littering a nearby park.

❋ ❋

Technology and Society

As technology advances, so does people's ability to deal with environmental challenges. For example, wireless technology makes it possible to monitor pollution levels around the world.

Global, regional, and local environmental problems can be put into several **categories,** or groups.

A Growing Population. More than 6.4 billion people live on Earth. Each year, that population increases by about 85 million people. That is like adding another New York City each month or another India every nine years. Experts estimate that by 2050, the population could grow to more than 9 billion. Both China and India already have populations of over a billion. This worldwide population increase has put pressure on the environment. You will learn more about population issues and how population affects the environment in Chapters 6 and 11.

Using Too Many Resources. Population growth is directly connected to **overconsumption.** When people use natural resources, they consume them. Overconsumption means using more resources than can be replaced.

Natural resources include everything people get from the environment that helps them survive. They include things such as water, air, wood, food, coal, oil, gas, minerals, and metals. Overconsumption will be discussed in more detail in Chapter 6.

Pollution and Climate Change. The use of resources produces waste. You have probably seen examples of this waste where you live. It can be waste in the air from burning trash. It can be chemicals spilled along the coast, or overflowing dumps. Sometimes people cannot see the waste, but its harmful effects show it is there. Poisonous chemicals in the water or air can cause health problems for humans and animals. Too much heat in the water can kill fish.

All of these are examples of pollution. Since the Industrial Revolution, the amount of pollution has increased along with the human population. Global temperatures are also rising, in a trend called **global warming.** Global warming is an increase in Earth's average surface temperature. This is partly caused by increased amounts of carbon dioxide escaping into the air. You will learn more about pollution in Chapters 8, 9, and 10.

Biodiversity

The variety of life on Earth; another name for nature

Extinct

When no members of a species remain

Value

What is important to a person

Loss of Biodiversity. Biodiversity is the variety of life on Earth. It includes all the living things on the planet, from trees to tigers. Loss of biodiversity is another serious problem. Many species have already become **extinct** in the past 200 years. When a species becomes extinct, it no longer exists.

Today, many species and ecosystems are in danger of becoming extinct. You will learn more about loss of biodiversity in Chapters 4 and 12.

Unequal Division of Resources. Earth's natural resources are not spread out evenly. Some countries have many natural resources and others have only a few. Some countries have much higher populations per square kilometer than other countries. All this adds up to some countries having more wealth per person than others.

People living in wealthier countries often use a greater share of Earth's natural resources. On average, people from the United States use more resources than people from any other country. These resources make life easier for people living in the United States. However, this unequal resource use can create hardships in other parts of the world. More than half of the people in the world do not have what they need to survive. They do not have enough food or clean drinking water. They also lack health care, jobs, and education. People in less wealthy countries often overuse local resources because they have no other choice. This puts more pressure on the environment.

The Role of Values

Scientific research can help people understand more about environmental problems and possible solutions. Research can help people understand the possible results of different decisions. However, scientists usually do not tell people what to do. They leave those decisions to society. Decisions about the environment often involve **values.** A value is what is important to a person. Values are shaped by people's view of the world.

Values play an important role in creating a sustainable global society. They help people decide what to do. How will a solution affect people's lives? Will it hurt some people more than others? Is the solution fair? How will it affect people in the short-term? How will it affect future generations? People making environmental decisions need to think about what is most important.

In this textbook, you will find out more about these major environmental challenges. You will learn what problems scientists have discovered and what creative solutions they have found. You will also see how you can help create a more sustainable world. Learning more about these issues and getting involved in your community are both important. In these ways, you can help protect the environment.

Science in Your Life

Consumer Choices: Reducing Global Warming

The amount of carbon dioxide released into the air increases each year. This trend began during the Industrial Revolution. Carbon dioxide is one possible cause of global warming, an increase in global temperatures. Many scientists are working to reduce the amount of carbon dioxide being released. You can also make choices at home that can help reduce global warming.

Carbon dioxide is released when fuels such as oil, coal, and gasoline are burned. The electricity that you use probably comes from a power plant that burns these fuels. You can lower the amount of carbon dioxide that goes into the air by using less electricity.

Appliances that use less energy can reduce your electricity use. Most products have labels that list their energy use. A flat-screen computer monitor uses less than half the electricity of a cathode ray tube monitor. Front-loading washing machines use less energy than those that load from the top. It also helps to keep size in mind. An oversized air conditioner or refrigerator wastes energy and money. By choosing an energy-efficient product, you can make a difference every day.

1. How does reducing the use of electricity help reduce global warming?

2. What are two ways you can reduce your use of electricity?

Based on standard U.S. Government tests
ENERGY USAGE
Refrigerator-Freezer   XYZ Corporation
With Automatic Defrost   Model ABC-33
With Side-Mounted Freezer   Capacity: 23 Cubic Feet
Without Through-the-Door Ice Service
Compare the Energy Use of this Refrigerator with Others before you Buy.

This Model Uses
776 kWh/year

Energy Use (kWh/year) range of similar models

Uses Least   Uses Most
Energy   Energy
709   823

kWh/year (kilowatt-hours per year) is a measure of energy (electricity) use. Your utility company uses it to compute your bill. Only models with 22.5 to 24.4 cubic feet and the above features are used in this scale.

Refrigerators using more energy cost more to operate. This model's estimated yearly operating cost is:
$78

Word Bank

extinct

overconsumption

values

On a sheet of paper, write the word from the Word Bank that completes each sentence correctly.

1. Using more resources than the environment can support is called _____.

2. A species that is _____ has no more living members.

3. People use their _____ to make decisions.

On a sheet of paper, write the letter of the answer that completes each sentence correctly.

4. The population of Earth grows by about _____ each year.

   A 8 million **B** 18 million **C** 80 million **D** 8 billion

5. Pollution problems in your neighborhood are _____ problems.

   A national **B** local **C** regional **D** global

6. _____ is any human-caused change in the environment that harms living things.

   A Energy **B** Pollution **C** Diversity **D** Farming

Critical Thinking

On a sheet of paper, write the answers to the following questions. Use complete sentences.

7. Describe how overconsumption harms the environment.

8. Explain how the division of resources can influence how different societies affect the environment.

9. What role do values have in finding solutions to environmental problems?

10. Explain why it is important for people to work for a sustainable society.

Lesson 5 · How Science Works

Objectives

After reading this lesson, you should be able to

◆ understand why scientists use the scientific method

◆ define each step of the scientific method

Coral bleaching

A process in which a coral dies and turns white

Algae

Tiny organisms that make their own food

Scientific method

A series of steps used to test possible answers to scientific questions

Bias

A personal belief that can affect an experiment's results

In the late 1980s, scientists and underwater divers noticed that many coral reefs were dying. When corals are under stress, they turn white. This is known as **coral bleaching.** It happens because of the **algae** that live in the coral. Algae are tiny organisms that make their own food. They give corals their bright colors and also provide them with food. When corals are stressed, they expel the algae, almost like spitting them out. Without their food source, the corals start to die. All that is left are the white skeletons that once housed tiny, living corals.

When scientists first noticed the problem, they started asking questions. What was causing the increased stress? Why did it happen in only some places? How could they stop it?

The Scientific Method

Like all scientists, environmental scientists follow a process to answer questions and find solutions. This process is called the **scientific method.** Scientists may skip steps or not follow steps in order, but they all use this process.

Scientists use the scientific method for many reasons. The steps help make sure that people's **biases** do not affect the results of their research. Scientists anywhere in the world should have the same results if they repeat the experiment. Science depends on facts that can be tested and retested by other scientists.

The scientific method requires that scientists use many skills. These skills include predicting, observing, organizing, classifying, modeling, measuring, inferring, analyzing, and communicating. The steps of the scientific method are:

1. Observation
2. Question
3. Hypothesis
4. Experiment
5. Analysis
6. Communication

Figure 1.5.1 shows the steps in the scientific method. You will learn about each step below.

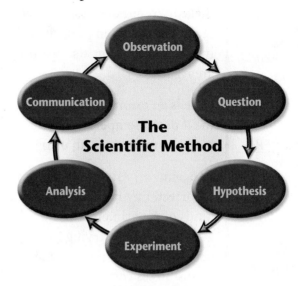

Figure 1.5.1 *The scientific method is a constant cycle scientists use to find answers to many questions.*

Observation. You perform this step without even being aware of it. Look at your classmates and all the objects in the room. The first step is simply looking at the world around you, watching life. While scientists are watching, or observing, they may see something they do not understand. If it interests them, they move to the next step of the scientific method.

In the example above, people observed that coral reefs were turning white. This led many scientists to start asking questions about why.

Question. When scientists see something they do not understand, they ask a question. Environmental scientists ask questions about how living things interact with their environment. They work to find answers to questions like, "Why are frogs and toads around the world disappearing?" or "Why are so many children in cities having trouble breathing?" Once environmental scientists have questions, they can begin looking for answers.

Hypothesis

An educated guess; also the third step of the scientific method (plural: hypotheses)

Field study

A study conducted in a natural environment

Control group

The group in an experiment that has no variable changed

Experimental group

Similar to the control group, except for the variable being tested

Variable

What is tested in an experiment

Hypothesis. A **hypothesis** is an educated guess. After asking a question, scientists try to guess the right answer. Scientists make their guesses based on what they already know. They also read what has been published about the topic or collect other information. Scientists then use experiments to see if they are right.

Here is an example. A scientist's hypothesis might be that corals die if ocean temperatures rise more than 1.5°C. This statement could be tested in a lab using corals from around the world.

Experiment. An experiment is used to test whether a hypothesis is correct. Environmental scientists perform many different kinds of experiments. The kind they perform depends on the question they are trying to answer. Scientists might conduct a survey, an experiment, or a **field study** to gather information. A field study is conducted in a natural environment.

Scientists design experiments to test possible answers to the question. There are two groups in a scientific experiment: a **control group** and an **experimental group.** In the control group, nothing is changed. The experimental group is similar to the control group, except for one part that is changed. That part is called the **variable.** Scientists control the variables in their experiments to get information they can use.

For example, an environmental scientist might want to test the hypothesis above. It states that corals will die if ocean temperatures rise more than 1.5°C. To test this hypothesis, the scientist would put corals of the same species into two groups of tanks. Both groups of tanks would be the same size and have the same amount of seawater in them. Then the scientist would raise the temperature of the water in one group of tanks 1.5°C. The water in the other group of tanks would stay the same temperature. The scientist would then record what happened to the corals.

Data

Information collected during experiments

Analysis

The process of making sense of an experiment's results; also the fifth step of the scientific method

Internet

A worldwide network of computers

Scientific journal

A science magazine

Scientists usually perform their experiments many times. They need to be sure that they get a similar answer every time. They also need to keep track of all the **data,** or information, they collect. Scientists use different tools to keep track of information, such as computers and calculators. They also use special equipment that is designed for their experiments. Math is also important in experiments. Scientists use math to gather data, analyze data, and communicate results.

Analysis. Analysis is the process of making sense of the results. Scientists look at the information and ask questions: Does the information collected support the hypothesis? Were there any unexpected results? If the results do not agree with the hypothesis, scientists may ask a different question. Sometimes the results answer the question but do not agree with the hypothesis. A hypothesis is an educated guess and can be wrong. The answers scientists find often lead to more questions. Say that scientists discovered that raising the water temperature 1.5°C caused corals to die. Then the scientists might ask what caused the ocean to become warmer.

Communication. After scientists have tested their hypothesis and checked their results, they share their results. Other scientists may be interested in the same questions. Scientists use the **Internet** to share their data. The Internet, a worldwide network of computers, helps scientists communicate.

Scientists also communicate their methods and results in **scientific journals.** Scientists publish their results in journals that are reviewed and read by other scientists. These journals help scientists keep up on advances in science. By publishing the results of their research, scientists contribute to what is known about a subject.

Sharing data not only allows others to know what one scientist did. It also allows scientists to review the data and check for mistakes. It also allows other scientists to suggest new questions or interpret the data in a different way. Environmental scientists share their data to help other scientists working on similar problems. When more scientists study a question, it increases the chances that it can be answered.

Field Research Technician

Field research technicians run experiments and gather data. They often set up experiments and make observations outside the laboratory. Field research technicians usually work with a professor or a chief researcher throughout the experiment.

Field research technicians must master many skills. Before setting up an experiment, the technician must often research past experiments and techniques. The technician writes up the experimental procedure and sets up the experiment. Often a field investigation takes several weeks, or even months, to run. During that time, the technician runs the experiment and collects data. Then the technician helps to analyze the data and write up the results.

It is common for a field research technician to have a bachelor's degree or be working toward one. However, many field research technicians have only an associate's degree.

Lesson 5   R E V I E W

Word Bank
control group
data
hypothesis

On a sheet of paper, write the word or words from the Word Bank that complete each sentence correctly.

1. The _____ in an experiment has no variable changed.

2. Forming and testing a _____ is an important part of the scientific method.

3. Information collected from experiments and research is called _____.

On a sheet of paper, write the letter of the correct answer.

4. Which of the following is not a step in the scientific method?

   A observation   **C** copying
   B experiment   **D** analysis

5. A scientist who is _____ experimental data checks to see if it supports the hypothesis.

   A communicating   **C** creating
   B questioning   **D** analyzing

6. Scientists publish their results in scientific journals and on the Internet to _____ their results.

   A question   **C** communicate
   B analyze   **D** check

Critical Thinking

On a sheet of paper, answer the following questions. Use complete sentences.

7. Describe how a scientist develops a hypothesis to test.

8. How does the control group help scientists test a hypothesis?

9. What should a scientist do when an experiment does not support a hypothesis?

10. Describe one method that a scientist could use to keep track of experimental data.

Materials

- ◆ safety goggles
- ◆ lab coat or apron
- ◆ 2 plastic cups
- ◆ 20 bean seeds
- ◆ potting soil
- ◆ water
- ◆ vinegar
- ◆ lamp
- ◆ paper towels
- ◆ eyedropper

Using the Scientific Method

Scientists answer questions and solve problems in an orderly way. They use a series of steps called the scientific method. How can you use the scientific method to answer questions? You will find out in this lab.

Plants need several things to grow well. Among them are light, space, and air. Also, plants require liquid, but the amount and type of liquid used can vary. How important are these variables for plant growth?

Procedure

1. In a small group, discuss the question in the second paragraph above. Then write a hypothesis that you can test with an experiment. Choose one variable to test: amount of light or water, or the type of liquid used.

2. Write a procedure for your experiment, including any Safety Alerts. Use materials from the Materials list. The experiment should take eight days to complete.

3. Be sure your experiment changes, or tests, only one variable at a time. Include a control group in which you do not change any variables.

4. Draw a data table to record your data for eight days.

5. Have your entire procedure approved by your teacher. Then carry out your experiment.

Cleanup/Disposal

Before leaving the lab, clean up your materials and wash your hands.

Analysis

1. What variable did you change in this experiment?

2. What changes did you see among the bean seeds after Day 4? What changes did you see after Day 8?

Conclusions

1. Was your hypothesis supported by the results of your investigation? Explain.

2. What problems did you have in performing the experiment? What part of the procedure would you change to be more successful?

Explore Further

In your group, discuss the variables of plant growth that you did not test. Pick one of these variables to investigate in the future. Write a procedure to carry out your investigation.

Objectives

After reading this lesson, you should be able to

◆ list three characteristics of a good scientist

◆ define theory and principle and give an example of each

◆ describe why environmental science is important to society

Theory

A well-tested hypothesis that explains many scientific observations

Principle

A basic law or truth

Science is important to human society. It provides information that helps people make better decisions. It helps people understand what effect decisions can have today, as well as in the future.

Theories and Principles

Scientific information is based on centuries of work. It is through sharing information that human knowledge grows. As new evidence is discovered, scientific ideas and **theories** may change. A theory is a well-tested hypothesis that explains many scientific observations. One example is the theory of gravity. With so much evidence, there is almost no chance that this theory could be proved wrong.

Scientists often add to the understanding of a theory. This may refine the theory, but not prove it wrong. Theories are believed to be some of the greatest achievements in science. They show how far humans have come in understanding how the world works.

After years of research, some theories can become **principles** of science. A principle is a statement of a basic law or truth. Principles about the laws of motion have been tested and retested. Scientists will tell you, though, that even principles may be questioned. Everything can change as humans learn more about the universe.

Science Myth

Myth: Theories are scientific ideas that are often proven wrong.

Fact: For an idea to become a theory, it must be tested and proven repeatedly. Scientific theories are supported by evidence and accepted by other scientists.

What Makes a Good Scientist?

Good science depends on good scientists. A good scientist may be described as curious, honest, patient, and creative.

Many people become scientists because they are curious about the world. They start by asking questions. They are also **skeptical,** meaning they do not just accept all that they read or hear. If something does not seem to make sense, they will question it. Being skeptical also means that scientists constantly question their own beliefs, research methods, and results. This questioning leads to more knowledge and understanding.

Ethics also are an important part of science. Ethics are a set of **moral** principles that help a person decide what is right. They are guidelines for how a scientist should act. Scientists must be honest about what they learn and what it means. Sometimes this is difficult. People who pay them or work with them might be expecting different results. For example, the results of an experiment might show that a scientist's hypothesis was wrong. The scientist might want to change his or her results to appear correct. A scientist must remember that honesty is critical to good science.

Patience is another characteristic of a successful scientist. Good science takes time. Most of the changes in people's understanding of the world happen in bits and pieces. Major changes in thinking have happened, but discovery is usually a slow process. Each new finding adds another piece of the puzzle of how the world works.

Scientists also try to be **objective** when making observations or collecting data from experiments. That means that they focus on facts and scientific measurements. They try not to include personal feelings or opinions, which are **subjective.** Although no one can be completely objective, scientists try not to be biased. They need to make sure their observations are accurate. Subjective observations are important in art, music, and literature, but not in science.

Skeptical

Questioning or doubting

Ethics

A set of moral principles

Moral

Helping to decide between right or wrong

Objective

Not influenced by personal feelings or opinions

Subjective

Influenced by personal feelings or opinions

Many universities and research labs have an ethicist working there. Ethicists make sure experiments do not harm people or the environment.

Environmental Science and Society

Environmental scientists often work on issues, or problems, that affect people and society. They might focus on issues such as:

◆ How to create new energy sources that do not pollute

◆ How to provide clean water to the billions of people who need it

◆ How to provide enough food for Earth's 6.4 billion people without harming the environment

◆ How to protect wild tigers or reintroduce wolves into Yellowstone National Park

Environmental scientists do not make decisions for society. Instead, they provide information to the members of governments, communities, and businesses who make decisions. This information can help people understand the possible **consequences,** or effects, of different actions. It can influence people's decisions about how they interact with the environment. In this way, environmental scientists can make a difference.

Figure 1.6.1 _Environmental scientists work to find solutions to problems that affect society._

Environmental Justice

Environmental justice

Dealing with environmental problems in a way that treats people equally

Environmental problems also create many social problems around the world. **Environmental justice** means dealing with environmental problems in a way that treats everyone equally.

Knowing the consequences of decisions helps to answer many questions:

- ◆ How will the solution affect people's daily lives?
- ◆ Will it hurt some people more than others?
- ◆ Is the solution ethical?
- ◆ How will it affect people in the short-term?
- ◆ How will it affect people in the future?

In a world that practices environmental justice, all of these questions would be equally important. Every environmental decision would try to balance the positive and negative effects for all groups. These groups include people from different countries and people who make different amounts of money. They also include people of different races and people with different backgrounds. The whole world benefits when everyone is treated equally.

❀ ❀

Technology and Society

The catalytic converter was invented in 1976. It reduces the amount of pollution that is released by an automobile's exhaust system. The converter changes engine exhaust into harmless materials. This helps reduce the amount of dangerous pollution in the air.

Lesson 6 **REVIEW**

On a sheet of paper, write the word from the Word Bank that completes each sentence correctly.

Word Bank
principle
subjective
theory

1. A _____ is a well-tested explanation that helps explain a variety of scientific observations.

2. A person's feelings or opinions help them make _____ judgments.

3. "Energy cannot be created or destroyed" is a _____ because it is a basic law of science.

On a sheet of paper, write the letter of the correct answer.

4. Which of the following characteristics does not help a scientist perform good science?

   A disorganized   **C** curious
   B honest   **D** skeptical

5. A scientific theory _____ be disproved.

   A cannot   **C** might
   B should not   **D** will always

6. _____ are moral principles that guide people's actions.

   A Objectives   **C** Ethics
   B Relationships   **D** Theories

Critical Thinking

On a sheet of paper, answer the following questions. Use complete sentences.

7. Which two characteristics of a good scientist do you think are most important? Explain your answer.

8. How are scientific principles and theories different?

9. Explain why it is important for scientists to be as objective as possible when doing research.

10. Give an example of how science works to improve society.

A Cleaner America

The U.S. Environmental Protection Agency (EPA) started in 1970. Its job is to protect human health and the environment. Before 1970, the U.S. government had few laws against releasing harmful chemicals into the environment. As a result, the EPA had to clean up a lot of pollution.

The EPA's headquarters are in Washington, D.C. Approximately 18,000 EPA employees work throughout the United States. Some workers research ways to reduce air and water pollution. Other workers run educational programs for communities and businesses. EPA workers also measure pollution coming from businesses and make sure they follow environmental laws.

The EPA runs several types of waste programs. These programs make sure that dangerous chemicals are disposed of properly. Chemicals such as paint thinner and gasoline can pollute water and soil. That means these chemicals must be disposed of differently than other wastes.

The EPA also gives money and direction to help repair areas damaged by pollution. Through this effort, polluted land becomes a place where people can live and work again.

1. What is the mission of the Environmental Protection Agency?

2. Describe two services that the EPA provides.

3. How might the environment be different if the EPA had not been established?

- Environmental science draws on many different sciences to help solve the world's environmental challenges.

- The environment has two parts: the natural environment and the built environment.

- Living things have basic needs, including energy, oxygen, nutrients, and water. In addition, living things also need shelter, space to raise their young, and a place to live.

- Almost all energy comes from the sun.

- Scientists estimate that the earliest life forms appeared about 3.5 billion years ago. Humans emerged about 100,000 years ago.

- Human societies first survived as hunters and gatherers. Later societies learned to farm and use machines to produce goods and services.

- Since the 1800s, the world population has grown from 1 billion people to more than 6 billion.

- In a sustainable society, natural resources are used in ways that ensure that there will be enough for current and future generations.

- Environmental problems include population growth, overconsumption, pollution, climate change, biodiversity loss, and unequal distribution of resources.

- Scientists use the scientific method to understand the universe.

- A theory is an idea explaining many events that has been tested and retested. A principle is a basic law of science.

Vocabulary

Agricultural Revolution, 13	dissolve, 8	global warming, 20	pesticide, 10
agriculture, 13	diversity, 19	habitat, 14	pollution, 14
algae, 24	ecosystem, 19	*Homo sapiens,* 12	principle, 32
analysis, 27	electromagnetic radiation, 9	hunter-gatherer, 12	regional, 19
applied science, 3	energy, 9	hypothesis, 26	reproduce, 9
bias, 24	environment, 2	Industrial Revolution, 14	scientific journal, 27
biodiversity, 21	environmental justice, 35	Internet, 27	scientific method, 24
built environment, 3	environmental science, 2	landscape, 13	skeptical, 33
category, 20	ethics, 33	local, 19	species, 9
cell, 8	experimental group, 26	mass-produce, 14	subjective, 33
consequence, 34	extinct, 21	moral, 33	sustainable society, 19
control group, 26	field study, 26	natural environment, 3	theory, 32
coral bleaching, 24	global, 19	natural resource, 3	value, 21
culture, 4		nutrient, 9	variable, 26
cycle, 13		objective, 33	
data, 27		organism, 2	
		overconsumption, 20	

Word Bank

Agricultural Revolution

applied science

built environment

electromagnetic radiation

energy

Homo sapiens

hunter-gatherers

hypothesis

Industrial Revolution

natural resources

nutrients

organisms

overconsumption

pesticides

scientific method

species

sustainable society

theory

Vocabulary Review

On a sheet of paper, write the word or words from the Word Bank that best complete each sentence.

1. The _____ includes buildings where people live, work, and play.

2. Environmental science is called a(n) _____ because scientists apply scientific knowledge to solve environmental problems.

3. Soil, water, and plants are all examples of Earth's _____.

4. Two organisms that can breed together and produce offspring belong to the same _____.

5. It changes forms, but _____ is never created or destroyed.

6. Most living things on Earth need water, energy, _____, and oxygen to survive.

7. Environmental science studies the interaction between _____ and their environment.

8. Heat waves and light waves are types of _____.

9. When farmers use _____ on their crops, they can harm more than just the pests.

10. The scientific name for humans is _____.

11. The first humans were _____, who lived off the land and moved from place to place to find food.

12. During the _____, people started raising crops and animals.

13. During the _____, machines were used to provide goods and services to society.

14. A(n) _____ is one that uses resources in a way that meets the needs of current and future generations and other living things.

Continued on next page

15. When people use more resources than the environment can support, it is called _____.

16. The _____ is a series of steps that scientists follow to test possible answers to scientific questions.

17. An educated guess in science is called a(n) _____.

18. A(n) _____ has been well-tested and makes sense of a great variety of scientific observations.

Concept Review
On a sheet of paper, write the letter of the answer that completes each sentence correctly.

19. The human population has grown from 1 billion in the 1800s to more than _____ billion today.

   A 2   **B** 6   **C** 9   **D** 12

20. A road is part of the _____.

   A applied environment   **C** organic environment
   B natural environment   **D** built environment

21. _____ are basic laws or truths that have been tested and retested over time.

   A Variables   **C** Values
   B Principles   **D** Hypotheses

22. The Industrial Revolution increased the amount of _____ released into the air.

   A carbon dioxide   **C** oxygen
   B ozone   **D** water vapor

Critical Thinking

On a sheet of paper, write the answers to the following questions. Use complete sentences.

23. List each step of the scientific method along with a short description of what happens during the step. Then explain why scientists use the scientific method.

24. Describe how people's lives changed as a result of the Industrial Revolution.

25. Describe five major environmental problems.

Test-Taking Tip When studying for a test, work with a partner to write your own test questions. Then answer each other's questions. Check your answers.

2

The Dynamic Earth

What does this photo show? Is it the strange surface of another planet? No. It shows the broken surface of a glowing lava flow. The hot, liquid lava underneath slowly cools and hardens into rock. Early in Earth's history, its surface probably looked much like this. Over time, the oceans and atmosphere formed, followed by living things. Today, Earth continues to change. In Chapter 2, you will learn about Earth's formation and how Earth has changed in the past. You will also learn about natural cycles that continue to shape Earth today.

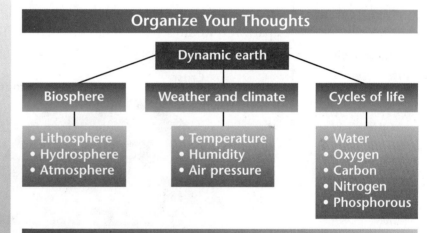

Organize Your Thoughts

Dynamic earth

Biosphere
- Lithosphere
- Hydrosphere
- Atmosphere

Weather and climate
- Temperature
- Humidity
- Air pressure

Cycles of life
- Water
- Oxygen
- Carbon
- Nitrogen
- Phosphorous

Goals for Learning

◆ To describe the origins of Earth

◆ To identify and describe Earth's three major parts

◆ To describe how water, oxygen, and other elements move through the environment

◆ To define weather and climate

◆ To explain the changes that happen on Earth over short and long time periods

The earth travels through the universe at about 107,000 kilometers per hour. Some people have compared it to a spaceship. Like a spaceship, the earth has everything it takes to keep people alive. You can think of it as a giant **life-support system.**

The Solid Earth

Earth was not always so welcoming to life, though. Scientists believe Earth formed when gas and rocky **debris** circling the sun crashed together. This crash happened 4.6 billion years ago. Energy heated the new planet to high temperatures. Earth was so hot, in fact, that its surface was **molten,** or liquid, rock.

Over time, the earth began to cool. Its molten surface hardened into solid rock. Yet its interior kept some of that original heat. Imagine that you could hold the earth in your hands and pull it apart. You would see that it has three layers. Together they look something like the inside of a hard-boiled egg.

Life-support system

A system that provides everything needed to stay alive

Debris

The remains of something that was destroyed

Molten

Melted into a liquid

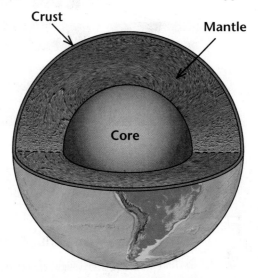

Figure 2.1.1 *The earth has three major layers.*

Crust

The outer layer of the earth

Continental crust

The lighter crust that makes up the continents

Oceanic crust

The heavier crust that makes up the ocean floor

Mantle

The layer of the earth that surrounds the core

Core

The hot center of the earth

Vent

An opening in the earth that lets out gases and other materials

Eruption

An explosion from beneath the earth's surface

Toxic

Poisonous

Meteorite

A piece of rock that hits the surface of a planet or moon after traveling through space

Comet

A ball of ice, rock, frozen gases, and dust that orbits the sun

The surface layer of rock and soil is called the **crust**. It is like the shell of the hard-boiled egg. Today, Earth's crust includes everything from high mountains to deep ocean floors. There are two types of crust. The lighter kind, called **continental crust,** makes up the continents. The heavier kind, the **oceanic crust,** forms the ocean floor.

Below the crust is a rock layer called the **mantle.** Think of it as the hard-boiled egg's white interior. Heat can make the mantle rock soften and move like warm butter.

The final section of the lithosphere is a round hot center called the **core.** It is a bit like an egg yolk that is not quite cooked. You will learn more about the layers of the earth in Lesson 2.

Gases and Liquids

Other major changes occurred as the earth cooled. Gases escaping from millions of volcanoes and **vents** formed a layer of air around the earth. As these gases cooled, some of them formed the oceans. Even so, this was not an environment where humans could have survived. Volcanic **eruptions,** or explosions from beneath the earth's surface, were violent. The air was **toxic,** or poisonous, to life. Rocky **meteorites** and icy **comets** battered Earth's surface. Damaging rays from the sun added to the dangerous conditions.

Link to ➤➤➤

Cultures

Mt. Vesuvius, Italy's most famous volcano, erupted explosively in A.D. 79. Ash and hot rocks from the volcano quickly buried the Roman town of Pompeii. As a result, everyday life in Pompeii was preserved for almost 1,700 years. Careful excavation of Pompeii has helped historians learn many details about ancient Roman culture.

Bacteria

The simplest organisms that carry out all basic life activities

Extremeophile

A tiny organism that lives in one of Earth's harshest environments

Extremeophiles live in the worst environments on Earth—for example, extreme heat, cold, or pressure. The ending *-phile* means "one that loves." These life forms thrive in conditions that no other living thing can stand.

The First Life on Earth

Still, life finally appeared on Earth. Tiny living things that resembled **bacteria** emerged in Earth's warm oceans. Bacteria are the simplest living things on Earth, made of a single cell. These early organisms could live without oxygen, a gas necessary for most life today. Some of them fed on chemicals in the environment. Others used hydrogen to make their own food.

Today, similar bacteria-like organisms known as **extremeophiles** still exist. They can thrive in Earth's harshest environments. They live in the hot springs of Yellowstone National Park. They are found around hot vents deep in the ocean and far underground. They live inside the stomachs of cows and other animals. These organisms help scientists understand how life existed early in Earth's history.

Figure 2.1.2 *These crabs and tube worms live in extreme conditions near an undersea vent. While they are not extremeophiles, they live in similar conditions.*

About 2 to 2.7 billion years ago, another form of life appeared on Earth: the first bacteria. These blue-green algae, or **cyanobacteria,** formed in shallow seas. With energy from the sun, they produced their own food. In the process, they released oxygen as a waste product. As the number of cyanobacteria grew, they began to change the chemicals in the air. Instead of toxic gases like methane and ammonia, the air became full of oxygen. This was air that animals could breathe.

Earth had changed from an unstable place too toxic for any life. It had solid surfaces, warm oceans, and oxygen-rich air. The planet now had the requirements for many different forms of life.

Express Lab 2

Materials
- safety goggles
- lab coat or apron
- cereal bowl
- pie pan
- small plastic or paper cup
- vinegar
- red food coloring
- spoon
- baking powder

Procedure
1. Put on safety goggles and a lab coat or apron.
2. Place the bowl upside down in the pie pan.
3. Fill the cup two-thirds full with vinegar. Add the food coloring and stir.
4. Set the cup on top of the bowl, and add a spoonful of baking powder.

Analysis
1. What caused the "lava" to flow out of this "volcano"?
2. What happened to the gases in the "lava" bubbles?

Lesson 1   R E V I E W

Word Bank

cyanobacteria

molten

toxic

On a sheet of paper, write the word from the Word Bank that completes each sentence correctly.

1. When Earth first formed, its surface was so hot it was liquid, or _____, rock.

2. For a long time, Earth's atmosphere was too _____, or poisonous, for life to exist.

3. The first life forms to use sunlight to make their own food were called _____.

On a sheet of paper, write the letter of the answer that completes each sentence correctly.

4. Earth is about 4.6 _____ years old.

   A thousand   **B** million   **C** billion   **D** trillion

5. Earth's atmosphere was formed by gases escaping from vents and _____.

   A meteors   **B** the sun   **C** earthquakes   **D** volcanoes

6. Earth's earliest life forms appeared in the _____.

   A oceans   **B** land   **C** air   **D** volcanoes

Critical Thinking

On a sheet of paper, write the answers to the following questions. Use complete sentences.

7. How did Earth form?

8. What were some of the reasons the young Earth could not support life?

9. What do today's extremeophiles have in common with Earth's earliest life forms?

10. How did cyanobacteria change Earth's air?

Lithosphere

The solid surface and interior of the earth

Hydrosphere

The water layer of the earth

Atmosphere

The layer of air surrounding the earth

Biosphere

The parts of the earth where living things are found

Plate tectonics

The study of plates and how they move

Continental drift

The theory of how continents move over time

Earth's life-support system still contains the three major parts described in Lesson 1. The **lithosphere** is Earth's solid surface and interior. The **hydrosphere** is the liquid layer where the earth's water is found. The **atmosphere** is the layer of air that surrounds the earth. Life can be found in parts of all three layers. Together, these living parts are known as Earth's **biosphere.**

The Lithosphere

The hard-boiled egg described in Lesson 1 was a model of the lithosphere. The crust, mantle, and core are all parts of the earth's solid surface and interior. Now imagine the hard-boiled egg from Lesson 1 with its shell cracked into pieces. That is what Earth's surface is like. Its crust and top layer of mantle are divided into huge, irregular slabs of rock called plates. Scientists believe Earth's surface cracked into plates millions of years ago. Ever since, they have been moving and shifting. This theory is called **plate tectonics.** Plate tectonics helps explain **continental drift,** a theory of how continents move over time. Today Earth has 12 major plates and hundreds of smaller ones.

The movement of Earth's plates has created many of its biggest land features. For example, mountains are formed when plates bump into each other and push upward. When two plates slide past each other, they can catch and create tension. Eventually, that tension is released and the ground shakes. This movement is known as an earthquake.

Volcanoes also form along the edges of plates. Some form where plates are moving apart and some form where plates collide. Either way, hot rock from inside the earth oozes or explodes from the volcano. It then flows onto the surrounding land or ocean floor.

Link to ➤➤➤

Earth Science

Plate movement caused the tsunamis of December 26, 2004. A resulting undersea earthquake raised a 1,500-km section of the seafloor 30 m. This change in the seafloor produced tsunami waves. The waves sped along the seafloor at 800 km/hr, the speed of a jet plane. In shallow waters near shore, the waves grew as high as a six-story building.

Plate movement has also created Earth's continents. Plates are not continents, however. They can carry both continental and oceanic crust. For example, most of North America and the Atlantic Ocean are part of the North American Plate. Hawaii and sections of Alaska, California, and the Pacific Ocean are part of the Pacific Plate.

Many people describe the lithosphere as the solid layer of the earth. Earthquakes, volcanoes, and plate movement itself are reminders that it is also an active layer.

Achievements in Science

Continental Drift and Plate Tectonics

The theory of plate tectonics is one of the most important theories in geology. This theory grew out of the study of maps of the world. Many people noticed that the outlines of several continents were similar. For example, North America, South America, Europe, and Africa appear to be able to fit together like pieces of a puzzle. Scientists began to wonder if these continents had once been joined together.

Many scientists studied the rocks and fossils of the continents. Others studied the features of the seafloor of the Atlantic Ocean. In 1915, German scientist Alfred Wegener proposed a hypothesis. He suggested that all the continents had been joined in one huge continent. This huge continent broke apart and the pieces moved slowly to their current locations. He is the one who first named these movements continental drift.

Scientists continued to add to Wegener's ideas. By 1960, scientists could explain continental drift, and many other parts of geology, with the theory of plate tectonics.

The Hydrosphere

The water layer of the earth is called the hydrosphere. It includes all the water on the earth's surface, such as oceans, ponds, lakes, and streams. The hydrosphere also includes water found underground, known as **groundwater.** It even includes the water in the air that forms clouds. Humans spend most of their time on solid ground. However, water covers about 70 percent of Earth's surface.

When scientists search for life on other planets, one of the things they look for is water. This is because water is necessary for life. Human bodies are between 50 and 75 percent water. A mushroom is more than 90 percent water. Water also helps **chemical reactions** take place. These reactions allow organisms to do things like grow, digest food, and sweat.

Water also helps the earth remain at temperatures that can support life. Water absorbs heat more slowly than a hard, rocky surface would. The oceans, which make up 97 percent of the hydrosphere, absorb most of this heat. They also release heat very slowly, and prevent the earth from getting too cold. That helps keep temperatures in a range that is neither too hot nor too cold.

Some planets may have ice, which is water that is frozen. Other planets may have water **vapor,** which is water in the form of a gas. So far, Earth seems to be the only planet in the universe with liquid water.

Groundwater

Water found underground

Chemical reaction

A chemical change

Vapor

Water or other materials in the form of a gas

❋❋❋❋❋❋❋❋❋❋❋❋❋❋❋❋❋❋❋❋❋❋❋❋❋❋❋❋❋❋❋

Technology and Society

Twenty-six countries around the Pacific Ocean participate in a tsunami warning system. The system consists of stations that detect earthquakes and gauges that measure changes in sea level. A center in Hawaii issues tsunami warnings. No such system existed for the Indian Ocean when tsunamis struck there in December 2004. Nations are currently working together to build a worldwide system.

The Atmosphere

The atmosphere is the ocean of air that surrounds Earth. It contains a mixture of gases, mostly nitrogen and oxygen, which organisms breathe. The atmosphere is made up of four layers. The layer where people can live and breathe is called the **troposphere.** It extends from Earth's surface up to a height of 16 km. The troposphere is also where weather happens. The next layer is the **stratosphere,** which is found between 16 and 50 kilometers up. The last layers are the **mesosphere** and **thermosphere.** See Figure 2.2.1 for their distances from the earth's surface. The farther a layer is from the earth's surface, the colder and thinner the air is.

The atmosphere also has other important duties. You can think of it as a protective blanket of air. During the day, the atmosphere allows some of the sun's rays to reach the earth. Living things stay warm but do not burn up. Without the atmosphere, daytime temperatures could reach more than 93°C. Then, during the night, the atmosphere holds warmth against the earth. Without the atmosphere, nighttime temperatures could drop to more than 173°C below zero.

Troposphere

The layer of the atmosphere people live and breathe in

Stratosphere

The layer of the atmosphere above the troposphere

Mesosphere

The layer of the atmosphere between the stratosphere and thermosphere

Thermosphere

The layer of the atmosphere above the mesosphere

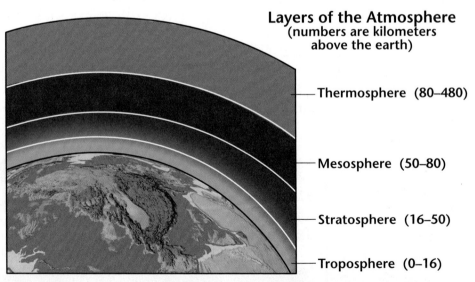

Layers of the Atmosphere
(numbers are kilometers above the earth)

Thermosphere (80–480)

Mesosphere (50–80)

Stratosphere (16–50)

Troposphere (0–16)

Figure 2.2.1 *The troposphere, stratosphere, mesosphere, and thermosphere are the four major layers of the atmosphere.*

Ozone layer

The layer of the atmosphere that protects Earth from harmful solar radiation

Ultraviolet radiation

High-energy radiation from the sun

The **ozone layer** is located in the stratosphere. It absorbs most of the harmful **ultraviolet radiation** produced by the sun. Ultraviolet radiation is a part of sunlight. Small amounts of ultraviolet radiation help your skin make vitamin D. Vitamin D helps your skin and eyesight, and supports bone and tooth growth. However, too much ultraviolet radiation can burn your skin and cause other damage, such as cancer.

In many ways, the atmosphere has helped make life on Earth possible. It shields the planet from many of the dangers that have existed since Earth first formed. Together with the lithosphere and the hydrosphere, it helps to make life on Earth possible.

Science in Your Life

Consumer Choices: Choosing Sun Protection

Exposing your skin to too much sun can be unhealthy. Most skin damage happens before the age of 18. While suntans fade, the skin damage does not. The effects of this damage will not be seen for many years.

Two kinds of ultraviolet rays damage the skin. UVA, which tans the skin, causes vision problems. It also causes allergic reactions to certain drugs and skin rashes. UVB, which burns the skin, causes skin cancer and ages the skin. By middle age, a person who has spent years in the sun may look much older.

Covering the skin with sunscreens or clothing is the best way to avoid sun damage. Choose a sunscreen that provides protection from both UVA and UVB. The higher the SPF, or sun protection factor, the better the protection. An SPF of 15 or greater is recommended. Clothing made of newer kinds of fabrics also provides sun

protection. The SPF is marked on the tags of these clothes. An SPF of 30 or greater is recommended for clothing.

1. How is a suntan different from the skin damage caused by the sun?

2. What is SPF? How is it rated?

3. How can you protect your skin from sun damage?

Lesson 2   R E V I E W

Word Bank

atmosphere

hydrosphere

lithosphere

On a sheet of paper, write the word from the Word Bank that completes each sentence correctly.

1. The _____ is the solid surface and interior of the earth.

2. The water layer of Earth is called its _____.

3. The blanket of air surrounding Earth is known as its _____.

On a sheet of paper, write the letter of the answer that completes each sentence correctly.

4. When two plates collide and push upward, they create a _____.

    A river   **B** mountain **C** earthquake **D** continent

5. _____ does not occur in the atmosphere.

    A Rainfall   **C** Plate movement

    B Breathing   **D** Airplane flight

6. Most of the water in the hydrosphere can be found in Earth's _____.

    A ice   **B** rivers   **C** air   **D** oceans

Critical Thinking

On a sheet of paper, write the answers to the following questions. Use complete sentences.

7. What is the biosphere? Identify its major parts.

8. Explain what makes the continents move across Earth's surface.

9. Describe two ways the hydrosphere affects your life.

10. Describe three things that might happen if the atmosphere did not exist.

Objectives

After reading this lesson, you should be able to

◆ describe the water cycle

◆ describe the oxygen and carbon cycles

◆ define element and name elements that are critical for life cycles

The Water Cycle

Every living thing on Earth needs water to survive. Think about how you feel when you do not take a drink for several hours. Notice how a house plant starts to droop if you do not water it enough. All plants and animals get their water through a process called the **water cycle.** The water cycle is the process of water moving from the air to the earth and back to the air. Figure 2.3.1 shows the parts of the water cycle.

Water can be found in oceans, lakes, and even puddles. When the sun warms this water, the water evaporates into the air. **Evaporation** is the process of heated water changing from a liquid into a gas. You have probably seen puddles dry up after a few hours in the sun. This is evaporation in action.

Water cycle

The movement of water between the atmosphere and the earth's surface

Evaporation

The process of water changing from liquid to vapor

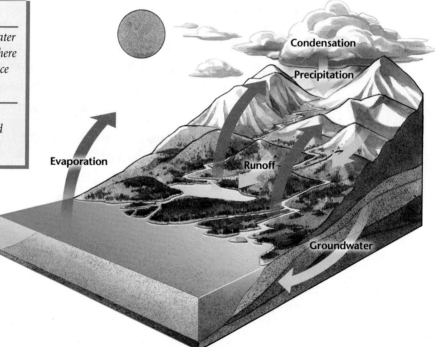

Figure 2.3.1 *The water cycle benefits all organisms on Earth.*

When water vapor rises up into the atmosphere, cooler temperatures cause it to form clouds. This process is called **condensation.** Have you ever noticed moisture forming on a cold glass on a hot day? That is condensation. The moisture was in the air all the time. The cold glass made some of it condense from vapor to liquid.

Eventually, clouds release water back to the earth as rain, hail, sleet, or snow. These are all different forms of **precipitation.** Some water falls directly into oceans, lakes, and streams. Some water soaks into the soil. At times, more water will fall than a surface can absorb. It forms puddles or flows over the ground into streams and other bodies of water.

Plants play a special part in the water cycle. When plants need water, they absorb it from the soil through their roots. The sun draws this water through the plants and out of their leaves. This process is called **transpiration.** The water then evaporates into the air.

One amazing thing about the water cycle is that it uses a set amount of water. For billions of years, there has been about the same amount of water on Earth. It is used over and over again. The water you drink today might once have been part of an ocean. It may also have been part of a mushroom or a dinosaur.

Even though water is used over again, people still need to take care of it. Less than 1 percent of Earth's water supply can be used for drinking. The rest is stored in the oceans or frozen in **polar ice caps.** Human activities can also drain and pollute available drinking water supplies. Chapter 8 will talk more about human impacts on the water supply.

Carbon and Oxygen Cycles

Elephant seals can dive down more than 1,500 meters in search of food. Yet they still swim back up to the ocean's surface about every 30 minutes. Like humans, elephant seals get oxygen from the air. Like all living things, elephant seals need oxygen to survive.

Oxygen is one of several **elements** that are necessary for life on Earth. Elements are matter that has only one kind of **atom.** All elements are made up of **particles,** or tiny pieces, called atoms. An atom is the smallest part of an element that still has the same qualities. They are the basic building blocks of matter. You will learn more about atoms in Chapter 7.

There are 92 elements found in nature, each made up of a different type of atom. The periodic table of elements in Appendix B, on pages 504 and 505, provides information about these and other human-made elements. Yet just six elements make up more than 95 percent of each living thing. These six elements are carbon, oxygen, hydrogen, nitrogen, phosphorus, and sulfur.

You take in oxygen from the air every time you breathe in. Every time you breathe out, or exhale, you release carbon dioxide. Carbon dioxide is a combination of carbon and oxygen. People cannot get oxygen from carbon dioxide, though. So why does the atmosphere not run out of oxygen?

Oxygen, like water, is used over and over again. Plants absorb carbon dioxide through tiny holes in their leaves called pores. They use this carbon dioxide to make sugars they use for food. In making these sugars, they release oxygen into the atmosphere. In this way, plants make it possible for every animal on Earth to live and breathe.

Carbon moves through the environment using the same process. The sugars plants make for food contain the carbon needed for their growth. Other organisms get the carbon they need by eating plants or the animals that eat plants. They then return this carbon to the atmosphere in the form of carbon dioxide.

Other Cycles

Ammonium

A form of nitrogen that some plants can absorb

Nitrate

A form of nitrogen that most plants can absorb

Nitrogen and phosphorous are two other elements that are very important to living things. Nitrogen helps living things grow. Most organisms cannot get nitrogen directly from the atmosphere. Instead they rely on bacteria in the soil to change nitrogen gas into **ammonium** or **nitrates.** Plants use their roots to absorb these forms of nitrogen from the soil. Humans and other animals get their nitrogen by eating plants or other animals. This nitrogen is then passed out again in animal waste. Tiny organisms that feed on the waste help return the nitrogen to the soil.

The element phosphorous also helps living things grow and develop. Phosphorous is one of the main elements in bones and teeth. It is also found in rocks on land and at the bottom of shallow oceans. Over time, water carries some of this phosphorous into the soil. Like nitrogen, phosphorous is absorbed from the soil by plants. It is then passed on to animals and returned to the soil in animal waste.

These and other cycles are taking place all the time. They are invisible processes that make life on Earth possible. Like the water cycle, though, they can be affected by human activities. In later chapters, you will learn more about impacts humans have on the cycles of oxygen, carbon, and other elements.

Lesson 3 REVIEW

Word Bank

elements

evaporation

transpiration

On a sheet of paper, write the word from the Word Bank that completes each sentence correctly.

1. When the sun heats water, some of that water goes into the air by _____.

2. Green plants release some water in a process called _____.

3. Carbon, oxygen, hydrogen, and nitrogen are all _____.

On a sheet of paper, write the letter of the answer that completes each sentence correctly.

4. The water _____ is the process of water moving from the air to Earth's surface and back into the air.

A supply   **B** gas   **C** cycle   **D** layer

5. When you breathe, you take in oxygen and let out _____.

A clouds   **C** condensation
B nitrogen   **D** carbon dioxide

6. Ammonium and nitrates are two forms of _____ that plants can absorb.

A nitrogen **B** hydrogen **C** oxygen   **D** carbon dioxide

Critical Thinking

On a sheet of paper, write the answers to the following questions. Use complete sentences.

7. Why does the water cycle not have a beginning or an end?

8. If you spill a cup of water on a sidewalk, what happens to it?

9. Why are plants so important to human life?

10. How do humans get the nitrogen they need to survive?

Materials

- safety goggles
- lab coat or apron
- 2-liter clear plastic bottle with cap
- water
- temperature strip
- matches

Cloud Formation

Cloud formation is a part of the water cycle. A cloud forms when water in the air condenses. The air always contains some water, but clouds are not always present. Why? In this lab, you will use a model to make a cloud. You will then observe the conditions that cause cloud formation.

Procedure

1. Put on safety goggles and a lab coat or apron.

2. Place a small amount of water and a temperature strip in the plastic bottle.

3. Strike a match, blow it out, and drop the match in the mouth of the bottle. **Safety Alert: Be careful when working with fire.**

4. To capture some of the smoke, put the cap on the bottle quickly and tighten it.

5. Squeeze the bottle and then release it.

6. Observe what happens and record what you see.

Cleanup/Disposal

Follow your teacher's instructions to clean up and dispose of your materials.

Analysis

1. What do you see inside the bottle when you squeeze it?

2. What do you see inside the bottle when you release it?

3. What does the smoke add to the bottle?

4. What happens to the temperature strip when you squeeze the bottle?

Conclusions

1. Under what conditions do clouds form?

2. What process is happening as the cloud forms?

Explore Further

Repeat the procedure with no smoke in the bottle. Try the procedure using a dry bottle with no water or smoke. Sit or stand on the capped bottle to apply more pressure. Observe how the temperature changes as you increase and decrease the pressure in the bottle.

Weather

The moment-by-moment conditions in the atmosphere

Climate

The average weather in a particular area

Equator

The imaginary line halfway between the North and South Poles

Tropics

Areas of land near the equator

Rotate

To turn in a circle

Axis

A straight line an object seems to rotate around

It is hard to ignore the weather. A sudden rainstorm can ruin a picnic or soak you on the way to school. A blizzard can dump piles of snow onto streets and sidewalks.

When people talk about **weather** they are referring to the moment-by-moment conditions of the atmosphere. Weather is the heat, cold, precipitation, wind, or fog affecting your day right now. **Climate,** on the other hand, is the long-term average of weather conditions in a particular place. For example, saying Phoenix, Arizona, has a dry climate does not mean it never rains there. It means that Phoenix tends to get much less rain than other places. As a student once said, "Climate tells you what kind of clothes to buy. Weather tells you what to wear."

Starting with the Sun

Where does weather come from? You can think of it as the result of several things coming together. These are the sun, the air, water (especially the ocean), and the solid earth.

The sun plays the largest role in weather production. The sun warms the ground, air, and water. It drives temperature changes, the water cycle, and air movement. Sunlight does not strike all parts of the world equally, however. The earth is tilted toward the sun. An imaginary line called the **equator** circles the earth halfway between the North and South Poles. The equator receives the most direct sunlight of any place on Earth. The sunlight at the poles is weaker. It comes in at an angle. That is one reason places on or near the equator are warmer than the poles. These areas are called the **tropics.**

The amount of sunlight each area receives depends on the time of day and the time of year. Every 24 hours, the earth **rotates** once on an imaginary **axis** that runs through the earth between the North and South Poles. This creates days and nights.

Revolve

To move in a circle around a point

Northern Hemisphere

The parts of the world north of the equator

Southern Hemisphere

The parts of the world south of the equator

Coriolis effect

The effect of Earth's spinning on the movement of air from the equator to the poles and back

At the same time, the earth **revolves** around the sun over the course of a year. For half the year, the **Northern Hemisphere** tilts toward the sun. That is when places north of the equator, such as Canada and Europe, experience spring and summer. It is also when the **Southern Hemisphere,** the southern half of the earth, experiences winter. When the Northern Hemisphere tilts away from the sun, the opposite is true. For example, December is a colder winter month in most of the United States. In Australia, December is a warm summer month.

Air on the Move

Air moves in response to temperature differences. You may have noticed strong winds when a hot summer day suddenly turned cool. Those winds were created by the big temperature difference between the hot and cool masses of air.

Air moves, or circulates, around the globe in a regular pattern. Sunlight at the equator creates warm air masses. When air is warmed, the atoms in it move faster and the air expands. This makes warm air less dense, or lighter, than cold air. These warm air masses rise, then move out toward the poles. There they are cooled, and then sink and move back toward the equator. The spinning of the earth makes this pattern more complicated. As Earth spins, it causes the winds to turn. This is known as the **Coriolis effect.**

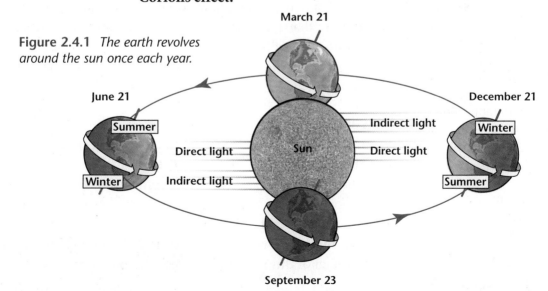

Figure 2.4.1 *The earth revolves around the sun once each year.*

The Coriolis effect results in three major patterns of global air movement, known as **prevailing winds.** These prevailing winds are called the trade winds, the prevailing westerlies, and the polar easterlies. See Figure 2.4.2 for a diagram of these winds.

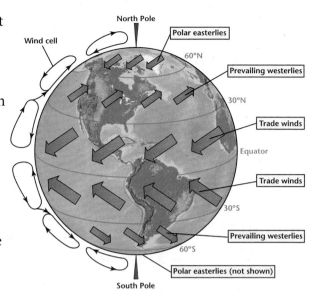

Figure 2.4.2 *Earth's prevailing winds include trade winds, prevailing westerlies, and polar easterlies.*

Prevailing winds do not cause every wind that forms. Many winds form because of local temperature differences. For example, differences in temperature between a cold ocean and warmer land create sea breezes. Huge temperature differences in the atmosphere create **jet streams.** Jet streams are powerful rivers of air that can cause big changes in the weather.

Air pressure also affects the weather. Air pressure is the weight of the atmosphere pushing down on the earth. Since cold air weighs more than warm air, its pressure is greater. Wind usually blows from areas of high pressure to areas of low pressure. This also means that wind usually blows from areas of cold air to areas of warm air.

Water Content

As air masses circulate around the globe, they carry moisture with them. The amount of moisture in the air is known as **humidity.** Where does this moisture come from? Evaporation draws moisture from the ocean and other bodies of water into the air. The warmer the air, the more moisture it can hold. As warm air masses move into colder regions, they cool. Then they release much of this moisture as precipitation.

Running into Land

The shape of the land can sometimes have an effect on weather, too. If moist air runs into a mountain, the air will rise over the mountain's peak. As it does, colder temperatures will make the moisture fall as precipitation. When the clouds descend, warm air will absorb a lot of the remaining moisture. Less rain will fall on the other side of the mountain.

Map Skills: Reading Weather Maps

Three conditions in the atmosphere act together to produce weather. They are air temperature, humidity, and air pressure. A weather map, such as the one here, shows these factors. Temperature can be written on the map with numbers or shown using color. Lines called isobars connect areas of similar air pressure. Humidity is higher in warm fronts and areas where precipitation is occurring.

Differences in air pressure cause air to move. In the Northern Hemisphere, cool air generally moves southward and warm air moves northward. Study the map and the legend, and answer the following questions about the weather.

1. Say you are given the air pressure at one point on an isobar. How do you know what the air pressure is at other points on that isobar?

2. This map shows the temperature at certain cities only. Is there enough information to find out the temperature between cities? Explain.

3. In which states is it raining?

4. What are the weather conditions near where you live?

Research and Write

Nearly every year, hurricanes cause billions of dollars of damage worldwide. Write a report about the causes of hurricanes and the effects of one famous hurricane. Be sure to discuss how the hurricane affected people as well as the environment.

Climate and Life

Humans have found ways to live in many different climates. They can keep their houses warm during cold winters. They can cool their living spaces during hot summers. They can even import water from wetter places. For most living things, though, climate determines where they can live. You would not see palm trees growing in Antarctica or polar bears living in a rain forest. That is because these living things cannot survive in those conditions. In general, average rainfall and average temperature have the biggest impacts on living things. You can learn more about weather by reading Appendix C, Weather and Weather Forecasting, on pages 506 and 507. In later chapters, you will learn more about the connections between climate and living things.

Science at Work

Meteorologist

Meteorologists study the weather. Some gather weather data and prepare weather maps. Others study climate data and look for trends. As a meteorologist gains experience, he or she prepares weather forecasts. Short-term weather forecasts are important in many ways. They help people plan what to wear. They help people prepare for heat, cold, and storms. Long-term weather forecasts help farmers and the military prepare for the future. They also help city officials predict power generation needs.

Most meteorologists work for the military or for government agencies such as the National Weather Service. Others work for TV or radio stations, newspapers, or airlines. Some work in research programs

at universities. Meteorologists spend at least some of their time working outdoors.

A meteorologist must have good math skills and computer skills. Most jobs in meteorology require either an associate's degree or a bachelor's degree. A master's or doctoral degree is required for working in research programs or weather forecasting.

Word Bank

climate

equator

prevailing winds

On a sheet of paper, write the word or words from the Word Bank that complete each sentence correctly.

1. The _____ of a place is its long-term average of weather conditions.

2. Halfway between the North and South Poles is an imaginary line called the _____.

3. The Coriolis effect creates global air patterns called _____.

On a sheet of paper, write the letter of the answer that completes each sentence correctly.

4. _____ is not an example of weather.

   A Hail   **B** Night   **C** Fog   **D** Cold

5. The part of the world south of the equator is called _____.

   A the Southern Hemisphere   **C** the Gulf Stream
   B Southland   **D** Europe

6. Warm climates usually have more _____ than cold climates.

   A clouds   **B** humidity   **C** hail   **D** wind

Critical Thinking

On a sheet of paper, write the answers to the following questions. Use complete sentences.

7. How is weather different from climate?

8. Why would you expect a city on the equator to have a warm climate?

9. Why should weather forecasters know about jet streams?

10. Why do you think the flat lands east of the Rocky Mountains have a dry climate?

After reading this lesson, you should be able to

◆ give examples of small and large environmental changes

◆ describe the impacts of ice ages and global warming

◆ give examples of the ways scientists learn about the past

Pangaea

The single landmass on Earth that began to break up 200 million years ago

Each of the previous lessons has described different kinds of environmental change. Some of these environmental changes are easy to notice. Earth's daily rotation is visible in the light changes from day to night. Weather changes are as obvious as a sudden blizzard or a bolt of lightning. Even the water cycle can be seen in action as evaporation, condensation, or cloud formation.

Some of the biggest environmental changes on Earth, however, have happened very slowly. Even today, many environmental changes are happening so slowly that humans may never notice them.

Changes in the Earth

Consider the lithosphere, for example. It took millions of years for Earth's surface to solidify into hard rock. Moving plates have kept this surface in a constant state of change. Over 200 million years ago, Earth had a single landmass scientists call **Pangaea.** Plate movement caused this landmass to break apart. It originally split into two major continents. Today there are seven continents.

Plate movement is continuing to change the position of oceans and continents. At this moment, the Pacific Ocean is getting smaller. Asia is being torn away from Africa. People cannot see these changes, but scientists can measure them with special instruments.

225 million years ago

180 million years ago

Present day

Figure 2.5.1 *The theory of continental drift states that major landmasses move over time.*

Ice age

A period of global cooling

Glacier

A thick mass of ice that covers a large area

Research and Write

Glaciers once covered most of North America. How do we know? They left behind many forms of evidence. Research the many different kinds of landforms that were made by glaciers. Make a poster or use a computer to present examples of these landforms to others.

Mountains are not as permanent as they appear to be, either. The Rocky Mountains began forming about 120 million years ago. Shock waves from two colliding plates cracked huge masses of rock and pushed them upward. After millions of years, the shock waves died down and the mountains stopped rising. Today, though, the Rocky Mountains are about half the height they once were. Bit by bit, wind, water, and ice have worn away the mountain rock.

Global climate, too, has gone through major changes in the last 4.6 billion years. For most of Earth's history, global temperatures were probably 5°C to 8°C warmer than they are today. Beginning about 925 million years ago, though, periods of severe cold began. These cold periods are known as **ice ages.** They produced enormous ice sheets, or **glaciers,** across much of the planet. The peak of the last ice age happened about 18,000 years ago. At that time, nearly one-third of Earth's land area was covered with ice. As these ice sheets advanced and retreated, they altered the landscape. The ice carved out hills and valleys, then melted to form lakes. During periods of global warming, parts of the polar ice caps melted and sea levels rose. Instead of being frozen under ice, many land areas were under seawater.

These climate changes greatly affected the types of organisms that could inhabit an area. The global warming that occurred between 120 and 90 million years ago made it possible for dinosaurs and coral reefs to thrive. The last ice age forced many northern animal species south to warmer regions.

Measuring Change

How do scientists know how Earth has changed in the last thousand, million, or even billion years? They do not find the answers in books. Earth has existed for much longer than people have been writing about it. If Earth's history were one day long, humans would not arrive until the last few seconds. Like a detective solving a mystery, scientists must piece together Earth's history by looking for clues.

Radioisotope

A radioactive element that helps scientists determine a rock's age

Sedimentary rock

A layered rock formed of sand, gravel, and mud

Fossil

The remains of animals and plants found in rocks

Origin

The source or beginning

Proxy data

Fossilized evidence that helps scientists understand past climate conditions

Math Tip

A graph can show the rate of change of a radioisotope. The graph's horizontal axis, or x-axis, shows the passage of time. The graph's vertical axis, or y-axis, shows the amount of isotope left.

Earth's rocks provide the best record of Earth's history. For one thing, they are very old. Since the early 1900s, scientists have had a special method for determining the age of rocks. They measure radioactive elements in the rocks called **radioisotopes.** Over time, radioisotopes change from one form of an element to another. Scientists can measure the amount of each form and determine the age of the rock. So far, the oldest rocks scientists have found are 4.3 billion years old.

Most rocks form in layers as bits of gravel, sand, and mud are pressed together. These rocks are called **sedimentary rocks.** Sedimentary rocks preserve a rough record of the past. Rock layers closest to the surface are usually the youngest. Each layer below is usually older than the one above.

Sometimes sedimentary materials trap living and dead animals and plants. These preserved traces or remains of plants and animals are called **fossils.** Fossils in Kansas reveal that it was once home to giant swimming and flying reptiles. In Kentucky, scientists have identified fossils of ancient caribou and musk ox. These fossils show that animals from the north lived in Kentucky during a past ice age.

The **origins,** or sources, of the rocks themselves also give clues to the past. Parts of the Guadalupe Mountains in western Texas are made of limestone formed from coral reefs. Scientists now know that a tropical sea flooded this region 250 million years ago.

The examples above show that rocks can provide fossil evidence of Earth's past climate. Scientists call this sort of information **proxy data.** It is not as precise as instrument readings. Yet it helps construct a picture of climate before these instruments were used.

Other sources of proxy data about Earth's past climate include trees, coral reefs, and ice.

◆ The rings in a cross section of a tree show the tree's yearly growth. The width of the rings can indicate warmer, wetter, colder, and drier years. An example can be seen in Figure 2.5.2.

◆ Corals are saltwater organisms that have existed on Earth for millions of years. Like trees, the growth rate of coral reefs reflects the climate conditions of the time.

◆ As glaciers form, bubbles of air are trapped in their layers. Scientists can analyze these bubbles to learn what the atmosphere was like when they formed.

Looking Ahead

Studying Earth's physical history teaches people many things. It shows when and how Earth's land, air, and water have changed. It also shows the impacts these changes have had on Earth's life forms.

In these ways, understanding Earth's past helps to imagine its future. What kinds of changes are likely to happen as part of Earth's natural cycles? How are human activities affecting natural processes, and what effects might they have? Humans emerged relatively recently on this planet. Yet, like wind, water, and volcanoes, humans are now a major force shaping life on Earth.

Figure 2.5.2 *Tree rings give scientists a better idea of past climate conditions.*

Lesson 5   R E V I E W

Word Bank

fossil

glacier

ice age

On a sheet of paper, write the word or words from the Word Bank that complete each sentence correctly.

1. A large sheet of ice is called a(n) _____.

2. A period of extreme cold is called a(n) _____.

3. A(n) _____ is a rock with the preserved imprint or remains of a plant or animal.

On a sheet of paper, write the letter of the answer that completes each sentence correctly.

4. Earth's continents were once part of a single landmass called _____.

  A Gaia   **B** Glacier   **C** Pangaea   **D** Earth

5. Measuring _____ elements in rocks helps scientists figure out their age.

  A loud   **B** radical   **C** radioactive **D** hyperactive

6. Scientists use evidence called _____ to learn about Earth's past climate.

  A radioisotopes   **C** recordings
  B proxy data   **D** rocks

Critical Thinking

On a sheet of paper, write the answers to the following questions. Use complete sentences.

7. What are some environmental changes you see every day?

8. Why is it difficult to notice mountains getting bigger or smaller?

9. Why do scientists study rocks to learn about the past?

10. What are some of the ways scientists learn about Earth's climate history?

DISCOVERY INVESTIGATION 2

Materials

- safety goggles
- lab coat or apron
- clear plastic box
- particle board
- dry sand
- metric ruler
- flour
- scoop

Mountain Building

Mountain building is a very slow process. However, the results are dramatic. In this lab, you will model one way that mountains form. Then you will develop a procedure for showing how mountains change over time.

Procedure

1. Put on safety goggles and a lab coat or apron.

2. Work with a partner. Place the particle board at one end of the box.

3. Pour enough sand in the box to make a layer about 2 cm thick. Use a ruler to level off the sand.

4. Spread a thin layer of flour across the sand.

5. Repeat Steps 3 and 4. Put a final layer of sand on top.

6. Hold the sides of the particle board tightly, and push it slowly to the center of the box.

7. In your lab group, discuss factors that could cause mountains to wear down. Write a hypothesis that could be tested with an experiment.

8. Write a procedure for your experiment. Include Safety Alerts.

9. Have your hypothesis, procedure, and Safety Alerts approved by your teacher. Then carry out your experiment. Record your results.

Continued on next page

Cleanup/Disposal

See your teacher for cleanup instructions.

Analysis

1. What happened to the layers of sand and flour as you pushed on the board? Make a drawing of the mountain you formed and the layers of "rock" inside it.

2. What happened when you tested your hypothesis?

Conclusions

1. What do the sand and flour layers represent?

2. Was your hypothesis supported by the results of your investigation? Explain why or why not.

Explore Further

Look for examples of the processes you modeled in the area where you live.

Changes in Sea Level

More than half of the world's population lives within 150 km of a coastline. Hurricanes and large sea waves called tsunamis are the most obvious risks of living near the coast. Both can cause serious property damage and loss of life. There is another danger for coastal cities and towns, however. The sea level is slowly and steadily rising.

The rise and fall of sea level is a natural cycle. The growing and shrinking of the Arctic ice caps and glaciers are the main causes of these changes. Over the past 18,000 years, sea level has varied by about 100 m. That is about the height of a 25-story building. The average elevation of New York City is less than 10 m above sea level.

Currently, sea level is rising worldwide at the rate of about 2 mm per year. That is about the width of your pencil tip. As global warming continues, however, that rate will increase. If the ice caps melted, sea level would rise rapidly. Scientists predict the melting of Greenland's ice cap alone would cause sea level to rise 6.5 m. A rise of 10 m would flood the homes of up to 25 percent of the U.S. population.

Communities along the coast have been battling seawater for a long time. Some built sea walls to protect buildings from the ocean.

Others raised the height of land by adding sand or soil. Building restrictions often prevent development in coastal areas that may flood. Any long-term solution must address global warming.

1. What causes the change in sea level?

2. What can people do to protect coastal cities from flooding by the ocean?

3. What are some other problems faced by cities built near the coast?

- Earth formed 4.6 billion years ago. The young Earth was not welcoming to life for almost a billion years.

- Cyanobacteria produced an oxygen-rich atmosphere.

- Earth has three parts called the lithosphere, the hydrosphere, and the atmosphere.

- Earth's lithosphere consists of a crust, mantle, and core.

- Earth's surface is broken into plates that move. These plates move the continents, form mountains, and cause volcanoes and earthquakes.

- The hydrosphere consists of water above ground, below ground, and in the air.

- Water in the hydrosphere helps maintain Earth's temperatures and allows living things to function.

- The water cycle is the process that moves water through the different parts of the biosphere.

- Oxygen and other elements move through the environment in continuous cycles.

- Weather is a word used to describe the moment-by-moment conditions in the air. Climate is the average weather in a particular place.

- Climate influences the kinds of plants and animals that can live in different places.

- Earth is still changing. People notice small changes, but most big changes happen too slowly for people to see.

- Scientists learn about Earth's past by studying rocks, tree rings, ice, and corals.

Vocabulary

air pressure, 64	cyanobacteria, 47	mantle, 45	radioisotope, 70
ammonium, 58	debris, 44	mesosphere, 52	revolve, 63
atmosphere, 49	element, 57	meteorite, 45	rotate, 62
atom, 57	equator, 62	molten, 44	sedimentary rock, 70
axis, 62	eruption, 45	nitrate, 58	Southern Hemisphere,
bacteria, 46	evaporation, 55	Northern Hemisphere, 63	63
biosphere, 49	extremeophile, 46	oceanic crust, 45	stratosphere, 52
chemical reaction, 51	fossil, 70	origin, 70	thermosphere, 52
climate, 62	glacier, 69	ozone layer, 53	toxic, 45
comet, 45	groundwater, 51	Pangaea, 68	transpiration, 56
condensation, 56	humidity, 64	particle, 57	tropics, 62
continental crust, 45	hydrosphere, 49	plate tectonics, 49	troposphere, 52
continental drift, 49	ice age, 69	polar ice cap, 56	ultraviolet radiation, 53
core, 45	jet stream, 64	precipitation, 56	vapor, 51
Coriolis effect, 63	life-support system, 44	prevailing winds, 64	vent, 45
crust, 45	lithosphere, 49	proxy data, 70	water cycle, 55
			weather, 62

Chapter 2 REVIEW

Word Bank

atmosphere

biosphere

climate

cyanobacteria

elements

evaporation

fossil

humidity

hydrosphere

ice ages

lithosphere

plate tectonics

precipitation

troposphere

vapor

water cycle

weather

Vocabulary Review

On a sheet of paper, write the word or words from the Word Bank that best complete each sentence.

1. Simple life forms called _____ filled Earth's early atmosphere with oxygen.

2. Earth's _____ includes its solid surface and interior.

3. All the water on Earth's surface makes up the _____.

4. The blanket of air that surrounds Earth is called the _____.

5. The areas on Earth where life is found are known together as the _____.

6. Someone who studies _____ studies Earth's plates and how they move.

7. The layer of the atmosphere where people live and breathe is called the _____.

8. When water is heated, it turns into a(n) _____, or gas.

9. The _____ is the continuous process of water moving from the ground to the atmosphere and back to the ground.

10. During _____, heated water turns into a gas.

11. The _____ are the basic building blocks of all the material on Earth.

12. Both rain and clear skies are examples of _____, the moment-by-moment condition of the atmosphere.

13. The average weather in a particular place is called _____.

14. A measurement of _____ tells you how much moisture is in the air.

15. Rain, sleet, snow, and hail are all examples of _____.

Continued on next page

16. Periods of extreme cold in Earth's history are known as _____.

17. A(n) _____ is the preserved remains of a life form that once lived.

Concept Review

On a sheet of paper, write the letter of the answer that completes each sentence correctly.

18. Earth's earliest life forms emerged in _____.

   A the air   **B** volcanoes   **C** soil   **D** the oceans

19. _____ can result from plate movement.

   A Meteors   **C** Earthquakes
   B Radiation   **D** Groundwater

20. Water forming on a bathroom mirror after a hot shower is an example of _____.

   A condensation   **C** transpiration
   B precipitation   **D** evaporation

21. Winds that blow from the equator out to the poles are turned because Earth _____.

   A tilts   **C** has an atmosphere
   B gets very hot   **D** spins

22. Changes in Earth's climate show in all of the following **except** _____.

   A radioactive dating   **C** coral growth
   B tree-ring growth   **D** fossil remains

Critical Thinking

On a sheet of paper, write the answers to the following questions. Use complete sentences.

23. In what ways has the atmosphere helped make Earth's environment more stable?

24. Some of the world's largest cities are located near plate boundaries. What are some possible dangers of living in those locations?

25. How can fossils of plants help scientists find out the climate of a particular place at a particular time?

Chapter

3

How Living Things Interact

The two tree swallows in the photo are clearly communicating. Communication between two members of a species is just one way that living things interact. Perhaps the birds are "arguing" over which one of them gets the nesting box. Providing nesting boxes is a way that humans, a different species, interact with tree swallows. In Chapter 3, you will learn about different ways that living things interact in ecosystems. You will also find out how these interactions can cause changes in ecosystems.

Organize Your Thoughts

Interactions

| Species interactions | Ecology | Energy |

- Competition
- Cooperation
- Symbiosis

- Biotic factors
- Abiotic factors

- Food chain
- Food web
- Energy pyramid

Goals for Learning

◆ To define ecology and identify biotic and abiotic factors

◆ To describe the parts of an ecosystem

◆ To identify the roles of producers, consumers, and decomposers

◆ To describe food chains and food webs

◆ To define niche, habitat, and predator-prey relationships

◆ To explain succession and how ecosystems change over time

In the 1960s, scientists noticed that the numbers of peregrine falcons were declining. After years of research, they discovered the cause: a chemical pesticide called DDT. DDT helped farmers by killing the insects that fed on their crops. However, when birds ate dead insects that contained DDT, the chemical poisoned them. When peregrine falcons ate these poisoned birds, they got even more DDT. DDT did not kill adult falcons. Instead, DDT caused females to lay eggs with weak shells. The weight of the parent crushed the eggs, and the chicks died.

Eventually, DDT was **banned,** and peregrine falcon populations started to recover. It turned out that DDT hurt many living things, including honeybees, bald eagles, and even people. It took scientists years to discover the connections between DDT and the problems it caused. This is because it is often difficult to know how different environmental factors interact.

The Study of Interactions

The word **ecology** was first used by a German biologist in 1869. It comes from two Greek words: *eco,* meaning house, and *logy,* meaning study. Ecology, then, is the study of interactions between organisms and their "house"—their environment. By studying these interactions, **ecologists** can learn what organisms need to survive. They can also learn how organisms affect other living things and the environment.

Ban

To forbid by law

Ecology

The interactions among living things and the nonliving things in their environment

Ecologist

A scientist who studies ecology

❁❁❁❁❁❁❁❁❁❁❁❁❁❁❁❁❁❁❁❁❁❁❁❁❁❁❁❁❁❁

Technology and Society

Scientists can reduce the need for pesticides by changing the DNA of some crops. For example, corn containing genes from the bacterium *Bacillus thuringiensis* has been created in a lab. This corn, called Bt corn, produces a chemical that kills a common pest called the corn borer.

| **Biotic factor** |
| A living part of the environment |

| **Abiotic factor** |
| A nonliving part of the environment |

| **Microorganism** |
| An organism too small to be seen without being magnified |

| **Domain** |
| The highest level of classification of living things |

| **Kingdom** |
| The second level of classification of living things |

Environmental science is one branch of ecology. Environmental scientists focus mostly on the interactions between humans and the environment. They study what humans need to survive and their effects on their environment.

For example, when farmers used DDT, they did not know it harmed more than pests. Scientific studies were needed to discover what other damage DDT was causing. That is one of the reasons environmental science is so important. It helps people learn how to prevent harmful changes to the environment.

Biotic Factors

Ecologists divide everything that makes up the earth into **biotic factors** and **abiotic factors.** The living parts of the earth are called the biotic factors. These include all the different types of life, such as animals, plants, fungi, and **microorganisms.** Microorganisms are living things too small to be seen without being magnified. The biotic factors in an environment also include the wastes organisms produce.

All of these types of living things are made up of cells. Some organisms, like yeast, are made up of a single cell. Other organisms, like humans, can be made up of trillions of cells.

Biotic factors are divided into a number of categories, beginning with **domains** and **kingdoms.** A domain is the highest level of classification, or organization, of living things. The three domains are Bacteria, Archaea, and Eukarya. A kingdom is the second level of classification. Most living things are included in Kingdom Protista, Kingdom Fungi, Kingdom Plantae, or Kingdom Animalia. These kingdoms are located within Domain Eukarya.

After being placed in a kingdom, organisms are organized by phylum (for animals) or division (for plants and fungi). The next levels of classification are class, order, family, genus, and species. Assigning organisms to these different levels of classification is one way to identify them. This is important for many types of scientific research.

Abiotic Factors

The nonliving parts of an ecosystem are called abiotic factors. These include rocks, **minerals,** water, air, sunlight, wind, and temperature. A mineral is an element or combination of elements found in the earth. These examples of abiotic factors contain no living material. Some abiotic factors were once alive, like leather or wood used for building. They still contain cells that are no longer alive.

Living things depend on the nonliving parts of the environment. They also depend on other living things. Every time you take a breath, you are interacting with the atmosphere. When you eat an apple, you are interacting with plants. When you take a drink, you are interacting with water systems. These are just a few examples of how biotic and abiotic factors are connected.

Express Lab 3

Materials
- aquarium with fish
- pencil
- paper

Procedure
1. Observe the fish tank in your classroom.
2. Draw all the parts of the fish's environment.
3. Label each item as biotic or abiotic.

Analysis
1. What are some ways that the abiotic factors in the fish's environment affect the biotic factors?
2. Describe the environment of the fish in terms of the atmosphere, lithosphere, and hydrosphere.

Lesson 1   R E V I E W

Word Bank

abiotic

biotic

ecology

On a sheet of paper, write the word from the Word Bank that completes each sentence correctly.

1. Environmental science is one branch of _____.

2. Leather and wood are _____ factors that have cells.

3. The different kinds of life are part of the _____ factors in an environment.

On a sheet of paper, write the letter of the answer that completes each sentence correctly.

4. _____ is a pesticide that caused serious problems for birds, insects, and people.

   A DDT   **B** Carbon   **C** Iron   **D** Chlorophyll

5. Examples of biotic factors in an ecosystem include _____.

   A butterflies and rocks   **C** squirrels and fungi
   B water and sunlight   **D** weather and grass

6. Examples of abiotic factors in an ecosystem include _____.

   A sunlight and minerals   **C** flowers and leaves
   B microorganisms and soil   **D** rocks and moss

Critical Thinking

On a sheet of paper, write the answers to the following questions. Use complete sentences.

7. Give an example of how organisms depend on nonliving parts of an ecosystem.

8. Explain how DDT caused the numbers of peregrine falcons to decline. What caused their numbers to rise again?

9. Describe how ecology can help protect organisms and their environments.

10. List three abiotic factors and three biotic factors in an ecosystem where you live.

Objectives

After reading this lesson, you should be able to

◆ name the five levels of interaction in the environment

◆ describe how energy is transferred between living things and ecosystems

◆ explain how ecosystems reuse matter

All biotic and abiotic factors are part of an ecosystem. They are connected by the flow of energy and nutrients in an ecosystem. A coral reef, desert, forest, grassland, and rotting log are all examples of ecosystems. Together, these and other ecosystems make up the biosphere, the parts of the earth where life can exist.

Levels of Interaction in the Environment

Figure 3.2.1 shows the different levels of interaction in the environment. At the bottom level are individual organisms, such as a single-celled fungus or lowland gorilla. Individuals of the same species often interact with each other. If you look around you outside, you might see examples of members of a species interacting. You might see two squirrels mating, raising their young, searching for food, or chasing away a threat. You might also see individuals from two different species interacting, such as a robin eating a worm. Individuals interact with their own species and other species in many different ways.

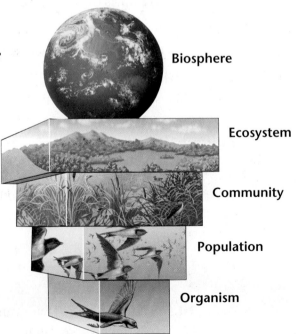

Figure 3.2.1 *There are five levels of interaction in the environment.*

Biosphere

Ecosystem

Community

Population

Organism

The next level of interaction is a **population.** A population includes all the members of one species living in the same area. Blue crabs in the Chesapeake Bay and black bears in Yellowstone National Park are examples of populations. Members of a population interact when they compete for food, water, and shelter. The males and females also interact when they mate.

The word *population* can refer to a group of species in general, such as a population of pandas. It can also refer to a number, such as the population of your city. The population of the world is the total number of people on all continents.

Map Skills: Population Density

When scientists study populations, they usually make maps that show the locations of the populations. The area of the map might cover an entire region or a small plot of land. Scientists often want to know the density of a population. Population density measures how many individuals are in a unit of area, such as a square meter. The formula for density is:

density = number of individuals/area.

The map to the left shows populations of three different kinds of wildflowers. Use the map to answer the questions.

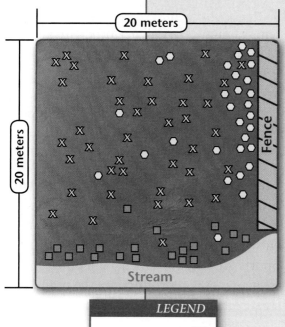

1. Which type of flower do you think favors a wet ground environment?

2. Describe how clover and dandelions differ in how they are grouped in this area.

3. What is the total area shown on this map?

4. Which type of flower in this area has the largest population?

5. What is the density of each population of wildflowers?

LEGEND

Violet ▪

Dandelion ⬡

Clover ✕

The third level of interaction in the environment is a **community.** A community is a group of different populations that live and interact in the same area. A forest community includes the trees, birds, squirrels, and other organisms that live in the forest. A beach community might include shorebirds, dune crickets, ghost crabs, and beach grass.

The next level of interaction is an ecosystem. An ecosystem is made up of living and nonliving things and how they interact. A beach ecosystem would not only include living things, but also the sand, the tides, and sunlight.

The highest level of interaction is the biosphere, which is made up of all of Earth's ecosystems. It is the part of earth where organisms can live and the organisms that live there. Even though it includes a lot, the biosphere is only a small part of the earth. That is why it is so important to protect it.

Energy Transfer

Though each ecosystem is unique, they all perform two important processes. First of all, they transfer energy from one organism to another. Second, they deal with **matter.** Matter is anything that has mass and takes up space. Ecosystems work to move different types of matter through different cycles. These two processes link living and nonliving things.

Sunlight is the source of energy for almost all ecosystems on Earth. Energy is transferred from the sun to green plants, then to animals. In a few ecosystems, energy is transferred from chemicals to bacteria, then to animals. Energy from chemicals, in the form of nutrients, and energy from the sun fuel living cells. This energy supports growth, movement, and other activities. One of these activities is **reproduction,** the process by which living things create offspring.

Cellular respiration

The process cells use to release energy from food

Molecule

The smallest part of a substance that has the same properties of the substance

Recycle

To reuse the same matter in different forms

Living things get the energy they need for these activities through a process called **cellular respiration**. Every time one organism eats another organism, a transfer of energy takes place. Think about the last meal you ate. Once the food entered your stomach, it was broken into smaller bits called **molecules.** The blood carried these molecules to your cells along with oxygen and water. Inside your cells, the food molecules were combined with oxygen. In this chemical reaction, carbon dioxide, water, and energy were released. This process happens every time you eat. It gives you the energy you need to live. Every time you run, walk, read, dance, or think, you use energy.

Nutrient Recycling

The second job of ecosystems of every size is to cycle matter. In Chapter 2, you learned about the cycles of different elements. Ecosystems can use carbon, oxygen, and other elements many times. These elements are being **recycled.** To recycle means to use the same matter in different forms. Ecosystems can also help the elements move from one form to another. The carbon in a tree can be recycled to become the carbon in a human body. The oxygen a fish absorbed could become the oxygen needed for a fire to burn.

Energy transfer and nutrient recycling are linked processes. Without energy, the different elements could not be recycled into new forms. Without elements like carbon, oxygen, and hydrogen, energy could not be stored or released from food. Cycling matter and transferring energy depend on the interaction of biotic and abiotic factors.

Link to ➤➤➤

Chemistry

The chemical reaction for cellular respiration is:
oxygen + glucose → energy + carbon dioxide + water.

Lesson 2   R E V I E W

Word Bank

cellular respiration
community
ecosystem
sun

On a sheet of paper, write the word or words from the Word Bank that complete each sentence correctly.

1. The _____ is the source of almost all of Earth's energy.

2. Cells use the process of _____ to get energy from food.

3. Different species that live in the same area form a(n) _____.

4. Plants, animals, and other living things in a(n) _____ are connected by the cycles of energy and nutrients.

On a sheet of paper, write the letter of the answer that completes each sentence correctly.

5. A _____ includes all the members of one species that live in the same area.

   A community   **C** population
   B niche   **D** kingdom

6. Examples of _____ include coral reefs, deserts, forests, and grasslands.

   A communities   **C** populations
   B ecosystems   **D** species

Critical Thinking

On a sheet of paper, write the answers to the following questions. Use complete sentences.

7. Why is the biosphere considered the highest level of interaction in the environment?

8. What are the two major processes that occur in an ecosystem and how do they support each other?

9. Do you think that different foods give you different amounts of energy? Explain your answer.

10. Draw a picture that shows how these words are related: population, community, biosphere, ecosystem, organism. Write a caption that explains your drawing.

Objectives

After reading this lesson, you should be able to

◆ describe the process of photosynthesis

◆ explain how carnivores and omnivores get energy

◆ describe the role of decomposers

Producer

An organism that makes its own food

Photosynthesis

A process plants use to change energy from the sun into stored sugars

Pigment

A chemical that absorbs certain kinds of light energy

Chlorophyll

A green pigment in plants that absorbs sunlight

Chloroplast

A structure in a cell that harvests energy from the sun

All living things get the energy they need from food. Different organisms have different food sources. Some make their own food. Some eat other living things. Some eat dead organisms. Depending on how they get their food, organisms are divided into one of three groups.

Producers

Every time you eat fruits or vegetables, you are eating **producers.** Producers, such as lettuce, broccoli, and apple trees, are organisms that make their own food.

Most producers are green plants and algae. They make food using a process called **photosynthesis.** *Photosynthesis* comes from two Greek words that mean "putting together with light." Carbohydrates, which are food for plants and many animals, are created during photosynthesis.

There are four things that green plants and algae need for photosynthesis to take place. First, they need a source of energy, which is sunlight. Second, they need water. Third, they need carbon dioxide. Fourth and last is a special green **pigment** called **chlorophyll.** A pigment is a chemical that can absorb certain kinds of light. Chlorophyll, which is stored in special cell structures called **chloroplasts,** absorbs sunlight.

During photosynthesis, chlorophyll absorbs light energy from sunlight. This breaks water molecules into hydrogen and oxygen. The oxygen is given off as waste. The hydrogen combines with carbon dioxide to create a simple sugar called glucose.

Science Myth

Myth: Animals get energy through cellular respiration, but plants get energy through photosynthesis.

Fact: Both plants and animals get energy through cellular respiration. Plants also change energy from the sun into stored chemical energy through photosynthesis.

Green plants and algae can change glucose into other sugars, as well as starch. They can also create more complex molecules such as proteins and fats. These molecules provide energy that helps plants grow. Plants also store some of the sugar and starch in their roots. Root vegetables such as potatoes and carrots are made this way.

Humans and other animals rely on producers for more than just food. They also rely on the oxygen that producers give off as waste during photosynthesis. The oxygen in the atmosphere comes from plants and algae. More than 50 percent of that oxygen comes from green plants in the ocean.

Some deep ocean and cave ecosystems do not rely on sunlight for energy. Instead, they get their nutrients from chemicals formed inside the earth. **Chemosynthesis** is a process in which bacteria and other life forms use chemicals to create nutrients. These organisms are also producers. They use hydrogen sulfide and other **inorganic** molecules to make their own food. Inorganic molecules do not contain carbon atoms.

Consumers

What do people, deer, and sharks have in common? They are all **consumers.** Consumers are organisms that depend on producers for food. All animals are consumers. Unlike green plants and algae, they cannot make their own food.

Some animals feed directly on producers. These consumers are called plant eaters, or **herbivores.** Cows, rabbits, deer, sheep, and grasshoppers are all herbivores.

Other animals, such as wolves and eagles, are **carnivores.** Carnivores feed on herbivores or other carnivores. For example, frogs are carnivores because they eat insects and small fish. Snakes are also carnivores. Some snakes eat other carnivores, such as frogs. Others eat herbivores, such as mice and rats.

Carrion

A dead animal or
rotten meat

Scavenger

An animal that feeds
on dead animals

Omnivore

An animal that eats
both plants and animals

Decomposer

An organism that breaks
down dead organisms
and other organic waste

Organic

Living or once-living
material containing
carbon

Some carnivores do not feed on living things. Instead, they eat dead animals that they find. Rotting meat is called **carrion.** Carnivores that feed on carrion are called **scavengers.** Carrion beetles, lobsters, shrimp, vultures, coyotes, and gulls are all scavengers. Some scavengers, such as gulls, eat living things as well. They eat live animals some of the time and are scavengers at other times.

Some consumers eat both animals and plants. These consumers, including people, bears, pigs, and raccoons, are called **omnivores.** Many omnivores eat a large variety of foods. Raccoons, for example, eat eggs, fish, frogs, berries, and whatever else they can find.

Eating a variety of foods can be an advantage in the wild. It means an animal can use many food sources at different times of the year. Bears often eat fish and berries in the summer. They will also eat roots and other plants when fish and berries are not available.

Some animals also eat different things during different stages of life. Caterpillars of monarch butterflies feed on milkweed leaves. When the caterpillars change into butterflies, the adults get their food from flowers instead.

Decomposers

Some consumers get the energy they need by breaking down dead organisms. These consumers are called **decomposers.** Without decomposers, dead animals and plant material would pile up everywhere. Fungi and bacteria are some of the most common decomposers. Both get nutrients from dead animals and **organic** matter, such as fallen leaves and tree trunks. Organic matter is material containing carbon that is alive or was once alive.

Link to ➤➤➤

Cultures

An animal that can only eat plants is called an herbivore. However, people that choose not to eat other animals are called vegetarians. People may choose this diet for ethical, environmental, religious, nutritional, or political reasons.

The words *carnivore, herbivore,* and *omnivore* are each formed from two Latin words. The verb *vorare,* "to eat," is part of all three words. Carnivore includes *caro,* which means "meat." Herbivore includes *herba,* which means "vegetation." Omnivore includes *omnis,* which means "all."

Decomposers play an important role in ecosystems. For example, fungi break down leaves and dead animals. Some of the nutrients are absorbed by the fungus. Others are recycled, often in a simple form that plants can use. In this way, decomposers make sure matter passed from plants to animals is recycled again. This is the ongoing cycle of matter.

■◆❖◆■◆❖◆■◆❖◆■◆❖◆■◆❖◆■◆❖◆■◆❖◆■◆❖◆■◆❖◆■

Science in Your Life

Consumer Choices: Home Composting Bins

Many people use special bins to turn grass, leaves, and other organic waste into a material called compost. Compost is rich in nutrients and can be added to soil. Composting helps the environment in two ways. First, it gets rid of yard waste that would otherwise be thrown out with the trash. Second, it provides a free, organic fertilizer which can replace chemical fertilizers. Chemical fertilizers can cause health and pollution problems.

Composting requires moisture, air, yard and food wastes, and time. The fungi and bacteria in the air and wastes decompose the dead plant material and recycle the nutrients. All you have to do is add water regularly and turn the yard waste. Turning allows air and moisture to reach all the material so the decomposers can do their work. You can buy a compost bin or you can also make your own.

1. What type of organisms work in a compost bin?

2. What is necessary for composting to take place?

3. What are some benefits of composting?

Word Bank

chlorophyll

consumer

omnivore

photosynthesis

On a sheet of paper, write the word from the Word Bank that completes each sentence correctly.

1. A(n) _____ is an animal that eats a variety of plant and animal material.

2. In _____, plants use sunlight, water, and carbon dioxide to produce food and oxygen.

3. A green pigment in plants that absorbs sunlight is _____.

4. A(n) _____ cannot make its own food and must feed on other organisms.

On a sheet of paper, write the letter of the answer that completes each sentence correctly.

5. Cows, deer, rabbits, and sheep are _____.

   A producers   **C** omnivores
   B herbivores   **D** decomposers

6. _____ are needed for photosynthesis to occur.

   A Sunlight and carbon dioxide
   B Salt water and oxygen
   C Sunlight and oxygen
   D Salt water and carbon dioxide

7. _____ is a waste product of photosynthesis.

   A Carbon dioxide **B** Oxygen **C** Fat **D** Energy

Critical Thinking

On a sheet of paper, write the answers to the following questions. Use complete sentences.

8. What is the nutrient source for producers that live in the dark, deep ocean?

9. Are you a carnivore, an herbivore, or an omnivore? Explain your answer by describing the types of food you eat.

10. How are decomposers important to an ecosystem?

Objectives

After reading this lesson, you should be able to

◆ explain how energy is transferred in a food chain

◆ explain how a food web differs from a food chain

◆ identify the different roles in a food chain or food web

Food chain

The feeding order of organisms in a community

When an animal eats a plant, energy is transferred from the plant to the animal. The same thing happens when an animal eats another animal. The energy stored in one organism is transferred to the organism that eats it. The transfer of energy through an ecosystem can be traced. This helps scientists see how organisms are connected by feeding relationships. Using this information, scientists can also calculate how much energy is transferred.

Food Chains

A **food chain** shows how organisms in an ecosystem get their food. Each organism is a link in the chain, and provides food for the next link. A food chain always starts with a producer and ends with a consumer. A simple food chain in the grasslands of Africa would start with acacia trees. As producers, they make their own food using sunlight. Giraffes eat the leaves and get some of the energy stored in the leaves. Finally, lions feed on the giraffes, and get the energy stored in the giraffe's cells. This example demonstrates how energy moves in a food chain from one link to the next. Another example of a food chain can be seen in Figure 3.4.1.

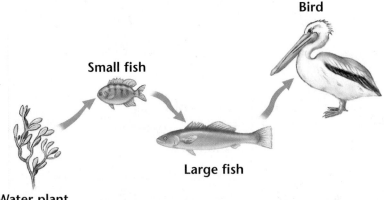

Figure 3.4.1 *A food chain shows the sequence of organisms that feed on each other.*

Food Webs

There are millions of food chains in nature. Each of them demonstrates one way that organisms are linked together in an ecosystem. In most ecosystems, however, energy transfer is much more complicated. That is because most organisms are part of more than one food chain. In a meadow, for example, grasshoppers feed on many different kinds of plants. A variety of birds, amphibians, and reptiles feed on grasshoppers. These animals are in turn eaten by raccoons, bears, hawks, and other creatures. This network of feeding relationships is called a **food web.** A food web shows many different feeding relationships in an ecosystem. Figure 3.4.2 is an example of a food web.

Eating many different foods can help a consumer make sure it can find enough food. A few species feed on only one thing. If something happens to their food source, they could die out. Australian koalas, for example, feed on the leaves of eucalyptus trees. When land is cleared for new houses, many of these trees are destroyed. If all eucalyptus trees disappear, koalas will have to find new sources of food and shelter. If they cannot, their populations will decline. When that happens, other parts of their ecosystem's food web can also be disturbed.

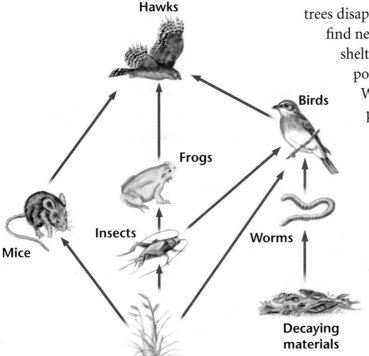

Figure 3.4.2 *A food web shows the different food chains an organism is part of in a community.*

Trophic Levels

Beyond food webs, you can see how energy is transferred by looking at feeding relationships. A **trophic level** is a feeding level in a food chain or web. In most ecosystems, producers such as green plants make up the first trophic level. In a grassland ecosystem, this level would include grasses and other plants. In an ocean ecosystem, algae forms the first trophic level. In a few ecosystems, bacteria form the first level.

The second trophic level is made up of herbivores, which are also called **primary consumers.** Giraffes in the African plains and squirrels in North American forests are primary consumers. **Secondary consumers** make up the third trophic level. Lions, eagles, and snapping turtles are all secondary consumers because they feed on primary consumers.

In some food chains there is a fourth or fifth level of consumers that eat other consumers. These carnivores or omnivores are called **tertiary consumers.**

Most consumers eat several types of food and feed at more than one trophic level. A bear is a primary consumer when it feeds on berries. It can also be a secondary consumer when it eats fish.

Energy Pyramids

How do the numbers of species in each trophic level compare? Would you expect there to be more producers or carnivores? If you guessed more producers, you are right.

You can use an **energy pyramid** to picture how trophic levels relate to each other. Look at the energy pyramid in Figure 3.4.3 on page 99. Producers form the bottom of the pyramid. Trophic levels form a pyramid because there are many more producers than primary consumers. There are also more primary consumers than there are secondary or tertiary consumers. Think about it this way. A field of grass can only support a certain number of rabbits. The number of rabbits can support a smaller number of bobcats. The bobcats can only support an even smaller number of cougars.

An energy pyramid shows more than the relative numbers of species. It also shows the amount of energy available at each trophic level. Each time energy is transferred from one level to the next, about 90 percent is lost. Some of that energy is lost as heat and escapes into the atmosphere. An animal uses most of the energy it receives to live. That means only 10 percent of the energy gets stored in the animal. This is the energy available to the consumer that eats the animal. As you move up the pyramid, there is less food energy available. Scientists call this the 10 percent rule, even though the amount of energy lost varies between ecosystems.

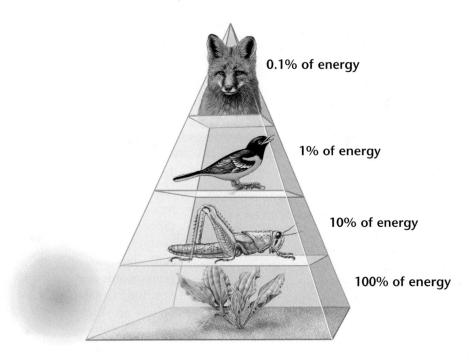

0.1% of energy

1% of energy

10% of energy

100% of energy

Figure 3.4.3 *The energy pyramid represents the percentage of energy transferred from one trophic level to another.*

Math Tip

To figure out the amount of energy in the next level of an energy pyramid, multiply the previous amount by $\frac{1}{10}$.

Look back at the energy pyramid on page 99. You can see that the first trophic level is the largest. This level has the most energy and the most species. Each level above it has less energy and fewer species. The top level of tertiary consumers has the smallest amount of energy. There is about 1,000 times more energy in the first trophic level than at the top. This is why there are more small animals than large animals in an ecosystem. It is also why most food chains do not have more than four or five links. There is not enough energy at the top level to support another level of consumers.

Energy pyramids, food chains, and food webs all show how energy travels from one organism to another. In every interaction illustrated in a food chain or web, energy is transferred. An ecosystem depends on this transfer of energy to maintain all forms of life.

Science at Work

Animal Caretaker

Do you have an interest in wild animals? Then you might want to explore a career as an animal caretaker. Zoos, aquariums, and other wildlife organizations are the main employers of animal caretakers. Handling the large number and variety of wild animals requires skilled and trained professionals.

Animal caretakers are responsible for the daily well-being of the animals in their care. Caretakers maintain feeding and grooming programs for the animals and are responsible for keeping their environment clean. Caretakers must become very familiar with the appearance and behavior of their animals as well.

The caretaker is responsible for recognizing health problems and alerting the medical staff. They also keep records on how the animals behave and their feeding habits.

To become a caretaker, you must show responsibility in dealing with animals. Some zoos require a college degree in biology or animal science. Others may require a high school diploma and completion of a certified training program.

Word Bank

energy

food chain

food web

producers

On a sheet of paper, write the word or words from the Word Bank that complete each sentence correctly.

1. In a(n) _____, energy is passed along from a producer to a consumer, and then sometimes to another consumer.

2. A(n) _____ shows many feeding relationships in an ecosystem.

3. The first trophic level in an ecosystem includes _____.

4. An energy pyramid shows the number of species and the amount of _____ available at each trophic level.

On a sheet of paper, write the letter of the answer that completes each sentence correctly.

5. A(n) _____ is considered a secondary consumer.

   A tree   **B** mouse   **C** eagle   **D** fungus

6. Each time energy is transferred from one trophic level to the next, energy _____.

   A increases by 10 percent   **C** stays about the same
   B is lost   **D** doubles

Critical Thinking

On a sheet of paper, write the answers to the following questions. Use complete sentences.

7. How can a bear be a primary and a secondary consumer?

8. Draw and label a food chain you would find in a lake or stream.

9. Why do ecosystems constantly need new energy?

10. Would it make sense to use another shape other than a pyramid to show energy changes at each trophic level? Explain your answer.

Materials

- data table
- pencil
- $300 of play money
- calculator

The Energy Pyramid

An energy pyramid shows how the amount of available energy decreases as it moves through trophic levels. In this lab, you will track this energy. You will use money to represent the energy as it moves between trophic levels.

Procedure

1. Form a group of four students. Choose someone to be the sun bank, the grass bank, the rabbit bank, and the fox bank.

2. Make a data table like the one on the next page.

3. The grass bank represents 300 grass plants. Each plant makes $1 a day through photosynthesis. Have the sun bank pay $300 to the grass bank. Record this amount in your data table under the "Amount earned." The grass bank does not lose money in this transfer, since no energy is "spent." Record the same amount under "Amount saved."

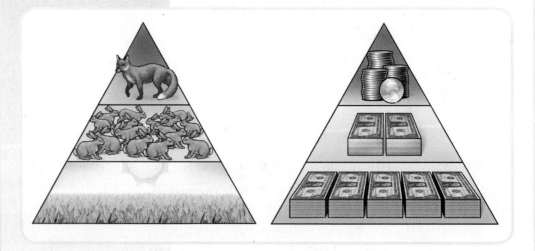

4. Have the grass bank pay the rabbit bank the money it has saved. Record this in the data table under "Amount earned." According to the 10 percent rule, the rabbit bank "spends" 90 percent of this money right away. Record this amount in your table. Then calculate and record the total amount that is saved.

5. A rabbit needs $2 a day to survive. Calculate how many rabbits can be supported by the amount of money saved in the rabbit bank. Record this number in your data table.

6. Have the rabbit bank pay the fox bank the money it has saved. Record this amount, the amount that is spent (remember the 10 percent rule), and how much is saved.

7. A fox needs $3 a day to survive. Calculate how many foxes can be supported by the amount of money saved in the fox bank. Record this number in your data table.

Cleanup/Disposal

Put away the materials and make sure your lab area is clean.

Analysis

1. How much money is remaining at the end of this lab?

2. What does the money that was spent represent?

Conclusions

1. What happened to the grass plants that provided energy for the rabbits? How will this affect the energy available the next day?

2. If the rabbit population grew very large, how would other organisms be affected?

Explore Further

Calculate how many more grass plants and rabbits would be needed to support 10 more foxes.

Trophic level	Amount earned	Amount spent	Amount saved	Number of organisms
Grass				
Rabbits				
Foxes				

Niche

The role an organism plays in an ecosystem; an organism's way of life

Every living thing lives somewhere. Earthworms live underground. Fleas live on cats, dogs, and squirrels. Cacti live in the desert. An organism's habitat can be large, like the grasslands in Africa. Habitats can be small, like the inside of a sheep's nostril. The size depends on how big the organism is and how much space it needs. Inside this space, the organism must find the food, shelter, water, and other things it needs to survive.

There can be many different habitats within every ecosystem. That is because one part of an ecosystem can have very different conditions from another part. Species living in the deep ocean are used to colder and darker conditions than those near the surface. Species living inside a sheep's nostrils experience different conditions than those that cling to its hair.

The Perfect Niche

Every organism has special ways to survive within its habitat. It needs to find food, find a mate, and reproduce. It also needs to avoid dangers and find the water and minerals it needs. The unique role that an organism plays in its ecosystem is called its **niche.** A niche includes where a species lives and how it interacts with other species. It also includes what conditions it depends on for survival. You can think of a habitat as an organism's address. Then its niche is its job. In other words, a niche is everything an organism does in its habitat to survive.

One way to see different niches is to watch what a species eats. Red-tailed hawks and kestrels can both live in the same field. Red-tailed hawks feed on mice and snakes. Kestrels feed on insects, lizards, and other small creatures. Even species that eat the same type of food have different niches. Cardinals and indigo buntings both feed on seeds. They have different niches because cardinals eat bigger seeds than indigo buntings. They also depend on different plants to survive.

No two species in the same habitat have exactly the same niche. It might look like they do, but there are many differences. Different species have very different life cycles and ways of reproducing. They are also eaten by different creatures and have different methods of defending themselves.

For example, monarch butterflies, honeybees, and ruby-throated hummingbirds all feed on nectar. Yet each species has its own way of getting nectar and prefers different flowers. They also have different ways of avoiding predators. Hummingbirds can fly the fastest of the three. Honeybees have a poisonous sting that can hurt an attacker. Monarch butterflies are poisonous to many would-be predators.

Competing for a Niche

Sometimes, two species compete for the same niche. The species that is best suited to the niche usually wins. The species that loses either moves, adapts to a new niche, or dies out. In the late 1800s, a bird lover imported birds called starlings from England. He released them in Central Park in New York City. The starlings competed with native birds in the area for nesting sites. Today there are millions of starlings all over North America. They fill niches that belonged to other birds before the starlings forced them out.

For all living things, **competition** is a normal part of life. Competition happens when two species compete for the same resources. Competition can occur between individuals, such as two lions competing over a mate. It can also occur between different populations. A population of gulls may compete for the same food as a flock of crows.

Individual members compete with each other. When praying mantis young hatch, they all compete for the same food. Some will even eat each other to stay alive. Some species that compete find ways to **coexist** in the same space. In some marshy areas, bats and dragonflies both feed on mosquitoes. They compete with each other, but they have different niches. Bats hunt at night. Dragonflies hunt during the day. People also compete with other species. When people fish for salmon, they may compete with bears and eagles for the same food. People also compete with wildlife for space to build their homes. This often forces species to move, adapt, or die.

Predators and Prey

When a fly is caught in a spider web, the spider feels it shake the web. The spider wraps the insect in a silklike case. When it is hungry, the spider will suck out the insect's liquids to get **nourishment.** A spider feeding on a fly is an example of a **predator** in action. A predator is an organism that hunts and feeds on another organism. The animal that a predator eats is called its **prey.** This kind of interaction between species is called **predation.** Road runners, sea otters, rattlesnakes, and lizards are all examples of predators.

★ ✹ ★ ✹ ★ ✹ ★ ✹ ★ ✹ ★ ✹ ★ ✹ ★ ✹ ★ ✹ ★ ✹ ★ ✹ ★ ✹ ★ ✹ ★ ✹ ★ ✹ ★ ✹ ★ ✹ ★ ✹ ★ ✹

Achievements in Science

Learning by Observing

What is the best way to learn about chimpanzees? Watch them at a zoo? Read a book about them? Jane Goodall thought the best way was to watch them in the wild. In 1960, she started living with a population of chimpanzees in East Africa.

When Dr. Goodall first started her studies, the chimpanzees would run from her. Then they slowly accepted her. Dr. Goodall became a member of their community. She gave the chimpanzees names and got to know their different personalities.

By observing their daily life, Dr. Goodall was able to make important discoveries. For example, she discovered that chimpanzees use tools. One such tool is a stick used to "fish" termites out of the ground. She learned that chimpanzees act as small family groups. She even witnessed a four-year war between chimpanzee tribes.

Jane Goodall's work has been an example for other scientists. Much of what is now known about animals comes from observing them in their natural environments.

Predator and prey populations are linked. More prey can support more predators. If the number of prey decreases, then the number of predators will shrink too. If a new predator joins an ecosystem, there might be less prey for native species. In some ecosystems, top predators, such as tigers or jaguars, are overhunted or face other threats. This can lead to an increase in prey species and cause changes in the ecosystem.

Many populations go through **boom-bust cycles.** In these cycles, the number of prey can affect the number of predators. When the population of prey grows, the population of predators grows. This is a population boom. Over time, the number of predators becomes too high for the prey to support. Predators begin to starve and die. This is a population bust. When the number of predators goes down, the number of prey increases. Then the cycle starts again.

Figure 3.5.1 *The thorn mimic treehopper avoids being eaten because it looks like a sharp thorn.*

Staying Alive

Over time, many prey species have found ways to defend themselves against predators. One way species protect themselves is with **camouflage.** Camouflage helps a species hide or look like something it is not, like the thorn mimic treehopper in Figure 3.5.1. Some frogs and insects look just like leaves or tree bark. Some caterpillars look like twigs or bird droppings.

Warning coloration

The bright colors or patterns on animals that scare off predators

Mimicry

A method of defense in which a species looks, sounds, or acts like a more dangerous species

The shingleback lizard's tail and head are the same shape and size. Because of this, predators often attack the wrong end. This increases the lizard's chances of survival. An attack on the lizard's tail does not injure it as much as an attack on its head.

Some species contain toxic chemicals that harm predators. Many of these animals have bright colors called **warning coloration.** These bright colors warn predators to stay away. Poison dart frogs, coral snakes, skunks, wasps, bees, and monarch butterflies all have warning coloration.

Species also use **mimicry** to protect themselves. In mimicry, one species looks, sounds, or acts like a more dangerous species. For example, several species of snake copy the bright colors of a coral snake. The viceroy butterfly has the same colors and patterns as a monarch butterfly.

Predators may also be camouflaged. This lets them hide from prey and have a better chance of catching them. Crab spiders can change color to match the color of the flowers where they hide. When prey passes by, it may not see the camouflaged spider. The spider then easily captures its prey. Camouflage, warning coloration, and mimicry help both predator and prey species survive.

Technology and Society

Humans have copied the way animals use camouflage. The military uses camouflage patterns on tanks, uniforms, and other equipment. A new technology allows soldiers to become almost invisible while wearing special reflective clothing. A photographic image of their surroundings is projected onto the soldiers. Optical camouflage creates the illusion that the soldiers are part of their surroundings.

Lesson 5 REVIEW

Word Bank

boom-bust cycle

camouflage

niche

predator

On a sheet of paper, write the word or words from the Word Bank that complete each sentence correctly.

1. The unique role that an organism plays in its environment is called its _____.

2. In a _____, the numbers of predators and prey rise and fall depending on each other.

3. An animal that actively hunts and kills its prey is called a _____.

4. A caterpillar disguised as a bird dropping is an example of _____.

On a sheet of paper, write the letter of the answer that completes each sentence correctly.

5. A snake feeding on a mouse and a frog eating a fly are two examples of _____.

   A competition   **C** camouflage

   B predation   **D** mutualism

6. The _____ of a species can be called its address in an ecosystem.

   A home **B** trophic level **C** niche **D** habitat

Critical Thinking

On a sheet of paper, write the answers to the following questions. Use complete sentences.

7. Describe an example of warning coloration.

8. Explain how predator and prey populations are linked.

9. Name three things that animals or plants might compete for in an ecosystem.

10. Describe the niche of an animal in your area.

DISCOVERY INVESTIGATION 3

Materials
- variety of plastic utensils
- tweezers
- toothpicks
- chopsticks
- watch, stopwatch, or timer
- multicolored pasta

Predator-Prey Interactions

All predators and prey have ways to be successful in their environments. Hawks, for example, have sharp beaks and talons to help them catch prey. Rabbits move quickly to escape capture. Some predators and prey use camouflage to survive. In this lab, you will explore how these factors benefit predators and prey.

Procedure

1. Your teacher will lead you to an outdoor site. Note the environmental conditions around you. **Safety Alert: Be careful around plants and animals. Let your teacher know if you are bitten, scratched, or stung.**

2. The colored pasta represents the prey. Your teacher will provide a selection of tools to "capture" prey. Examine these tools.

3. Work in pairs. With your partner, write a hypothesis that describes how successful a "predator" will be at capturing the pasta "prey." Your hypothesis can include information on the type of pasta, the environment, or the tools used.

4. Test your hypothesis. Spread out the pasta while one partner is not looking. The "predator" should choose a tool and capture as much "prey" as possible.

5. Stop the predator after 30 seconds. Count the number of prey captured successfully.

6. Repeat the process five times. Vary the tool used and the test site. Record your data.

Cleanup/Disposal

Before returning to the classroom, clean up your materials. Wash your hands afterward.

Analysis

1. What was your hypothesis?

2. Was your hypothesis supported by the data you collected? Explain your answer.

Conclusions

1. How did the tools of the "predator" affect its success at predation?

2. How did the color of the "prey" affect success?

3. How did the environment affect success?

Explore Further

Choose a different type of prey and different tools. Write a hypothesis with these new factors and test it.

After reading this lesson, you should be able to

◆ describe how primary and secondary succession differ

◆ give examples of species found in different stages of succession

◆ describe how climax communities can change

Succession

The process of ecological change in a community over time

Ecosystems are always changing. Some of the changes can happen quickly. Hurricanes, volcanoes, floods, and fires can change a habitat overnight. Change also happens on a smaller scale. In a forest, conditions might change if a tree gets hit by lightning and falls. Sunlight can now reach the forest floor. Seeds that have been buried in the soil can grow. Small flowering plants and shrubs soon appear. This creates a new layer of plants on the forest floor. Over time, the bigger plants will block sunlight from the species below them. Finally, shrubs and flowering plants will be replaced by trees. This process can take many years.

Some changes in ecosystems can take hundreds or even thousands of years. What is a forest today might have been a swamp. A field might once have been a forest that was destroyed by a fire.

Communities of life are not created overnight. They form over time, through several different stages. This process of ecological change in a community over time is called **succession.** In many ecosystems, one community of life is replaced by another. Succession usually refers to how the plant life changes. Still, each stage in succession also has its own animals and other organisms. Succession can also happen in water environments.

Primary Succession

On November 14, 1963, a volcano erupted underwater off the coast of Iceland. The eruption pushed a new island out of the water. The island was named Surtsey, after a Norse god of fire. At first, Surtsey was just a lifeless black rock. Over the next few years, the eruptions continued. The island grew to about 2.6 square kilometers and rose more than 171 meters above sea level.

Lichen

An organism made up of a fungus, a green alga, and a cyanobacterium

Primary succession

Succession in a lifeless environment that creates a community

Erode

To break apart or wear away

Pioneer species

The first species to arrive in an area

The first signs of life on the island were bacteria and fungi. Soon mosses and **lichens** began to colonize the island. Seeds carried by birds, the wind, or the sea started to sprout. Three years after the eruption, birds started nesting on the island. Insects and other small creatures arrived, along with new plants.

Today, there are about 60 kinds of plants growing on the island. Ten different kinds of birds nest there, including puffins and gulls. There are also thousands of insects and other small organisms. Seals now live on the island. The rocks are covered with algae and starfish.

Primary succession is the process of succession in what was once a lifeless environment. Recently exposed rock or newly formed sand dunes are two examples of lifeless environments. Primary succession also happens after a volcano leaves an area almost without soil. Primary succession usually follows a pattern. First, new soil is formed when rocks **erode,** breaking into smaller pieces. This is caused by wind, water, and frost. In most areas, soil forms with the help of lichens. Lichens are tiny organisms made up of fungi, algae, and cyanobacteria living together. Unlike many producers, lichens can live on bare rock. The algae create their own food through photosynthesis. The fungi absorb water and nutrients from rocks. Together they make and give off acids that can break down rocks. These plants, which are often the first to arrive, are called **pioneer species.**

Science Myth

Myth: Lichens harm trees.

Fact: Lichens live on a tree's bark without interacting with the tree. Often green or gray-colored, lichens are sensitive to pollutants such as sulfur dioxide. This means that the presence of lichens can signal clean air and a healthy environment.

Climax community

The last step in the succession of an ecosystem

Distribution

The location of species in a community

Secondary succession

Succession in an environment that was disturbed by humans or natural causes

Once soil starts to form, small plants like mosses and grasses begin to grow. Seeds and spores are carried in by animals or the wind. Insects, small mammals, and other creatures start to arrive. As the soil gets deeper, shrubs with longer roots can grow. These larger plants will crowd out the grasses. The shrubs will eventually be replaced by trees.

The last step in the succession of an ecosystem is called a **climax community.** Scientists once thought each climax community was stable. They now realize that these communities also experience change. Over time, a climax community typically has the same kinds of species. Yet the numbers and **distribution,** or location of species in a community, can change. Different species make up climax communities in different areas of the world.

Secondary Succession

Secondary succession is the process of change in communities that have been disturbed. Human activities, fires, floods, and other events can all lead to secondary succession.

Secondary succession is similar to the later stages of primary succession. When farmland is abandoned, grasses and wildflowers are the first plants to grow. They are followed by larger shrubs and then fast-growing trees, such as pines. Slow-growing trees, such as maples, oaks, and beeches, eventually outcompete the pines and smaller shrubs. Over time, a climax community forms. It may resemble the forest that was originally cleared to create the farm.

During succession, animal species change along with the plant species. Some species might be found in all stages. Other species will enter or leave a community as it moves through different stages. In a field, you would find species that depend on grasses, wildflowers, and small shrubs. As it becomes a forest, finches, squirrels, and other species would join the community.

Old-growth forest

A forest containing trees
that can be hundreds or
thousands of years old

Diverse

Varied

Protecting Species and Spaces

Over hundreds of years, an abandoned farm can become a forest through succession. However, the new forest might never recover the species and relationships the original one had. Many people are concerned about how fast ecosystems are changing. Farming, road building, and other human activities cause changes that can affect the species of an area.

Many people are working to protect natural communities that have not been changed by humans. One example of this type of community is an **old-growth forest.** An old-growth forest contains trees that are hundreds or thousands of years old. Certain species of animals need these ecosystems to find food and a place to live.

Natural communities such as old-growth forests are some of the most **diverse** that exist today. A diverse area has many different plants and animals. If these ecosystems are disturbed, it can take them hundreds or thousands of years to recover. In some cases, the original forest will never recover.

Link to ➤➤➤

Earth Science

Rocks and soil made from volcanic lava are especially rich in minerals and nutrients. That is one reason why crops grow so well on the volcanic Hawaiian Islands.

On a sheet of paper, write the word or words from the Word Bank that complete each sentence correctly.

1. Primary and secondary _____ are two kinds of change in an ecosystem over time.

2. The first organisms to move into a lifeless area are called _____.

3. A(n) _____ can have trees that are hundreds of years old.

On a sheet of paper, write the letter of the correct answer.

4. Which of the following is an example of primary succession?

  A lichens, mosses, grasses, shrubs, then trees
  B forests, shrubs, weeds, algae, then flowering plants
  C forests, fields, rocks, soil, then deserts
  D fields, wetlands, bare rock, then grasses

5. On the island of Surtsey, _____ happened after the volcano erupted.

  A nothing   **C** secondary succession
  B primary succession   **D** distribution

6. Secondary succession would probably occur after _____.

  A abandoning a farm   **C** a comet hits Earth
  B a volcanic eruption   **D** a nuclear explosion

Critical Thinking

On a sheet of paper, write the answers to the following questions. Use complete sentences.

7. What is special about lichens?

8. Why is it important to preserve old-growth forests?

9. Describe how a human activity can cause secondary succession.

10. In primary succession, what happens after plants appear?

Integrated Pest Management

For many years, farmers have depended on chemical pesticides to keep crops safe. However, these pesticides can cause health problems in humans and other animals. Now, many agricultural scientists advise using several different methods to defeat weed and insect pests. This approach is called Integrated Pest Management (IPM).

IPM does not try to replace pesticides. Instead, its goal is to help people use less of them.

IPM begins by looking at each crop and the pest that is threatening it. Once the problems are identified, IPM scientists look for many different solutions. Often, natural predators can be introduced to fight a problem insect or weed. For example, some farmers add ladybugs to their crops. The ladybugs eat the insect pests, but do not damage the crops. Another method is to rotate crops from year to year. Crops that are not affected by particular pests and diseases replace those that are.

An IPM program may include using small amounts of pesticides. However, they are used only when and where they are necessary.

Combining these different tools works better than chemicals alone. At the same time, it reduces pollution from pesticides. IPM also improves the effectiveness of the chemical pesticides that are used. When farmers use fewer chemicals, the pests have less exposure to them. This means they cannot become resistant to the chemicals as easily. Finally, when farmers use fewer chemicals, the cost to produce crops is lowered.

1. What does IPM include?

2. How does IPM actually improve the ability of chemicals to reduce pests?

3. Describe two advantages of using IPM.

Chapter 3   SUMMARY

- The environment is made up of living, or biotic, factors and nonliving, or abiotic, factors that interact.

- Ecosystems transfer energy from the sun to green plants to animals.

- Ecosystems recycle matter. This allows atoms of carbon, oxygen, and other elements to be used over and over.

- The environment is organized into five levels: organisms, populations, communities, ecosystems, and biosphere.

- Living things can be divided into three groups depending on how they get their food. Producers make their own food. Consumers eat other living things. Decomposers break down waste.

- Consumers can be divided into three groups. Herbivores eat plants. Carnivores eat animals. Omnivores eat both plants and animals.

- Food chains and food webs show the feeding relationships in an ecosystem.

- Energy pyramids show the amount of energy transferred from one trophic level to the next.

- Species compete for resources, including food, shelter, water, and living space.

- Predators are species that feed on prey. Camouflage, warning coloration, mimicry, and defensive behaviors help protect prey from predators.

- Ecosystems follow a pattern of change over time called succession. Primary succession happens in areas that were once lifeless. Secondary succession occurs in areas that were once inhabited by living things.

Vocabulary

abiotic factor, 83	consumer, 92	matter, 88	predator, 106
ban, 82	decomposer, 93	microorganism, 83	prey, 106
biotic factor, 83	distribution, 114	mimicry, 108	primary consumer, 98
boom-bust cycle, 107	diverse, 115	mineral, 84	primary succession, 113
camouflage, 107	domain, 83	molecule, 89	producer, 91
carnivore, 92	ecologist, 82	niche, 104	recycle, 89
carrion, 93	ecology, 82	nourishment, 106	reproduction, 88
cellular respiration, 89	energy pyramid, 98	old-growth forest, 115	scavenger, 93
chemosynthesis, 92	erode, 113	omnivore, 93	secondary consumer, 98
chlorophyll, 91	food chain, 96	organic, 93	secondary succession, 114
chloroplast, 91	food web, 97	photosynthesis, 91	succession, 112
climax community, 114	herbivore, 92	pigment, 91	tertiary consumer, 98
coexist, 106	inorganic, 92	pioneer species, 113	trophic level, 98
community, 88	kingdom, 83	population, 87	warning coloration, 108
competition, 105	lichen, 113	predation, 106	

Chapter 3   R E V I E W

Word Bank

abiotic factors
chemosynthesis
competition
consumers
decomposers
ecology
energy pyramid
food web
niche
photosynthesis
population
predators
prey
producer
scavenger
succession
trophic level

Vocabulary Review

On a sheet of paper, write the word or words from the Word Bank that complete each sentence correctly.

1. The process of ecological change in a community over time is _____.

2. The study of how living things interact with each other is called _____.

3. Through a process called _____, plants use energy from the sun to make food.

4. When predators eat _____, it is known as predation.

5. A(n) _____ is a group of organisms of the same species that live in the same area.

6. A(n) _____, such as a gull or vulture, feeds on carrion.

7. Every _____ is made up of food chains that are connected.

8. When resources such as food, shelter, and water are limited, _____ occurs between living things.

9. Wind, water, temperature, and minerals are among the _____ that are part of the environment.

10. When there is no sunlight available, some organisms make food using _____.

11. Some _____ feed directly on producers. Others feed on animals that feed on producers.

12. Without _____, the world would be full of plant and animal waste.

13. Every food chain begins with a(n) _____.

14. Scientists use a(n) _____ to show the amount of energy at each trophic level in an ecosystem.

Continued on next page

15. Cats, lions, hawks, and praying mantises are called _____ because they actively hunt and eat other animals.

16. A(n) _____ is a layer of a feeding relationship and a link in a food chain.

17. Each organism's role in an ecosystem, or _____, is different.

Concept Review

Choose the answer that best completes each sentence.
Write the letter of the answer on your paper.

18. The numbers and _____ of species can change in a climax community.

  A colors   **B** types   **C** habitats   **D** distribution

19. A(n) _____ would eat both fish and lettuce.

  A carnivore   **C** omnivore
  B herbivore   **D** producer

20. An example of _____ is lichens and mosses growing on bare rock after a volcanic eruption.

  A competition   **C** primary succession
  B population   **D** secondary succession

21. Trophic levels describe _____ in a community.

  A the energy available
  B succession
  C predator-prey relationships
  D competition

22. Most of the energy that fuels ecosystems on Earth comes from _____.

  A chemicals **B** water   **C** sunlight   **D** bacteria

Critical Thinking

On a sheet of paper, write the answers to the following questions. Use complete sentences.

23. Is a decomposer a predator or prey? Explain your answer.

24. Draw a local food web or use the example from the book. Are there more producers or consumers? Why?

25. List the levels of interaction in the environment and give examples of each level.

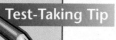

Test-Taking Tip Restate the test directions in your own words. Tell yourself what you are expected to do.

The Diversity of Life

Bundles of colorful flowers fill this photo of a flower shop. Flowers from three different groups of flowering plants are shown. The bundles in the lower left corner contain tulips. Above them are two kinds of daisies. Most of the other bundles hold roses, another plant species. You can see many different colors of roses in this picture. This is just a small sample of all the variation, or diversity, in this kind of flower. In Chapter 4, you will learn about diversity in living things. You will find out how this diversity is important.

Organize Your Thoughts

Biodiversity

Species diversity

Genetic diversity

Ecosystem diversity

- Evolution
- Speciation

- Mutation
- Natural selection
- Adaptation

- Ecosystem services

Goals for Learning

- ◆ To identify the three levels of biodiversity
- ◆ To explain how biodiversity is measured
- ◆ To describe how biodiversity has developed
- ◆ To understand the concept of a web of life
- ◆ To explain how biodiversity benefits the planet

Species diversity

The diversity of species on Earth

Earth supports a tremendous variety of life. It is home to five-centimeter hummingbirds and a fungus the size of 1,600 football fields. It supports yellow and blue fish, fish with spikes, and fish that walk on land. These organisms live in Earth's many wild spaces, including warm seas, frozen tundra, and mountain meadows.

As you learned in Chapter 1, biodiversity refers to this variety of life. You can think of biodiversity as *bio,* meaning "life," plus *diversity,* or variety. Biodiversity exists in every part of Earth's biosphere. One handful of soil holds many kinds of insects, worms, and plants. A city park can contain more than a thousand kinds of plants and animals. Even human bodies are home to millions of tiny organisms and bacteria.

Species Diversity

Biodiversity occurs on three levels. You are probably most familiar with the level of species. Members of a species can reproduce with others of the same species, but usually not with other species. **Species diversity,** then, is the variety of species on Earth. Eastern bluebirds, African lions, great white sharks, and sugar maples are all examples of species.

To appreciate species diversity, consider a familiar animal such as a frog. Perhaps you have seen a bullfrog or heard the calls of spring peepers. Still, you may be surprised to learn that Earth contains more than 5,400 different species of frogs. Tiny poison dart frogs range in color from yellow to bright blue. Goliath frogs are the world's biggest frogs and can grow to be more than 30 centimeters long. Gastric brooding frogs are famous for how they reproduce. The mother frog swallows her fertilized eggs and turns off her stomach acids. Six to seven weeks later, she spits out fully formed babies.

Frogs are not the only organisms represented by many species. About 36 species of wild cat pad through Earth's forests, grasslands, and mountain areas. More than 9,500 ant species have been identified. Earth is also home to more than 2,500 kinds of palm trees and more than 20,000 species of orchids.

Genetic Diversity

Genetic diversity is the variety of genes found in living things. **Genes** are information found in an organism's cells. That information is passed from parents to their offspring. Genes are largely responsible for how an organism looks and behaves. In humans, for example, genes determine hair and eye color. These features are called **traits.** Not all traits are visible on the outside. For example, organisms can carry nonvisible traits that make them vulnerable to particular diseases.

Genetic diversity causes the wide range of sizes, colors, and shapes of organisms. Even individuals of the same species have some differences in their genes. This kind of genetic diversity helps the species survive.

For example, some individuals of a species might be good at storing fat. Some might be better at staying lean and fast. Some might survive colder temperatures. Some might be less likely to get certain diseases. This variety makes it likely that at least some individuals will survive an environmental change. These changes could include the arrival of a new predator or rising global temperatures. Even if individuals die, the survivors can slowly rebuild the population.

Figure 4.1.1 *Genetic diversity causes differences in animals of the same species.*

Cheetahs are wild cats that provide an example of weak genetic diversity. As their numbers decreased, cheetahs began breeding with close relatives. Now the remaining cheetahs have very similar genes. A disease that could harm one cheetah could harm them all. Increasing genetic diversity among cheetahs would increase their chances of long-term survival.

Ecosystem Diversity

Grasslands, deserts, lakes, and caves contribute to Earth's **ecosystem diversity.** Ecosystems can be as small as a mud puddle or as large as an ocean. These differences of scale mean that ecosystems can be found within other ecosystems. For example, a log inhabited by moss and insects is an ecosystem. At the same time, this log is part of a larger forest ecosystem.

Among Earth's many other ecosystems are coral reefs, tundra, swamps, and savannas. You will learn more about these types of ecosystems in Chapter 5. Each of these places offers different living conditions for different species. Some ecosystems are warmer and some are colder. Some ecosystems receive a lot of precipitation, while some are very dry. Some are found on land, while some are found in the water. The diversity of ecosystems is necessary for supporting species diversity.

The Whole Picture

Species, genetic, and ecosystem diversity can each be defined separately. In the real world, though, they are not really separate. Each level affects and is affected by the other levels. For example, a wild cat called the lynx lives in the forests of the Rocky Mountains. Human activities have destroyed much of the lynx's forest ecosystem. With fewer places to live, the number of lynx has dropped. The remaining lynx live in small groups. These groups may be too far apart for members to reach and breed with other groups. Scientists worry that this may be reducing their genetic diversity.

This example is not unique. Species diversity, genetic diversity, and ecosystem diversity are connected everywhere.

Conservationists are people who want to protect species and ecosystems. They are concerned with the **conservation,** or protection and care, of natural resources. These natural resources include both living and nonliving parts of the earth. Conservationists work to maintain biodiversity at all three levels.

Express Lab 4

Materials

◆ paper
◆ pencil

Procedure

1. Work with a partner to determine three of your genetic traits.

2. Make a data table like the one shown below.

3. Record your traits in the table.

4. List all the different combinations of the three traits that are possible.

5. Count the total number of classmates with each combination.

Analysis

1. How many combinations of these three traits are possible?

2. How many students had each type of combination?

Name	Eye color (dark or light)	Hair (curly or straight)	Little finger (straight or bent)

Word Bank

biodiversity

ecosystem

genetic

On a sheet of paper, write the word from the Word Bank that completes each sentence correctly.

1. The word _____ refers to the many different kinds of life on Earth.

2. Differences between members of the same species are caused by _____ diversity.

3. The many different kinds of wild places on Earth are part of _____ diversity.

On a sheet of paper, write the letter of the answer that completes each sentence correctly.

4. A _____ is an example of an ecosystem.

    A lynx   **B** swamp   **C** gene   **D** population

5. An example of an inherited trait is _____.

    A hair length   **C** a sunburn

    B a job   **D** eye color

6. A(n) _____ is one example of a species.

    A tree   **C** eastern bluebird

    B fish   **D** desert

Critical Thinking

On a sheet of paper, write the answers to the following questions. Use complete sentences.

7. How could a handful of soil show biodiversity?

8. Why do cheetahs have weak genetic diversity?

9. How does ecosystem diversity support species diversity?

10. How can a forest stream be both an ecosystem and part of an ecosystem?

Objectives

After reading this lesson, you should be able to

- give the estimated number of species on Earth
- explain why scientists do not know the exact number of species
- name several ways that scientists learn about new species

Mollusk

A soft-bodied animal that lives inside a hard shell

Specimen

An example of a species

Taxonomy

A branch of science that deals with classifying species

Just how much diversity does the planet have? When scientists measure diversity, they are usually measuring species diversity. So far, they have identified about 1.7 million species worldwide. Species diversity is greater among some groups of animals than others. For example, scientists have identified about 4,500 mammals and 9,700 birds. They have counted 10,500 species of reptiles and amphibians, 24,000 species of fish, and more than 260,000 species of plants. There are about 1 million known species of insects. The remaining species include worms, spiders, **mollusks,** and microorganisms.

Discovering New Species

The number 1.7 million refers to species actually named by scientists. That means scientists have seen the species. They have probably also collected an example of the species called a **specimen.** Scientists have compared the specimen to similar species to make sure it is unique. They have then classified it and given it a Latin name that is used by scientists worldwide. **Taxonomy** is a branch of science that deals with the classification of species.

There are many more species than those that have been named. In fact, scientists estimate that there are between 3 to 100 million species total. They simply have not been able to find and identify everything yet.

For example, scientists have identified nearly 370 species of sharks. Every year, though, they find about three to five new shark species. Scientists have actually discovered new shark species by walking through fish markets. Other times, the new sharks wash up on shore. In 1976, a new shark species was discovered when it swallowed part of a navy ship's anchor. This enormous shark with rubbery lips is now known as the megamouth shark.

Link to >>>

Social Studies

In 2004, a kayaker in eastern Arkansas spotted an ivory-billed woodpecker. This species had been considered extinct since the 1940s. Immediately, a team of researchers began searching for more of them. Efforts are now under way to preserve the species and the habitat it needs to survive.

Few of the millions of undiscovered species are likely to be as large as sharks. Most will be tiny microorganisms and **invertebrates.** Invertebrates are species without a backbone such as insects and mollusks. Finding and identifying these species is very difficult. Imagine trying to find every microscopic organism in your city. You can then understand why this task would be so challenging given the size of the earth.

Figure 4.2.1 *The megamouth shark is one of many species discovered by chance.*

When scientists discover larger animals, it is global news. In 1965, scientists discovered a new wild cat they called the Iriomote cat on a Japanese island. Japan considers this rare cat to be a national treasure. In 1992, scientists in Vietnam discovered the horns of a species now called the saola. Saola are believed to be related to oxen and antelopes. Only 11 of these animals have been seen alive. In 2004, researchers discovered a new bird species on an island in the Philippines. The researchers believe the Calayan rail is probably flightless and may number fewer than 200 pairs.

In these and other cases, local people were probably already familiar with the "newly discovered" species. Trained scientists simply proved that the species was unique. Then they shared its existence with the rest of the world.

A Moving Target

While more species are discovered every year, the total number of species is getting smaller. Every year, thousands of species become extinct. This means there are no more members of those species. **Extinction** is the complete loss of a species. Many other species are **endangered,** which means they are at risk of extinction. When many species disappear in one time period, scientists call it a **mass extinction.**

Species have always come and gone. About 99 percent of all species that have existed since the earth formed are now extinct. Mass extinctions have occurred about five times in Earth's history. The end of the age of the dinosaurs is one example. Another mass extinction is happening right now. Some scientists estimate that up to two-thirds of Earth's species will disappear by the year 2100. Identifying species as they disappear, then, is like hitting a moving—or shrinking—target.

Extinction

The loss of all members of a species

Endangered

At risk of extinction

Mass extinction

A period of time when high numbers of species are becoming extinct

Science at Work

Taxonomist

Taxonomists study the classification and identification of living things. The science of taxonomy is based on evolutionary relationships, which are based on genetic makeup. When a new life form is discovered, taxonomists study its body structure and genetic makeup. This information is then compared with what is known about other life forms. Once the closest relatives of the new life form are agreed on, a scientific name is assigned. Finally, the new species is carefully described. Correct classification and identification are needed for all biological studies.

Taxonomists work for museums, universities, and government agencies including state and national parks and wildlife services.

Many taxonomists work outdoors at least part of the time. They often oversee collections of specimens that help educate others about the diversity of life.

A taxonomist must have good observation skills. To become a taxonomist, you need a bachelor's degree in science. Many taxonomists have a master's or doctoral degree.

Counting Tools

Scientists use many tools for finding new species. Natural places often disappear quickly, so some scientists conduct high-speed surveys of local species. This process is called a **rapid assessment.** Experts in plants, mammals, birds, and other areas visit a threatened place together. In a short amount of time, they attempt to identify every species living there. Most of these species have already been discovered and named. However, rapid assessment teams sometimes discover new species.

If these species are found in one place and nowhere else on Earth, they are **endemic** species. The golden lion tamarin, shown in Figure 4.2.3, is endemic to the country of Brazil. Some areas, such as Brazil, have high numbers of species, high numbers of endemic species, or both. These areas are centers of biodiversity.

Figure 4.2.3 *Because the golden lion tamarin is endemic to one small area in Brazil, it has become endangered as its habitat is destroyed.*

Sample

A small part of a larger unit

Math Tip

Counting very large numbers of things takes a long time. Estimating can be used instead of counting or calculating the exact amount. Counting a sample amount is a quick way to make an educated guess.

To locate areas with new species, scientists sometimes use planes and satellites to take pictures. These technologies give them detailed pictures of a large area. By carefully inspecting these images, scientists can find promising sites. They can then visit these sites to see what is there.

Estimating the total number of species on Earth is difficult. One method is to measure numbers of different species in a small area, called a **sample.** This number can be used to estimate diversity across a larger area. Biologist Terry Irwin, for example, studied small sections of tropical rain forest. He counted all the insect species in a certain number of trees. Many were new to science. Based on his findings, he estimated that there are 30 million insect species. Only a million or so have been named so far. Irwin's estimate surprised the scientific community and is still being debated.

Expert scientists and ground-breaking technologies are needed to measure biodiversity. In Chapter 12, you will learn about how scientists are using what they learn to protect biodiversity.

Technology and Society

Remote sensing is a technology for studying something from a distance. Studying images of reflected or radiated light is one example. Different materials reflect and radiate different colors of light. Satellites, such as the Landsat, can take photos of any place on Earth. The colors are clues to the kind of material that reflected or radiated the light.

Lesson 2   R E V I E W

Word Bank

endangered

endemic

extinct

On a sheet of paper, write the word from the Word Bank that completes each sentence correctly.

1. An _____ species is found in only one place on Earth.

2. All members of an _____ species have died.

3. Species that are at risk of disappearing are _____.

On a sheet of paper, write the letter of the answer that completes each sentence correctly.

4. Scientists think there are _____ more species yet to be discovered.

   A dozens   **B** hundreds   **C** thousands   **D** millions

5. To estimate numbers of species, scientists count species in a small _____ of a larger area.

   A picture   **B** sample   **C** map   **D** pond

6. Some scientists do quick studies of biological diversity called _____.

   A speed reads   **C** estimates
   B rapid assessments   **D** samples

Critical Thinking

On a sheet of paper, write the answers to the following questions. Use complete sentences.

7. Why do scientists not know the exact number of species on Earth?

8. What is one example of a mass extinction?

9. Why is it sometimes incorrect to say that a new species has been "discovered"?

10. How have scientists used technology to find new species?

Lesson 3 — Evolution and Adaptation

Objectives

After reading this lesson, you should be able to

◆ define evolution

◆ explain how species adapt and evolve

◆ understand that biodiversity is the result of evolution

Evolve

To develop and change genetically over time

Scientists estimate that the first single-celled organism appeared on Earth about 3.5 billion years ago. Today, as many as 100 million different organisms may exist on Earth. How did this diversity develop? To answer that question, it helps to know a bit about an English scientist named Charles Darwin.

Evolution

In 1835, Charles Darwin visited the Galápagos Islands off the coast of Ecuador. While there, he discovered 13 different species of small birds called finches. What caught his attention were the birds' beaks. The beaks of each species were a different size or shape. After his journey, Darwin wrote that there must have been one original species of finch in the Galápagos. Over thousands of years, this species developed, or **evolved,** into 13 species.

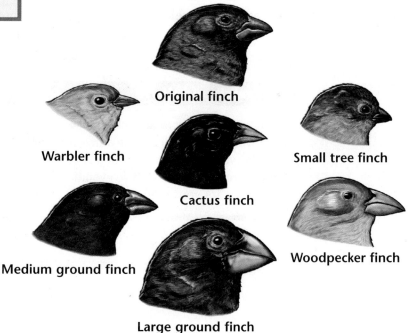

Figure 4.3.1 *The beaks of the Galápagos finches inspired Darwin's theory of evolution.*

Darwin's observations led to his theory of **evolution.** Evolution is a process of genetic change in a population over time. This change happens in response to a population's environment.

Darwin recognized that individuals of the same species are not exactly the same. Genetic differences make some individuals bigger, faster, and so on. An individual inherits most of these traits from his or her parents. Your genes are a combination of your two biological parents' genes. The exception to this rule is a genetic **mutation.** A mutation is a sudden change in an organism's genes. For example, two orange tigers will sometimes produce a white tiger cub. The white color is caused by a mutation in the cub's genetic material.

Natural Selection

Genetic mutations can create new or different traits. Traits that make individuals better suited to their environment are known as **adaptations.** Individuals with these traits are more likely to survive and pass on their genes to offspring. Darwin called this process **natural selection.** Over time, the more successful traits become more widespread in a population. The genetic makeup of the individuals in the population changes.

Research and Write

Whales evolved from animals that lived on land. Their land-based relatives are members of the antelope family. Research the story of whale evolution. Work with others in a small group to prepare a visual presentation on whale evolution. You might use posters or a computer for your presentation.

Biology

All plants grown for food are products of selective breeding. The same is true for farm animals and pets. Selective breeding works like natural selection, but faster. People, not nature, choose the parents for the next generations of the plants and animals they raise. The result is a huge variety of useful plants and animals.

Evolution gives organisms a way to deal with their unstable environment. It helps them survive changes in climate, new diseases, and predators. As you read in Lesson 1, genetic diversity is important. Diversity makes it more likely that some individuals will survive an environmental change.

Science in Your Life

Consumer Choices: Pet Breeding

Pets are more popular today than ever. The many different recognized breeds of dogs and cats are the result of selective breeding. People began breeding dogs about 14,000 years ago. They were bred to have certain desirable characteristics. For example, some were bred to be guard dogs. Others were bred to assist in hunting or herding.

A new trend in breeding is hybridizing. This is the practice of mating two distinct breeds. Some examples of hybridized dogs are cockapoos, schnoodles, and labradoodles. You might have figured out that poodles are one part of each of these "designer dogs." The reason is that people have fewer allergies to poodles than to other breeds of dogs. That is a very desirable trait if you happen to be allergic to other dogs, yet still want one as a pet.

1. How did humans develop the many breeds of dogs?

2. What is one reason you might want a designer pet?

Interbreed

To breed together

Distinct

Separate; not the same

Speciation

The evolution of a new species

Math Tip

A rate is an amount measured in relation to something else. One example is kilometers per hour, which is a measurement of speed.

Evolution happens at different rates for different species. Some organisms, such as cockroaches, reproduce very quickly. In one year, a female cockroach and her offspring can produce more than 30,000 individuals. Other species reproduce very slowly. A female African elephant reproduces once every four to five years. She only has about seven offspring in her lifetime.

Different reproductive rates play a role in how quickly species can adapt to change. Species with fast reproductive rates can evolve quickly. That is why, for example, it is so hard to get rid of pest cockroaches. Even if only a few individuals survive, they will quickly produce many offspring. These offspring will share the traits that allowed their parents to survive. Elephants, though, could not recover so easily from a disease or other threat. Since they reproduce slowly, they adapt to environmental changes very slowly. Having slow reproductive rates is one characteristic that makes species more likely to become endangered.

Speciation

How, then, has evolution added to the diversity of species on Earth? Remember, species usually exist in separate groups, or populations. Sometimes these populations become separated by physical barriers and can no longer **interbreed.** Interbreed means to breed together. These barriers might include bodies of water, mountains, and roads. Other times populations have no barrier between them, but they occupy separate niches. Either way, these different populations can experience different environmental conditions. When that happens, they may begin to evolve in different ways. After thousands of years, this may result in two **distinct,** or different, species. This process is called **speciation.**

Science Myth

Myth: Species choose to evolve.

Fact: The members of a species cannot choose to evolve. Species evolve in response to changes in the environment. In order to survive, a living thing must be born with a genetic makeup that helps it survive. Living things cannot change their genetic makeup.

A tiny deer called the key deer is endemic to the Florida Keys. Scientists believe this species is related to the white-tailed deer living in other parts of the United States. A small deer population may have reached these islands by a land bridge thousands of years ago. A land bridge is a strip of land connecting two bigger areas of land. There the deer were exposed to unique environmental conditions. They became used to more salt in their drinking water. Smaller individuals were more successful at surviving than larger individuals. Eventually they evolved into a unique species of pygmy, or very small, deer.

The finches Darwin found in Ecuador went through a similar process. Most likely, one species of finch arrived at the Galápagos thousands of years ago. Over time, different populations settled on several islands. Different beak characteristics made individuals in each population better at obtaining certain foods. These more successful individuals passed along their traits to their offspring. Populations evolved differently depending on the available food. Eventually, 13 different, closely related species evolved on the islands. The cactus finch, for example, has a long beak for reaching into cactus flowers. The ground finch has a short beak for getting seeds out of the soil.

From these stories, you can begin to see how Earth became so diverse. The populations of Earth's earliest plants and animals spread out across land, air, and water. Different parts of the earth had different environmental conditions. These conditions also changed dramatically over time, in different ways. As a result, populations of plants and animals evolved differently. The result is a world full of diversity.

Word Bank

adaptation

mutation

speciation

On a sheet of paper, write the word from the Word Bank that completes each sentence correctly.

1. A(n) _____ is a sudden change in the genes of a living thing.

2. A(n) _____ is a trait that makes a living thing better suited to its environment.

3. The formation of a new species is called _____.

On a sheet of paper, write the letter of the answer that completes each sentence correctly.

4. Through natural selection, individuals best suited to their environment pass on their _____ to their offspring.

    A mutations   **B** species   **C** genes   **D** diet

5. New species can form when an isolated _____ is exposed to new environmental conditions.

    A individual   **B** family   **C** trait   **D** population

6. Charles Darwin developed a theory of _____.

    A evolution   **B** climate   **C** extinction **D** ecosystem

Critical Thinking

On a sheet of paper, write the answers to the following questions. Use complete sentences.

7. Why was Charles Darwin so interested in the beaks of the Galápagos finches?

8. Why can cockroaches evolve more quickly than elephants?

9. How do new species form?

10. Why does Earth have so much species diversity?

INVESTIGATION 4

Materials

- paper
- pencil
- 20 dried white beans
- 20 dried black beans
- 20 dried kidney beans
- sheet of black construction paper
- sheet of white construction paper

Modeling Natural Selection

Natural selection acts on the genetic diversity in the populations of a species. Different combinations of genes carried by individuals provide advantages or disadvantages in a given environment. An individual's genes are passed on if the individual survives long enough to reproduce. The environment determines which combinations of genes are the most successful. How does natural selection work? You will model the process in this lab.

Procedure

1. Make a data table like the one shown below.

2. Scatter 10 of each bean type on black paper.

3. Close your eyes. After five seconds, open your eyes and pick up the first bean you see. Repeat until you have 10 beans.

4. Record your observations in your data table.

5. Repeat Steps 2–5 using white construction paper.

Environmental conditions	Number of white beans remaining	Number of black beans remaining	Number of kidney beans remaining
Black paper			
White paper			

Continued on next page

Cleanup/Disposal

Before leaving the lab, return your materials and wash your hands.

Analysis

1. How many kidney beans were left on the black paper?

2. How was the number of remaining beans different for each paper color?

Conclusions

1. What would eventually happen if you continued the selection process using only the beans remaining on the paper?

2. How does this activity model natural selection?

Explore Further

Repeat the investigation using different colors of paper and different combinations of beans.

Objectives

After reading this lesson, you should be able to

◆ understand the idea of a web of life

◆ describe some of the ways organisms interact

◆ explain why the loss of one species can affect many other species

Pollination

The transfer of pollen between plants for reproduction

Pollen

The male reproductive cells of plants

Nectar

A sweet liquid produced by many flowers

A spider's web is made up of individual strands linked together. Tugging on any part pulls the rest of the web. Ecosystems are like a web because they are also made up of many connected pieces. Every species, from tigers to tarantulas, depends on other living things to survive. These connections can be described as a web of life.

Perhaps you have seen a squirrel burying acorns or insects eating fallen fruit. Maybe you have seen birds nesting in trees. All of these examples illustrate the ways organisms are connected to other organisms.

Food, Reproduction, and Shelter

Food chains and food webs are a key part of the web of life. They represent feeding relationships between organisms in a community. As you learned in Chapter 3, organisms can be producers, consumers, and decomposers. They can be predators and they can be prey. All of these roles are linked, connecting one organism to another.

Pollination is another important way that species in an ecosystem interact. Pollination is the transfer of **pollen** from one plant to another for reproduction. Plants often depend on insects and other animals to pollinate them. Perhaps you have seen bees crawling on flowers. Flowers produce a sweet liquid called **nectar.** As the bees feed on the nectar, they bump against parts of the flower covered with pollen. The pollen attaches to the bees, and the bees carry the pollen to other flowers. In the process, they pollinate those flowers. Bees, flies, birds, and bats are a few of the many animals that pollinate plants.

Science Myth

Myth: Bats are dangerous pests that suck blood.

Fact: Only three species of bats actually eat blood, usually that of weakened animals. Most bats eat insects. This adds up to millions of tons of insects each year. As a result, bats can help reduce a farmer's need for pesticides.

Sometimes only one type of organism can pollinate a particular plant. The hawk moth keeps its very long tongue coiled beneath its head. Its tongue is long enough to reach the nectar of the Angraecum orchid. This nectar lies at the base of a tube that can be up to 30 centimeters long. These two species have evolved together. Today, hawk moths are the only species that can pollinate Angraecum orchids.

Some plants also depend on animals for **seed dispersal.** Seed dispersal is scattering seeds away from a parent plant. Squirrels and other animals that bury acorns help disperse these seeds. Birds, rhinos, and other animals that eat seeds help disperse them through their waste.

Some organisms also depend on other living things for shelter. For example, small seabirds called marbled murrelets nest mostly in coastal old-growth trees. Other animals use the holes and burrows of other species for shelter. Gopher tortoises make burrows in southern pine forests. Many animals use these burrows, including mice, snakes, and frogs. Some use them to escape forest fires. Others use them for long-term shelter.

Research and Write

Plants and their pollinators have, in many cases, evolved together. This process is called coevolution. For example, Hawaiian honeycreepers have beaks that are shaped to fit specific flowers. Fuchsias are flowering plants that are a specific color of red that attracts hummingbirds. Bats are the most efficient pollinators of many species of agave plants and cactuses. Write a report about one of these examples of coevolution.

Survival by Association

Even without providing shelter, some organisms help protect other species. For example, the clownfish stays safe by swimming among the stinging **tentacles** of sea anemones. Tentacles are armlike body parts used to capture food. The clownfish is not affected by the poison in these tentacles. Swimming near the anemone, it can avoid predators that are harmed by the poison. Scientists call relationships like this **commensalism.** One organism benefits from a special relationship with another organism. The second organism is neither helped nor harmed. Commensalism is an example of **symbiosis,** which includes all close relationships between organisms.

New research suggests that clownfish may help protect sea anemones from certain predators. If this is correct, their relationship is really an example of **mutualism.** Mutualism is a relationship between two organisms that benefits both of them.

Tentacle

An armlike body part used to capture food

Commensalism

A relationship between two species where one benefits and the other is not affected

Symbiosis

A close relationship between two species

Mutualism

A relationship between two species where both species benefit

---

Link to >>>

Physics

Some plants spread their own seeds. The Himalayan balsam's seed-dispersal method is very effective. The pods explode and eject seeds several meters away from the parent plant. Due to this plant's height and the force behind the explosion, Himalayan balsams have invaded the habitats of other plants.

Figure 4.4.1 *Cattle egrets feed on insects disturbed by large grazing animals, such as elephants.*

A keystone is the stone at the top of an arch. It is important because it holds the other stones in place. The arch will fall if the keystone is removed.

A third kind of relationship between two species is called **parasitism. Parasites** depend on a **host** organism for their survival. They often harm the host in the process. For example, strangler fig seeds grow in cracks in other trees. The seeds sprout and send roots downward. The plant roots itself in the ground. In time, the fig can grow to cover the host tree and smother it.

Commensalism, mutualism, and parasitism are different kinds of relationships between species. These relationships show some of the many ways that species depend on each other.

Keystone Species

Some animals shape their entire habitats. Beavers build dams across fast-flowing streams. As water gets trapped behind these dams, it floods the surrounding forests. The resulting lakes and wetlands support different kinds of plants and animals. In this way, beavers can change landscapes and the life found in them. In fact, beavers are so important to their ecosystems that scientists call them **keystone species.** Keystone species can increase the diversity of life around them. Without them, many other species could become extinct.

Another example of a keystone species is the North American prairie dog. More than 200 other species live in or around prairie dog colonies. Burrowing owls, black-footed ferrets, and salamanders find shelter in prairie dog burrows. Hawks, coyotes, and badgers eat the prairie dogs. Also, prairie dogs churn up the soil and increase plant growth. Elk and bison feed on these plants.

The loss of any species will affect the lives of other species. This is especially true of keystone species. Without prairie dogs, the Great Plains could lose much of its species diversity.

Species other than keystone species can also affect other species and ecosystems. The loss of old-growth trees endangers the marbled murrelets. The loss of gopher tortoises endangers the animals that use their burrows. Without hawk moths, Angraecum orchids would soon disappear. Each loss of a species can cause other losses.

Biodiversity, then, depends on all the interactions among species, and between species and their ecosystems. It is this web of relationships that makes such diversity possible.

★ ✦ ★ ✦ ★ ✦ ★ ✦ ★ ✦ ★ ✦ ★ ✦ ★ ✦ ★ ✦ ★ ✦ ★ ✦ ★ ✦ ★ ✦ ★ ✦ ★ ✦ ★ ✦ ★ ✦ ★ ✦ ★ ☆

Achievements in Science

The Keystone Species Hypothesis

In the 1960s, ecologist Robert Paine began running tests to see what would happen after the main predator was removed from an ecosystem. He discovered that a single species can affect the biodiversity of an entire ecosystem.

The basic idea of Paine's keystone species hypothesis is that predators control the populations of prey. If the prey populations stay small, different species do not have to compete for resources. As a result, the diversity of a community increases. This idea was originally tested when starfish—the main predators— were removed from an ocean community. This upset the feeding relationships in the community. The biodiversity of the community dropped quickly.

A keystone species has a much greater effect on its ecosystem than its population size would suggest. Recently, the keystone species hypothesis has been expanded. Now, many ecologists call any species that greatly affects its ecosystem a keystone species.

Lesson 4   R E V I E W

Word Bank

commensalism

mutualism

parasitism

On a sheet of paper, write the word from the Word Bank that completes each sentence correctly.

1. In _____, one life form benefits and the other is harmed.

2. Lichens are a combination of cyanobacteria, algae, and fungi. These life forms help each other to survive. This relationship is called _____.

3. In a relationship called _____, one life form benefits and the other is neither harmed nor helped.

On a sheet of paper, write the letter of the answer that completes each sentence correctly.

4. Bees help plants reproduce through _____.

   A pollination   **C** parasitism
   B mutation   **D** hatching

5. By carrying acorns away from an oak, squirrels are helping the tree with _____.

   A pollination   **C** seed dispersal
   B decomposition   **D** shelter

6. The burrow of a gopher tortoise can become important _____ for other species.

   A shelter   **C** landscape
   B food   **D** pollination

Critical Thinking

On a sheet of paper, write the answers to the following questions. Use complete sentences.

7. How is biodiversity like a spider web?

8. What would happen if hawk moths became extinct?

9. Give an example of a keystone species, and explain why it is important.

10. Why does the loss of one species affect other species?

Ecosystem service

A benefit provided by Earth's ecosystems

In the previous lessons, you have learned more about biodiversity. You have learned where it comes from and how it is supported by connections between organisms. What may be less clear is why diversity is important. What do microorganisms and bears and palm trees have to do with human life?

Believe it or not, biodiversity contributes to your life every day. You may live in a city and feel far removed from wild plants and animals. Still, you could not exist without them.

Ecosystem Services

Earth's green plants produce all the oxygen we breathe. A large amount of this oxygen is produced by green plants in the ocean. The trees, vines, and flowers of tropical rain forests also release a lot of oxygen. Even the trees and weeds on your block change carbon dioxide into carbon and breathable oxygen.

Without these plants, humans could not exist on Earth. Oxygen production is one of many **ecosystem services.** An ecosystem service is a benefit provided by Earth's ecosystems.

Biodiversity supplies other important ecosystem services. Plants anchor themselves in the soil with their roots. In the process, they help keep soil from eroding due to wind or water. Sand dunes, for example, would erode without beach grass and other plants. Riverside trees help keep stream banks from eroding during floods.

Plants help slow down rainwater as it rushes over ground and into streams. Slower water does not carry away as much soil. As a result, the land stays more fertile and the water stays clearer. Plants also prevent pollutants from entering bodies of water. These pollutants can become trapped by plants and their roots. The pollutants can also be absorbed by the plants through their roots.

Animals, too, can help clean water. Oysters, for example, filter water as they feed. In the process, they remove dirt and pollutants and make the water cleaner. Two hundred years ago, oysters filtered the volume of the Chesapeake Bay in one week. Now there are fewer oysters and there is more pollution. It may take a year for oysters to filter the Chesapeake Bay's waters.

Resources from the Planet

Do you enjoy oranges, walnuts, coffee, or tuna? Have you ever taken aspirin for a fever? Many foods, medicines, and other resources are possible because of Earth's biodiversity.

Figure 4.5.1
Apples, bananas, beans, carrots, walnuts, and fish are all part of Earth's biodiversity.

Humans have always relied on biodiversity for their food. Animals also help farmers produce food through pollination. Insects and other animals pollinate 75 percent of the world's **staple crops.** Staple crops provide most of the food for people around the world. Biodiversity also contributes to food production by providing diverse genetic material. The genes of some wild plants, for example, have been used to improve common foods. A wild Peruvian tomato has twice the sugar content of other tomatoes. It was used to produce a breed that is better for making canned tomato paste.

Compound

A combination of two or more elements

The biodiversity of Earth also provides people with many different medicines. At least 25 percent of all medicines people use come from plant and animal materials. The Pacific yew tree contains **compounds** that help fight ovarian cancer. Vampire bat saliva contains compounds that thin the blood, which can help heart attack patients. Shark cartilage contains compounds that can help people who have suffered burns.

Scientists who develop new medicines often investigate natural compounds. To discover these medicines, scientists sometimes turn to native healers. These healers have often used local plants to treat sicknesses for centuries.

Other times, scientists look at the successful traits of certain species. Remember the gastric brooding frog from Lesson 1? It turned off its stomach acids while its young developed inside. Scientists hoped this frog would provide clues for treating people with stomach ulcers. Not long after its discovery, though, the frog disappeared. Scientists believe it may now be extinct. When a species disappears, the information scientists would have gained from it is lost.

Foods and medicines are only a few of the resources the natural world provides. The shine of some kinds of makeup comes from crushed fish scales and insect wings. Wood furniture is made from trees. It is possible to harvest too much of these resources, of course. Still, with careful management, biodiversity can be used to improve human life over the long term.

Technology and Society

Genetic engineering is a technology used to increase biodiversity. This is done by taking genes from one life form and putting them in another. For example, a gene from a cold-water fish was placed in one kind of tomato plant. The gene protects the fish from cold. In tomato plants, the gene allows tomatoes to last longer without rotting.

Quality of Life

Many people enjoy fishing, hiking, and spending time on the beach. Many Americans spend time bird watching. People from **rural** and **urban** areas flock to parks for picnics, games, and sports. All of these activities reflect the recreational benefits biodiversity provides.

Human culture has benefited from biodiversity. The masks, carvings, and textiles of many groups often contain images of local plants and animals. Many famous paintings and photographs show landscapes or nature scenes. Wild animals are often used as the mascots of sports teams. Nature is often pictured in television and magazine advertisements. The natural world may seem far away, but people's daily lives continue to bring it closer.

Some scientists have suggested that humans may have a genetic need to interact with other species. They believe people's physical, emotional, and **spiritual** health is supported by interacting with nature. This idea is not easy to test. However, the popularity of zoos, pets, and parks provides evidence this is true.

Biodiversity also provides many **economic** benefits. Economic benefits have to do with money or finances. They affect an area's **economy,** which is a system of production, distribution, and consumption. The three levels of biodiversity each provide their own economic benefits. For example, species diversity contributes to the economy through pollination of crops. It also contributes through the money people spend to visit zoos and botanical gardens. Genetic diversity contributes to greater sales for food companies by creating healthier crops. Ecosystem diversity saves communities money by providing ecosystem services that would cost money to replace. In these and many other ways, biodiversity supports humans and their quality of life.

Rural

Away from the city

Urban

Inside a city

Spiritual

Having to do with religion or the soul

Economic

Having to do with money or finances

Economy

A system of production, distribution, and consumption

Map Skills: Nature Preserves

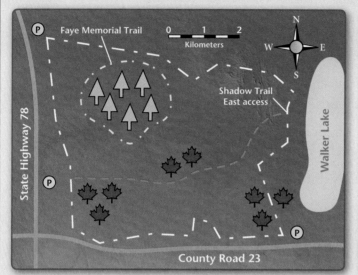

LEGEND

Preserve boundary	– – –
General parking	P
Big Sandy Trail	
Evergreen forest	
Red maple tree areas	

Nature preserves are designed to protect wild habitats and species. Many nature preserves are open to the public. There are trails to guide visitors around the preserve. People can see the points of greatest interest from these trails. It is often important to stay on the trails to reduce impacts on habitat and wildlife. Maps like the one above show the preserve's features and trails.

1. What road borders the south end of the preserve?

2. Which trail would be best for viewing an evergreen forest?

3. What is another name for the Shadow Trail?

4. About how long is the Shadow Trail?

5. Is Walker Lake inside or outside of the preserve?

On a sheet of paper, write the word or words from the Word Bank that complete each sentence correctly.

<table>
</table>

Word Bank

economic

ecosystem services

staple crops

1. Biodiversity provides _____ benefits, such as greater sales of foods.

2. Corn, rice, and wheat are _____ that provide most of the food for people around the world.

3. Many different _____ are provided by healthy ecosystems.

On a sheet of paper, write the letter of the answer that completes each sentence correctly.

4. The healing properties of natural compounds can be used to make _____.

   A genes   **C** soil

   B oxygen   **D** medicines

5. The _____ of wild plants can be used to improve food crops.

   A smell   **C** locations

   B genes   **D** recipes

6. Bird watching, hiking, and fishing are examples of biodiversity's _____ benefits.

   A recreational   **C** medicinal

   B noise   **D** ecosystem

Critical Thinking

On a sheet of paper, write the answers to the following questions. Use complete sentences.

7. Explain how humans depend on plants.

8. What are some ways plants and animals keep water cleaner?

9. Why might doctors be concerned about decreasing biodiversity?

10. What evidence suggests that humans need to interact with other species?

Materials

- latex gloves
- field notebook
- 4 1-meter pieces of string
- 4 dowels or tent pegs
- magnifying glass
- plastic bag

Conducting a Biodiversity Survey

Think of a time when you walked across a lawn or a field at school. You might have noticed just one kind of living thing, grass. Is that all that is there? What diversity of life is found under your feet and above your head? Find out in this lab.

Procedure

1. Form a group of three students. Decide who will be a data recorder, an animal surveyor, and a plant surveyor. A surveyor is someone who surveys, or examines, the land.

2. At the survey site, put on protective gloves if you are a surveyor. Lay the 1-meter pieces of string in a square on the ground. You may secure the ends to wooden dowels or tent pegs.

Continued on next page

3. Look for and record every kind of plant or animal inside the square. Use descriptions or draw pictures if you do not know the name of something. Also record any signs of living things, such as seeds or animal waste.

4. In your lab group, discuss factors that affect biodiversity in different areas. Write a hypothesis that could be tested with an experiment. Include the way you will measure biodiversity. Your experiment should use sampling.

5. Write a procedure for your experiment. Include Safety Alerts.

6. Have your hypothesis, procedure, and Safety Alerts approved by your teacher. Then carry out your experiment. Record your results.

Cleanup/Disposal

Make sure to collect all materials when you leave your survey site. Wash your hands with warm, soapy water.

Analysis

1. Work with your group to summarize your data in a table or chart.

2. How does biodiversity vary among the sites?

Conclusions

1. Was your hypothesis supported by the results of your experiment? Explain.

2. How does the amount of human activity affect biodiversity?

Explore Further

Conduct biodiversity surveys in other locations, such as your backyard or a local park.

Ecotourism

Ecotourism is a popular trend in vacation travel. The destinations are remote areas that are undisturbed by modern human culture. Destinations include rain forests, islands, and coral reefs. Ecotourists want to see and learn about these natural environments.

Ecotourism has two main goals. The first is to encourage responsible behavior to preserve the natural environment. Motorized travel is limited. Instead, visitors often hike, canoe, kayak, or climb to reach their destinations. They camp or stay in conditions similar to those of the local people. Often, visitors help with local conservation efforts. For example, they may help with research programs or help build trails.

The second goal of ecotourism is to improve the lives of the local people. Ecotourists visiting a remote area spend money, which helps the local economy. Ecotourism has been important to the economies of Costa Rica, Kenya, and parts of Australia. It also helps local people see the value in protecting biodiversity.

Ecotourists usually want to preserve nature. However, conservationists have some concerns about ecotourism. Any time people enter a natural area, some parts of it will be disturbed. The more visitors there are, the more damage that is done. Some countries and companies that offer ecotourism are not prepared to handle these problems.

Ecotourism is one way to educate people about biodiversity and problems it faces.

1. What are the goals of ecotourism?

2. What are some of the activities that ecotourists do?

3. Why does the popularity of ecotourism concern some conservationists?

Chapter 4 SUMMARY

- Biodiversity is all the different forms of life on Earth.

- The three levels of biodiversity are genetic diversity, species diversity, and ecosystem diversity.

- Scientists estimate that Earth may have between 3 million and 100 million species. So far, about 1.7 million species have been identified.

- Since Earth formed, millions of species have come and gone. Periods of huge losses of species are called mass extinctions.

- The current rate of species loss is so high that it can be called a mass extinction.

- Evolution happens through natural selection. In this process, individuals best suited to the environment survive and pass their genes to offspring.

- Speciation happens when different groups of a species stay separated for a long time. The groups evolve differently by adapting to different environments.

- Some ways that species interact include feeding relationships, pollination, seed dispersal, and shelter.

- Removing any species can change an ecosystem. Removing a keystone species can destroy an ecosystem.

- Biodiversity supports human life in many ways. It provides food, oxygen, medicine, and shelter.

- Biodiversity also provides economic, recreational, and personal benefits to humans.

Vocabulary

adaptation, 136
commensalism, 145
compound, 151
conservation, 127
conservationist, 127
distinct, 138
economic, 152
economy, 152
ecosystem diversity, 126
ecosystem service, 149

endangered, 131
endemic, 132
evolution, 136
evolve, 135
extinction, 131
gene, 125
genetic diversity, 125
host, 146
interbreed, 138
invertebrate, 130
keystone species, 146
mass extinction, 131

mollusk, 129
mutation, 136
mutualism, 145
natural selection, 136
nectar, 143
parasite, 146
parasitism, 146
pollen, 143
pollination, 143
rapid assessment, 132
rural, 152
sample, 133

seed dispersal, 144
speciation, 138
species diversity, 124
specimen, 129
spiritual, 152
staple crop, 150
symbiosis, 145
taxonomy, 129
tentacle, 145
trait, 125
urban, 152

Chapter 4 REVIEW

Word Bank

commensalism

conservation

ecosystem diversity

ecosystem service

endemic

extinction

genetic diversity

keystone species

mutation

mutualism

parasitism

pollination

seed dispersal

species diversity

trait

Vocabulary Review

On a sheet of paper, write the word or words from the Word Bank that complete each sentence correctly.

1. Efforts in _____ help to protect species and ecosystems.

2. The different forms of genes in living things, or _____, adds to Earth's biodiversity.

3. Marshes, beaches, rivers, and forests are part of Earth's _____.

4. The many different kinds of animals in a forest represent _____.

5. An inherited property of a living thing is called a(n) _____.

6. The complete loss of a species is called _____.

7. A(n) _____ species is one found in a particular place and nowhere else.

8. A sudden change in a living thing's genetic material is called a(n) _____.

9. Squirrels, birds, and other animals help with _____, or scattering seeds away from a parent plant.

10. Bees and birds are two animals that help plants reproduce by providing _____.

11. A relationship between two living things is called _____ if it benefits both of them.

12. A relationship between two living things that helps one and harms the other is called _____.

13. A clown fish and a sea anemone are connected by _____. In this relationship, one living thing benefits and the other is neither harmed nor helped.

Continued on next page

14. A(n) _____ increases the diversity of its ecosystem.

15. A benefit provided by Earth's ecosystems is called a(n) _____.

Concept Review

On a sheet of paper, write the letter of the answer that completes each sentence correctly.

16. Charles Darwin studied _____ while visiting the Galápagos Islands in 1835.

   A orchids   **C** prairie dogs
   B finches   **D** bison

17. Scientists have identified about 1.7 _____ species worldwide.

   A hundred   **C** million
   B thousand   **D** billion

18. The process by which individuals with successful traits survive and pass on their traits to their offspring is called _____.

   A mutations   **C** growth
   B natural selection   **D** ecosystem services

19. Earth's history shows five _____, or losses of very large numbers of species.

   A mass extinctions   **C** endangered species
   B endemics   **D** evolutions

20. _____ include producing oxygen, preventing erosion, and purifying water.

   A Traits   **C** Ecosystem services
   B Ecosystems   **D** Issues

Critical Thinking

On a sheet of paper, write the answers to the following questions. Use complete sentences.

21. How do the three levels of biodiversity interact?

22. Why is it difficult to know how many species exist on Earth?

23. Explain the relationship between evolution and environmental change.

24. Why might conservationists be especially interested in protecting keystone species?

25. What are some of the ways biodiversity benefits people?

Test-Taking Tip Before you begin a test, look it over quickly. Try to set aside enough time to complete each section.

5

Biomes of the World

The mountain lake in the photo is a freshwater ecosystem. A coniferous forest ecosystem covers the mountain slopes that surround the lake. Each ecosystem supports a unique set of living things. These organisms are all adapted to the conditions in which they live. Large areas that contain ecosystems with similar conditions are called biomes. Freshwater lakes are one kind of biome. Coniferous forests are another. In Chapter 5, you will learn more about the different types of biomes found on Earth. You will also learn about the factors that affect the kinds of life forms that inhabit each biome.

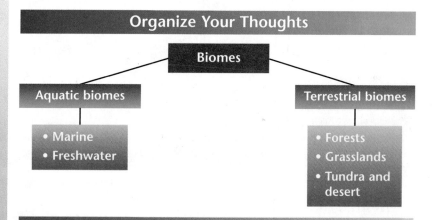

Organize Your Thoughts

Biomes

Aquatic biomes

- Marine
- Freshwater

Terrestrial biomes

- Forests
- Grasslands
- Tundra and desert

Goals for Learning

◆ To define biome and compare and contrast terrestrial and aquatic biomes

◆ To describe characteristics and locations of rain forests, coniferous forests, and deciduous forests

◆ To describe characteristics and locations of grasslands, tundra, and deserts

◆ To describe characteristics and locations of marine and freshwater biomes

Lesson 1 — What Is a Biome?

Objectives

After reading this lesson, you should be able to

◆ compare and contrast terrestrial and aquatic biomes

◆ explain the effects of precipitation and temperature

◆ explain the effects of latitude and altitude

◆ describe how salinity and water depth affect aquatic biomes

Biome

A group of ecosystems with similar temperature and rainfall, or salinity and water depth

Terrestrial

Living or growing on land

Aquatic

Living or growing in water

The earth is covered by many types of ecosystems. Scientists group ecosystems into larger areas called **biomes.** Biomes are the largest category of ecosystem that scientists use.

Deserts, forests, grasslands, and oceans are all examples of biomes. The map in Figure 5.1.1 shows the major biomes on Earth. The two main categories of biomes are **terrestrial** (land) biomes and **aquatic** (water) biomes.

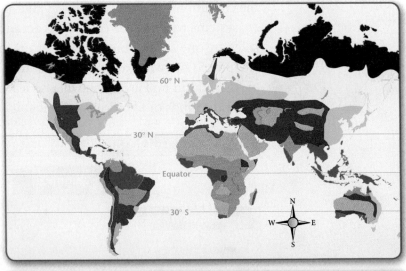

LEGEND

Polar ice	Coniferous forest	Chaparral	Mountains
Tropical rain forest	Savanna	Desert	Marine
Deciduous forest	Temperate grassland	Tundra	Freshwater

Figure 5.1.1 *The earth has 12 major biomes. This includes both terrestrial and aquatic biomes.*

Terrestrial Biomes

The earth has 10 major land biomes: tropical rain forests, deciduous forests, coniferous forests, temperate grasslands, savannas, chaparral, deserts, tundra, mountains, and polar ice. Each of these biomes is characterized by a particular climate. Average annual temperatures and amounts of precipitation are the aspects of climate that define terrestrial biomes. That is because both help to determine the types of plants that can grow there. Plants have special adaptations to help them survive in particular conditions. The plants, in turn, help determine what types of animals can live in each biome.

The total diversity of biomes is determined largely by the amount of precipitation they receive and the average temperature. For example, deserts and tundra both get very little precipitation. As a result, they have less diversity than other biomes. Rain forests, however, get a lot of rain and have a hot, humid climate. These conditions make rain forests the most diverse ecosystems on Earth.

Figure 5.1.2 shows the relationships between the rainfall and average temperature of the major land biomes. Biomes found on the left side of the pyramid get more precipitation than biomes found on the right. Biomes at the top of the pyramid are colder than those on the bottom.

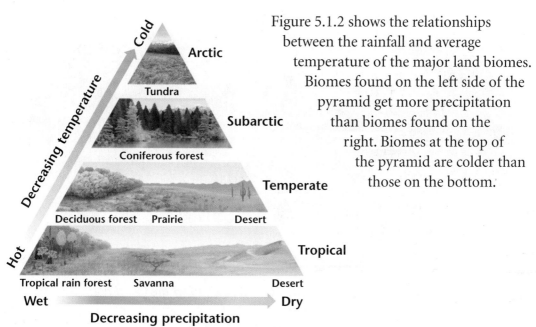

Figure 5.1.2 *Temperature and precipitation determine the vegetation found in a terrestrial biome.*

The right side of the pyramid on page 165 also shows that average temperatures are related to **latitude.** Latitude is the distance north or south of the equator. It is measured in degrees. Biomes nearer to the equator have higher temperatures than land biomes farther north or south. Figure 5.1.3 shows the different climate zones, which are divided by latitude. Biomes found near the equator, in the tropical zone, are warmer than those in the temperate zone. The temperate zone is warmer than the polar zone. As the latitude of a place increases, its temperature decreases.

The type of **vegetation,** or plants, found in different biomes is also affected by **altitude.** Altitude is how high a place is above sea level. As you climb higher up a mountain, for example, it gets colder. The vegetation is different at different stages of the climb. First, you might pass through forests, then small shrubs. Higher up, there are low-growing plants, such as mosses and lichens. On the snowy mountain peak, there is almost no vegetation.

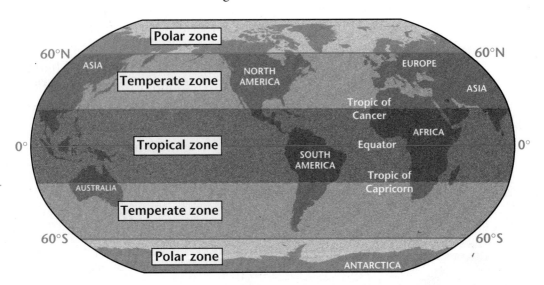

Figure 5.1.3 *The tropical, temperate, and polar zones are found north and south of the equator.*

Salt water is water with high salinity. *Saltwater* is an adjective describing something as relating to or consisting of salt water.

Aquatic Biomes

Aquatic biomes make up more than 70 percent of the earth's surface. So it is not surprising that many of Earth's organisms live in or on water. Algae, fungi, frogs, fish, and giant blue whales can all be found in aquatic biomes.

Unlike land biomes, aquatic biomes are not grouped into biomes by climate. Instead, they are grouped according to water depth and **salinity.** Salinity is the amount of salt dissolved in the water. Oceans, lakes, rivers, streams, marshes, and swamps are all examples of aquatic habitats. Although rainfall and temperature affect aquatic ecosystems, they are not as important.

There are two main groups of aquatic biomes: **saltwater** biomes and **freshwater** biomes. All water biomes contain some dissolved salt and other minerals. However, oceans contain more dissolved salt than the water that is found in freshwater systems. This salinity is usually measured in parts per thousand. The salinity of ocean water is about 30 parts per thousand. The salinity of freshwater biomes is about 0.5 parts per thousand or less.

Saltwater biomes include oceans, estuaries, coral reefs, saltwater marshes, and mangrove swamps. Freshwater biomes include rivers, streams, ponds, lakes, swamps, and freshwater marshes. You will learn more about these freshwater and saltwater biomes in Lessons 6 and 7.

The depth of water in an aquatic biome also determines what kinds of organisms can survive there. In areas where sunlight can reach, there is more life. Aquatic plants use sunlight to create food. These plants form the base of aquatic food chains. In many freshwater ecosystems, sunlight can reach all the way to the bottom. In shallow ecosystems, such as ponds and streams, there is life at all depths. As sunlight decreases with depth, however, the amount of plant and animal life also decreases. In the deep ocean, the water is too dark for photosynthesis.

The Importance of Studying Biomes

Scientists study terrestrial and aquatic biomes to learn more about how organisms survive in different habitats. They investigate how organisms have adapted to temperature, rainfall, water depth, and salinity. They also study how land biomes affect aquatic biomes. For example, pollution from farming, industry, and other human activities ends up affecting aquatic biomes. To protect aquatic environments, it is important to control pollution on land. Studying biomes can also help scientists learn more about how to protect fragile environments. The next lesson will introduce one fragile biome: rain forests.

Express Lab 5

Materials
- flashlight
- globe
- cash register paper
- toilet paper tube
- masking tape

Procedure

1. Tape a strip of cash register paper on a globe from a little below the equator to the North Pole.

2. Tape the end of a toilet paper tube to the flashlight so that the beam of light will be better focused.

3. Hold the flashlight about 30 cm away from the globe. Turn it on and shine it directly at the equator.

4. On the paper, have a partner draw the shape of the area the light shines on.

5. Move the flashlight up so that it shines on the middle latitudes. Then move it so it shines near the North Pole. Repeat Step 4 each time.

Analysis

1. How do the shapes of the lighted areas change?

2. The flashlight represents the sun. How do you think the way the sun shines on Earth affects temperatures in different places?

Word Bank

aquatic

biome

salinity

On a sheet of paper, write the word from the Word Bank that completes each sentence correctly.

1. A(n) _____ is a group of ecosystems that share similar characteristics.

2. The _____ in saltwater ecosystems is higher than in freshwater ecosystems.

3. The two major types of biomes are terrestrial and _____.

On a sheet of paper, write the letter of the answer that completes each sentence correctly.

4. As the _____ increases, the temperature gets colder.

    A density   **B** altitude   **C** precipitation   **D** salinity

5. Swamps, rivers, and streams are examples of _____ biomes.

    A saltwater   **C** small

    B freshwater   **D** terrestrial

6. The two most important characteristics that influence land biomes are _____.

    A salinity and temperature   **C** salinity and latitude

    B precipitation and depth   **D** temperature and precipitation

Critical Thinking

On a sheet of paper, write the answers to the following questions. Use complete sentences.

7. How are aquatic biomes grouped?

8. Describe how vegetation changes as you climb up a mountain.

9. Do freshwater biomes contain salt? How are they considered different from saltwater biomes?

10. Explain how life changes in aquatic biomes as depth increases.

Materials

- safety goggles
- lab coat or apron
- 2 plastic jars
- water
- table salt
- stir stick
- spoon
- 2 eggs

Salinity and Density

Saltwater and freshwater biomes have different levels of salinity. Another difference between these biomes is the density of the water. In this lab, you will compare water that has different levels of salinity. You will observe how salinity and density are related and how density affects flotation.

Procedure

1. Put on safety goggles and a lab coat or apron.

2. Fill both jars about two-thirds full of water. Add about 2 teaspoons of salt to one of the jars. Stir until the salt is dissolved in the water. **Safety Alert: Do not taste or drink the saltwater solution.**

3. Using a spoon, gently place an egg in the freshwater. **Safety Alert: Be careful when handling the eggs.** Observe and record what happens.

4. Gently place the second egg in the salt water. Observe and record what happens.

Cleanup/Disposal

Before leaving the classroom, clean up your materials. Wash your hands afterward.

Analysis

1. What happened to the egg in the freshwater?

2. What happened to the egg in the salt water?

3. Which type of water has the higher salinity?

4. Density is measured by the weight of a given volume. Which has the higher density, freshwater or salt water?

Conclusions

1. Explain how the different salinities and densities of the water affected the eggs.

2. How might a change in salinity affect life in an aquatic biome?

Explore Further

Add one ice cube at a time to the jar of freshwater. Record your observations. What can you conclude about the effect of temperature on water density?

Objectives

After reading this lesson, you should be able to

◆ describe the characteristics of rain forest biomes

◆ describe how rain forest organisms have adapted to survive

Research and Write

Tropical rain forests contain an enormous variety of organisms. Research some plants and animals that can only be found in tropical rain forests. Create a poster that describes the organisms that you researched. Include photographs and drawings. Hang your poster where other classes can view it.

Forests cover about 30 percent of the earth's land surface. They contain more species than any other type of biome. The trees are what make these biomes different from others. Trees are the most important form of life in forest biomes. The types of trees determine what kinds of animals and other plants live in each forest biome.

As you learned in Chapter 4, forests provide many ecosystem services. For example, forests produce more than 40 percent of the world's oxygen. They help cool the earth's surface, absorb pollutants, and clean the water. Humans also depend on forests for food, wood, and paper.

There are many kinds of forests in the world. The three main forest biomes are rain forests, deciduous forests, and coniferous forests. In this lesson, you will learn more about rain forest biomes. In Lesson 3, you will find out more about deciduous and coniferous forests. Both lessons will explain some of the threats that all forests face.

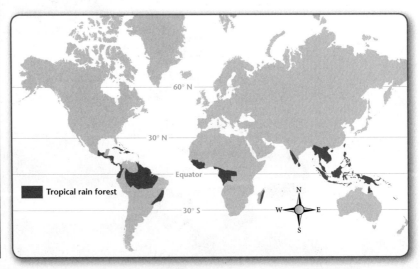

Figure 5.2.1 *Tropical rain forests are located in a belt around the equator.*

Tropical Rain Forests

Tropical rain forests are hot, humid, and full of life. They are found in a belt around the equator. See Figure 5.2.1 for the location of rain forests around the world. The largest rain forests are found in South America, Asia, and Africa. By definition, rain forests get more than 200 cm of rain a year. Some areas, however, can get more than 500 cm. Temperatures are hot all year, with averages between 20° and 30°C. Rain forests also get more energy from the sun than other biomes. Since rain forests are located near the equator, they get more direct sunlight. They also have long days all year.

Not all rain forests are in the tropics. There are also **temperate rain forests** in North America, South America, and Australia. These forests get a lot of rain, but are not warm year-round. Instead, these forests are usually mild in the winter and cool in the summer.

The warm, wet climate of tropical rain forests supports abundant vegetation. The vegetation, in turn, supports a wide variety of animal life. Rain forests are the most diverse ecosystems on Earth. Though they cover less than 7 percent of Earth's land surface, they contain more than 50 percent of all species. Scientists studying rain forests are constantly finding new species. They also believe that there are many more species waiting to be discovered.

Rain Forest Nutrients

Given the diversity in rain forests, you might think the soils are full of nutrients. However, rain forest soils are not very fertile. Most of the nutrients in a rain forest are stored in the plants. When a plant or animal dies, it is quickly broken down by decomposers living in the soil. The nutrients are soon absorbed by nearby trees and other plants. In other types of forest biomes, more nutrients are stored in the soil.

Canopy

The layer formed by the leaves and branches of the forest's tallest trees

Emergent

A tree that grows taller than the canopy trees around it

Buttress

Special root structures that support a tree and make it more stable

The thin, infertile soil creates problems when rain forests are cut down for farms or ranches. With so few nutrients, the land cannot support crops. In a few years, farmers must find new areas to farm.

Plant and Animal Diversity

One reason rain forests are so diverse is because they are so old. Many have existed for millions of years. During that time, the warm, wet climate encouraged a diversity of plants to thrive. Animal species evolved to live among these plants. Some insects, for example, look just like leaves and are hard to see. Slow-moving animals called sloths are also well camouflaged. They have algae growing in their hair, which give their fur a greenish color.

In most rain forests, there are four main layers, as shown in Figure 5.2.2. The forest **canopy** is the "roof" of the rain forest, acting like a giant umbrella. It catches most of the sunlight, letting only about 1 percent reach the ground. Giant trees called **emergents** stick up through the canopy. Some grow to heights of more than 50 m tall. Many of these giant trees have **buttresses,** or special root structures, that help support them. Monkeys and toucans are examples of species found in the canopy layers.

Figure 5.2.2 *A rain forest is divided into several layers, including the canopy, understory, and forest floor.*

The **understory** of the rain forest is made up of smaller trees and shrubs. These plants try to catch as much sunlight as they can. Some of the understory trees will eventually grow to become part of the canopy. Others will stay in the shadows of the giants.

The **forest floor** is about 20 m below the canopy. Unlike the canopy, the forest floor is in the shadows. Without much sunlight, the vegetation is sparse. There is almost no wind and the humidity is very high. Deer and Indian cobras are examples of species that can be found on the forest floor.

Protecting Rain Forests

In the last 50 years, thousands of square kilometers of tropical rain forest have been cut down. When large areas of forest are destroyed, it is called **deforestation.** Many of these forests have been turned into farmland and pastures. Some have also been **logged,** which means they were harvested for their wood. Others were cut down for natural resource exploration.

The loss of so many square kilometers of forest is creating serious problems for people and wildlife. Many species are being lost, often before scientists can identify and learn more about them. People are also concerned about the **indigenous,** or native, people that depend on forests to survive. Deforestation causes them to lose their homes and their ways of life. Unfortunately, because rain forests are so complex, it is almost impossible to replace them. Deforestation can destroy the relationships that make up a rain forest.

Link to ➢➢➢

Social Studies

More than 15.5 million square kilometers of rain forest once covered Earth. Today, only about 6.5 million square kilometers exist.

Lesson 2   R E V I E W

Word Bank

equator

rain forests

soil

On a sheet of paper, write the word or words from the Word Bank that complete each sentence correctly.

1. Tropical rain forest biomes get more than 200 cm of rainfall a year and are located near the _____.

2. Most tropical rain forests have poor _____. The land cannot support crops.

3. Asia, South America, and Africa contain the largest _____ in the world.

On a sheet of paper, write the letter of the correct answer.

4. Which of the following is **not** an ecosystem service that tropical rain forests provide?

   A absorbing pollutants   **C** making fertile soil for crops
   B providing oxygen   **D** providing food and wood

5. The tallest trees in the tropical rain forest are called _____.

   A emergents   **B** conifers   **C** shrubs   **D** mosses

6. Tropical rain forests are characterized by _____.

   A high temperatures and high salinity
   B low temperatures and low rainfall
   C low temperatures and high humidity
   D high temperatures and high rainfall

Critical Thinking

On a sheet of paper, write the answers to the following questions. Use complete sentences.

7. Why are tropical rain forest soils so infertile?

8. Describe how some animals' adaptations help them live in the rain forest.

9. What are the two main reasons for deforestation in tropical rain forests?

10. Why are tropical rain forests important to people?

Tropical rain forests are found in areas that are near the equator. If you traveled north or south from the equator, you would find two other types of forest biomes. They are temperate deciduous forests and coniferous forests. In this chapter, you will learn more about these forest biomes and what makes them special. See Figure 5.3.1 for the locations of these two biomes.

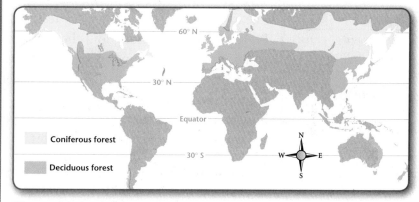

Figure 5.3.1 *Deciduous forests are located in temperate zones, while coniferous forests are located farther north.*

Temperate deciduous forest

A deciduous forest that grows in temperate regions of the world

Deciduous tree

A tree that sheds its leaves at the end of the growing season

Temperate Deciduous Forests

Most of the forests in the eastern half of North America are **temperate deciduous forests.** These forests are mostly made up of **deciduous trees,** which shed their leaves every autumn. Deciduous forests are some of the most photographed in the world, especially in autumn. When the weather starts getting colder, their leaves show bright shades of red, orange, and yellow. Eventually, they fall to the ground.

Science Myth

Myth: Leaves change color in the autumn.

Fact: The different "autumn colors" of leaves are present throughout the summer. They are hidden by the green pigment that is used for photosynthesis. In the autumn, however, deciduous trees stop producing the green pigment. Without this pigment, the leaves show their other colors.

Hibernate

To pass the winter in a sleeplike condition

Migrate

To move from one region, climate, or environment to another

Dormant

Inactive

Humus

Decomposed plant and animal material that is part of fertile soil

Reptile

A scaly, egg-laying animal that breathes with lungs

Amphibian

An animal that spends part of its life in water and part on land

Temperate deciduous forests are located in the temperate zones, between 30° and 50° north latitude. Outside North America, they are found in Europe, Asia, Australia, New Zealand, and South America. These forests are very different from tropical rain forests. Instead of having hot temperatures all year, they have four seasons: spring, summer, autumn, and winter. The average yearly temperature in a deciduous forest is 10°C. The average rainfall is 75 to 150 cm a year, less than in tropical forests.

Life in Deciduous Forests

Life in deciduous forests has adapted to changing seasons. Precipitation falls throughout the year. However, during the winter the precipitation is usually snow. Most water is frozen and harder for animals to drink. Animals living in this biome adjust to cold winters and hot summers in many ways. Some **hibernate,** or become inactive in the winter. Others **migrate,** moving to areas with warmer climates.

When the days get shorter in autumn, this causes changes in the forest. The trees shed their leaves and become **dormant,** which means they are inactive. This allows them to save water during the cold winter months. They also use food stored in their roots and trunk. The fallen leaves create a rich layer of soil called **humus.** The humus and fallen leaves provide a home for many organisms, including earthworms and fungi. When the days get longer and the ground warms, new leaves grow and photosynthesis begins again.

Deciduous forests do not have the diversity found in tropical rain forests. However, they still support a large variety of plants and animals. Foxes, raccoons, and deer live in these forests. Owls, hawks, and other birds nest here. These forests are also home to many kinds of **reptiles, amphibians,** and insects. Reptiles are scaly, egg-laying animals that breathe with lungs, such as snakes and turtles. Amphibians are animals, such as frogs and salamanders, that spend part of their lives in water and part on land. All of these creatures can be found in deciduous forests.

Coniferous forest

A forest in northern latitudes dominated by conifers

Taiga

Another name for a coniferous forest

Conifer

A cone-bearing tree that has needles instead of leaves and stays green all year

Evergreen

A tree that keeps its leaves or needles all year

Link to ≫≫≫

Earth Science

Forest fires can destroy thousands of trees. However, forest fires can also bring life to some trees. Some types of pine trees, such as jack pine, require the extreme heat of a fire to open their cones and release seeds.

Coniferous Forests

In northern latitudes, there are vast **coniferous forests.** Coniferous forests are also called the **taiga.** While there are some deciduous trees in a coniferous forest, most are **conifers.** Conifers are cone-bearing trees, meaning they produce their seeds in cones. They also stay green all year. Because of this, they are also known as **evergreens.** Unlike deciduous trees, they have needles rather than broad leaves. Coniferous forests are characterized by tight groups of smaller trees. They include spruces, hemlocks, firs, larches, and pines. Large coniferous forests can be found in Europe, North America, and Asia.

Coniferous forests are the largest terrestrial biome in the world. These forests are located between 50° north latitude and the Arctic Circle. They are also found at high altitudes in many parts of the world. The winters in these biomes can get very cold. The average temperature is below 0°C for six months of the year.

▼◄▲▼◄▲▼◄▲▼◄▲▼◄▲▼◄▲▼◄▲▼◄▲▼◄▲▼◄▲▼◄▲▼◄▲▼

Science at Work

Park Naturalist

Park naturalists work for federal agencies, such as the National Park Service, as well as for state parks. They work to protect the natural resources on public lands. They may also lead hikes in national parks or treat injured visitors. Park naturalists work in cities and suburbs, as well as large wilderness areas.

A person who likes to work outdoors and with others might enjoy being a park naturalist. Good communication and teaching skills are helpful, as naturalists may run tours or teach classes. A bachelor's degree in forestry or botany provides a good background for this career. Park naturalists may start their career as volunteers before being hired as full-time employees.

Coniferous forests get less rainfall than tropical and deciduous forests, about 25 to 200 cm a year. Most precipitation falls during the summer months. As a result, coniferous forests have fewer animal species than rain forests and deciduous forests.

Conifers are well adapted to their habitat. Their needlelike leaves are not large and flat leaves like deciduous trees. Instead, they are thin and waxy. They lose less water and shed snow more easily than the leaves of deciduous trees. The needles also do not fall off in autumn. Most conifers keep their leaves for two to three years. Some keep their needles for more than 10 years. Since most evergreens lose their leaves a few at a time, the change is often not noticed.

Life in Coniferous Forests

Plants and animals in coniferous forests are adapted to long winters and the resources conifers provide. Many small animals, such as squirrels and mice, feed on the seeds inside the cones. Larger herbivores, such as elk and moose, feed on bark and berries. Bears, wolves, and lynx feed on the herbivores. When the conditions get really tough, some species will migrate to warmer areas. Others will hibernate or live under the protective blanket of snow.

With such long, cold winters, decomposition is very slow in coniferous forests. Vegetation builds up on the forest floor, making it feel like a sponge. The soil is very thin and **acidic,** containing more acids because of the needles. Like rain forest soils, coniferous forest soils also lack nutrients. Few plants grow on the forest floor because of poor soil and lack of sunlight.

❋ ❋

Technology and Society

Most banks offer online banking. Instead of sending out monthly statements, banks post account information on a protected Web site. Banks also provide online bill paying. Bank customers can have money transferred electronically. These services save paper by limiting the use of paper statements, envelopes, and checks.

Threats to Forest Biomes

Forests around the world are being developed, or changed from natural environments into built environments. Many deciduous forests have been cut down to make way for farms, cities, and roads. Coniferous forests are also disappearing as they are cut down and sold for timber. Timber is wood used to build and make everyday items. Wood is also ground up, or pulped, to make paper. Many forests have been replanted, but few have the same diversity of the original forest.

Losing forests means losing habitat for the species that live there. In Chapter 12, you will learn more about how losing forests causes loss of biodiversity. You will also learn about what people are doing to help protect forest biomes.

Science in Your Life

Technology: Environmentally Friendly Books

Forests are getting help from book publishers. Until recently, printing books meant that old trees would be cut down to provide paper. Now, books can be printed on paper that does not affect forest biomes.

One way that book publishers help is by using recycled paper. Recycled paper can be made from scraps produced during regular papermaking. It can also be made from paper that has already been printed on. This second type of paper is called post-consumer paper. The more post-consumer paper used, the better it is for forests.

In the future, publishers may use paper made from farm crops instead of trees. This papermaking process uses parts of the plant that are not eaten. For example, fiber from a banana plant can be made into paper. Look at the next book you read to see if it is printed on recycled paper.

1. Why is it important to find new processes for printing books?

2. How might using young trees be another way for publishers to help forests?

3. How do environmentally friendly books affect you?

Lesson 3   R E V I E W

<table>
<tr><td>Word Bank</td></tr>
<tr><td>coniferous</td></tr>
<tr><td>deciduous</td></tr>
</table>

On a sheet of paper, write the word from the Word Bank that completes each sentence correctly. Each word will be used more than once.

1. Maples, dogwoods, and oaks are all examples of _____ trees, which shed their leaves every year.

2. Pines, spruces, and hemlocks are all examples of _____ trees, which have needles and shed their leaves over time.

3. Boreal forests and taiga are other names for _____ forests.

4. Known for their brightly colored leaves in fall, _____ forests are found in temperate areas of the world.

On a sheet of paper, write the letter of the answer that completes each sentence correctly.

5. The dark, organic matter in the soil of deciduous forests is _____.

   A the understory   **B** humus   **C** minerals   **D** compost

6. The annual rainfall in temperate deciduous forests is about _____ a year.

   A 30–60 cm   **C** less than 10 cm
   B more than 200 cm   **D** 75–150 cm

Critical Thinking

On a sheet of paper, write the answers to the following questions. Use complete sentences.

7. Contrast the temperatures of coniferous forest and temperate deciduous forest biomes.

8. Describe the changes that deciduous trees experience when weather gets cold.

9. Why are coniferous trees known as "evergreens"?

10. Give some examples of the threats that forests face.

After reading this lesson, you should be able to

◆ describe how grassland biomes are different from forest biomes

◆ describe the characteristics of savannas, temperate grasslands, and chaparral

◆ describe how species have adapted to life in grassland biomes

Grassland biomes are found on every continent except Antarctica. Figure 5.4.1 shows the locations of grassland biomes throughout the world. These are large, open spaces without many shrubs or trees. Some grasslands are mostly grass. Others have small shrubs mixed with other dry weather plants.

Grasslands

Grasslands are found where it is too wet for deserts but too dry for forests. Grassland biomes receive less than 75 cm of precipitation per year. Scientists estimate that about 25 percent of the earth's land area is covered with grasslands. About 70 percent of the food people eat comes from grassland areas. This lesson explains more about the major grassland biomes and why each is unique.

Grassland

A large, grassy biome with few shrubs or trees

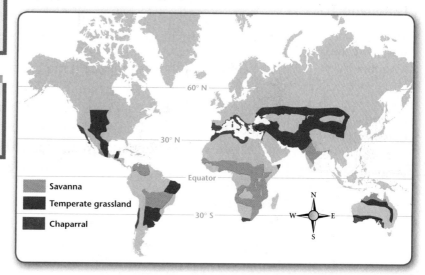

Figure 5.4.1 *Grassland biomes include savannas, temperate grasslands, and chaparral.*

Savanna

A tropical grassland with scattered trees or clumps of trees

Temperate grassland

A grassland biome found in temperate areas of the world; also called steppes, pampas, veldts, and prairies

Prairie

A temperate grassland with very fertile soil

Link to ➤➤➤

Language Arts

The word *temperate* means "moderate temperatures." Biomes such as temperate grasslands and temperate forests are neither very cold nor very hot.

Savannas

Some grasslands are found in and just outside tropical areas. These grasslands are called **savannas.** Savannas are found near the equator between tropical rain forests and desert biomes. They have grassy areas with scattered trees.

When many people think of Africa, they think of the savannas. You have probably seen movies of the savannas in Africa. Herbivores such as elephants, giraffes, and rhinoceroses are some savanna animals you might recognize. Savannas have a wet and a dry season. The climate is usually warm, with temperatures ranging from 20°C to nearly 30°C. The total rainfall is about 50 to 150 cm per year. Most of this precipitation falls during the six- to eight-month wet season.

Savanna plants have adapted to survive the dry season. Many plants have large, horizontal root systems that grow out instead of down. They have also adapted to sprout and grow quickly after fires. Many of the trees and shrubs have thorns to try to keep hungry herbivores away.

The animals of the savanna often migrate to find water and food. Many species share the limited food by feeding on plants at different heights. Giraffes feed on taller plants, while smaller herbivores, such as zebras, feed on low-growing grass. Many predators, such as lions and hyenas, follow the herbivores and feed on them.

Temperate Grasslands

Many of the world's grassland biomes are found in temperate areas. These **temperate grasslands** are called different names in different parts of the world. In Asia they are called steppes. In South America they are called pampas. In South Africa they are called veldts. In North America, they are called **prairies.** These biomes get about 25 to 60 cm of precipitation per year.

Prairies are covered by grasses. Unlike the savannas, there are very few trees in prairies. A few trees, such as cottonwoods, oaks, and willows, grow in river valleys. These grassy plains have hot summers and cold winters. Short-grass prairies receive the least amount of rain. Tall-grass prairies get the most rain and have the tallest grasses. Sunflowers and other tall-grass prairie plants can grow up to 1.5 m tall.

Prairie animals include the American bison, badgers, and coyotes. You can also find black-tailed prairie dogs and endangered black-footed ferrets there. Birds, such as meadowlarks and quail, also live in prairies. They feed on insects, such as crickets, grasshoppers, and caterpillars.

Prairies grow on some of the most fertile land in the world. The soil is deep and rich. That is why so many prairies have been turned into farmland and ranches. Many people call prairie lands the "breadbaskets of the world." This is because so many grains and cereals come from prairie lands, including flour.

Unfortunately, farming has changed the prairies. Crops do not hold the soil in place as well as native grasses. As a result the top layer of soil, called **topsoil,** often washes away. This also happens due to **overgrazing.** Overgrazing is allowing farm animals to eat more of the native vegetation than is healthy for the soil. During overgrazing, animals also pack down the soil, making it hard for new plants to grow.

Today, less than 1 percent of North America's original prairie lands remain. The good news is that people are working to protect and restore these important biomes. They are doing so by setting aside areas of prairie lands as national parks. They are also replanting areas of prairie lands with native vegetation.

Chaparral

Have you ever seen a picture of the famous "Hollywood" sign in Los Angeles? If so, you have seen the **chaparral.** These dry grasslands are found in coastal areas. They are found in the United States, South America, South Africa, Australia, and the Mediterranean. Chaparral biomes are characterized by tight groups of evergreen shrubs and short, scrubby plants. Some areas of chaparral have flat plains. Others have rocky hills or mountain slopes.

Chaparral biomes are found in temperate areas. However, they do not get enough rain to support trees or a diversity of plants. They have hot, dry summers, and mild, wetter winters. Temperatures can soar to more than 38°C in the summer.

Most plants in the chaparral have small, hard leaves that help **conserve,** or save, water. Scrub oak, yucca, cacti, and sage are all plants adapted to life in the chaparral. They have root systems that are designed to absorb as much water as possible. They pull water from the surface and from underground. Many of these plants have also adapted to survive periodic fires.

The animals that live in these environments have also adapted to hot, dry weather. Some, like jackrabbits and mule deer, have large ears to help cool their bodies. Others stay out of the heat during the day and look for food when it cools off. You might see coyotes, lizards, hawks, quail, and horned toads in these biomes.

The biggest threat to chaparral biomes around the world is human activities. The chaparral is often near the coast, where many people prefer to live. Many areas of chaparral have been developed for homes and businesses. This includes much of southern California.

The U.S. Forest Service protects and maintains many national forests and grasslands for everyone to use. These lands total 781,000 square kilometers—about the size of Texas. The forests managed by the U.S. Forest Service are used for recreation, research, logging, and other activities. They also provide homes to a variety of wildlife. Use the map to answer the following questions.

LEGEND

National forests
National grasslands

1. Which type of protected land does the United States have more of, national forest or national grassland?

2. Where are most of the national forests in the United States located?

3. Name one state that does not contain a national forest or grassland.

4. Which state has the most national forest land?

5. Why are the grasslands mostly located in different parts of the United States than the forests?

Lesson 4   R E V I E W

Word Bank

chaparral

temperate
grasslands

savannas

On a sheet of paper, write the word or words from the Word Bank that complete each sentence correctly.

1. Pampas, veldt, and steppes are names for _____ in different parts of the world.

2. Animals living in _____ have adapted to dry weather, and often migrate to find food or water.

3. Coastal grasslands, also called _____, have scrubby plants and evergreen shrubs.

On a sheet of paper, write the letter of the answer that completes each sentence correctly.

4. Less than _____ percent of North America's original prairies still remain.

   A 25   **B** 10   **C** 5   **D** 1

5. Grasslands are found on all of the following continents except _____.

   A Africa   **B** Antarctica   **C** Europe   **D** North America

6. Savannas are grasslands that are found _____.

   A near the equator   **C** on the coast
   B in the mountains   **D** in temperate areas

Critical Thinking

On a sheet of paper, write the answers to the following questions. Use complete sentences.

7. What do some animals do to survive life in the chaparral?

8. Describe the location of prairies.

9. Why are trees not found in the chaparral?

10. What has caused the decline in prairie lands?

DISCOVERY INVESTIGATION 5

Materials

- 2 aluminum pie plates
- soil
- grass seeds
- radish seeds
- balance or scale
- water
- watering can

Grassland Erosion

Rainfall and streams can cause soils to erode. This can harm habitats on land and in the water. Planting grasses and other plants keeps the soils from washing away. In this lab, you will test how well different plants prevent land from eroding.

Procedure

1. In a small group, review the characteristics of grassland biomes. Note the type of vegetation and the amount of rainfall.

2. Write out a procedure for comparing how well certain plants prevent grasslands from eroding.

Continued on next page

3. Have your procedure approved by your teacher. Include Safety Alerts and a data table with headings.

4. Label the two pie plates. Fill each with a layer of soil, then plant grass seeds in one and radish seeds in the other. Place the pie plates in a sunny area.

5. Wait a few weeks for the plants to grow, watering them regularly. Then begin your experiment.

6. Follow your procedure for testing how well different types of plants prevent erosion. Record your results in your data table.

Cleanup/Disposal

Follow your teacher's instructions for disposing of your soil and plants.

Analysis

1. Which plant did the best job of preventing erosion? Explain.

2. How could you change the experiment to compare erosion from wind?

Conclusions

1. What types of plants do you think landscapers might plant on a hill?

2. How do the roots of different plants affect erosion?

Explore Further

Use your procedure to measure the erosion of bare soil with no plants. Compare the measurements with your results above.

Objectives

After reading this lesson, you should be able to

◆ compare and contrast desert and tundra biomes

◆ describe tundra plants and animals and their adaptations

◆ describe desert plants and animals and their adaptations

◆ describe threats to desert and tundra biomes

Tundra

A treeless plain that stays frozen most of the year and receives very little precipitation

Arctic tundra

Tundra located north of the Arctic Circle

Alpine tundra

Tundra located above the tree line of high mountains

At first, you might think that tundra biomes have little in common with desert biomes. The tundra is the coldest of all the biomes. Deserts are the hottest. So what do they share? These biomes get the least precipitation of all the biomes. Figure 5.5.1 illustrates where these biomes are located. In this lesson, you will learn more about each of these dry areas. You will also learn how the organisms in each biome have adapted to life without rain.

Tundra Biomes

The word **tundra** comes from the Finnish word *tunturia*, which means "treeless plain." Tundra biomes are frozen landscapes, with low temperatures and few plants or animals. Tundra biomes have very short growing seasons. They get less than 25 cm of rain per year and stay frozen most of the year.

There are two types of tundra biomes. **Arctic tundra** is located north of the Arctic Circle. **Alpine tundra** is located on mountains above the tree line, at high altitudes where trees cannot grow. Both the Arctic tundra and alpine tundra have short summers and long winters. The major plants are grasses, lichens, and other plants that can survive without much soil.

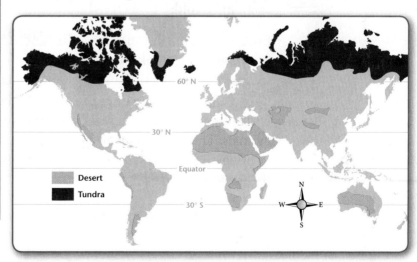

Figure 5.5.1 *Tundra and desert biomes get the least amount of precipitation, though they are found in very different locations.*

Permafrost

Permanently frozen ground at high latitude and high elevation

Bog

An area of wet, spongy ground full of decomposing plant matter

Arctic Tundra

Arctic tundra is known for its short growing season, desertlike conditions, and cold temperatures. These biomes extend from the Arctic to the coniferous forests. They stay so cold that underneath the topsoil there is a permanently frozen layer of soil. This layer is called the **permafrost.** During the summer, the top layer of soil thaws, forming **bogs** and shallow ponds. A bog is an area of wet, spongy ground full of decomposing plant matter. These marshy areas breed swarms of mosquitoes, black flies, and other insects that attract birds. Birds feed on these insects until the weather gets too cold.

Although conditions are harsh, the tundra supports a wide variety of plants. These plants have adapted to little precipitation and cold climates. They have also adapted to winds that sweep across the frozen land. Lichens, mosses, grasses, small shrubs, and short flowers are typical plants of the tundra biomes.

Some animals hibernate to survive the lack of food in the winter. Many have adapted to breed and raise their young quickly during the short, cool summers. Many birds migrate south to warmer weather and more food. Some species have an extra layer of fat or extra-thick fur for more protection against the cold.

Even with its harsh conditions, the tundra has more species than you might think. Herbivores, including lemmings, musk ox, caribou, and arctic hares, feed on the plants and shrubs. Carnivores, such as arctic foxes and polar bears, feed on the herbivores. They also eat seals, walruses, and other marine animals. There are many birds, such as falcons and snow buntings. There are even arctic bumblebees that pollinate the flowering plants.

Extract

To take out or harvest

The tundra has harsh conditions, yet it is actually a very fragile environment. Footprints and tire tracks can remain on the ground for years, as seen in Figure 5.2.2. Soil forms very slowly. People have moved to the tundra to work for companies that remove, or **extract,** oil and minerals. Oil pipelines now stretch long distances across the tundra. New towns and roads have been built in many parts of the tundra. Scientists are concerned that the arrival of more people is harming the native species. For example, pesticides used to control the insects during the summer are affecting birds. Oil spills have also affected many species on land and in the ocean. Oil pipelines have changed the migration routes of caribou and other large animals.

Alpine Tundra

Alpine tundra is found on the tops of mountains throughout the world. Although these environments are similar to the Arctic tundra, alpine habitats have longer growing seasons. There are many types of grasses, small trees, and shrubs with small leaves. Alpine animals include mountain goats, mountain sheep, and elk.

Alpine tundra is similarly fragile. Activities such as grazing sheep can damage native vegetation. Alpine vegetation can take hundreds of years to recover because there is so little precipitation. The growing season is also very short because the areas are so cold. Activities like off-road driving can damage the alpine ecosystem for years.

Figure 5.5.2 *Human damage to tundra ecosystems can remain for many years.*

Desert Biomes

Some **desert** biomes are sandy. Others are covered with smooth stones or dry, cracked mud. Some are very hot. Others can be covered by a blanket of snow. However, like the tundra, deserts share one important characteristic: they are all very dry. Deserts are defined as areas that get less than 25 cm of precipitation a year.

Deserts are spread out on five continents: Africa, Asia, North America, South America, and Australia. They cover about one-fifth of the earth's land area. There are about 20 major deserts, most of which are **hot deserts.** That means they have hot temperatures most of the year. The Chihuahua Desert in North America and the Sahara Desert in Africa are two examples. The rest of the world's deserts are called **cold deserts.** Although these deserts can be hot during parts of the year, their temperatures can drop below freezing. Many cold deserts get more than half their moisture from snow. The Patagonia Desert in South America and the Great Basin Desert in North America are examples.

In addition to lack of rainfall, many deserts have a high rate of evaporation. In some deserts, rain evaporates before it even hits the ground. One reason is that deserts have very little cloud cover. The sun's radiation strikes the desert floor directly. Many deserts also have strong winds that increase the rate of evaporation. Another characteristic of many deserts is that rain may not fall for long stretches of time. Weeks or even months may pass without precipitation.

Many deserts have soils that are rich in minerals. That is because there is limited rainfall. The minerals are not washed out of the soil. Deserts also have almost no topsoil because there is very little organic material.

Desert

An area with a high rate of evaporation that receives very little precipitation; can be hot or cold

Hot desert

A desert where temperatures are hot all year

Cold desert

A desert where temperatures can drop below 0°C

Link to ➤➤➤

Biology

Most desert plants have characteristics that allow them to live with little water. For example, the leaves of a cactus plant are in the form of spines. If the leaves were large and flat, they would dry out quickly in the desert environment.

Life in the Desert

Everything that lives in the desert has adapted to conserve water. In hot deserts, species have also adapted to survive high temperatures and lack of shade.

Desert plants have many adaptations that help them store and find water. Some desert plants have seeds that do not grow until there is enough rain. Many desert plants have small leaves and stems that are covered with a coating like wax. This coating helps keep water from escaping.

Some desert plants have long roots to reach water underground. Others have shallow roots that absorb as much water as possible when it rains. Some species also can store water in their leaves and stems. When there is no rain, they can use the stored water.

Animals that live in deserts have as many adaptations for survival as plants do. Kangaroo rats, pocket mice, and other small animals rarely drink. They get the moisture they need from the food they eat. Larger animals, such as antelopes in African deserts, travel long distances to find water. Some desert creatures, such as spadefoot toads, snails, and spiders, "sleep" through dry times. This is just like other animals hibernating during cold weather.

With so little water, desert ecosystems are very difficult to repair once disturbed. When the plants disappear, the animals that use them for food and shelter also disappear. This affects all desert animals, from hummingbirds to mountain lions. Without protection, desert ecosystems can become just as lifeless as many people think they are.

On a sheet of paper, write the word from the Word Bank that completes each sentence correctly.

Word Bank
desert
permafrost
tundra

1. The _____ is a layer of soil underneath the topsoil that is always frozen.

2. The _____ biome can be hot or cold, and can be found in Africa, Asia, North America, South America, and Australia.

3. A _____ biome is a frozen landscape, with few plants or animals.

On a sheet of paper, write the letter of the answer that completes each sentence correctly.

4. In many deserts, the rate of _____ is extremely high. This causes many plants to conserve water.

   A evaporation   **C** freezing
   B condensation   **D** flooding

5. All deserts are _____.

   A hot   **B** lifeless   **C** dry   **D** windy

6. The major plant life found in a tundra includes _____.

   A trees   **B** vegetables   **C** seaweeds   **D** grasses

Critical Thinking

On a sheet of paper, write the answers to the following questions. Use complete sentences.

7. Describe some of the characteristics of desert plants that help them conserve water.

8. How can extracting oil harm the tundra?

9. How are hot and cold deserts alike? How are hot and cold deserts different?

10. Describe how animals survive in the tundra environment.

Objectives

After reading this lesson, you should be able to

◆ define the vertical and horizontal zones in the ocean

◆ explain why coral reefs are important habitats

◆ describe three types of coastal wetlands

Marine biomes are aquatic ecosystems that contain larger amounts of salt than freshwater biomes. They are divided into three general types of ecosystems. The first is the open ocean, which is the largest ecosystem. Coral reefs are the second major ecosystem. They are found near the equator and are some of the richest ecosystems on Earth. The coastal wetlands, where the ocean meets the land, are the third type of ecosystems. Figure 5.6.1 shows the locations of marine biomes throughout the world.

Marine Biomes

Marine biomes are made up of a variety of plant and animal communities. They are affected by salinity, water depth, and temperature. They are also affected by the amount of sunlight and nutrients they receive.

Marine biome

An ocean or other saltwater ecosystem

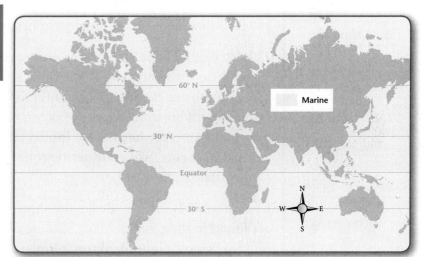

Figure 5.6.1 *Marine biomes cover most of the earth.*

The World's Oceans

More than 97 percent of all the water on Earth is salt water. Oceans cover more than three-quarters of the earth's surface. They affect people everywhere, even those living far from the coast. Huge amounts of water evaporate from the oceans every day. This evaporated water is carried by the wind around the globe. Eventually, the water falls as rain or snow. Without this precipitation, life on land would not be possible.

Oceans also help organisms to breathe. Trillions of tiny plants called algae continually give off oxygen through photosynthesis. The oceans also absorb huge amounts of carbon dioxide. This may slow down the rate of climate change.

Ocean Zones

To study the ocean, scientists divide it into several zones. **Vertical zones** are based on water depth. Each zone is home to a different community adapted to life at that depth. **Horizontal zones** are classified by the distance from shore. See Figure 5.6.2 on page 199 for a diagram of these different zones and their organisms.

The top vertical zone is called the **photic zone,** or sunlit zone. It gets the most solar energy. This is the zone where aquatic plants can thrive, because photosynthesis can take place here. Two different horizontal zones of ocean life are found only in the photic zone: the **neritic** and **intertidal zones.** The intertidal zone is near shore, while the neritic zone stretches along the continental shelf.

Marine animals such as whales, dolphins, squid, and fish are found in these zones. Many of these creatures feed on microscopic **phytoplankton, zooplankton,** or **krill.** Phytoplankton are producers that are the base of the marine food chain. Zooplankton and krill are microscopic animals that provide food for larger marine organisms.

Vertical zone

An ocean zone classified by water depth

Horizontal zone

An ocean zone classified by the distance from shore

Photic zone

The top zone of ocean life, which gets sunlight all year

Neritic zone

The zone between the intertidal zone and the edge of the continental shelf

Intertidal zone

The zone between the high and low tide marks

Phytoplankton

A microscopic plant that forms the base of the marine food chain

Zooplankton

Microscopic animals that float freely in the water

Krill

Tiny, shrimplike animals that provide food for marine creatures

---

About 200 m below the surface, the **disphotic zone,** or twilight zone, begins. This zone receives very little or no sunlight, and the water is cold. Many creatures living in this zone have large eyes to capture enough light to see. Many are also well camouflaged so that prey cannot see them in the dim light. This zone is included in the **oceanic zone** of ocean life, a horizontal zone that includes the open ocean.

About 1,000 m below the surface, the **aphotic zone** begins. The water here is very cold and completely dark. The water pressure, or the weight of the water, is high enough to crush a person. Sea cucumbers, sea spiders, and sponges can be found in these habitats. Unusual fish with weird shapes and glowing body parts also live there. Many creatures that live in the aphotic zone feed on tiny pieces of dead plants and animals that fall from above. These bits of organic material are called **detritus.**

The **abyss** is more than 4,000 m below the surface. Although some creatures can survive, it is very cold and dark. Hot, mineral-rich water shoots through vents in some parts of the ocean floor. This provides food and a home for bacteria, tube worms, clams, and crabs. Creatures of the aphotic zone and abyss are part of the oceanic zone of ocean life.

Figure 5.6.2 *The photic, disphotic, and aphotic zones divide the ocean into different zones of life.*

Coral Reefs

Coral reefs are some of the largest and oldest ecosystems. Reefs are made up of **colonies** of tiny animals. Colonies are groups of the same type of organism living and growing together. These living things, called coral polyps, create "skeletons" out of calcium carbonate. Over hundreds and thousands of years, these polyps build up giant reefs. These diverse and colorful places are home to one-third of all known fish species. They also contain thousands of other species, including shellfish and sea horses.

There are many types of coral and many types of reefs. Most coral reefs are found in warm, shallow ocean waters near the equator. Some, called **barrier reefs,** grow parallel to the coast. The Great Barrier Reef, for example, is found off the coast of Australia. Barrier reefs help protect the land from storms and rough waves.

In Chapter 1, you learned how coral reefs around the world are dying. They are affected by changes in water temperature and quality. Global warming continues to threaten these ecosystems. You will learn more about the problem of global warming in Chapter 9.

Coastal Wetlands

Coastal wetlands include several different types of marine ecosystems. **Wetlands** are low areas that are **saturated** with water for at least part of the year. Some of these areas are washed by the tides several times a day. Others are covered by salt water all of the time or are a mix of freshwater and salt water.

Estuaries

Estuaries are areas where freshwater streams or rivers mix with ocean waters. They are very nutrient-rich because nutrients are constantly added from both freshwater sources and the ocean. Seaweeds, marsh grasses, and mangrove trees thrive here. These plants, in turn, support diverse populations of fish, worms, oysters, barnacles, and waterfowl.

Coral reef

A marine ecosystem formed from the skeletons of corals

Colony

A group of the same kind of organisms growing and living together

Barrier reef

A long coral reef that acts as a barrier against tides and winds

Coastal wetland

A wetland washed by tides, always under salt water or under a mix of freshwater and salt water

Wetland

A low area that is saturated with water

Saturated

Unable to hold more liquid

Estuary

A marine ecosystem where freshwater and salt water meet

Many of the world's major ports, such as New York, are built on estuaries. Because they are connected to rivers, they offer access to oceans. Many estuaries suffer from serious pollution problems due to wastes from these cities and rivers. Sewage, pesticides, and sediment are harming the organisms that live in these ecosystems.

Salt Marshes and Mangrove Swamps

Like all coastal wetlands, **salt marshes** and **mangrove swamps** are washed by the tides. For part of the day, these coastal wetlands are flooded. When the tide retreats, the plants and animals become exposed to the air again. Rising and falling tides affect the temperature and salinity.

Salt marshes are open, grassy wetlands. They are covered with salt-tolerant grasses and other low-lying plants. These areas are very rich in nutrients. Salt marshes are important **nurseries** for many species of fish. Saltwater nurseries are areas where marine organisms hatch and grow. Many larger animals, such as raccoons, use the marshes as hunting grounds. Migrating birds also depend on these important habitats.

Instead of grasses, mangrove swamps are covered by mangrove trees. Mangrove trees have adapted to conditions that few other trees can survive. The wet ground is very unstable. Mangrove trees have shallow roots the form a "raft" to keep them upright. Also, salt water is poisonous to most plants. The mangrove survives by filtering salt out of the water it takes in.

Mangrove swamps are only found in warm climates. Mangrove swamps can help protect coastlines from storm damage and prevent erosion. Unfortunately, many mangrove swamps around the world have been destroyed. Many are being cut down to make way for shrimp farms and other types of development.

Marine biomes cover most of the earth. This fact may make it difficult to believe they can be harmed. However, pollution and global warming are damaging many marine ecosystems around the world. Chapter 8 will cover the issues of water resources and water pollution.

Salt marsh

A marsh periodically flooded by marine water

Mangrove swamp

A saltwater swamp dominated by mangrove trees

Nursery

A place where marine organisms hatch and grow

Lesson 6   R E V I E W

Word Bank

coastal wetlands

coral reefs

freshwater

salt water

On a sheet of paper, write the word or words from the Word Bank that complete each sentence correctly.

1. More that 97 percent of all water on Earth is _____.

2. An estuary is where _____ mixes with ocean water.

3. Three marine biomes include the ocean, _____, and _____.

On a sheet of paper, write the letter of the answer that completes each sentence correctly.

4. Oceans absorb large amounts of _____.

    A ozone   **C** carbon dioxide

    B oxygen   **D** hydrogen peroxide

5. Coral reefs are made up of tiny animals called coral _____.

    A polyps   **B** shells   **C** leaves   **D** cells

6. The deepest part of the ocean is the _____.

    A abyss   **C** disphotic zone

    B aphotic zone   **D** photic zone

Critical Thinking

On a sheet of paper, write the answers to the following questions. Use complete sentences.

7. Explain how oceans produce oxygen.

8. Describe how giant coral reefs form.

9. Can all ocean life live in the disphotic zone? Explain your answer.

10. Many cities and ports are built on estuaries. How might this cause problems for estuary wildlife?

Objectives

After reading this lesson, you should be able to

◆ explain the importance of freshwater biomes

◆ describe the two categories of freshwater biomes

◆ compare and contrast ponds and lakes

◆ describe two examples of freshwater wetlands

Finite

Having an end, limited

Standing-water ecosystem

A body of freshwater surrounded by land that does not have flowing water

Flowing-water ecosystem

A freshwater ecosystem that has flowing water, such as a river or stream

Unlike marine biomes, freshwater biomes have a salt concentration of less than half a percent. People and wildlife depend on freshwater biomes for their survival. However, freshwater is a **finite** resource, which means it can run out. Only about 3 percent of the water on Earth is freshwater. Figure 5.7.1 shows where freshwater is found in liquid form.

Most of that freshwater is not available to living things. It is stored in the ice caps of Antarctica and Greenland or as groundwater. The small amount that is left is about 1 percent of the earth's water supply. This 1 percent is what makes up rivers, streams, lakes, ponds, and wetlands. It is also the water available for everything from drinking to bathing.

Freshwater biomes are divided into **standing-water ecosystems** and **flowing-water ecosystems.** Lakes and ponds are the most common standing-water ecosystems. Freshwater bogs, swamps, and freshwater marshes also fall into this group. Flowing-water ecosystems include examples of water on the move, like rivers, streams, and creeks.

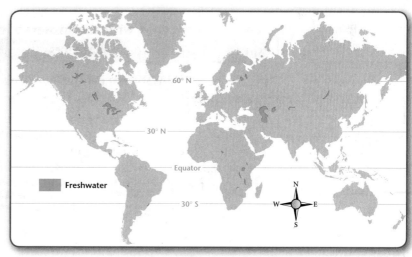

Figure 5.7.1 *Freshwater biomes are the smallest biomes on Earth.*

Lakes and Ponds

Lakes and **ponds** both have standing water all year. The main difference is size. Ponds are smaller than lakes. They are shallow enough to support plants with roots, such as cattails and reeds. A lake is larger and deeper. It is too deep for plants with roots to grow, except along the shore.

Ponds usually have fairly even water temperatures from top to bottom. When the air temperature changes, the water temperature changes. Most also have mud-covered bottoms that support plant life. The amount of dissolved oxygen in ponds can change during the day. Because they are so shallow, some ponds freeze completely during the winter. Also, some ponds are **seasonal,** which means they dry up during part of the year.

Lakes are deep enough that during the summer there are layers with different temperatures. The top layer stays warm, the middle is cooler, and the bottom is the coldest. Lakes are deep enough that light cannot reach all the way to the bottom. That means that photosynthesis is limited to the top layer. Most lake organisms spend the summer in the upper layers. However, plankton and organisms such as fish are found throughout all the layers of the lake.

❋ ❋

Technology and Society

Sources of freshwater are constantly examined for changes that may affect people and wildlife. The Environmental Monitoring and Assessment Program (EMAP) is a research program created by the U.S. Environmental Protection Agency. EMAP's technology allows multiple water tests to be combined and analyzed. Then scientists can notice trends and make predictions about future effects on freshwater biomes.

Lake

An inland body of freshwater, larger than a pond and too deep for plants to grow on the bottom

Pond

An inland body of freshwater, smaller than a lake and shallow enough for plants to grow on the bottom

Seasonal

Existing only at certain times during the year

Most lakes contain freshwater, but the Great Salt Lake in Utah is full of salt water. Streams empty salt and minerals into this lake. Many early explorers believed that it was connected to the ocean.

Rivers and Streams

Rivers and streams are bodies of water that flow over the land. In general, rivers are larger than streams, brooks, and creeks. However, all of them empty into a lake, another river or stream, or the ocean.

River and stream ecosystems are diverse freshwater habitats. They begin at their **headwaters,** which are often natural springs. Springs are areas where freshwater from underground flows to the earth's surface. Rivers and streams can also get their start from melting snow in mountains and hills. At their start, rivers and streams are often cold, fast moving, and rich in oxygen. The water flows through a **channel** or riverbed. As their journey continues down a mountain, rivers and streams may widen and slow down. The amount of oxygen often decreases and the water warms up. Eventually, rivers and streams will empty into another body of water. This end point of a river or stream is called the **mouth.**

Life in the headwaters has adapted to swift currents and cool temperatures. Mosses cling to rocks, and fish must be strong swimmers to fight against the current. In the slower parts of a river or stream, plankton and other kinds of plants can survive. Catfish, carp, and other scavengers thrive. Many creatures also live along the shores of these freshwater biomes. Raccoons and bears feed on crawfish, fish, and other river creatures.

Headwaters

The upper part of a river or stream, near its source

Channel

The bed of a river or stream that directs flowing water

Mouth

The place where a stream or river enters another, larger body of water

---

Science Myth

Myth: Rivers run from north to south.

Fact: Rivers run in all directions. All rivers run from higher ground to lower ground. They empty into other rivers, lakes, or oceans.

Generate

To create by physical process

Waterlogged

Saturated with water

Environmental problems in rivers and streams can affect people and wildlife. Pollution from homes, factories, and farms is a serious problem in many rivers. Dams are often built to **generate** electricity, or create it using physical processes. However, dams can destroy or harm wildlife habitat. They can make it difficult for fish to swim to the areas where they lay their eggs. Dams can also change the quality and temperature of the water.

Freshwater Wetlands

Freshwater biomes also include freshwater wetlands such as swamps, marshes, and bogs. A freshwater wetland is defined as an area that has **waterlogged** soils. Waterlogged soils are saturated with water. Freshwater wetlands can also be covered with a shallow layer of water. Wetlands support aquatic plants and many organisms that are adapted to wet conditions.

Many wetlands are wet because they are found in low-lying areas. Some are in places where groundwater is close to the surface. That means they are constantly being fed with water from underground. Some are also next to rivers that flood, creating marshes or other types of wetlands.

Research and Write

Your local water supplier runs tests to make sure that the drinking water is clean and safe. Work with a partner to find out what substances are tested for in the water. Request a copy of the supplier's latest test report. Then write a summary of the report's details.

Wetlands are important to people and wildlife. They help prevent floods by slowing down fast-moving water. They also catch sediment and prevent it from polluting rivers and streams. Wetlands also reduce the impact of storm waves and wind. Many types of wildlife depend on healthy wetlands to survive. Migrating birds flock to wetlands, where there are rich supplies of food. Wetlands also serve as important nurseries for young fish.

Achievements in Science

The Establishment of National Parks

In 1870, General Henry Washburn led an expedition to the Yellowstone area in northwestern Montana. Fur trappers had told him fantastic stories of steaming geysers and bubbling pools of mud. To his amazement, their stories were true.

Another expedition followed in 1871. Then, in 1872, the U.S. Congress established the area as Yellowstone National Park. This was the first national park in the United States. This act of Congress guaranteed that the land would be set aside for everyone to enjoy.

Over the next 30 years, Congress created many other national parks. They included Sequoia and Yosemite in California and Glacier in Montana. These lands were preserved largely because of their natural beauty and wildlife.

In 1916, President Woodrow Wilson approved the creation of the National Park Service (NPS). This new department became responsible for managing all the national parks and monuments. At that time, there were 14 national parks and 21 national monuments. Today, the NPS manages more than 375 public areas. They include national parks, monuments, historic sites, and seashores.

Match the phrase in Column A with the term in Column B.
Write the letter of your answer on a sheet of paper.

Column A

1. examples include lakes and ponds

2. upper part of a river or stream, near its source

3. the area where water flows into another body of water

4. examples include rivers and streams

5. having an end

6. bed of a river or stream that directs flowing water

Column B

A channel

B finite

C flowing-water ecosystem

D headwater

E mouth

F standing-water ecosystem

Critical Thinking

On a sheet of paper, write the answers to the following questions. Use complete sentences.

7. What are some problems that rivers and streams are facing?

8. Compare and contrast lakes and ponds.

9. Why is so little of Earth's water usable for drinking?

10. Compare and contrast freshwater and saltwater wetlands. How are both important for humans and wildlife?

ENVIRONMENTAL ISSUES IN THE WORLD

Protecting Earth's Rain Forests

In a 0.01-square-kilometer area of rain forest in South America, scientists have counted more than 200 species of trees and 40,000 species of insects. Rain forests are being destroyed very rapidly, however. Farmers and loggers clear out approximately 158,000 square kilometers of land every year. Once cut, it is almost impossible to replace a rain forest, even if new trees are planted. The biodiversity of the rain forest disappears, as well as its ecosystem services. Losing this resource affects the entire world.

There are many efforts underway to save rain forests. Many environmental groups sponsor rain forest preservation efforts. They work at the local level to increase awareness of rain forest issues. International organizations also support conservation activities. They set aside, protect, and manage areas of rain forest. They also advise businesses and governments on conservation efforts.

Several countries in South America have banded together to buy rain forest land and protect it from development. They hire people who live in or near rain forests to serve as caretakers. However, it is sometimes difficult to find people to take the job. Local people are often poor and have few options for making money. Instead, they take jobs with the loggers and farmers that are destroying the rain forest.

Still, progress is being made. An international conservation organization, the Brazilian government, and other organizations are working to protect 10 percent of the Amazon rain forest. New parks are being established, creating a park system larger than the National Park System in the United States.

1. What benefits do the rain forests offer the rest of the world?

2. Why should efforts to save rain forests include the people who live near them?

3. Why do efforts include people who live outside of countries where rain forests are found?

- Terrestrial biomes are grouped by the amount of precipitation and average temperatures.

- Aquatic biomes are grouped by water depth and the amount of dissolved salts found in the water.

- Rain forests are highly diverse, hot and humid forests with poor soils.

- Temperate forests are dominated by deciduous trees. Coniferous forests are dominated by trees that have needles instead of broad leaves.

- Savannas are tropical and subtropical grasslands found near the equator. The chaparral are dry grasslands found along coastal areas. Most of North America's prairies have been converted to farmland.

- Tundra is very fragile and sensitive to pollution and human development. All deserts have little precipitation and a high rate of evaporation.

- Coastal wetlands and coral reefs are some of the most diverse marine habitats in the world. Freshwater biomes include lakes, ponds, rivers, streams, and freshwater wetlands.

Vocabulary

abyss, 199
acidic, 180
alpine tundra, 191
altitude, 166
amphibian, 178
aphotic zone, 199
aquatic, 164
Arctic tundra, 191
barrier reef, 200
biome, 164
bog, 192
buttress, 174
canopy, 174
channel, 205
chaparral, 186
coastal wetland, 200
cold desert, 194
colony, 200
conifer, 179
coniferous forest, 179
conserve, 186
coral reef, 200
deciduous tree, 177

deforestation, 175
desert, 194
detritus, 199
disphotic zone, 199
dormant, 178
emergent, 174
estuary, 200
evergreen, 179
extract, 193
finite, 203
flowing-water
  ecosystem, 203
forest floor, 175
freshwater, 167
generate, 206
grassland, 183
headwaters, 205
hibernate, 178
horizontal zone, 198
hot desert, 194
humus, 178
indigenous, 175
intertidal zone, 198

krill, 198
lake, 204
latitude, 166
log, 175
mangrove swamp,
  201
marine biome, 197
migrate, 178
mouth, 205
neritic zone, 198
nursery, 201
oceanic zone, 199
overgrazing, 185
permafrost, 192
photic zone, 198
phytoplankton, 198
pond, 204
prairie, 184
reptile, 178
salinity, 167
salt marsh, 201
salt water, 167
saturated, 200

savanna, 184
seasonal, 204
standing-water
  ecosystem, 203
taiga, 179
temperate deciduous
  forest, 177
temperate grassland,
  184
temperate rain forest,
  173
terrestrial, 164
topsoil, 185
tropical rain forest,
  173
tundra, 191
understory, 175
vegetation, 166
vertical zone, 198
waterlogged, 206
wetland, 200
zooplankton, 198

Chapter 5 REVIEW

Word Bank

aquatic

biomes

canopy

chaparral

deciduous forest

deforestation

desert

estuary

humus

marine

prairie

salinity

savanna

taiga

terrestrial

tundra

understory

Vocabulary Review

On a sheet of paper, write the word or words from the Word Bank that complete each sentence correctly.

1. Freshwater and saltwater systems combine in a(n) _____.

2. A(n) _____ is a grassland located near the equator.

3. A biome that is _____ is located on land.

4. Fertile soil contains a large amount of _____.

5. A(n) _____ may be hot or cold, but is generally very dry.

6. The _____ of a forest is made up of the tops of large trees which capture most of the sunlight.

7. Cutting down large forest areas for development contributes to _____.

8. The _____ is filled with evergreen trees.

9. The _____ has a layer of soil called permafrost that is always frozen.

10. A saltwater ecosystem is known as a(n) _____ biome.

11. A(n) _____ grassland is very fertile.

12. Trees in a(n) _____ lose their leaves when the weather gets cold.

13. Ecosystems are grouped into different _____.

14. The amount of salt that is dissolved into water is called its _____.

15. Trees in the forest _____ receive little light.

16. Dry, coastal grasslands are called the _____.

17. More than 70 percent of Earth's surface is covered with _____ biomes.

Continued on next page

Concept Review
On a sheet of paper, write the letter of the correct answer.

18. Biomes that are close to the equator have _____.

   A low rainfall   **C** low temperatures

   B no rainfall   **D** high temperatures

19. The chaparral are _____ biomes.

   A grassland   **C** marine

   B desert   **D** tundra

20. Which of the following biomes usually contains the greatest diversity of life?

   A tundra   **C** rain forest

   B deciduous forest   **D** desert

21. Most of the food that people eat comes from _____ biomes.

   A rain forest   **C** ocean

   B grassland   **D** forest

22. The difference between a lake and a pond is _____.

   A salinity   **C** altitude

   B temperature   **D** size

Critical Thinking

On a sheet of paper, write the answers to the following questions. Use complete sentences.

23. Describe how temperature, speed, oxygen level, and organisms change as a freshwater river ecosystem goes from the headwaters to the mouth.

24. Why is it important to study biomes?

25. What conditions cause tropical rain forests to have so much life?

Test-Taking Tip   To study for a chapter test, use the headings within the chapter to write an outline. Review this outline to help you recall and organize the information.

People and the Environment

How many different kinds of food can you count in the photo? Each of these postcards shows something that can be consumed. People consume these and other foods for energy and for growth. They also consume many other natural resources. For example, they consume land by using it for crops or development. As the human population grows, humans consume more and more of Earth's resources. In Chapter 6, you will learn about how the human population is growing. You will also find out how increased consumption affects Earth's resources and human health.

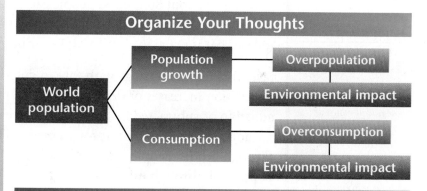

Organize Your Thoughts

World population
- Population growth
  - Overpopulation
  - Environmental impact
- Consumption
  - Overconsumption
  - Environmental impact

Goals for Learning

◆ To describe major trends in world population

◆ To understand the link between population growth and environmental impact

◆ To understand the link between consumption and environmental impact

◆ To describe some ways that people can reduce their impact on the environment

World population

The total number of people on Earth

Growth rate

The rate at which a population is increasing or decreasing

Migration

A large movement of people from one place to another

The earlier chapters in this book introduced parts and processes of the natural environment. Until now, though, one major part of the environment has hardly been discussed: people. Humans are a force that is shaping and changing the natural environment. The rest of this textbook describes the links between humans and major environmental issues.

One reason humans greatly affect the environment is because there are so many of them. The problem of population size was introduced in Chapter 1. Today the **world population,** the total number of people on Earth, is more than 6.4 billion. By 2050, the population could be more than 9 billion. Meeting the needs of all these people has a huge impact on Earth's natural environment.

Growth Rates

The world population is not just large, it is also growing very fast. In Chapter 1, you learned that the world population is growing by about 85 million people each year. At the current rate of growth, nearly 233,000 people will be added to the world today. That is equal to about 10,000 per hour, or 3 per second.

Scientists use the term **growth rate** to describe how quickly a population increases or decreases. It is the number of people added to or subtracted from a population each year. People are added to a population through births. They are subtracted through deaths. People can also be added or subtracted from a population through **migration.** Migration is a large movement of people from one place to another. Florida's population, for example, is growing very fast because people are moving there from other states.

Exponential growth

Growth that increases by larger and larger amounts

J-curve

A J-shaped curve

Link to ▶▶▶▶

Biology

With most populations, growth rarely forms a J-curve. That is because there are not enough resources to support an ever-growing population. Eventually, the population stops growing. Graphing this growth over time produces an S-shaped curve.

Usually, growth rate is expressed as a percent. In the year 2000, the world's growth rate was 1.4 percent. That means the population was increasing by 1.4 percent a year. There were 6.1 billion people at the start of 2000. Multiply that number by 1.4 percent (0.014): 6.1 billion × 0.014 = about 85 million. About 85 million people were added to the population by the end of 2000.

If the growth rate never increased, would the population continue growing by just 85 million a year? No. That is because each year there are more people to start with. Remember that about 85 million people were added in 2000. The population at the start of 2001 was: 6.1 billion + 85 million = about 6.2 billion.

To calculate the number of additional people for 2001, multiply 0.014 by 6.2 billion, not 6.1 billion: 6.2 billion × 0.014 = about 87 million. In 2002, the population would grow by about 88 million people. This steady increase would continue each year.

This kind of growth is called **exponential growth.** Exponential growth means the population is growing by larger and larger amounts each year. With exponential growth, a population may grow slowly for a while. In time, though, the population explodes. This pattern can be shown on a graph. It takes a shape known as a **J-curve,** which you can see in Figure 6.1.1.

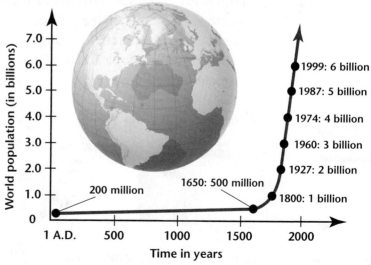

Figure 6.1.1 *A J-curve results when you graph exponential growth.*

This pattern can be shown with exponents as 2^{n-1}, where n is the number of the square.

$n = 1: 2^0 = 1$
$n = 2: 2^1 = 2$
$n = 4: 2^3 = 8$
$n = 8: 2^7 = 128$
$n = 13: 2^{12} = 4{,}096$
$n = 30: 2^{29} = 5.37 \times 10^8$
$n = 64: 2^{63} = 9.22 \times 10^{18}$

A legend from Persia in the Middle East may help you see how exponential growth takes off. A young man offered a beautiful chess set to his king. He said he wanted just a bit of rice in return. He wanted one grain for the first square. He wanted two grains for the second square. He wanted four for the next square and eight for the next one. In other words, he wanted twice as much rice for each additional square. Figure 6.1.2 illustrates this progression.

Unfortunately, the king did not understand math. He agreed to the trade. At first, he did not seem to owe much rice. By the eighth square, he owed the young man 128 grains. By the thirteenth, though, he owed 4,096 grains. By the thirtieth, he owed more than 536 million grains. Long before the sixty-fourth square, he was out of rice. All the rice grown in the world today would not be enough to keep this promise.

This pattern shows how the population can grow so quickly. Once the population is large enough, even a small growth rate adds lots of people. Think of it this way. It took 3 million years for the human population to reach one billion. That happened around 1800. Just 127 years later, another billion were added. Then the intervals, or years between adding another billion people, grew even shorter. First 33 years, then 14 years, and then 13 years.

The world's population growth rate has actually been decreasing over the last 40 years. In the 1960s, the growth rate was about 2 percent. By 1990 it was 1.5 percent. Some experts believe the growth rate will only be at about 1 percent by 2015. Still, when that rate is applied to a huge population, the results are enormous.

Figure 6.1.2 *The king paid twice as much rice for each square of the chess board.*

Carrying capacity

The largest number of living things an area can support

Death rate

The number of deaths per 1,000 people in a given year

Birth rate

The number of births per 1,000 people in a given year

Science Myth

Myth: Increasing birth rates cause greater population growth.

Fact: Increasing birth rates and decreasing death rates cause greater population growth. If death rates increased along with birth rates, population growth would remain the same.

The population will not grow forever, however. An area's environment can support only so many living things. The largest number of living things that an area can support is its **carrying capacity.** Estimates of Earth's human carrying capacity vary, depending on many factors. They average between 7.7 and 12 billion people. However, some scientists believe there are already more people than Earth can support.

Understanding the Numbers

You may wonder why population growth rates have increased and decreased over human history. The answer is tied to factors that affect human survival and reproduction. Problems such as food shortages and diseases increase **death rates.** Death rates are the numbers of deaths in one year per 1,000 people. Medical discoveries and other technologies help decrease death rates and increase **birth rates.** Birth rates are the number of births in one year per 1,000 people.

Consider the life of Earth's early hunter-gatherers, which you learned about in Chapter 1. The challenge of finding food and staying alive kept their numbers quite small. The population did not increase much until the Agricultural Revolution. When food was easier to obtain, people lived longer and produced more children.

Another jump in the population happened after the Industrial Revolution. Improvements in medicine and food production made people less likely to die from sickness and hunger. Death rates decreased and birth rates increased. This pattern continued for many years.

There are several reasons for the recent decrease in the world growth rate. Women in many parts of the world are choosing to have smaller families. Also, diseases such as AIDS are increasing death rates in many areas. In the next lesson, you will learn more about these regional differences in population growth.

Lesson 1   R E V I E W

Word Bank
death rate
growth rate
world population

On a sheet of paper, write the words from the Word Bank that complete each sentence correctly.

1. The rate at which a population increases or decreases is called the _____.

2. The _____ is expressed as deaths per 1,000 people per year.

3. The _____ is the total number of people on Earth.

Critical Thinking

On a sheet of paper, write the answers to the following questions. Use complete sentences.

4. Why does migration not affect the growth rate of the world population?

5. Under what conditions would the population growth rate be zero?

Express Lab 6

Materials
◆ paper
◆ pencil
◆ dried beans

Procedure

1. Create two piles with two beans each. Label each pile. One will be the Arithmetic Growth pile. The other will be the Exponential Growth pile.

2. Create a data table to record the number of beans in each pile. Record your starting numbers.

3. Add two more beans to the Arithmetic Growth pile. Double the number of beans in the Exponential Growth pile.

4. Record the new totals.

5. Repeat Steps 3 and 4 four more times.

Analysis

1. What do the beans in each group represent?

2. Which population grew the fastest?

3. How could this activity be changed to model real population growth?

Objectives

After reading this lesson, you should be able to

◆ define overpopulation

◆ explain regional trends in population growth

◆ explain how rapid population growth can affect human health and biodiversity

Overpopulation

When a population is too large to be supported by local resources

Demographer

A scientist who studies population

Population trend

A change in population over time

In 1798, a British man named Thomas Malthus wrote "An Essay on the Principle of Population." In this famous essay, he wrote that the human population was growing too fast. Living conditions were getting worse. In time, he said, there would not be enough food for everyone.

Many people believe that Malthus's warnings never came true. New ideas and technologies solved many of the problems he described. For example, farmers learned how to grow more food on less land. The world population is more than six times larger than it was in Malthus's time. Yet a high percentage of the population is still able to get enough food to survive.

Other people think that Malthus described a very real problem called **overpopulation.** Overpopulation means the population is too large to be supported by the resources available. Many of Earth's resources are finite. The more a population grows, the fewer the resources available for each person. Parts of China and India do not have enough freshwater. Nigeria, Ethiopia, and Iran are running out of land for growing grain. These and other countries are experiencing overpopulation.

Regional Trends

People who study population are called **demographers.** They work to figure out how many people live in different parts of the world. They study changes in population over time, also called **population trends.** They predict how the population will change in the future. They also look at how these population changes will affect each person's quality of life.

Stabilize

To remain the same

Reproductive age

Neither too old nor too young to have children

Industrialized nation

A nation with well-developed industries and economies

Standard of living

The way of living that is usual for a person, community, or country

Most African countries have a population growth rate (PGR) of nearly 3 percent per year. The PGR of the United States is less than 1 percent per year. Some European countries have negative PGRs.

Demographers know that the world population is growing very fast. They also know that there are large differences in growth rates between countries. Demographers describe three main ways that growth is occurring in different countries.

Some countries have populations that are staying about the same size. These countries have **stabilized** their population growth. This group includes all the countries in Europe. In a few countries, including Japan and Russia, the population may soon start to decrease.

Some countries have lowered their growth rates, but will continue growing for many years. This is happening for two reasons. First, their populations are already very large. Second, a major part of their population is or will soon be of **reproductive age.** That means the females are old enough—but not too old—to begin having children. Both China and the United States are included in this group of countries.

The last group of countries is experiencing the fastest population growth. They have high birth rates and many people of reproductive age. Nations such as Nigeria and Pakistan may double their populations by 2050.

All of the countries where populations are stabilizing are industrialized nations. **Industrialized nations** have strong economies based on manufacturing and technology. In general, citizens of industrialized nations enjoy high **standards of living.** A country's standard of living is the quality of life its people enjoy.

Developing nation

A nation that has not yet become industrialized

Sanitation

Disposal of waste

Subsistence agriculture

Growing just enough food to meet immediate local needs

Poverty level

The amount one must earn to afford what is needed to live

Life expectancy

The total number of years a person is expected to live

By contrast, most of the countries with fast growth are **developing nations.** Developing nations are countries whose economies are not as strong. Health care, education, and **sanitation,** or disposal of waste, may be inadequate. Many people who live in developing nations rely on **subsistence agriculture.** Subsistence agriculture means producing just enough food to meet day-to-day needs. Most developing countries are located in the Southern Hemisphere. They include all the countries in Africa, Latin America, Asia (except Japan), and the Caribbean.

The terms "industrialized" and "developing" can be helpful. They provide an average of living conditions in different parts of the world. Keep in mind, though, that they make things too simple. Both kinds of countries have both wealthy and poor citizens. Consider the United States, for example. The United States has one of the strongest economies on Earth. Yet about one in eight U.S. citizens lives below the **poverty level.** The poverty level is the amount one must earn to afford what is needed to live.

Life expectancy is also different in industrialized and developing nations. Life expectancy is the total number of years someone is expected to live. It is affected by a person's birth year, country of birth, gender, and other factors. Citizens of industrialized nations usually have higher life expectancies than those of developing nations. This reflects a difference in their standards of living.

Link to ➤➤➤

Cultures

As of 2005, the life expectancy in the United States is 77.7 years. Swaziland, in Africa, has the lowest life expectancy at 33.2 years. Andorra, a tiny country between France and Spain, has the world's highest life expectancy at 83.5 years.

Problems and Solutions

Starve

To die because of hunger

Fast population growth can make many other problems worse. It makes it harder for everyone to find jobs. It makes it harder to keep people safe. It makes it harder to educate everyone. Where people are poor, fast population growth can make them poorer. Children may **starve,** or die because of hunger. People may get sick from drinking unclean water. Families may live in temporary shelters on the streets of crowded cities.

Often, people living in poverty continue having large families. You may wonder why. It is certainly harder to feed seven or eight children than one or two. These parents know, though, that children can also help them survive. They can help them work and find food. They can take care of their parents when they are older. Most of these parents also know they will lose some of their children. Some will probably starve or die of diseases. Having more children can be a way to make sure that at least a few survive. Unfortunately, having large families continues the problem of overpopulation.

▼◄▲▼◄▲▼◄▲▼◄▲▼◄▲▼◄▲▼◄▲▼◄▲▼◄▲▼◄▲▼◄▲▼◄▲▼◄▲▼◄▲▼◄▲▼

Science at Work

Demographer

Demographers collect and study information about populations. They study the numbers of births, deaths, and marriages in communities. They also gather data on age, sex, race, education, and income. Then they use the data to predict changes in the makeup of a population. Governments and businesses use this information to make plans for the future. Therefore, facts about populations are important data, and demographers must be as accurate as possible.

Demographers are interested in social issues and enjoy working with numbers. They usually work in an office and

may travel to different areas to collect information. Most demographers have a bachelor's degree in statistics, sociology, economics, or political science. Some have degrees in marketing or computer science. Research in demography may require an advanced degree.

Rapid population growth affects more than just human health and well-being. It also affects the natural environment. Many areas with fast population growth are located in areas rich in biodiversity. The island country of Madagascar is one example. Madagascar is home to rare species such as lemurs, tortoises, and baobabs. It also has a high population growth rate. Growing populations here and elsewhere put local biodiversity at risk. People may burn forests to make room for farms. They may cut down trees for fuel wood. They may hunt rare animals for food or to sell for money. It may be difficult for them to see other ways to meet their day-to-day needs. Unfortunately, these choices destroy the natural environment they depend on.

Demographers do see signs of hope, however. In the mid-1900s, all nations were growing rapidly. The recent decrease in population growth in industrialized nations could be repeated in other nations. Sometimes families have many children because they do not have the option of **family planning.** Family planning involves controlling reproduction. It allows parents to make decisions about when they want children and how many they want. When given this option, they may choose to have fewer children.

Education also helps lower the birth rate. Women who have chances to learn and get jobs usually choose to have fewer children. Consider the example of Bangladesh, a country near India. Between 1980 and 1996, the average number of children per woman dropped from 6.1 to 3.4. This number is known as the **fertility rate.** Why did the fertility rate go down? The women in Bangladesh received more schooling during these years. They were given more business opportunities. The government also worked to balance the rights of men and women.

Many countries are working to control their population growth through education and information. They know that a large part of the population is entering reproductive age. The decisions these young people make about family size will affect population growth for years to come.

Lesson 2 REVIEW

Word Bank
demographers
developing
overpopulation

On a sheet of paper, write the word from the Word Bank that completes each sentence correctly.

1. Scientists called _____ study population.

2. In _____, there are too many people and too few resources.

3. A _____ nation has a low standard of living and little industry.

On a sheet of paper, write the letter of the answer that completes each sentence correctly.

4. Canada, France, and Australia are all examples of _____ countries.

   A industrialized   **C** island
   B developing   **D** overpopulated

5. In _____, people produce just enough food to meet their day-to-day needs.

   A family planning   **C** subsistence agriculture
   B industrialized nations   **D** poverty

6. The _____ rate is the average number of children per woman.

   A fertility   **B** birth   **C** growth   **D** family

Critical Thinking

On a sheet of paper, write the answers to the following questions. Use complete sentences.

7. How well did Thomas Malthus predict population trends? Explain.

8. Describe population growth trends in the United States.

9. Compare the population growth trends of industrialized and developing nations.

10. How does human population growth threaten biodiversity?

Objectives

After reading this lesson, you should be able to

◆ define consumption

◆ explain how population and consumption rates affect resource use

◆ describe the links between overconsumption and the environment

Consumption

The process of using resources and producing waste

All animals affect the environment in which they live. Elephants tear down trees to get more food. Termites build tall mounds of dirt. Sea birds cover rocky islands with piles of droppings.

In some ways, humans are just like other animals. They use resources for food. They change the environment around them to create safe shelter. They create waste. In other ways, though, humans are very different from other animals. They use more resources and create more waste than any other species. The process of using, or consuming, resources and creating waste is known as **consumption.**

One reason humans consume so many resources is that their population is so large. A larger population will generally use more resources and produce more waste. Here is one way to understand the link between population and consumption. Imagine you are hosting a party. A party for six people requires a certain amount of food, drinks, and space. If you invite twice as many people, you might need to double the amounts.

Consumption is affected by more than population size, however. Think about the party mentioned above. If you increased the number of guests from six to 12, would you really need exactly twice as much of everything? Not always. If your six extra guests were small children, you would need fewer resources. If your six extra guests were very hungry, you would need more resources. How *much* a person consumes is as important as how *many* people are consuming.

Research and Write

Consumption in North America has changed greatly over the past century. Interview your parents, grandparents, and great-grandparents. Find out about their consumption habits when they were your age. For example, ask them how often they bought new clothes or a new car. Share your findings in an oral report to the class.

Consumption Trends

Right now, people are consuming huge amounts of resources. In fact, people used more resources in the last 50 years than in all of human existence. People today use five times as much plastic as they did 50 years ago. They use three times as much water. They burn four times the amount of **fossil fuels,** such as oil and coal, for energy. They use six times as much paper. Some of this increase is the result of population growth. Much of it, though, is caused by increasing levels of consumption.

Some level of consumption is necessary for survival. People need to buy clothes, eat food, and live in some kind of building. It is also true that consumption is an important part of the economy. When people consume resources, they contribute to jobs and the economic health of the nation. When people buy things, they also help provide jobs for people who make the items. But resource use today is so high that some people call it overconsumption. As you learned in Chapter 1, overconsumption means using resources faster than they can be replaced.

Unlike population growth, high rates of consumption are found mostly in industrialized nations. Consider the United States, for example. The United States is home to just 4.6 percent of the world's population. Yet Americans eat 16 percent of the world's grain and 21 percent of its beef. They use 32 percent of the world's paper and buy 16 percent of all shoes. Americans drive nearly one-third of all the motor vehicles in the world. They also generate almost three-quarters of the world's **toxic waste.** Toxic waste is waste that is poisonous to living things. You can see some of these amounts compared in Figure 6.3.1.

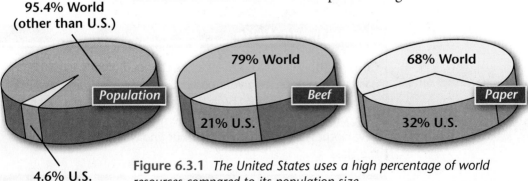

95.4% World (other than U.S.)

Population

4.6% U.S.

79% World

Beef

21% U.S.

68% World

Paper

32% U.S.

Figure 6.3.1 *The United States uses a high percentage of world resources compared to its population size.*

All of this resource use adds up. A child born in the United States will consume about 35 times more resources in its lifetime than a child born in India. Some experts believe the United States and most other industrialized nations are overpopulated. They may not seem to have too many people. Yet their high rates of consumption mean the population cannot be sustained by local resources.

Map Skills: Population Density Maps

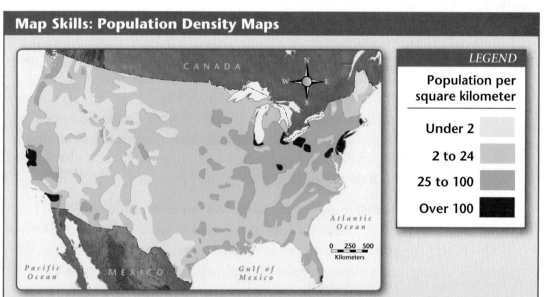

Wherever people live, they affect the land, air, and water around them. As the number of people increases, these effects can increase too. Consider what would happen if an island population tripled. Would water use increase? Would trash multiply?

Population density is the number of people living in an area. For example, a red area on the map indicates more than 100 people living in every square kilometer. Use the map to answer the following questions.

1. What do you think the areas of densest population are?

2. What color shows areas that have very few people living in a large area of land?

3. What areas of the United States would have the greatest consumption overall? Does this necessarily mean they have the greatest per-person consumption? Explain.

4. Generally, which part of the United States is least populated?

Mine

To extract minerals from the earth

Renewable

Able to be renewed by natural processes

Fishery

An industry that catches and sells fish

Impacts of Consumption

High levels of consumption are using up natural resources around the world. Wild forests are disappearing to satisfy demand for fuel wood and paper. Population growth in dry places is reducing supplies of fresh water. Wild plant and animal species are becoming extinct as human communities expand into their habitat.

The effects of consumption are often hard to see. They happen in distant oceans and forests and they affect people in other nations. Consider the example of cell phones. Companies use a mineral called coltan to make cell phones. Coltan is found mostly in eastern Congo in Africa. High demand for cell phones has led coltan **mining** in parts of eastern Congo. To mine is to extract minerals from the earth. Much of this coltan mining occurs illegally in protected areas. Important gorilla habitat has been destroyed and many gorillas have died.

Not all resources are finite, like minerals or fossil fuels. Some are **renewable,** or able to be replaced by natural processes. More of these resources can be created if they are not used too quickly. Fish and forests, for example, are renewable resources. However, current levels of consumption often make it hard for them to be renewed. That means people today may be using resources that future generations may need. For example, **fisheries** are industries that catch and sell fish. Fisheries now catch about five times as much fish as they did 50 years ago. As a result, many fish species are being caught faster than they can reproduce. Now 11 of the world's 15 major fisheries are having trouble meeting demand. If their populations continue to decrease, these fish may no longer be available in 20 or 50 years.

Figure 6.3.3 *As human communities grow in population, they often expand into wildlife habitat.*

Link to >>>

Health

A syndrome is a group of symptoms that are signs of a specific disease. The damage to the environment caused by overconsumption is sometimes called "Carson's syndrome." This name was given to honor Rachel Carson, author of *Silent Spring*.

High consumption produces lots of waste. This waste affects the quality of air, land, and water. Already, the effects of this waste are being felt by humans and natural communities. For example, driving cars produces pollution that affects air quality in major cities. This also contributes to major changes in Earth's climate. These changes could affect all living things in the coming years.

Finding ways to decrease the impacts of consumption is an important goal. Lesson 4 discusses new approaches to consumption that may benefit people and the environment.

Achievements in Science

The Tragedy of the Commons

Who is responsible for a resource that everyone owns? In 1968, Garrett Hardin explored that question in his essay "The Tragedy of the Commons." The tragedy of the commons describes the conflict between individual interest and the common good. Say there is a pasture where everyone brings cows to graze. Every individual benefits from adding more cows to his or her herd. Yet if everyone increases his or her herd size, the pasture will begin to be damaged. Still, this damage is shared by the group. So individuals tend to keep increasing his or her own benefits even if it hurts the pasture. In time, though, the pasture will become so damaged that no cows can graze there.

Hardin believed many environmental problems resulted from this conflict of interests. For example, there is too much carbon dioxide in the air. However, few individuals are motivated to give up activities that burn fossil fuels. Fish stocks are declining, but every fishery benefits from continued fishing. These and similar "tragedies," according to Hardin, are the result of human nature coupled with human population growth.

Lesson 3 R E V I E W

Word Bank

consumption

poisonous

renewable

On a sheet of paper, write the word from the Word Bank that completes each sentence correctly.

1. Using resources and producing waste is known as _____.

2. Cattle, forests, and crops are _____ resources.

3. Toxic waste is _____ to living things.

On a sheet of paper, write the letter of the answer that completes each sentence correctly.

4. Cars, factories, and many homes burn _____ for energy.

    A peat moss   **C** sugar

    B fossil fuels   **D** wood

5. Freshwater, fish, and fuels are all examples of _____.

    A wastes   **B** services   **C** resources   **D** products

6. Consumption rates are _____ worldwide.

    A about the same   **C** decreasing

    B hard to measure   **D** increasing

Critical Thinking

On a sheet of paper, write the answers to the following questions. Use complete sentences.

7. What could cause fish to become a resource that is not renewable?

8. What is a benefit of consumption? What is a drawback to consumption?

9. How can overconsumption in one country affect the resources of another?

10. How can human consumption cause the extinction of a wild species?

INVESTIGATION 6

Materials

◆ paper
◆ pencil
◆ population data
◆ calculator
◆ ruler

Making an Age-Structure Histogram

A population's age structure is the number of males and females in each age group. A bar graph called a histogram is used to display age structure data. You will make an age-structure histogram in this lab. But first, you will collect data on the age structure of a population.

Procedure

1. Collect data on the ages of your living family members. Include parents, siblings, cousins, aunts, uncles, grandparents, and great-grandparents.

2. Make a data table like the one below on your paper. Include a row for every 10 years of age up to 81+.

3. Enter the pooled numbers of males and females in each age group.

4. Calculate what percent of each age group are males and females. Enter this data.

Pooled Class Data

Age group	Males		Females	
	Number	Percent	Number	Percent
0–10				
11–20				
21–30				
• • •				
81+				

Continued on next page

5. Begin building a histogram. Label each age group, starting with the youngest group on the bottom. Arrange your labels as shown in the diagram.

6. Draw a bar that represents all the people in the 0–10 age group. Draw a vertical line that divides the bar into two parts, one for males and one for females.

7. Repeat Step 6 for each age group. Place each bar on top of the last. Line up the dividing lines to make one solid vertical line.

Cleanup/Disposal
Before leaving the lab, put away all your materials.

Analysis
1. Which age groups have more males, and which have more females?

2. Describe the general shape of the histogram you created.

Conclusions
1. How do the life expectancies of males and females compare?

2. How does your histogram compare with the one for the United States?

Explore Further
Make age-structure histograms for other populations.

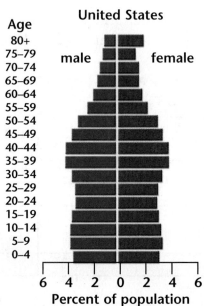

Objectives

After reading this lesson, you should be able to

◆ describe an equation for measuring human impact on the environment

◆ discuss equity and the gaps between wealthy and poor populations

◆ describe some ways that people are reducing the impacts of consumption

Affluence
Wealth

People everywhere depend on the natural environment. It is their source of food, water, oxygen, and shelter. Yet throughout the world, people are pushing the limits of what the environment can provide.

Population scientist Paul Ehrlich studies people's impact on the environment. He has created the following equation, called IPAT, to measure this impact. *I* is the impact of any human group on the environment. This impact can be measured by the equation:

$I = P \times A \times T$, where

P = Population, or the number of people

A = **Affluence,** or wealth. People's affluence reflects how much they consume.

T = Technology, or how much damage is caused by the technologies providing goods

In this equation, T measures how much environmental damage a technology causes. However, different technologies can increase or decrease environmental impacts. For example, technologies that recycle materials can decrease environmental impacts. Technologies that create pollution increase impacts.

Equity and the Environment

Many experts believe that consumption and its impacts will get worse. First, the world population is still growing rapidly. Second, consumption rates are increasing even in developing nations. People everywhere are buying more televisions, refrigerators, and washing machines. These products make life easier, but they also increase resource use. Many more people are also buying cars. Pollution increases as cars replace bicycles and other cleaner forms of transportation.

Equity

Fairness

Obesity

The state of being
significantly overweight

Malnutrition

Not getting enough
calories or nutrients
from one's food

Link to ➤➤➤

Math

In the IPAT equation, if P, A, or T increase, then so does the impact, I. An increase in P is an increase in population. An increase in A is an increase in consumption. An increase in T is an increase in environmental damage due to production of goods.

Most people agree that everyone has a right to live like people in industrialized nations. Yet there are not enough resources on Earth for everyone to consume at this level. Suppose everyone lived like North Americans do now. Experts have calculated that it would take the resources of four Earths to meet this demand.

Dealing with these issues raises questions of **equity.** Equity is another word for fairness. What is the most fair, or equitable, way to share Earth's resources? Should they go to the people who have the most money? Should they go to the people who need them most? It is true that many people are increasing their consumption rates. At the same time, others are not even consuming enough resources to meet their basic needs.

As one example, consider how **obesity** rates are increasing in many affluent populations. Obesity is a term doctors use to describe people who are significantly overweight. Obese people usually have more than 20 percent more body weight than is recommended. Yet millions of people living in poverty worldwide suffer from **malnutrition.** They are not getting enough calories or nutrients from their food to keep them healthy.

Many people believe it is necessary to close the gap in resource use. They are looking for ways to reduce consumption in some populations and increase it in others.

Science Myth

Myth: Modern agriculture can feed a growing population.

Fact: Modern agricultural methods can feed more people using less space. However, these methods are not widely used in areas with the highest population growth rates. In these areas, environmental damage also decreases the amount of land available for agriculture.

Reducing Human Impacts

Already, individuals in many nations are choosing to change their consumption habits. People in developing nations now recycle much more of their paper, plastic, and glass. When they recycle, they use waste products to create new products. A growing number of individuals also choose goods that cause less of an environmental impact. For example, many people buy **nontoxic** cleaners that do not pollute the environment. Others buy fish that have been caught in ways that do not damage ocean habitats.

Nontoxic

Not poisonous to the environment

Science in Your Life

Technology: Plastic Recycling Codes

Petroleum is used to make plastics. Since petroleum is a resource that cannot be renewed, it will eventually run out. One way to slow this process is to recycle plastic. Recycling also reduces the amount of garbage thrown away. Before recycled plastics can be made into new plastic, several steps must take place. Used plastics need to be collected, sorted, cleaned, and reprocessed.

When it comes to recycling, not all plastics are the same. Different kinds of plastics cannot be processed together to make new plastic. Instead, plastics of the same type have to be grouped together. There are six main types of plastics in common use. Each type has a number. The number is usually labeled on the plastic. Around the number are arrows that form a triangle. This code helps people organize types of plastic. The recycling process can be very expensive. As a result, most U.S. plastics recyclers only use plastics with the codes 1 and 2.

1. What are the steps in the recycling process?

2. How can recycling plastics help save a natural resource?

3. Are there recycling programs in your community? If so, what types of plastic do they take?

Sustainably harvested

Harvested in a way that does not damage an ecosystem

Environmentally intelligent design

An approach that tries to change production so no harmful waste is created

Research and Write

To be sustainable, a society must use limited resources and/or replenish those resources. Research the topic of sustainability. Write a report about the sustainable use of an important resource. One example is sustainable agriculture.

Manufacturers are also changing how they produce goods. Many companies believe that it makes sense to use fewer resources. It saves them money as well as helping the environment. Many paper companies offer products made from recycled paper. Many furniture makers now use wood that has been **sustainably harvested.** This means the trees have been harvested in a way that does not damage the forest ecosystem. Trees are cut down in ways that do not damage surrounding trees. Also, once a tree is cut down, it is replaced with a new tree. This helps ensure the forest and its biodiversity will be maintained.

New ways of designing everything from products to buildings are also reducing the impact of consumption. Some clothing companies use naturally-colored cotton instead of chemical dyes. Some build office spaces that maximize natural sunlight to reduce energy use.

Some of the most promising advances come in the area of **environmentally intelligent design.** This approach tries to change production so no harmful waste is created. In this way, it imitates natural systems. For example, an oak tree like the one in Figure 6.4.2 produces more seeds than it needs to reproduce, but the extra seeds are not wasted. They are food for animals. They can also decompose and return nutrients to the soil.

Figure 6.4.2 *Environmentally intelligent design attempts to change production processes to imitate natural systems.*

Following this example, some companies use materials that can return safely to the environment. This work requires the efforts of engineers, chemists, and many other scientists. One company has produced fabrics with so few chemicals they would be safe to eat. The waste material from this process is full of nutrients. It can be sold to farmers as **compost.** Compost is decayed organic material used to add nutrients to soil.

People have a lot of choice about how much they affect the environment. Individuals can reduce their consumption rates. Manufacturers can reduce waste and produce items that cause less harm to the environment. Governments can lead the way with programs and policies that protect natural resources. All of these efforts go into reducing society's impact on the environment.

Technology and Society

New technologies can help prevent environmental damage. For example, turkey feathers can be used to keep soil from washing away. The soft parts of the feather are separated and mixed with latex. A "cloth" made from this substance can stabilize soil long enough for new plants to grow. When the cloth decomposes, it returns safely to the environment.

Word Bank

affluence

equity

nontoxic

On a sheet of paper, write the word from the Word Bank that completes each sentence correctly.

1. The measure of a person's use of resources is called _____. This helps to determine their environmental impact.

2. Another word for fairness is _____.

3. Products such as _____ cleaners reduce the impact of chemicals on the environment.

On a sheet of paper, write the letter of the answer that completes each sentence correctly.

4. In the equation, $I = P \times A \times T$, the letter I stands for _____.

   A individuals   **C** innovation

   B influence   **D** impact

5. In _____ design, companies create products that imitate natural processes.

   A equitable

   B environmentally intelligent

   C low-impact

   D sustainable

6. _____ is an example of not getting enough resources.

   A Malnutrition   **C** Pollution

   B Overconsumption   **D** Recycling

Critical Thinking

On a sheet of paper, write the answers to the following questions. Use complete sentences.

7. Do all technologies increase environmental impact? Explain.

8. Obesity is a growing problem among children and adults in the United States. What is obesity, and what is the cause?

9. In what kinds of societies is malnutrition common?

10. What kinds of materials are recycled, and how are these materials used?

DISCOVERY INVESTIGATION 6

Materials
- safety goggles
- lab coat or apron
- gloves
- spring scale
- plastic grocery bags
- marker
- 1 day's household trash, minus food wastes
- calculator

Analyze Your Trash

If people reduce the amount of waste they produce, they also reduce their environmental impact. How much waste do you produce from consumption? Are there ways you could produce less? To answer these questions, you need to know what kinds of materials you throw away. In this lab, you will analyze household trash. You will then use the data to make predictions and propose solutions.

Procedure

1. In a small group, discuss the kinds of materials that you throw away. Write a hypothesis in which you predict the amount of garbage produced in a typical household each day. You will test your hypothesis with an experiment using the materials listed.

Continued on next page

2. Write a procedure for your experiment. Include Safety Alerts for handling garbage.

3. Have your hypothesis, procedure, and Safety Alerts approved by your teacher.

4. Carry out your experiment. Record your results.

Cleanup/Disposal

Before you leave the lab, be sure your work area is clean. Wash your hands thoroughly.

Analysis

1. What is the average amount of trash thrown away by each person in the household?

2. Make a circle graph of your group's data.

3. How does the makeup of your group's trash compare with that of other groups?

Conclusions

1. At this rate, how much trash would each person throw away in a month? A year?

2. How can you explain any differences in the groups' trash?

3. What are three things you could do to produce less trash?

Explore Further

Analyze the contents of the trash in the classroom or the trash from an office.

Balancing Consumption and Productivity

Your ecological footprint is the amount of land needed to produce and absorb what you consume. On average, it takes about 2.2 hectares per person to produce what humans currently consume. A hectare is equal to 0.01 square kilometers. The problem is that Earth only has 1.8 hectares of productive land per person. Some populations have higher rates of consumption, however. For example, the average ecological footprint for North Americans is about 9.2 hectares per person.

A person's ecological footprint is determined by a number of factors, including:

◆ the amount of meat and processed foods eaten per week

◆ the amount of waste generated

◆ the kinds of transportation used, and amount of use

◆ home resource use, including electricity, heat, and water

As of 2001, humans were consuming at a rate 20 percent greater than Earth's productivity. The result is a decrease in worldwide reserves of food, fuel, water, and other goods. To maintain this rate with population growth, humans would need more planet Earths.

In a sense, people are already using part of another Earth to meet demands. They are using the part of Earth that would have otherwise been used by future generations. To become sustainable, human societies must find a way to balance consumption and productivity.

1. What is an ecological footprint?

2. Why is the average ecological footprint of North America higher?

3. Find out what your ecological footprint is. Several Web sites offer online quizzes.

- There are currently 6.4 billion people on Earth. This number may climb as high as 9 to 10 billion by 2050.

- Modern medicine and agriculture have increased birth rates and decreased death rates.

- In most industrialized nations, the population is decreasing and the population growth rate is stable or decreasing.

- Industrialized nations have economies based on manufacturing and advanced technologies.

- Developing nations have less well-developed economies. All the countries with highest growth rates are developing nations.

- Better access to education and jobs can help growth rates decline.

- Industrialized nations have the highest levels of consumption. The increase in consumption causes an increase in resource use and pollution.

- Worldwide consumption levels are also increasing because population is increasing.

- Paul Ehrlich's measure of environmental impact is $I = P \times A \times T$. In this formula, I is impact, P is population, A is affluence, and T is technology.

- People in many parts of the world do not have enough resources to meet their basic needs. Some people say uneven use of resources is not equitable.

- Materials in many products can be recycled. Products can be designed with less energy use and less waste. Materials can be harvested in ways that do not disrupt natural systems.

Vocabulary

affluence, 235
birth rate, 219
carrying capacity, 219
compost, 239
consumption, 227
death rate, 219
demographer, 221
developing nation, 223
environmentally
   intelligent design,
   238

equity, 236
exponential growth,
   217
family planning, 225
fertility rate, 225
fishery, 230
fossil fuel, 228
growth rate, 216
industrialized nation,
   222
J-curve, 217

life expectancy, 223
malnutrition, 236
migration, 216
mine, 230
nontoxic, 237
obesity, 236
overpopulation, 221
population trend, 221
poverty level, 223
renewable, 230

reproductive age, 222
sanitation, 223
stabilize, 222
standard of living, 222
starve, 224
subsistence
   agriculture, 223
sustainably harvested,
   238
toxic waste, 228
world population, 216

Chapter 6 REVIEW

Word Bank

affluent

birth rate

compost

consumption

death rates

demographers

equity

exponential growth

fertility rate

malnutrition

migration

nontoxic

overpopulation

population trend

renewable

reproductive age

Vocabulary Review

On a sheet of paper, write the word or words from the Word Bank that complete each sentence correctly.

1. Decomposed organic waste used to add nutrients to crops is called _____.

2. A change in population over time is called a(n) _____.

3. When people or animals move from one place to another, it is called _____.

4. Something that grows by larger and larger amounts shows _____.

5. Chemicals that are _____ do not harm the environment.

6. The number of births per 1,000 people each year is the _____.

7. When a population is too large to be sustained by available resources, _____ has happened.

8. Food shortages and disease can increase _____.

9. Scientists called _____ study population and population trends.

10. People of _____ are capable of having children.

11. The _____ is the average number of children produced by women in a certain area.

12. During _____, resources are used and waste is produced.

13. Some resources are _____, meaning they can regenerate if not used too quickly.

14. In _____ societies, there is often a high standard of living.

15. Another word for fairness is _____.

16. People who do not get enough to eat can suffer from _____.

Continued on next page

Concept Review

On a sheet of paper, write the letter of the answer that completes each sentence correctly.

17. Rapid population growth is now occurring mostly in _____.

    A industrialized nations   **C** Europe
    B the Northern Hemisphere **D** developing nations

18. Poverty and malnutrition occur when there are too many people and not enough _____.

    A births   **C** resources
    B medicine   **D** growth

19. Driving a car, eating an apple, and heating your home are all examples of _____.

    A resources   **C** affluence
    B consumption   **D** equity

20. People who are very wealthy and very poor often have the greatest environmental _____.

    A impact   **C** concern
    B knowledge   **D** values

21. _____ is a way to reduce one's environmental impact.

    A Driving   **C** Polluting
    B Consuming   **D** Recycling

Critical Thinking

On a sheet of paper, write the answer to each of the following questions. Use complete sentences.

22. What are some reasons growth rates increased after the development of agriculture and again after the Industrial Revolution?

23. China's growth rate is quite low. Yet its population is still growing rapidly. How is this possible?

24. Why are consumption rates so high in industrialized nations?

25. How does environmentally intelligent design try to imitate an oak tree?

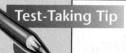

Test-Taking Tip When studying for a test, learn the most important points. Practice writing this material or explaining it to someone.

7

Energy

The tall machines in the photo are wind turbines. These machines can generate electricity wherever and whenever the wind blows. Wind energy is a renewable form of energy that comes from Earth's natural systems. Unlike wind energy, the energy in fossil fuels is used up once they have been burned. In Chapter 7, you will learn about sources of energy that can power human activities. You will learn about the advantages and disadvantages of each of these sources. You will also learn about ways to meet people's energy needs in the future.

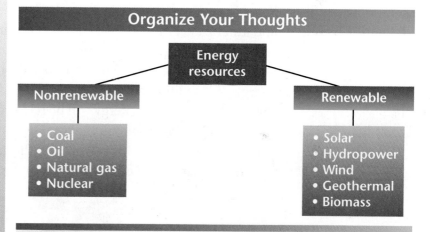

Organize Your Thoughts

Energy resources

Nonrenewable
- Coal
- Oil
- Natural gas
- Nuclear

Renewable
- Solar
- Hydropower
- Wind
- Geothermal
- Biomass

Goals for Learning

◆ To understand what energy is

◆ To name three fossil fuels and their advantages and disadvantages

◆ To describe nuclear energy and its benefits and risks

◆ To name five types of renewable energy and their advantages and disadvantages

◆ To explain how energy experts expect to meet future energy demand

Potential energy

The energy stored in an object

Kinetic energy

The energy of motion

All living things need energy to survive. In Chapter 1, you learned that energy is the ability to do work. Energy helps people and other animals walk, stay warm, breathe, and more. In today's world, energy fuels many other kinds of work, too. Energy makes cars move, heats homes, and lights buildings. Energy keeps factories running, radios humming, and computers powered.

Energy use has a big effect on the environment. This lesson introduces some energy terms and laws. These basic ideas will help you better understand the energy options discussed in later lessons.

Potential and Kinetic Energy

Scientists separate energy into two basic types: **potential energy** and **kinetic energy.** Potential energy is the energy stored in an object. That energy comes either from where the object is or what is inside it. Suppose you lift a rock off the ground. The energy used to lift it is now stored in the rock. The rock has potential energy. That energy will be released when you drop the rock. A liter of gasoline is full of potential energy. That energy will be released when you burn the gasoline in the car's engine. You can see an example of this in Figure 7.1.1.

Figure 7.1.1 *The potential energy in a liter of gasoline moves a car forward.*

Kinetic energy is the energy of motion. When you drop the rock, it has kinetic energy. A moving car has kinetic energy, too.

Laws of Energy

Scientists have come up with two principles, or **laws,** of energy. These laws help explain how energy is **transformed** in living systems, such as an ecosystem. They also relate to how energy is transformed in human inventions, such as car engines. To transform is to change from one form to another.

The **first law of energy** is also called the law of conservation of energy. This law states that energy is neither created nor destroyed. Instead, it changes from one form to another.

You can see this law at work in many situations. The energy in a rock held above the ground came from someplace else. It came from you, when you lifted it. The energy in a campfire log came from someplace else. It came from sunlight that the tree absorbed to help it grow. Dropping the rock and burning the log release the energy. The energy does not disappear, though. It just changes form. The dropped rock releases its energy as noise and **vibration,** or movement, in the ground. The burning log releases its energy as heat and light.

This first law of energy can be confusing. You might think it means that there will always be enough energy. If energy cannot be destroyed, the supply should not run out, right?

Link to ➤➤➤

Physics

The kinetic energy of an object depends on the object's mass and speed. The formula for kinetic energy is mv^2, where m = mass and v = velocity.

The answer is yes, and no. Energy is not destroyed, but it changes from high-quality to low-quality forms. This is the **second law of energy.** Every time energy is used, some of it changes to a less useful form. This less useful form is usually heat, which is given off at low temperatures. A perfect example of this law is a lightbulb. Put your hand above a lightbulb when it is on. Do you feel heat? This heat is energy given off by the lightbulb. Believe it or not, only 5 percent of the energy that goes into a lightbulb creates light. The remaining 95 percent is given off as heat. This is not high-quality heat, either. The heat released by a lightbulb would not keep you warm on a cold day. This heat is mostly waste.

The second law of energy shows how **inefficient,** or wasteful, energy use can be. When a car burns gasoline, only 10 percent helps the car move. The remaining 90 percent is lost as heat that goes into the environment. In other words, every time humans use energy, they waste energy. Nothing is 100 percent efficient. However, some uses waste more energy than others. Also, people's energy use changes high-quality energy sources into lower-quality sources. The total supply of these high-quality sources, then, is decreasing.

Express Lab 7

Materials

◆ tennis ball

Procedure

1. Place the ball on top of a desk. Push the ball just enough so that it falls off the edge of the desk.

2. Hold the ball at shoulder height, then drop it.

3. Hold the ball at waist height, then drop it.

Analysis

1. When does the ball display kinetic energy?

2. When does the ball display potential energy?

3. At what point does the ball have the most potential energy?

Renewable and Nonrenewable Energy

Human society currently makes use of many sources of potential energy. Many of these sources are considered **nonrenewable.** Nonrenewable means that there is only a limited supply of them. They cannot be replaced naturally as fast as they are being used. Coal, oil, and natural gas are all nonrenewable resources.

Other sources of energy are renewable. As you learned in Chapter 6, renewable means the resources are renewed by natural processes. That means they could possibly be available forever. Energy from the sun, water, and wind are all renewable sources of energy. Figure 7.1.2 shows the different fuels U.S. **utilities** used to generate electricity. A utility is a company that provides a public service, such as water or electricity.

The choices a society makes about energy affect the environment in different ways. Every source of energy has costs and benefits. Some are easier to find and use. Some are cheaper to **transport,** or move from one place to another. Using some causes less pollution than using others. Some meet the needs of more people. The following lessons explore these issues as they relate to many different energy options.

Fuels That U.S. Electric Utilities Used to Generate Electricity in 2004

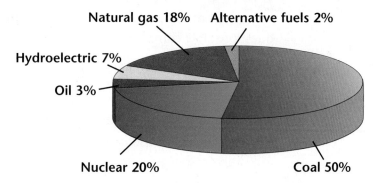

Figure 7.1.2 *U.S. electric utilities use both renewable and nonrenewable fuels to create electricity.*

Word Bank

first

kinetic

potential

second

On a sheet of paper, write the word from the Word Bank that completes each sentence correctly.

1. The energy stored in an apple or a log is _____ energy.

2. The energy of motion is _____ energy.

3. The _____ law of energy states that whenever energy is used, some of it decreases in quality. The _____ law of energy states that energy cannot be destroyed.

On a sheet of paper, write the letter of the answer that completes each sentence correctly.

4. Most of the energy used by burning gasoline in an engine is spent as _____.

    A motion   **B** light   **C** potential   **D** heat

5. Coal, natural gas, and oil are all _____ forms of energy.

    A renewable   **C** nonrenewable

    B kinetic   **D** waste-free

6. A person standing on a diving board best illustrates _____ energy.

    A kinetic   **B** potential   **C** nonrenewable   **D** thermal

Critical Thinking

On a sheet of paper, write the answers to the following questions. Use complete sentences.

7. How are a person and a car similar in terms of their energy needs?

8. List some of the sources that supply renewable energy.

9. Why is the second law of energy important to human society?

10. Give an example of a nonrenewable energy source that you use in your daily life.

Deposit

A layer of material laid down naturally

Crude oil

A thick liquid fossil fuel found underground

Petroleum

Another word for crude oil

Diatom

A tiny alga found in the ocean millions of years ago

Refinery

A place where crude oil is turned into usable forms of oil

Turbine

A device with blades that can be turned by steam, water, or wind

Generator

A machine that generates electricity

Whatever you did today, you probably benefited from the use of fossil fuels. Maybe you rode in a gasoline-fueled car. Maybe the energy used to turn on your computer came from burning coal. Maybe your home was heated by burning heating oil.

As you know, fossil fuels come from the remains of ancient plants and animals. Heat and pressure in the earth changed these remains over hundreds of millions of years. They became **deposits,** or layers, of fossil fuels. Oil, coal, and natural gas are all fossil fuels.

Fossil fuels provide about 90 percent of the energy used in the United States. They are also used widely in other parts of the world. These fuels are all easy to obtain. They are also inexpensive compared to other sources of energy. This is partly because there are already systems in place to support their use. A major disadvantage, however, is that they are nonrenewable. In one year, people consume the amount of fossil fuels made in about one million years. At this rate of consumption, fossil fuel supplies will eventually run out.

Oil

Crude oil, or **petroleum,** lies in deposits deep underground and under the sea floor. It is a thick, liquid mixture of hydrogen, carbon, and other elements. Like other fossil fuels, oil comes from the remains of ancient organisms. Most were tiny algae called **diatoms** that floated in the ocean millions of years ago.

Oil wells extract oil from the ground or sea floor. Then the oil is transported to **refineries.** Refineries convert crude oil into gasoline, heating oil, diesel fuel, and other substances. Each of these forms of oil is burned to produce energy. For example, power plants burn oil to heat water and create steam. That steam turns a **turbine,** which is a device with blades that can spin. When they spin, they drive a **generator** that generates electricity. Figure 7.2.1 on page 256 shows a steam turbine.

Contaminate

To pollute

Sulfur oxide

A pollutant produced by burning fossil fuels

Nitrogen oxide

A pollutant produced by burning fossil fuels

Combustion gases

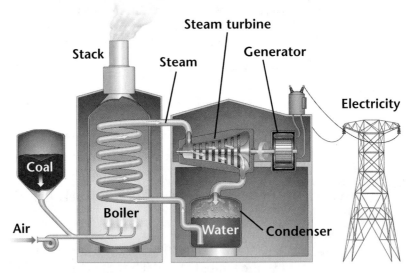

Figure 7.2.1 *A steam turbine is used to generate electricity.*

Each stage of oil use creates different environmental impacts. Constructing and using oil drills can disrupt local habitats and wildlife. Pipelines used to transport oil can sometimes get in the way of migrating animals. More than 322,000 kilometers of pipeline crisscross the United States alone. Pipelines can also leak oil. Transporting oil by ship has led to many accidental oil spills. Oil spills can kill wildlife and **contaminate,** or pollute, ecosystems. Cars that leak oil can also contaminate water supplies.

Finally, burning oil releases air pollutants such as **sulfur oxides** and **nitrogen oxides.** These pollutants greatly reduce air quality. They contribute to smog, acid rain, and global climate change. These and other problems caused by air pollution will be covered in Chapter 9.

Oil is considered an inexpensive source of energy. The current price is kept low in part because of tax breaks for oil companies. Yet some experts argue that the price should be higher. This might cause people to use less oil. It would also reflect the damage oil does to the environment.

Reserve

An amount of a natural resource known to be available

Coal

A solid fossil fuel made up of almost pure carbon

Strip mining

A form of mining in which the surface layer of rock is removed

Tunnel mining

A form of coal mining in which "rooms" of coal are extracted; also called pit mining

Mountaintop removal

A form of coal mining in which the entire top of a mountain is removed

Oil is found in many parts of the world, both on land and under the ocean. The United States has many oil **reserves.** These are places where a certain amount of oil is known to be available. However, at the rate North Americans use oil, the reserves could be used up by 2050. Therefore, the United States relies on imported oil, which is bought from other countries. The U.S. dependence on oil greatly affects its relations with these nations.

Coal

Coal is a solid material made of almost pure carbon. It comes from decomposing plant material that has been under pressure for millions of years. Coal is the most commonly available kind of fossil fuel. It is found in large amounts in the United States and many other countries. It is the source of one-third of the energy used in the world.

Coal is found underground between layers of rock. There are several different ways to remove it. In **strip mining,** the top layer of plants, soil, and rock is removed. The exposed coal can then be taken out. In **tunnel mining** or pit mining, heavy machinery carves out "rooms" within coal deposits. Pillars are left to hold up the rock overhead. In **mountaintop removal,** the entire top of a mountain is destroyed with dynamite. The exposed coal layer can then be removed. Extracting coal is dangerous work.

Coal is carried by trucks and trains to coal-burning power plants. As with oil, these power plants burn coal to heat water and produce steam. The steam spins turbines that generate electricity.

Miners can die from explosions, cave-ins, and lung diseases. Extracting coal also causes several kinds of environmental damage. Both strip mining and mountaintop removal seriously damage the natural environment. Trees and other plants are removed. Natural habitat is lost. Soil erodes and severe water pollution results. Tunnel and pit mines sometimes collapse. This makes the land above them dangerously unstable.

Natural gas

Underground deposits of gas, mostly methane

Methane

A gas released by decaying organisms

Burning coal releases huge amounts of pollutants into the air. These include sulfur dioxide, nitrogen dioxide, and mercury. Coal plants also produce carbon dioxide. In fact, three-quarters of the carbon dioxide released by power plants comes from coal. This contributes greatly to global warming.

Natural Gas

Natural gas is a combination of several gases, mostly **methane.** As ancient plants rotted, they released methane gas. The gas was trapped underground. It is often found near oil deposits. Natural gas can be extracted easily with drills. It can be burned to heat homes and businesses. That heat can also be used by power plants to turn a turbine that generates electricity.

▼◀▲▼◀▲▼◀▲▼◀▲▼◀▲▼◀▲▼◀▲▼◀▲▼◀▲▼◀▲▼◀▲▼◀▲▼◀▲▼◀▲▼

Science at Work

Power Plant Technician

Power plant technicians supervise the activities at power plants. They monitor the processes that produce power and make adjustments to the machinery. Power plants must maintain a steady flow of energy. A technician has to monitor and enforce safety regulations in the plant as well. Technicians are also responsible for writing reports and communicating with government and safety officials.

A power plant technician must have a high school degree. It is also helpful to have a strong math and technology background. Most technicians complete some technical training or have previous experience working in a power plant. A power plant technician should be skilled in working with machines and have good communications skills.

Natural gas has several advantages over other fossil fuels. First, it does not need to be processed. Once it is cleaned of **impurities,** it is ready to be used. Natural gas burns hotter and cleaner than other fossil fuels, too. It does not produce as much carbon dioxide as coal or oil.

Natural gas is relatively cheap. That makes it a promising way to heat homes and buildings. Natural gas supplies are limited, however. Those in the United States are likely to run out by 2050.

Today, fossil fuels are the most widely used sources of energy. At the current rate of consumption, these nonrenewable resources may only last a few more decades. To prepare for the future, humans must seek out other sources of energy.

Technology and Society

Coal-burning power plants are required to use filters that reduce the amount of pollution they produce. These filters are called "scrubbers" because they clean the air. Thanks to the widespread use of scrubbers, power plants produce much less pollution than they did decades ago.

Lesson 2 REVIEW

Word Bank

coal

fossil fuels

natural gas

On a sheet of paper, write the word or words from the Word Bank that complete each sentence correctly.

1. The remains of ancient plants and animals form sources of energy called _____.

2. A fossil fuel that is found as a solid mass of almost pure carbon is _____.

3. A fossil fuel made up mostly of methane is _____.

On a sheet of paper, write the letter of the answer that completes each sentence correctly.

4. Another word for crude oil is _____.

   A petroleum   **B** diesel   **C** heating oil   **D** gas

5. In _____ mining, machinery is used to dig out large rooms within coal layers.

   A strip   **C** mountaintop removal
   B tunnel   **D** natural

6. Oil wells, mines, and drills are all used to _____ fossil fuels.

   A renew   **B** create   **C** extract   **D** replace

Critical Thinking

On a sheet of paper, write the answers to the following questions. Use complete sentences.

7. Compare the length of time it takes to create fossil fuels and to use them.

8. Choose an animal. How might the use or extraction of fossil fuels affect it?

9. Why is coal mining dangerous work?

10. Which fossil fuel would be the hardest to do without? Explain your answer.

Objectives

After reading this lesson, you should be able to

◆ explain the process of nuclear fission

◆ describe the benefits and risks of nuclear energy

Subatomic particle

A proton, neutron, or electron

Proton

A tiny particle in the nucleus of an atom with a positive electrical charge

Neutron

A tiny particle in the nucleus of an atom with no electrical charge

Electron

A tiny particle with a negative charge that moves around the nucleus of an atom

Nucleus

The center of an atom

Isotopes

Atoms of the same element that have different numbers of neutrons

Nuclear power provides about 8 percent of the energy used in the United States. In some European nations, it provides more than half. Nuclear power comes from a process called nuclear fission. To understand nuclear fission, you must first understand atoms.

Nuclear Fission

In Chapter 2, you learned that elements are made up of tiny particles called atoms. Atoms themselves are made of three kinds of even smaller particles, called **subatomic particles.** These are **protons, neutrons,** and **electrons.** Inside the center, or **nucleus,** of an atom are protons and neutrons. The protons have a positive charge. The neutrons have no charge. Traveling around the nucleus are electrons. They have a negative charge. The total number of protons and electrons in an atom are always the same. That means that the atom has no electrical charge. Figure 7.3.1 shows a diagram of a helium atom. It has two protons, two neutrons, and two electrons.

All atoms of the same element have the same number of protons and electrons. For example, all hydrogen atoms have just one proton and one electron. All uranium atoms have 92 protons and 92 electrons. Sometimes atoms of the same element have different numbers of neutrons, though. These are called **isotopes.**

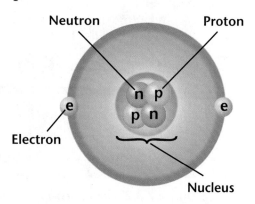

Figure 7.3.1 *An atom is made up of protons, neutrons, and electrons.*

Nuclear fission releases energy trapped inside an atom. Fission means a split. When the nucleus of an atom is split, the neutrons inside are released. They then split the nuclei of other atoms. This starts a **chain reaction** that produces lots of energy. Some is light energy. Some is heat energy. If the energy is released all at once, it can produce an explosion like in an atomic bomb. If it is released slowly, it can be used to make electricity. The heat boils water and creates steam. The steam turns a turbine to generate electricity.

Causing the chain reaction described above requires the use of **radioactive** isotopes. Radioactive means an element turns into another element over time, releasing energy in the process. Nuclear fission uses radioactive **uranium** isotopes. Uranium is dug out of the ground. Then it is processed into tiny cylinders called pellets. The pellets are then loaded into long rods called **fuel rods.**

Nuclear energy is produced inside a **nuclear reactor.** One is shown in Figure 7.3.2. Inside this reactor, fuel rods are combined with **control rods.** Control rods are made of materials that capture neutrons. These control rods interrupt the chain reaction of nuclear fission. In so doing, they control the speed of the reaction. There are one or more nuclear reactors in a **nuclear power plant.** A nuclear power plant converts the energy from nuclear fission into electricity.

Figure 7.3.2 *Nuclear energy is produced inside a nuclear reactor.*

Uranium Mining

The impacts of nuclear energy begin with the mining of uranium. Uranium is found around the world. About 20 countries, though, produce most of the uranium used for nuclear power. Australia, Kazakhstan, Canada, South Africa, and Namibia produce much of this uranium.

Uranium is dug out of the ground from uranium mines. Then, in **uranium mills,** it is processed into forms that can be used for nuclear fission. Both the mines and the mills produce debris called **tailings.** These tailings give off radioactive gas for hundreds of thousands of years. Millions of tons of these wastes now exist. Some have been left in piles near uranium mills. Some have been left in town dumps. Some have even been used to make roads, homes, and buildings.

Being exposed to radioactive materials over long periods of time can cause serious health problems. For example, tailings went into the construction of 5,000 homes in Grand Junction, Colorado. For years, inhabitants were exposed to large amounts of radiation. The **leukemia** rate in Grand Junction is now twice as high as in other parts of the state. Leukemia is a form of cancer that affects blood cells.

People who mine uranium are also exposed to radiation. In some mines, miners have six times the normal death rate from lung cancer. Better **ventilation** has helped clean the air in most mines. It has also increased the radioactive gases outside the mines.

Uranium mill

A place where uranium is processed for use in nuclear fission

Tailings

Debris produced by mining

Leukemia

A cancer of the blood cells

Ventilation

A means of supplying fresh air

Science Myth

Myth: Nuclear radiation causes animals and people to mutate.

Fact: Radiation from nuclear accidents and leaks can harm people in two ways. The radiation can burn, like a fire. Nuclear radiation can also damage DNA in cells. If DNA is damaged, sicknesses such as cancer can occur. Damaged DNA can also cause mutations in new generations but does not change the current generation.

Reactor Safety

Nuclear reactors produce huge amounts of heat, even after they are shut down. For this reason, water or another material is used to cool down the nuclear reactor **core.** The core is the center of the reactor where fuel and control rods are placed. If the core is not cooled, a **meltdown** can occur. A meltdown is the complete melting of a nuclear reactor's core. It can release huge amounts of radioactive materials into the environment.

Nuclear reactors have many safety features to help avoid a meltdown or explosion. Many people say that these make nuclear reactors completely safe. Yet a number of nuclear accidents have happened because of mechanical or human errors. In 1979, one reactor at Three Mile Island in Pennsylvania had a partial core meltdown. Small amounts of radiation escaped.

In 1986, a nuclear power plant in Chernobyl, Russia, caught fire. Radioactive materials were spread more than 2,000 kilometers from the plant. People in more than 20 countries were exposed. Thirty-one plant workers and firefighters died within five months after the accident. Experts disagree on the total number of people who will end up dying early from this exposure. Estimates range from 4,000 to over 100,000 people.

Research and Write

Nuclear power was more popular before the accidents at Three Mile Island and Chernobyl. Research these two incidents in history. What actually happened at each nuclear power facility? Try to find old news reports. Write a report with a partner, explaining how these incidents affected attitudes about nuclear power.

There are two types of waste produced at nuclear power plants. The fuel rods are considered high-level waste. Low-level waste includes all the clothing, tools, and filters that have been contaminated.

Nuclear Waste

Another impact of nuclear energy is the production of radioactive waste. Each fuel rod lasts only about three years. After that, they are cooled at the plant for several years. Then they are sealed in containers and can be transported to nuclear waste storage sites.

People disagree about the safety of these storage sites and where they should be located. Many people are concerned that the waste could leak and contaminate land and water. Others are concerned about accidents that could occur when the waste is transported. There are no permanent waste storage sites in the United States. Radioactive waste is stored at power plants, where space is running out.

Evaluating Nuclear Energy

People who support the use of nuclear energy point out that it has many benefits. For one thing, nuclear energy produces no carbon dioxide. Therefore, it does not contribute to global warming.

In addition, uranium is widely available. A small amount produces a huge amount of energy. This means nuclear energy is a good long-term option. Some people also believe it may soon be possible to recycle used fuel rods. This would avoid a major source of radioactive waste.

Today, producing nuclear energy is very expensive. This is one of the reasons why fossil fuels are used more widely than nuclear power. Also, some people are concerned about the health risks of nuclear power plants and waste storage. They feel it is necessary to address these financial costs and safety concerns before nuclear power is used more widely.

On a sheet of paper, write the word or words from the Word Bank that complete each sentence correctly.

Word Bank
atoms
fuel rods
tailings

1. Elements are composed of tiny particles called _____.

2. Debris from uranium mines and mills is known as _____.

3. Uranium pellets are packed into tubes called _____.

On a sheet of paper, write the letter of the answer that completes each sentence correctly.

4. Nuclear fission is the splitting of the _____ of an atom.

   A neutron   **B** nucleus   **C** proton   **D** electron

5. Nuclear reactors slow the fission process with _____.

   A fuel rods   **C** chain reactions
   B pellets   **D** control rods

6. A _____ is the melting of a nuclear reactor's core.

   A meltdown   **C** burner
   B heat wave   **D** chain reaction

Critical Thinking

On a sheet of paper, write the answers to the following questions. Use complete sentences.

7. What types of pollution does nuclear energy produce?

8. Why might a country without many fossil fuel reserves choose to use nuclear power?

9. What is a chain reaction? Explain its role in creating nuclear energy.

10. What are the advantages of using nuclear power as an energy source?

Solar energy

Energy from the sun

Passive solar energy

Energy produced directly by sunlight, without extra machinery

Passive solar heating

Heating a building directly by sunlight

Passive solar cooling

Cooling by blocking sunlight from a building

Daylighting

Using sunlight to replace or supplement artificial light

The sun is the main source of energy on Earth. Think about your own home. During the day, do you need to turn on electric lights in every room? If not, that is because the sun lights your home for you. During many months of the year, you probably do not need to heat your home. That is because the sun heats it for you.

Solar energy, or energy from the sun, is nothing new. Yet people have found new ways to capture and use solar energy. Solar energy has many benefits. It is available just about everywhere. It produces no pollution. It often makes use of simple technology. It can be used in many settings. Finally, solar energy systems cost money to set up, but the energy itself is free. The biggest disadvantage of solar power is that sunlight is not always available. Cloudy days provide less solar power and nights provide none.

Solar energy can be used to provide heat, light, mechanical power, and electricity. The following sections describe the three main forms of solar power. They are passive solar energy, active solar systems, and photovoltaics.

Passive Solar Energy

Passive solar energy is the most basic form of solar energy. It means capturing the sun's energy directly. No extra machinery or energy is needed. There are three types of passive solar energy use. **Passive solar heating** happens when sunlight is absorbed and converted to heat. **Passive solar cooling** keeps sunlight and heated air away from a building. **Daylighting** finds the best use of available sunlight to light a building.

Insulation

A material that prevents heat or cold from escaping into or out of a space

These forms of passive solar energy are made possible by the design of a building. First, buildings are laid out so that their longest sides receive the most direct sunlight. In the Northern Hemisphere, this means the longest side faces south. Windows are placed on this south side. They let in lots of heat and light in the winter months. In the summer, shades and shutters are used to block the light. This keeps the building cooler. Deciduous trees can also be planted on the south side to provide shade in summer.

Passive solar heating systems also use dense building materials. Walls and floors are constructed of materials such as brick, concrete, tiles, and stones. These materials absorb a lot of heat and release it slowly. Sometimes, passive solar systems even use containers of water for this purpose. Heat is stored in the water, then slowly let out into the air.

Finally, **insulation** is very important in passive solar heating and cooling systems. Insulation is any material that prevents heat or cold from passing in or out. In passive solar systems, heavy insulation keeps hot air inside a building during the winter. It keeps cool air inside during the summer.

Passive solar energy is the cheapest way to heat a home. Unfortunately, it can cost a lot to install passive solar systems. If families move a lot, they may not want to pay to install these systems in each home. Passive solar heating has another disadvantage. In very cold climates, another heating system is also needed. In very hot climates, homes using passive solar energy are difficult to keep cool.

Active Solar Systems

Active solar system

A system that collects and delivers solar energy

Solar collector

A device that captures solar energy and converts it to heat

Photovoltaics

Devices that convert solar energy into electricity; also called solar cells

Active solar systems have two main features. First, they absorb the sun's energy with **solar collectors.** Solar collectors are flat panels that can be mounted on rooftops or on the ground. They have black absorbers inside that convert the sun's energy into heat. Second, active solar systems require electric pumps or fans to distribute the absorbed heat. This heat can be used right away. It can also be stored for later use. Either way, these pumps and fans require additional energy.

Active solar systems can be used to heat homes. They can also be used to heat water to use at home. In fact, active solar systems currently heat half of the hot water in Israel. They are especially useful for heating water for big apartment buildings and businesses. Some people even use active solar systems to heat their swimming pools.

Active solar systems are currently expensive to use at home. The cost can decrease, though, if more people begin to use these systems.

Active solar systems can also be used on a much larger scale. Their biggest disadvantage is that they require a lot of land. Many solar collectors are installed together across a large area. Mirrors concentrate sunlight to heat liquid to very high temperatures. The steam is then used to turn turbines and generate electricity. In California's Mojave Desert, 1.6 square kilometers are used for these solar collectors. They supply electricity to Los Angeles.

Photovoltaics

If you have ever had a solar-powered calculator, then you have used **photovoltaics.** Photovoltaics are also known as PVs or solar cells. They are devices that convert sunlight into electricity. These devices contain elements such as silicon that react to sunlight by releasing electrons. This produces a small amount of electrical current. Wires transfer the current to storage batteries or machines.

Photovoltaics are currently used to light highway signs and lighthouses. They are often used in calculators and watches. It takes many photovoltaics to provide electricity for a home or other building. First, many cells are mounted together on a panel. Then several panels can be put on a rooftop.

Photovoltaics are most cost-effective in regions far from major cities. That is because it costs a lot to extend power lines out to these areas. Many people living in rural Canada and the United States use photovoltaic power.

Photovoltaics are also a good option in developing nations. Many of these areas have lots of sunshine. Most also have a large rural population without access to an electrical **power grid**. An electrical power grid is used to distribute electricity to a region.

Solar energy will be available as long as the sun keeps shining. Solar energy is free, though systems that collect this energy cost money to set up. The energy can also be undependable, especially on days with little sunlight. However, solar energy does not pollute the environment. It does not consume nonrenewable resources to generate energy. Because of this, solar energy may be used more and more in the years to come.

Science Myth

Myth: Solar energy is only available when the sun is shining.

Fact: Solar energy systems often have batteries. The solar cells charge the batteries and provide energy when the sun is shining. The batteries then provide energy when the sun is not out.

Map Skills: Solar Energy Availability

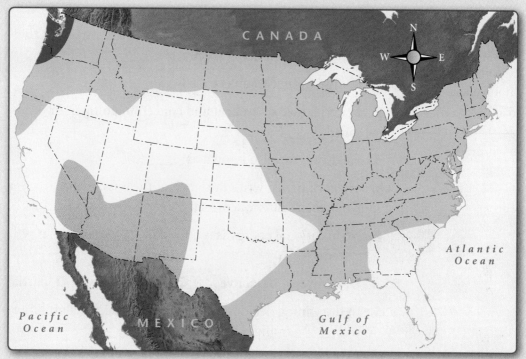

Solar energy is a resource that is available to everyone. However, as with other forms of energy, there is more available in some places. Because solar systems can be expensive to set up, it helps to know how much of this resource is available. This can help people decide whether to use it.

The map shows the average amount of solar energy available in the United States. Solar energy is represented in kBtu (kilo British thermal units) generated for each square foot of solar panel. Use the map and its key to answer the following questions.

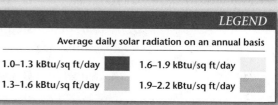

LEGEND

Average daily solar radiation on an annual basis

1.0–1.3 kBtu/sq ft/day	1.6–1.9 kBtu/sq ft/day
1.3–1.6 kBtu/sq ft/day	1.9–2.2 kBtu/sq ft/day

1. In general, which parts of the country receive the most solar energy?

2. What is the total range of kBtu/sq ft/day found in the United States?

3. Which two states would benefit the most from using solar panels to generate electricity?

Lesson 4   REVIEW

Word Bank

insulation

photovoltaics

solar

On a sheet of paper, write the word from the Word Bank that completes each sentence correctly.

1. Energy from the sun is called _____ energy.

2. Material that keeps heat and cold from going in or out is called _____.

3. Solar cells are also known as _____.

On a sheet of paper, write the letter of the answer that completes each sentence correctly.

4. No additional energy is required in _____ solar energy systems.

    A passive   **B** active   **C** photovoltaic   **D** partial

5. In the winter, deciduous trees planted next to a building will _____ sunlight.

    A block   **B** reflect   **C** let in   **D** replace

6. Active solar systems use either pumps or _____ to distribute heat.

    A drills   **B** fans   **C** collectors   **D** panels

Critical Thinking

On a sheet of paper, write the answers to the following questions. Use complete sentences.

7. In what ways does every person rely on solar energy?

8. In what kinds of climates do you think solar energy systems would work best?

9. Describe the advantages and disadvantages of using solar energy.

10. How does passive solar cooling help to save energy?

Hydropower

Energy that comes from moving water

Dam

A barrier built across a river to control the flow of water

Upstream

In the opposite direction of the way that water is flowing in a stream or river

Downstream

The direction water in a river or stream flows, away from its source

Fish ladder

A series of pools that allow fish to move upstream over a dam

Solar energy is one of several kinds of renewable energy used today. Others include water energy, wind energy, geothermal energy, and biomass energy. All of these share many of the same benefits as solar energy. They are widely available. They can last for a long time if managed carefully. They also produce much less pollution than fossil fuels.

Right now, about 7 percent of U.S. energy comes from water power. Another 3 percent comes from other forms of renewable energy.

Water Energy

If you have ever canoed down river rapids, you know that moving water has energy. This kinetic energy can be used to produce electricity. Power produced by moving water is called **hydropower.** The force of falling water makes turbines rotate. This energy is sent into a generator that makes electricity.

Hydropower often relies on **dams.** Dams are barriers built across rivers. The water collects behind the dam. When it is released, it falls with greater force than it did before. Dams are not always necessary, though. Natural waterfalls, such as Niagara Falls, produce a lot of energy without dams. Niagara Falls provides electricity for both the United States and Canada.

Hydropower is renewable. It does not produce pollution. Yet using dams does cause major environmental problems. Changing the flow of a river alters local ecosystems. Wildlife can lose their habitats. The largest dam in the world is on China's Yangtze River. Scientists believe flooding from this dam threatens the habitat of clouded leopards and other species. Dams can also interfere with the movement of migrating fish. Salmon, for example, swim **upstream** to lay and fertilize their eggs. The young salmon then swim **downstream** to the sea. **Fish ladders** are sometimes used to help the salmon. They are a series of pools that allow fish to swim upstream over a dam.

Research and Write

Research the fish ladders that are used to help fish get around dams. Use the library and Internet. Write a description in your own words. Present your findings to the class. Include a drawing or photo of how the fish ladder works.

The ocean provides another form of water power. The daily rising and falling of ocean **tides** produces energy. Dams can be built where the tides are especially high. These dams have been successful in China, Norway, Canada, and France. Large communities usually require additional power systems, however. Dams also must be built carefully to avoid harm to coastal habitats.

Wind Energy

Wind power has been used for thousands of years. Long ago, people realized they could move boats by catching the wind with their sails. They also built windmills to capture the wind's energy. This energy was used to grind grain and pump water.

Wind power has been used to generate electricity since the early twentieth century. Large **wind turbines** are placed on top of high towers. As the wind hits their blades, it turns a shaft that is connected to a generator. This generator produces electricity.

There are many advantages to wind power. It is renewable. It produces no pollution beyond what is caused by making and transporting the turbines. Connected groups of turbines called **wind farms** can produce large quantities of energy. These wind farms can be built on land used for more than one purpose. For example, they can go on land used for farms or raising cattle. They can also be located in ocean waters just off the coast.

Wind turbines have caused a few environmental problems in the past. The spinning blades were known to kill birds and bats. They also made a lot of noise. Design changes have reduced both these problems. Today, the biggest impact is one of **aesthetics,** or visual appearance. Some people believe wind turbines spoil beautiful views. For example, many people oppose a large wind farm now proposed for Nantucket Sound. They believe it would ruin the view of the ocean.

Geother...

As you kr... hot.
Sometir... ... of
volcar... ...s a natural
flow ... geyser is a jet of
he... in Earth's crust.

...duce **geothermal**
...side the earth." Water
is ... ...nes into contact with hot
rocks. ... and creates steam, which a
pipe carries ... ...t spins the turbine to generate
electricity. The he... ...an also be used to heat homes.

Geothermal energy powe... Italy's railway trains. It produces electricity for San Francisco. It also heats most of the houses in Iceland, which has many volcanoes.

Geothermal energy has several advantages. Geothermal power stations require very little land. Once a power station has been built, the energy is nearly free. Currently tapped sources will last hundreds of years if they are not overused. No carbon dioxide is produced.

Geothermal energy also has some major disadvantages. It is only easy to access in certain geographic areas. The energy cannot be used to power motor vehicles. Finally, it does produce other forms of air and water pollution. Hazardous gases and minerals can come up from underground. They can be difficult to dispose of safely.

Hot spring
A natural flow of groundwater heated inside the earth

Geyser
A jet of hot liquid or steam that shoots out of a crack in Earth's crust

Geothermal
Heat from inside the earth

Link to ➤➤➤

Cultures
Many people in Europe and northern Canada use peat as fuel. Peat comes from layers of moss that have been buried in wetlands. The peat can be harvested and burned like coal. Peat, however, is more renewable than coal because it takes much less time to form. Peat can form in thousands of years instead of millions.

Biomass

Biomass

Plant material that is burned for fuel

Peat

Partly decomposed plant material found in wetlands

Ethanol

A fuel made from corn or sugar cane

If you have ever burned a log on a fire, you have used **biomass** energy. Biomass is organic material made by plants and animals that is burned for fuel. Wood is the most common source of biomass energy. Other examples include cow droppings and **peat.** Peat is a spongelike brown material made of partly decomposed plants. It is found in marshes and other wetlands.

Around the world, billions of people get the fuel they need from wood. Used carefully, wood could provide an endless supply of energy. Yet population growth in many areas is causing wood supplies to be used up. People are taking wood faster than the trees can grow back. As a result, rain forests and other forests are disappearing. Now, many people do not have enough wood to meet their fuel needs. Burning wood also creates a lot of air pollution. Carbon dioxide, smoke, and ash are all released when wood is burned.

There are new ways of converting biomass into a cleaner-burning gas or liquid. Corn or sugar cane can be used to make a liquid fuel called **ethanol.** Ethanol fuels about half the cars in Brazil. However, it takes many square kilometers to grow enough plant material for large amounts of ethanol.

Link to >>>

Biology

Ethanol is made from corn or other crops. It is produced when living yeast cells consume and process the grain extract. Ethanol is often added to gasoline to reduce the amount of pollution produced.

❀ ❀

Technology and Society

The grass plant Miscanthus, which can be burned as fuel, stands more than four meters high. It can be burned alone in a power plant or mixed with coal. According to one estimate, if 8 percent of Illinois's land were used to grow Miscanthus, this grass could provide for all the electricity used in the state.

The Future of Renewable Energy

As the world population continues to increase, so will the demand for energy. The rise in individual energy consumption will also increase the demand for energy. This increase will place more pressure on fossil fuel reserves. Renewable energy sources provide opportunities for relieving some of this pressure.

There are many different sources of renewable energy to choose from. Although each has disadvantages, they will all become more important in the future. In Lesson 6, you will read about energy use in the future, and what role renewable sources of energy will play.

Achievements in Science

Denmark Leads the World in Wind Power

Currently, the country of Denmark gets more than 20 percent of its power from wind. This figure may soon increase to 29 percent. Denmark has improved its ability to harvest wind power by setting up offshore wind farms. Wind speeds over the ocean are often faster and more consistent than over land.

Denmark does more than use the wind to get a large amount of its power. Danish companies have also spent the last several years developing better, more efficient wind turbines. Denmark's economy has benefited from marketing wind power to the rest of the world.

Denmark's economy may also receive a boost from the health and environmental benefits of wind energy. Using clean energy means that there is less money spent on treating pollution-related illnesses. Also, Denmark does not have to purchase large amounts of coal or oil. Denmark's use of wind power is an important achievement in a world powered mostly by fossil fuels.

On a sheet of paper, write the word or words from the Word Bank that complete each sentence correctly.

Word Bank

fish ladder

hydropower

turbine

1. Another word for water power is _____.

2. A wind _____ converts wind energy to electricity.

3. A _____ can help salmon get past a dam.

On a sheet of paper, write the letter of the answer that completes each sentence correctly.

4. Hot springs and geysers are two sources of _____.

    A hydropower   **C** solar power

    B geothermal energy   **D** biomass energy

5. Wood is a source of _____.

    A hydropower   **C** solar power

    B geothermal energy   **D** biomass energy

6. Hydropower requires building dams on rivers except where there are powerful _____.

    A waterfalls   **B** winds   **C** geysers   **D** turbines

Critical Thinking

On a sheet of paper, write the answers to the following questions. Use complete sentences.

7. Why is geothermal energy not used more often? Explain your answer.

8. What problems are caused by building a dam to harness power from a river?

9. Why do people sometimes object to building wind farms to produce power?

10. Describe at least two ways that geothermal energy is used today in the world.

INVESTIGATION 7

Materials

- 1- or 2-liter plastic bottle
- sand
- paper
- pencil with an eraser
- thumbtack
- string
- large paperclip
- assortment of washers

Using Wind Energy to Do Work

Wind power is the wind's kinetic energy. Modern wind turbines take this energy and produce electricity. How did early windmills use wind power? Most did work, such as pumping water, which was powered directly by the wind. In this lab, you will model how early windmills worked.

Procedure

1. Create a pinwheel from a square of stiff paper by cutting diagonally from the corners to the center. Do not cut through the center. Then take the left corner of each triangle formed and fold it into the center. Pin the corners down with a thumbtack pushed into a pencil's eraser.

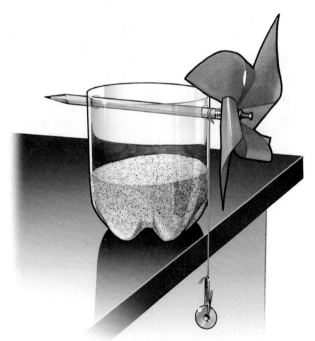

Continued on next page

2. Cut the top half off a 1- or 2-liter bottle. Fill the bottom fourth of the bottle with sand. Punch two holes across from each other in the rim of the bottle. Push the pencil through the holes.

3. Tightly tie or tape one end of the string to the pencil. Bend the paperclip into an S shape and tie one end of it to the other end of the string. Hook a washer on the paperclip.

4. Blow gently until the pinwheel turns and winds up the string.

5. Add another washer to the paperclip and repeat Step 4. Continue adding washers until the pinwheel can no longer lift them without you blowing harder.

6. Add a second student blowing against the pinwheel. Add washers to find out how much weight the pinwheel can lift now.

Cleanup/Disposal
Return the materials and make sure your area is clean before you leave the lab.

Analysis
1. How many washers were you able to lift by blowing gently?

2. How many washers were you able to lift with two people blowing?

Conclusions
1. What type of energy makes the pinwheel turn?

2. How does the amount of wind affect the amount of energy that can be produced by the windmill?

3. How can wind be used to make electricity?

Explore Further
Observe two pinwheels of different sizes next to each other in front of a fan. Describe what you observe. How does the size of the pinwheel affect how much work it can do?

Energy conservation

Using less energy and wasting less energy

Carpooling

Sharing car rides with others to reduce energy use

Energy efficiency

The percentage of useful work from an input of energy

Compact fluorescents

Energy-efficient lightbulbs

Energy efficient

Wastes less energy

How will people use energy in the future? Where will their energy come from? Currently, the demand for energy is rising. Much of this demand is being met by fossil fuels. Yet fossil fuel reserves will run out some day. That means that something will have to change in order to meet future demand.

Many energy experts believe it will be important to increase the use of renewable energy. Solar and wind power create the least pollution. Improvements in design and wider use could make them less expensive. Solar, wind, water, geothermal, and biomass energy can all contribute to future energy needs. Some experts say they could provide up to 70 percent of U.S. energy within 40 years.

Energy Conservation

Energy conservation will be an important way to help meet society's increasing energy needs. Energy conservation means using less energy and wasting less energy. There are many simple things people can do to conserve energy. For example, turning out the lights when you leave the room conserves energy. Installing insulation at home to keep heat and cold from escaping saves energy. You save energy if you ride a bicycle someplace instead of driving in a car. Energy is even saved if people share a car ride rather than driving alone. This is called **carpooling.**

Energy can also be conserved through increased **energy efficiency.** Energy efficiency is the percentage of useful work from a certain amount of energy. As you learned in Lesson 1, some energy is always wasted when energy changes form. Standard lightbulbs convert only about 5 percent of electricity into light. The rest is wasted as low-quality heat. Changes in design can improve energy efficiency. For example, **compact fluorescents** use 25 percent less energy than standard lightbulbs. That makes them much more **energy efficient.** They use less energy to produce the same amount of light.

Hybrid vehicle

A vehicle that runs on both a gasoline engine and an electric motor

Mandated

Enforced by law

Link to >>>

Home and Career

Appliances sold in the United States may have an Energy Star label. This label tells you that the appliance is proven to be energy efficient. Choosing an efficient appliance saves money and reduces pollution.

Scientists in many fields are helping increase the energy efficiency of appliances, cars, and other products. One benefit is that people who buy the products often do not notice a difference. For example, refrigerators became 72 percent more energy efficient between 1972 and the late 1980s. Yet consumers did not complain that the refrigerators were not cooling well enough.

Perhaps you have heard of gasoline-electric **hybrid vehicles.** These vehicles are much more energy efficient than gasoline-powered vehicles. Many models get more than 17 kilometers per liter of gasoline (40 miles per gallon). The reason is that they have both a gasoline engine and a battery-powered electric motor. These cars use little or no power when they are sitting still or slowing down. The electric motor charges as the car drives.

Energy efficiency adds up to big savings on energy use. For example, suppose every exit sign in the United States were changed to an energy-efficient system. Each year, this would save the amount of energy produced by 985 million liters of gasoline. Or suppose everyone in the United States lowered their household temperature in cold months. A change of only 6 degrees on a cold day would save about 80 million liters of oil.

You may wonder how energy conservation happens. Sometimes it is an individual choice. Homeowners may choose to install insulation. Consumers may choose to buy a more energy-efficient car. Sometimes conservation is **mandated,** or enforced by law. For example, a government mandate forced automobile companies to increase fuel efficiency in the 1970s. As a result, cars were averaging nearly twice as many kilometers per liter by 1985. Sometimes companies choose to increase the energy efficiency of their products. They believe that consumers want these products and will buy them.

Energy Innovations

Scientists are working all the time to find new ways to address global energy needs. Some are working to make renewable energy sources cheaper and more efficient. Others are working to develop new sources of energy, such as the **fuel cell.** A fuel cell is a device for converting substances like hydrogen and oxygen to electricity. When these substances react, water and electricity are produced. Fuel cells work something like a regular battery. Yet they do not need to be recharged. They also produce far less pollution than burning fossil fuels.

Other discoveries are happening all the time. A scientist in Canada has recently found a way to "paint" tiny solar cells onto all sorts of surfaces. In the future, your house could be painted with cells that provide heat and electricity. Your shirt could be painted with cells that charge your cell phone.

New discoveries are also contributing to energy possibilities. Scientists have recently found frozen natural gas crystals on the ocean floor. It is possible that these could be harvested. This would provide another source of energy in the future.

No one knows exactly what the future of energy will hold. Most agree, though, that it will take some combination of all the ideas described above. People will need to reduce their energy demand though energy-efficient products and conservation. They will need to use more renewable sources of energy. More research and development will be necessary to continue to improve energy options. Individuals, communities, and industries will all play a role in shaping our energy future.

Lesson 6   R E V I E W

Word Bank

conservation

efficiency

fuel cell

On a sheet of paper, write the word or words from the Word Bank that complete each sentence correctly.

1. Using less energy and wasting less energy is known as energy _____.

2. Energy _____ means the amount of useful work you get from a certain input of energy.

3. A(n) _____ is a device that converts substances like hydrogen and oxygen into water and electricity.

Critical Thinking

On a sheet of paper, write the answers to the following questions. Use complete sentences.

4. Give two examples of an energy-efficient product. How do they conserve energy?

5. Describe one change you have made recently or could make in your life that would save energy.

■ ◆ ■ ◆ ■ ◆ ■ ◆ ■ ◆ ■ ◆ ■ ◆ ■ ◆ ■ ◆ ■ ◆ ■ ◆ ■ ◆ ■ ◆ ■ ◆ ■ ◆ ■ ◆ ■ ◆ ■ ◆ ■ ◆ ■

Science in Your Life

Consumer Choices: More Efficient Homes

Two of the biggest uses of energy are for heating and cooling our homes. Fortunately, newer furnaces and air conditioners are much more efficient than older ones. Furnaces are ranked according to how much of their fuel they turn into heat. This is given as a percentage. Older furnaces typically turned about 50 to 60 percent of their fuel into heat. The rest was wasted. Newer furnaces must be at least 78 percent efficient. Some high-efficiency models can be up to 97 percent efficient.

Air conditioners are given a Seasonal Energy Efficiency Rating (SEER) according to their efficiency. The higher the rating, the more efficient the unit is. The government requires that all new air conditioners must have a SEER rating of at least 13. Most older units have a SEER rating of only 7 or 8. Upgrading to a new unit usually cuts energy costs by about 30 to 40 percent each year.

1. How much fuel is wasted in older furnaces?

2. Why would you choose an air conditioner with a high SEER rating?

Materials

◆ notebook

How Can You Conserve Energy?

Energy conservation means using energy wisely and efficiently. Conserving energy benefits everyone. It means more fossil fuels are available for the future. It also means less pollution is produced today.

How can you conserve energy in your daily life? In this lab, you will create and follow an energy conservation plan.

Procedure

1. Form a small group. Discuss some ways that you can conserve energy at school and at home.

2. Use the library or the Internet to research the conservation methods you discussed. Where possible, find how much energy each method could save.

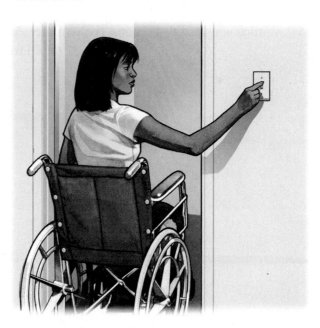

Continued on next page

3. Create an action plan that you can follow to conserve energy. Include the actions you will take.

4. Have your teacher approve your plan. Then follow your plan for one week.

5. Create a report about your energy conservation methods. Include data on how much energy you saved.

Analysis

1. Were you able to follow your plan? Why or why not?

2. What problems, if any, did you have with following your plan?

3. How much energy did you conserve?

Conclusions

1. Besides saving energy, in what other ways did your action plan benefit you and the environment?

2. How much energy would be saved if everyone in your classroom followed your action plan?

3. How much energy would be saved if everyone in the United States followed your action plan?

Explore Further

Design a campaign to encourage others to adopt one of your energy conservation methods. Include information that would help others understand how their participation would make a difference.

Turning Trash into Energy

What do coal and trash have in common? It may surprise you to find out that both can supply us with energy.

Most of the trash produced in the United States is buried in landfills. Afterward, some of these landfills are covered with soil and grass to become golf courses, parks, and other recreational areas. However, environmental scientists and utility companies have realized that these landfills can be used for another purpose—to make electricity.

Here is how it works. Trash that is buried in landfills breaks down to create methane gas. Methane gas released into the atmosphere contributes to air pollution.

Some utility companies realized that they could burn this methane to produce electricity. Landfills produce a lot of methane, and they produce methane for a long time. Even after a landfill is closed, it produces methane for another 20 years.

Today, many electrical utility companies are setting up small power stations on landfills. The gas is pulled from wells in the landfill. As the gas burns, it turns a turbine and electricity is produced. The electricity can be added directly to a city's electrical lines. Because landfills produce methane for decades, the cost of building the power station is well worth it.

The benefits help everyone. The city receives electricity from a source that previously was only wasted. The electric company produces electricity without having to pay for coal or oil. Finally, the environment benefits because additional fossil fuels were not burned to produce the electricity.

1. What are some ways landfills are used after they are closed?

2. Describe the process that allows landfills to produce electricity.

3. What are some benefits of producing electricity from landfills?

- Energy cannot be created or destroyed. Instead, it changes forms.

- Coal, oil, and natural gas are fossil fuels. Fossil fuels provide most of the world's energy but produce a lot of pollution.

- Nuclear energy is produced through nuclear fission. It produces no carbon dioxide, but it is expensive, produces radioactive waste, and carries the risk of accidents.

- The three major forms of solar energy are passive solar energy, active solar systems, and photovoltaics.

- Hydropower provides a clean source of electricity. However, hydropower dams alter river habitat and disrupt wildlife.

- Wind turbines can generate a lot of electricity, but some people object to them being in scenic areas.

- Geothermal energy is energy obtained from natural features in the earth.

- Biomass is energy from plant matter, such as wood, peat, or cow waste.

- Renewable sources of energy will be increasingly important for meeting energy needs. Experts also stress the importance of conservation.

Vocabulary

active solar system, 269
aesthetics, 274
biomass, 276
carpooling, 281
chain reaction, 262
coal, 257
compact fluorescents, 281
contaminate, 256
control rod, 262
core, 264
crude oil, 255
dam, 273
daylighting, 267
deposit, 255
diatom, 255
downstream, 273
electron, 261
energy conservation, 281
energy efficiency, 281
energy efficient, 281

ethanol, 276
first law of energy, 251
fish ladder, 273
fuel cell, 283
fuel rod, 262
generator, 255
geothermal, 275
geyser, 275
hot spring, 275
hybrid vehicle, 282
hydropower, 273
impurity, 259
inefficient, 252
insulation, 268
isotopes, 261
kinetic energy, 250
law, 251
leukemia, 263
mandated, 282
meltdown, 264
methane, 258
mountaintop removal, 257

natural gas, 258
neutron, 261
nitrogen oxide, 256
nonrenewable, 253
nuclear fission, 262
nuclear power plant, 262
nuclear reactor, 262
nucleus, 261
passive solar cooling, 267
passive solar energy, 267
passive solar heating, 267
peat, 276
petroleum, 255
photovoltaics, 269
potential energy, 250
power grid, 270
proton, 261
radioactive, 262
refinery, 255

reserve, 257
second law of energy, 252
solar collector, 269
solar energy, 267
strip mining, 257
subatomic particle, 261
sulfur oxide, 256
tailings, 263
tide, 274
transform, 251
transport, 253
tunnel mining, 257
turbine, 255
upstream, 273
uranium, 262
uranium mill, 263
utility, 253
ventilation, 263
vibration, 251
wind farm, 274
wind turbine, 274

Chapter 7 R E V I E W

Word Bank

active solar system

biomass

coal

conservation

crude oil

energy efficiency

generator

geothermal

hydropower

kinetic energy

mountaintop
    removal

natural gas

nonrenewable

nuclear fission

photovoltaics

potential energy

solar energy

subatomic particles

Vocabulary Review

On a sheet of paper, write the word or words from the Word Bank that complete each sentence correctly.

1. Neutrons, protons, and electrons are all _____.

2. Solar cells, or _____, are devices that transform sunlight into electricity.

3. The energy of movement is _____.

4. A fossil fuel that is found underground as a thick liquid is _____.

5. A(n) _____ uses pumps and fans to distribute solar energy.

6. A fossil fuel made of a solid mass of carbon is _____.

7. A(n) _____ is a machine that creates electricity.

8. Nuclear energy is created through a process called _____.

9. Energy called _____ comes directly from the sun.

10. Energy from water is called _____.

11. In a type of mining called _____, the entire top of a mountain is removed to expose layers of coal.

12. Energy sources that are _____ will someday run out.

13. A fossil fuel that is made up mostly of methane is _____.

14. Energy obtained from volcanoes, geysers, and hot springs is _____ energy.

15. Energy from burned plant or animal matter is called _____ energy.

Continued on next page

16. Energy _____ means using less energy and wasting less energy.

17. Stored energy is known as _____.

18. The percentage of work you get from a certain input of energy is known as _____.

Concept Review

On a sheet of paper, write the letter of the correct answer.

19. Which of the following is **not** an example of potential energy?

A a rock on the ground   **C** a liter of gasoline
B a log on a wood pile   **D** a ball in a ballplayer's hand

20. All of the following are fossil fuels except _____.

A oil   **C** natural gas
B wood   **D** coal

21. The element _____ is radioactive.

A oxygen   **C** nitrogen
B carbon   **D** uranium

22. Corn or sugar cane can be used to make a liquid fuel called _____.

A methane   **C** peat
B biomass   **D** ethanol

Critical Thinking

On a sheet of paper, write the answer to each of the following questions. Use complete sentences.

23. How does insulation contribute to energy conservation?

24. What are two advantages and two disadvantages of nuclear power?

25. Describe a place where photovoltaics might be a good option, and explain why.

Test-Taking Tip When studying for a test, review any previous tests or quizzes that cover the same information. Make sure you have the correct answers for any items you missed.

8

Water Resources and Water Pollution

F ew people realize what it takes to keep a lawn green. In many parts of the country, lawn grasses cannot survive the summer without frequent watering. The lawn sprinkler shown here is able to water large sections of the lawn. Over a summer, it can use hundreds or thousands of liters of water. In Chapter 8, you will learn about Earth's limited freshwater resources. You will learn about the ways they are used by people, farms, and industry. You will also learn about different sources of water pollution. Finally, you will find out how you can help conserve this important resource.

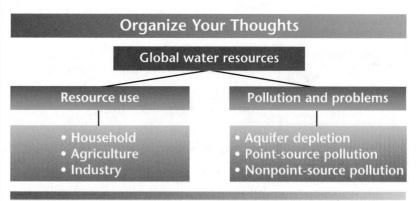

Organize Your Thoughts

Global water resources

Resource use	Pollution and problems
• Household • Agriculture • Industry	• Aquifer depletion • Point-source pollution • Nonpoint-source pollution

Goals for Learning

◆ To describe Earth's water resources and why they are important

◆ To identify the main ways water is used and how it is managed

◆ To define three major sources of water pollution

◆ To explain how people can conserve and protect water resources

Objectives

After reading this lesson, you should be able to

◆ describe how people and wildlife use water

◆ explain how water is distributed on Earth

◆ explain how pollution affects people living in a watershed

◆ describe how groundwater is stored, used, and recharged

Surface water

Water that is visible on the surface of the earth

Recreation

Play or amusement

When you turn on the water faucet, freshwater usually comes pouring out. Many people do not think about where the water comes from. There seems to be an unlimited supply. However, the world's freshwater supplies are actually very limited. In many parts of the world, freshwater is in short supply. The supplies can also be polluted. That makes it very important to know where freshwater comes from. Knowing this will help you learn how to better protect it.

As you learned in Chapter 5, only 3 percent of the earth's water is freshwater. Most of the freshwater on Earth is frozen or difficult to reach. That leaves about 1 percent that is in a form that humans can use. This small amount of water is found in lakes, rivers, and streams. It is also stored in special layers of rock underneath the ground.

Worldwide Water Supplies

Freshwater is divided into two types: **surface water** and groundwater. Surface water is water above the ground. It flows in rivers, streams, and creeks, and fills up lakes, ponds, and swamps. Oceans are also examples of surface water, although they contain salt water instead of freshwater. Unlike surface water, groundwater is hidden from view. It is water that fills the spaces between soil particles and rocks underground. Both surface water and groundwater are important to people and other living things. About half of the people in the United States rely on groundwater for their drinking water. The rest rely on surface water.

Surface Water

Throughout history, people have settled near rivers, streams, and other sources of surface water. These bodies of water provide humans with drinking water, food, electricity, transportation, and **recreation.** Recreation includes activities such as swimming, boating, and fishing. Some of the world's oldest cities have been built on major rivers. One well-known example is Cairo on the Nile River in Egypt.

Watershed

An area of land from which precipitation drains into a particular river, stream, or lake

Math Tip

You can use ratios to describe the amount of freshwater on Earth. The ratio of freshwater to salt water is 3:97. The ratio of drinkable water to all freshwater is 1:3. The ratio of drinkable water to undrinkable water is 1:99.

Where does surface water come from? As you learned in Chapter 2, water cycles through the lithosphere, hydrosphere, and atmosphere. As it cycles, it changes from liquid water to a gas. During condensation it returns to a liquid form. Surface water forms as precipitation falls on the earth's surface. This water flows down mountains, hills, and other land areas, forming fast-flowing streams. These streams combine with other streams, eventually emptying into rivers. Eventually, larger rivers empty into oceans or lakes.

Watersheds

No matter where you live in the world, you live within a **watershed.** In a watershed, all the rainwater and melting snow drains into the same stream or river. Watersheds can be small areas of land that drain water into small streams. They can also be huge areas of land that drain water into large rivers. Within every large watershed there are many smaller watersheds.

Watersheds are often named for the river that the water in the area drains into. For example, you might live in the Ohio River watershed or the Potomac River watershed. The Rio Grande watershed and several others are illustrated in Figure 8.1.1. Every person and organism living in a watershed has an impact on its future. Your watershed also has an impact on you.

As rain and melting snow flow into streams and rivers, they wash over the land. That means they wash through farmland, lawns, forests, roads, and industrial sites. As water flows over these places, it picks up different materials. In some cases, the water washes trash, dirt, chemicals, oil, and other waste into waterways. Pollution anywhere in a watershed can end up in a stream or river. It is then taken farther downstream.

Figure 8.1.1 *Surface water from the Rio Grande River area is included in the Rio Grande watershed.*

Groundwater

A large percentage of the earth's freshwater is stored as groundwater. Groundwater starts with rain or snow that **seeps,** or soaks, into the ground. The amount of water that seeps into the ground varies from place to place. In some areas, more than half of the rain or snow soaks in. In other areas, most of the water runs off into other bodies of water. It may also evaporate into the air instead of soaking into the soil.

As water soaks into the ground, some of it stays in the soil. The rest keeps moving down until it reaches the place where the ground is saturated. Saturated means that it cannot hold any more water. The top of this saturated zone is called the **water table.** You can think of the water table as the top boundary of the groundwater. Above the water table, water can still soak into the soil. Below the water table, all the cracks and spaces are filled with water.

Aquifers

The area underground that contains groundwater is called an **aquifer,** as seen in Figure 8.1.2. Aquifer is another name for the water-saturated area of the earth. It contains underground formations that can store water and also transport it. Aquifers are usually layers of rock, sand, or gravel where water builds up over time. Aquifers are found in most parts of the world.

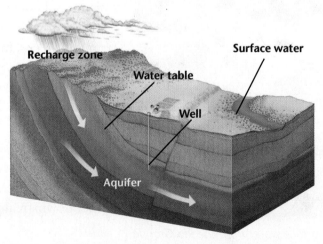

Figure 8.1.2 *An aquifer is an area that contains groundwater.*

Some states give landowners the right to pump all the water they want on their property. Other states limit the amount of groundwater that a landowner can pump from an aquifer.

Most of the groundwater people use comes from aquifers. They are important sources of water for wells and springs. In many areas, more than 50 percent of the population relies on groundwater for their drinking water. In rural areas, outside of cities, more than 80 percent of the people rely on groundwater.

In many parts of the world, people are pumping too much water from aquifers. Some are becoming **depleted,** or used up. The Ogallala Aquifer is under parts of eight states in the western United States. It contains water left from the time of the last glaciers. Many people are concerned that this water is being depleted faster than it can recover. The same thing is happening in many other parts of the world. As more water is pumped out of the ground, the level of the aquifer may fall. As the water table drops, it becomes harder and harder to reach the water.

Recharge Zones and Wells

Water that seeps into an aquifer **recharges** it, or refills it. The water that recharges an aquifer comes from sources including rain, melting snow, and streams. It can also come from groundwater flowing from other areas. The **recharge zone** is an area where water travels downward to become part of an aquifer.

In some places, people have built too many roads and parking lots. This affects the recharge area. Less water soaks into the ground. That means that an aquifer cannot recharge as quickly. Materials that allow water to flow through them are called **permeable** materials. Gravel, sand, and certain kinds of rock are permeable. They have holes or cracks that allow water in and out. Materials such as clay and concrete are **impermeable.** They stop the flow of water.

In some places the water table is deep below the surface of the earth. In other places, it is nearer to the surface. A **well** is a deep hole in the ground that allows people to reach the groundwater. In many parts of the world, people depend on wells for their water supplies. When digging a well, people search for the water table. People often dig below the water table. This means they will still have water if the height of the water table drops.

Science Myth

Myth: There is less freshwater today than in the past.

Fact: The total amount of freshwater is the same today as in the past. The growing world population is what creates shortages of freshwater.

Using Too Much Water

In many parts of the world, too much water is taken out of rivers and streams. Groundwater is also being used too quickly. Much of the water is used for businesses and farming, as well as drinking water. When too much water is used too quickly, aquatic life can suffer. Over time, groundwater sources can become threatened. Wells can dry up as the water table drops below the bottom of the well. In some places water is redirected upstream. People and wildlife living farther downstream are left with very limited amounts of water. This increasing water **scarcity** in many parts of the world is a huge problem.

Pollution of surface water and groundwater supplies is also a very serious problem. This can affect water supplies for entire regions. It takes years for groundwater to recharge. It can also take tens or hundreds of years for polluted groundwater to be recycled.

Express Lab 8

Materials
- safety goggles
- large glass container (aquarium or baking dish)
- rocks, 3–5 cm in diameter
- sand
- pea gravel
- water
- ruler

Procedure
1. Put on safety goggles.
2. Spread rocks, 5–10 cm thick, on the bottom of the container.
3. Make a layer of sand, 1–2 cm thick, on top of the rocks.
4. Make an uneven layer of gravel, 1–15 cm thick, on top of the sand.
5. Slowly pour about a liter of water onto different parts of the top layer.

Analysis
1. Which part of the model is the water table?
2. How does the water recharge this aquifer?

Lesson 1 REVIEW

Word Bank
depleted
recharging
scarcity

On a sheet of paper, write the word from the Word Bank that completes each sentence correctly.

1. Groundwater can be _____ because of pumping of water from wells.

2. A lack of freshwater resources is an example of _____.

3. The process of water going into an aquifer is called _____.

On a sheet of paper, write the letter of the answer that completes each sentence correctly.

4. Layers of rock that water can move through are said to be _____.

   A saturated   **B** rural   **C** permeable   **D** gravel

5. A(n) _____ is an area of land that drains into the same surface water.

   A aquifer   **B** watershed   **C** well   **D** drain

6. Most of Earth's freshwater is found in _____.

   A ice   **B** aquifers   **C** oceans   **D** lakes

Critical Thinking

On a sheet of paper, write the answers to the following questions. Use complete sentences.

7. How do surface water and groundwater compare as water resources in the United States?

8. What would keep the amount of water in an aquifer about the same over a period of time?

9. Why does a well need to be deeper than the water table?

10. How does development in cities affect water resources?

Objectives

After reading this lesson, you should be able to

◆ describe the three main uses of water

◆ explain why water is important to aquatic ecosystems

◆ name several ways humans manage water systems

Industry

The making and selling of a particular kind of good or service

Drought

An unusually long period of little rainfall

Think about the ways you used water today. Did you brush your teeth or wash your face? Did you water your lawn, wash a car, or flush a toilet? Maybe you used water to cook or give your pet a bath. On average, American households use more than 760 liters of water each day. Still, individuals use a small amount of the total water society uses. Agriculture uses the most water around the world. More than 67 percent of the global water supply is used for agriculture. **Industry** is the making and selling of a particular kind of good or service. It is the second largest use of water around the world.

All of these uses are affecting worldwide supplies of freshwater. In some areas, water is already scarce. Natural disasters, such as **droughts** and earthquakes, can increase water shortages. During a drought, there is very little rainfall, which puts more pressure on water supplies. Because of these issues, it is important to learn how to use and manage water.

Household Water Use

About 8 percent of the global water supply is used by households. The amount varies, depending on the country and community. On average, individuals in the United States use about 379 liters of water daily. In developing nations, water consumption averages as little as 15 liters per day. The world average is 60 liters per day.

Science Myth

Myth: Bottled water is safer than tap water.

Fact: The Environmental Protection Agency (EPA) regulates the quality of tap water in the United States. The Food and Drug Administration (FDA) regulates the quality of bottled water. Both agencies use similar standards, but neither requires drinking water to be 100 percent pure.

Household water is used for drinking, cooking, cleaning, watering gardens, and other activities. People need to drink about 1.9 liters of water a day to stay healthy. That is less than 1 percent of household water use. The rest goes to flushing toilets, taking showers, and washing clothes and dishes. People also use huge amounts of water to keep their lawns green. They also use water to fill up their swimming pools and water their gardens.

Water Treatment

Most water is treated to make it safe for drinking. **Water treatment** removes harmful chemicals, which can make people sick. Water treatment also removes bacteria, parasites, and other living things that can cause diseases. Living things that can cause diseases are known as **pathogens.** Harmful chemicals and pathogens are found in polluted rivers, streams, lakes, and ponds. They can also be found in groundwater.

Agricultural Use

The single biggest water user around the world is agriculture. It takes more than 181,700 liters of water to make an average Thanksgiving dinner for eight people. Just making a hamburger consumes a large amount of freshwater. Each hamburger takes more than 2,270 liters of water to create. That includes water needed to grow the grain that feeds the cow. It also includes the water the cow needs to survive. The water needed to process the hamburger is also added in. Americans eat more than 72 billion hamburgers a year. That can add up to a lot of water.

Link to ➤➤➤

Cultures

Humans began to use water from nearby rivers to irrigate crops about 7,000 years ago. The Egyptians were the first culture known to use irrigation. They dug short channels to direct yearly floodwaters from the Nile River to their fields. By B.C. 2000, cultures in Mesopotamia, Peru, China, and North America were irrigating crops.

Irrigate

To artificially supply land with water for agriculture or landscaping

Landscaping

Improving the natural beauty of a piece of land

Divert

To turn from one course to another

Sprinkler system

A device used to spray water, usually in a circular pattern

To grow more crops, many farmers **irrigate** their farmland. To irrigate means to artificially supply land with water for farming or **landscaping.** Irrigation uses the largest amount of water of any process in the world. In some cases, water is brought from other areas to farmland through ditches or pipes. Sometimes rivers are **diverted,** or turned from one course to another. Figure 8.2.1 shows how the Yangtze River in China has been diverted to supply water for industry and irrigation. Fields are often flooded with water. Many areas also use **sprinkler systems,** which spray water from above the ground. Sometimes, the water used to irrigate farms evaporates and never reaches the crops. Scientists are looking at how to grow crops by using water more efficiently.

Industrial Use

The second-biggest use of water is industry. More than 20 percent of water in the world is used for industrial purposes. Almost every product manufactured, or built, uses water during part of the production process. Water is used to cool substances as they are produced. It is also used for transportation, boiling or cooking, and preparing raw materials. For example, it takes about 147,600 liters of water to produce a car, including the tires. Water is also used to make many parts of products people use every day. This includes computers, semiconductors, clothing, paper, and soft drinks. More than half of the water industries use goes toward cooling power plants and other industrial areas.

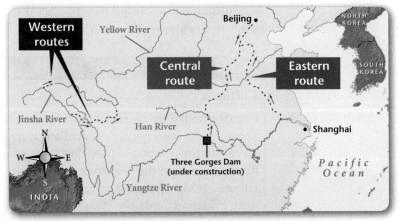

Figure 8.2.1 *Water is diverted from the Yangtze River in China for use in industry and irrigation.*

Purification

Cleaning by separating out pollutants or impurities

Ecosystem Use

Ecosystems use water to support living things. They also provide ecosystem services that manage water, such as flood control and water **purification.** As human water demands increase, however, many ecosystems are being changed or destroyed. In some cases, freshwater wetlands and swamps have been filled in. Dams have been built across streams and rivers. Instead of soaking into the ground to recharge aquifers, more water is being directed elsewhere. In many areas, water that used to support ecosystems has been drained or polluted.

This loss of ecosystems has many effects. Wild species decline, and ecosystem services are affected. Wetlands, for example, help prevent floods and filter water. In some places, people have built water treatment plants to replace these natural ecosystems. Some experts estimate that the services that wetlands provide are worth billions of dollars.

Science at Work

Irrigation Engineer

Irrigation engineers design and install irrigation systems. Some irrigation engineers specialize in large systems for agricultural crops. Others specialize in sprinkler irrigation systems for home or business landscapes.

Many irrigation engineers work in developing countries, where farming methods are being improved. Irrigation engineers spend a lot of time working outdoors. They survey areas, large or small, that need an irrigation system. They must understand the climate of the area and the needs of the plants. They must also understand how water behaves as it flows and moves through the soil. An irrigation engineer then uses all this information to design a system for the area.

Irrigation engineers work for government agencies as well as for private companies. Any kind of engineering career requires the study of math. Irrigation engineers also take courses in plant sciences, geology, and soil science. Most irrigation engineers have a bachelor's degree in civil or agricultural engineering or landscape design.

Overuse of groundwater in the southwestern and central United States is causing land to sink. Areas west of Phoenix, Arizona, have sunk more than 6 meters. Parts of California have sunk more than 10 meters.

Water Management Systems

For thousands of years, people have tried to change natural water systems. In some cases, these projects have been designed to bring more water to dry areas. In other cases, water storage areas called **reservoirs** have been built. Reservoirs store water to meet the needs of growing communities. Many rivers have been diverted into canals that carry water to new areas. For example, water from the Colorado River has been diverted to supply water to seven western states. This diverts a lot of water from the Colorado River. As a result, there is often not enough water for communities downstream. Communities in Texas and Mexico must find other sources of water.

Dams have also changed natural water systems. They have diverted rivers to help generate power. They have also been built to help control the flow of water and prevent floods. The power generated by dams is an important source of energy. However, there are some environmental and social problems with dams.

Dams often change environmental conditions downstream. This affects both wildlife and human communities. Sometimes human communities are forced to relocate because of changes dams have brought about, both upstream and downstream.

The number of dams being built has grown steadily since the 1950s. There are more than 45,000 large dams in the world. China alone has more than 22,000 large dams and more than 80,000 dams in total. More than 60 percent of the world's 227 largest rivers have been broken up by dams.

To help prevent problems with dams, many states and countries are looking at alternatives to dams. Some countries have decided that big dams are not environmentally sound investments. Instead, engineers are looking at ways to build smaller dams that have smaller environmental impacts.

Lesson 2   R E V I E W

Word Bank
agriculture
industry
reservoir

On a sheet of paper, write the word from the Word Bank that completes each sentence correctly.

1. The practice of _____ uses most of Earth's freshwater resources.

2. A(n) _____ is a place where water is stored.

3. The second-biggest user of water around the world is _____.

On a sheet of paper, write the letter of the answer that completes each sentence correctly.

4. A(n) _____ is a long period of little rainfall.

   A landscape   **B** irrigation   **C** pathogen   **D** drought

5. People irrigate in order to provide water for crops and _____.

   A industry   **C** reservoirs
   B landscaping   **D** pathogens

6. Much of the water used to manufacture goods is used for _____.

   A cooling   **C** sprinkler systems
   B water treatment   **D** ecosystems

Critical Thinking

On a sheet of paper, write the answers to the following questions. Use complete sentences.

7. How is most household water used in the United States?

8. Explain the many different ways water is used to make a hamburger.

9. How are wetlands valuable ecosystems?

10. How is the water that is diverted from rivers and streams used?

Materials

- safety goggles
- lab coat or apron
- gloves
- tap water
- outdoor water
- wax pencil
- 4 small test tubes and stoppers
- test tube rack
- pH test solution
- pH color card
- nitrate test solutions #1 and #2
- nitrate color card

Water Quality Testing

How do you know your drinking water is safe to drink? Experts test the water for many contaminants. In this lab, you will test water samples for two different contaminants.

Procedure

1. Copy the data table below onto a sheet of paper.

Water source	Kind of test	
	pH	Nitrate (ppm)
Tap water		
Outdoor water		

2. Put on safety goggles, a lab coat or apron, and gloves.

3. Place 5 mL of tap water in two test tubes. Label the test tubes A and B using a wax pencil. **Safety Alert: Do not taste any of the water samples.**

4. Add three to five drops of the pH test solution to Test Tube A. **Safety Alert: Be careful when handling glassware and chemicals.** Close the test tube with a stopper and gently shake the tube several times.

5. Find the pH of the water by matching the color of the solution to the same color on the pH color card. Record the pH.

6. Add 10 drops of nitrate test solution #1 to Test Tube B. Close the test tube and gently shake it several times.

7. Shake the bottle of nitrate test solution #2 forcefully for 30 seconds. Then add 10 drops of this solution to Test Tube B. Close the test tube again, and shake it forcefully for 1 minute. Let the test tube stand in the test tube rack for 5 minutes.

8. Find the amount of nitrate in the water in parts per million (ppm) by matching the color of the solution to the same color on the nitrate color card. Record the amount of nitrate.

9. Repeat Steps 3–8 for the outdoor water sample.

Cleanup/Disposal

Before you leave the lab, be sure your work area is clean. Wash your hands thoroughly.

Analysis

1. Summarize the results of your tests.

2. How do the two water samples compare?

Conclusions

1. Which water sample would be safest for aquatic life?

2. Can the water you tested be considered safe to drink? Explain.

Explore Further

Test more water samples from different sources such as a creek, a lake, rainwater, and different brands of bottled water.

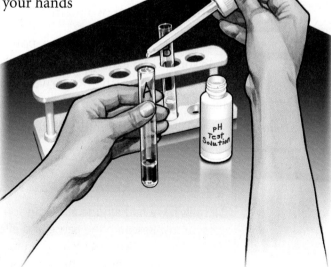

Many types of water pollution are easy to spot. Bottles, cans, tires, and other debris can wash up along the beach. Dead fish might be floating in a lake. Other types are invisible but are still serious threats to aquatic ecosystems. All types of aquatic ecosystems, from oceans to rivers, are affected by water pollution.

Water pollution is not new to human societies. For centuries, people threw their waste into the ocean and other large bodies of water. Today there are two important reasons why water pollution is more of a threat. The first is the rise in industry. More industry has caused massive amounts of waste. The second is the rapid increase in human population. More people create much more waste. Unfortunately, this waste often ends up in water systems.

Types of Water Pollution

There are many types of water pollution. Some pollution is caused by chemicals that get into water supplies. Some pollution is caused by human or animal waste that is dumped into the water. Water pollution can even be caused by heat. In fact, almost all the ways humans use water can create water pollution. There are two main categories of water pollution.

Point-source pollution is water pollution that comes from a single source. An example of point-source pollution is a pipe pouring waste directly into a river. This waste might come from a factory. Another example would be a tanker ship that spills oil into the ocean. Point-source pollution is easier to trace back to a source and to control.

Point-source pollution

Pollution that comes from a particular source

Research and Write

Oil spills have had a huge effect on some ocean and coastal ecosystems. Research the cause and effects of a major oil spill. Find out what measures were taken to clean up the oil spill. Write a report and present it to the class.

Nonpoint-source pollution

Pollution that cannot be traced back to a specific source

Runoff

Rain or melted snow that flows over land to streams, rivers, lakes, and the ocean

Nonpoint-source pollution is much more difficult to control. Nonpoint-source pollution comes from many sources. It is caused by a variety of human land uses. For example, farming, logging, construction, and other activities can all cause nonpoint-source pollution. What usually happens is that falling rain washes over farms and urban areas. As the water flows over the land, it picks up pesticides and other pollutants. Eventually, this water carries the pollutants into rivers, lakes, and other bodies of water. This water is called **runoff**. Runoff brings material that washes off roads, fields, lawns, and other surfaces with it.

Map Skills: Nonpoint-Source Pollution

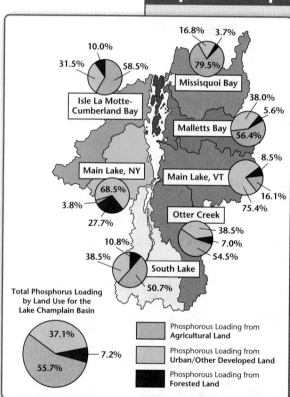

Total Phosphorus Loading by Land Use for the Lake Champlain Basin

Phosphorous Loading from **Agricultural Land**

Phosphorous Loading from **Urban/Other Developed Land**

Phosphorous Loading from **Forested Land**

It is difficult to find the origin of nonpoint-source pollution. This is because the pollutants are picked up from across a large area. Different areas of land contribute different types and amounts of certain pollutants. What matters is how the land is used. Three different types of land use are agricultural, urban and other development, and forest land.

The map shows the sources of phosphorous pollution emptying into Lake Champlain. This is also called phosphorous loading. The area is divided up into different lake segments. Each lake segment has different percentages of its phosphorous output coming from different sources.

These percentages depend on the watershed's land use. Use the map and its legend to answer the following questions.

1. Does the same land use cause the most phosphorous loading in each watershed? If not, give examples showing this is not the case.

2. What do you think causes the differences in the percentages between watersheds?

Major Water Pollutants

Many different chemicals and other types of pollutants get into surface water and groundwater supplies. Below are some of the major water pollutants and the problems that they cause.

Sewage. In many parts of the world, bacteria and **viruses** get into water supplies. When that happens, these pathogens can cause diseases, including **hepatitis, cholera,** and **dysentery.** The source of many of these organisms is untreated human waste from homes and factories. Water that carries waste from people and industries is called **sewage** or wastewater. Sewage comes from toilets, sinks, dishwashers, washing machines, and factories. It can carry everything from food scraps to soap to chemicals. It is the second-largest source of water pollution.

Sewage is usually cleaned at **sewage treatment plants** before being released into surface water. These facilities are designed to kill pathogens and get rid of other types of pollution. You can see a picture of a sewage treatment plant in Figure 8.3.2. Wastewater is carried to sewage treatment plants by an underground system of drains, pipes, and sewers. Unfortunately, sewage treatment plants can get overloaded during storms. When they back up, untreated waste can wash directly into surface water. There are also not enough sewage treatment plants to treat all the sewage in the world. In many places, the sewage is dumped into the ocean and other bodies of water.

Figure 8.3.2 *At sewage treatment plants, sewage is cleaned before it is released into surface water.*

Organic waste

Waste from living organisms

Herbicide

A chemical used to kill weeds

Fertilizer

An organic or inorganic plant nutrient

Eutrophication

The process by which plant nutrients increase plant growth and decrease available oxygen

Limestone aquifers can easily become polluted. Caves and sinkholes in recharge zones act as point sources for pollutants. They also lead nonpoint-source pollutants directly into aquifers.

Untreated human waste can do more than cause diseases. It can also decrease the amount of oxygen in the water. As bacteria break down **organic waste,** they use up the oxygen in the water. Organic waste is waste from living organisms. The more waste there is to break down, the less oxygen is left in the water. As a result, fish and other aquatic creatures do not have enough oxygen.

Organic waste can come from overflowing sewage treatment plants. It can also come from farms, ranches, and other sources of food and animal waste.

Fertilizers. The biggest source of water pollution is runoff from farms and ranches. One reason is that they produce so much animal waste. Another is that many pollutants are used to grow food and crops and raise livestock. These pollutants include pesticides and **herbicides,** chemicals that kill weeds. They also include **fertilizers,** which are nutrients to help plants grow.

Animal wastes and fertilizers both contain nutrients for plants. In small amounts, they can help crops and other plants grow. In the water, they can cause algae and other aquatic plants to grow too much. Over time, these plants start to die. As explained earlier, bacteria that break them down use up oxygen. Without enough oxygen in the water, whole communities of life can die. This process is called **eutrophication.** Eutrophication is actually a natural process. It becomes a problem when pollution speeds up the process.

❋ ❋

Technology and Society

Making water safe to drink requires several processes at a water treatment plant. Flocculation involves adding chemicals that cause substances in the water to form clumps. These clumps settle out during sedimentation. Filtration removes the remaining particles, such as soil and organic materials. Ion exchange and absorption are then used to remove metals, minerals, and other unwanted elements. Finally, disinfection with chlorine compounds or ozone kills harmful microbes.

Bioaccumulation

The process by which toxic chemical compounds accumulate through the food chain

Thermal pollution

Heat added to water by humans that causes ecological changes

Radioactive waste

Waste that contains or is contaminated by radioactive materials

Link to >>>

Biology

During bioaccumulation, some types of toxic chemicals may build up in the fatty tissues of consumers. When these tissues are used for energy, the chemicals are released and may poison the consumer.

Toxic Chemicals. Many water pollutants are toxic chemicals. Some are organic chemicals that come from living things. Although not all organic chemicals are toxic, many are poisonous to living things.

The most common and dangerous organic pollutant is petroleum. Oil often spills or leaks while being transported. It can enter water supplies when it is drilled out of the ocean floor. Accidents can happen along oil pipelines and at oil refineries. All of these accidental spills add up to enormous amounts of water pollution.

Other types of toxic chemicals are inorganic. Lead, mercury, sulfur, nickel, and arsenic are all inorganic chemicals. Even small amounts of these chemicals can cause brain, liver, and kidney diseases. This damage can be caused by **bioaccumulation.**

Bioaccumulation happens when these chemicals work their way up the food chain. For example, when mercury washes into a lake, the fish are exposed. When people eat the fish, they take the mercury into their bodies. The more contaminated fish people eat, the more chemicals they are exposed to. These chemicals can build up in their bodies and cause serious health problems.

Other Types of Water Pollution. There are many other types of water pollution that can affect living things. For example, heat can be a pollutant. **Thermal pollution** is heat added to a body of water. This heat often comes from factories or power plants as they release hot water. This heat can kill living things. It can also harm entire ecosystems by decreasing the amount of oxygen in the water.

Another serious water pollutant is **radioactive waste.** Radioactive waste comes from nuclear reactors, research institutions, or hospitals. In some cases, this waste is dumped illegally into the water, creating serious health risks.

The many types and sources of water pollution often make it difficult to protect water resources. In Lesson 4, you will learn about the efforts being made to control water pollution.

Lesson 3   R E V I E W

Word Bank

nonpoint-source
   pollution

point-source
   pollution

runoff

On a sheet of paper, write the word or words from the Word Bank that complete each sentence correctly.

1. A leaking gasoline pipeline is an example of _____.

2. Rain or melted snow that flows over land into bodies of water is called _____.

3. Farming and driving contribute to _____.

On a sheet of paper, write the letter of the answer that completes each sentence correctly.

4. Sewage is wastewater that comes from the activities of _____.

   A plants   **B** humans   **C** bacteria   **D** animals

5. Chemicals that are used to kill unwanted plants are _____.

   A radioactive wastes   **C** fertilizers
   B organic wastes   **D** herbicides

6. Excessive plant growth happens in lakes that are undergoing _____.

   A bioaccumulation   **C** eutrophication
   B decomposition   **D** pollution

Critical Thinking

On a sheet of paper, write the answers to the following questions. Use complete sentences.

7. How are leaking sewer pipes a threat to groundwater quality?

8. How is untreated human waste a threat to fish and other aquatic life?

9. Explain why oil pollution is so common.

10. Which do you think is more dangerous, oil pollution or radioactive waste? Explain your answer.

Materials

- safety goggles
- lab coat or apron
- gloves
- outdoor water
- 2 small test tubes and stoppers
- test tube rack
- nitrate test solutions #1 and #2
- nitrate color card
- soil
- sand
- gravel
- filter paper
- funnel
- jars

Testing Groundwater

Surface water soaks through one or more layers of soil and rock as it becomes groundwater. As water moves through the ground, soil and rock filter out some pollutants. How well do these materials remove nitrates? Find out by designing and conducting an experiment.

Procedure

1. In your lab group, discuss the kinds of pollutants that are found in water. Also discuss the kind of soil that is found in your area.

2. Write a hypothesis about how well different soil materials filter out pollutants. This hypothesis should be able to be tested with an experiment that uses the materials listed here.

3. Write a procedure for your experiment. Include Safety Alerts.

4. Have your hypothesis, procedure, and Safety Alerts approved by your teacher. Then carry out your experiment. Record your results.

Cleanup/Disposal
Before you leave the lab, be sure your work area is clean. Wash your hands thoroughly.

Analysis
1. Which kind of material was easiest for water to filter through?

2. What other differences do you notice in the water that has filtered through soil?

Conclusions
1. Which kind of material best filtered nitrates out of the water?

2. Think about the soil types in your area. How well would they filter nitrates out of water?

Explore Further
Repeat your experiment using another type of material such as potting soil, aquarium gravel, or crumbled modeling clay.

Objectives

After reading this lesson, you should be able to

◆ describe several ways that homes, businesses, and farms can conserve water

◆ explain how legislation has helped protect water resources

◆ give two examples of how technology can help protect water resources

Research and Write

Research some of the water-protection laws that followed the Clean Water Act. Find out why they were created, when they were passed, and what effects they have had. Write a report to summarize your findings.

How can people preserve water resources for the future? In this lesson, you will learn more about how people are preserving water resources. You will also learn what you can do at home to make a difference.

Controlling Water Pollution

In 1969, the Cuyahoga River in Cleveland, Ohio, caught on fire. It burned for several hours until the oil and other garbage had burned off. When many people saw the photograph of the burning river, they were shocked. It was not the first time this had happened, however. The river had caught fire several times before. These fires caused damage to the docks, ships, and factories along the river.

The fire on the Cuyahoga did bring about one good thing. It was one of the events that led to important water pollution laws. In 1972, Congress passed the Clean Water Act. This act has helped clean up many waterways around the country, including the Cuyahoga River. Its goal was to make all surface waters clean enough for fishing and swimming by 1983. Although that goal has not been achieved, the results have still been encouraging. Many rivers, lakes, and streams have been cleaned up. Many toxic chemicals are now removed as part of wastewater treatment.

The Clean Water Act led to other laws designed to improve water quality. These included laws that banned ocean dumping. Others required oil tankers to have stronger hulls to help prevent oil spills. Congress also passed the Safe Drinking Water Act in 1974. This helped to protect community drinking water supplies.

In addition to laws, new technologies help protect water resources. For example, in many areas, irrigation water contains salt. When the water evaporates, salt is left behind. This can harm crops and ruin the land. Farmers are exploring ways to reduce the salt and protect groundwater supplies and topsoil.

Drip irrigation

Irrigation in which water is delivered in drops directly to the plants' roots

Many countries have also built water treatment plants that remove salt from water. This is especially important in countries that do not have enough freshwater. Scientists are experimenting with ways to turn salt water from the ocean into drinking water.

Many countries are also banning toxic chemicals that can seep into water supplies. Recently, many countries have signed a treaty banning some of the most deadly pesticides.

Conserving Water

Conserving water is important for preserving water supplies for the future. This is especially true in areas that have limited supplies of freshwater. Water conservation can take place in homes, communities, farms, and industries.

Reducing Water Use in Farming. Since the 1960s, the amount of land that is farmed has increased by 12 percent. This increase in farmland has greatly increased worldwide water use. There are many new technologies that farmers are using to help conserve water. For example, some farmers are using **drip irrigation.** In drip irrigation, water tubing lets water drip directly over the roots of plants. It helps prevent evaporation, which can cause huge losses of water in fields. This system is still expensive, but it holds great potential for the future. An example of a drip irrigation system can be seen in Figure 8.4.1. Many farmers are also looking at the types of crops they grow. Many grow nonnative crops that require huge amounts of water. Now they are looking at more native and water-efficient options.

Figure 8.4.1 *Drip irrigation systems help reduce water use by preventing loss through evaporation.*

Gray water

Wastewater that does
not contain animal
waste and can be used
to water crops

Low-flow

Designed to use less
water

Xeriscaping

A type of landscaping
that uses native and
drought-tolerant plants

Reducing Water Use in Industry. As water supplies decrease, many industries are looking at ways to conserve. One of the most effective is recycling wastewater and reusing it. For example, many beverage industries use water to cool bottles or equipment. This water can be reused, which reduces the need for more water. In many plants, water that is used to clean equipment can be recycled. It can be used for many other things, including landscaping and washing vehicles.

Reducing Water Use at Home. Homes and communities can also do a lot to reduce water use. Many communities are exploring new ways to recycle water. For example, systems can be built that collect **gray water.** Gray water is water that has been used in sinks, showers, and washing machines. It can be recycled and used for things like flushing toilets and watering the lawn. There are also many new technologies that can help cut water use. **Low-flow** showerheads and low-flow toilets are both designed to use less water.

Individuals can take other steps to reduce water use, too. Turning off the faucet while brushing your teeth is one example. Watering the lawn at night can prevent evaporation and water loss. Another way to save water is to not use plants that need too much water. Many communities in very dry climates have banned nonnative plants that require more water. People are not allowed to plant vegetation such as grass and leafy shrubs. Instead, these communities encourage **xeriscaping.** Xeriscaping is designing a landscape that uses the least water possible. When one action is multiplied by all the people conserving, it saves a lot of water.

Figure 8.4.3 *Xeriscaping saves water by using native and drought-tolerant plants.*

Protecting Aquatic Ecosystems

Many countries are exploring new technologies that will provide more water for more people. Providing clean water for people living throughout the world is an important goal. At the same time, it is important to protect the ecosystems that help support all life.

There are a number of things being done to restore damaged habitats. In some cases, rivers are being returned to their original courses. Dams are being taken apart to create normal water flows. Vegetation is being planted along streams to prevent erosion. These efforts also help to restore damaged habitats and the ecosystem services they provide.

Science in Your Life

Technology: Water Conservation

Conserving freshwater is one way to help all people get enough water. Conserving water is something everyone can do. There are many products that reduce the amount of water used in households. Low-flow toilets, low-flow showerheads, and other fixtures are designed to cut water use. Xeriscaping and drip irrigation techniques also help households reduce their water use outdoors.

When it comes to conserving, personal responsibility is the key. This means realizing that you make a difference and doing what you think is right. You can decide to use the water-saving technologies that are available. Then you can take an active role in deciding how you and your household use water.

1. What are some ways that you can conserve water?

2. What are some ways that you can encourage others to conserve water?

Lesson 4   R E V I E W

Word Bank

dumping

recycling

technology

On a sheet of paper, write the word from the Word Bank that completes each sentence correctly.

1. The Clean Water Act led to laws that ban ocean _____.

2. Scientists are looking to new _____ to provide more water to a growing population.

3. Industry can conserve water by _____ wastewater.

Critical Thinking

On a sheet of paper, write the answers to the following questions. Use complete sentences.

4. What was an important result of the 1972 Clean Water Act?

5. What are some of the benefits of protecting watersheds and restoring aquatic ecosystems?

★ ★

Achievements in Science

Xeriscaping

Neatly trimmed green lawns were once the model for home landscaping. Lawn grasses are easy to grow and maintain, but they require huge amounts of water. Green lawns are not always practical because of water shortages. Xeriscapes are replacing many grassy lawns. The prefix *xeri-* is from the Greek word *xeros*, meaning "dry." The word *xeriscaping* was first used in Denver, Colorado, in 1981. At first, it referred to the use of drought-tolerant plants in landscaping. Since that time, xeriscaping has taken on a wider meaning.

Xeriscaping is the use of plants that are best adapted to local conditions for landscaping. In dry regions, this may mean using desert plants in the landscape. Scientists look in areas with similar climates for new landscape plants to use. Xeriscaping also involves using mulch as ground cover to hold in moisture. With xeriscaping, people can reduce water use and still have a pleasing landscape.

Illnesses Caused by Water Pollution

Waterborne diseases are caused by bacteria, viruses, and other pathogens in water. These diseases cause serious problems wherever there is water pollution or poor sanitation. In developing nations, waterborne diseases make up as much as 80 percent of illnesses. Most deaths of infants and young children in these countries are caused by waterborne diseases. Industrialized nations, such as the United States, sometimes experience waterborne diseases due to flooding.

Diarrhea is a symptom of waterborne bacterial diseases such as cholera, typhoid, and dysentery. The bacteria grow in the intestines. Waste material from infected individuals contains the bacteria. When people drink water or eat food that is contaminated with infected feces, the diseases spread. Diseases also spread when people use contaminated water for recreation. The resulting diarrhea can lead to dehydration and other physical problems that can cause death.

Hepatitis A is an example of a waterborne disease that is caused by a virus. The disease is most common in areas without safe drinking water. Much of the world's population does not have access to safe drinking water. Giardiasis is an example of a waterborne disease caused by a protozoan. It, too, causes diarrhea but is usually not a life-threatening disease.

Industrialized nations face other health problems that are caused by water pollution. Toxic chemicals and radioactive substances have been linked to cancers. Pollution in heavily industrialized areas has also been linked to birth defects and many other health problems.

Some developed nations have worked together to set safety standards. One goal is to have toxic waste treated and disposed of as close to its source as possible.

1. Why should world travelers be careful about what they eat and drink?

2. What could help reduce the incidence of waterborne diseases in the world?

3. How do you think treating toxic waste close to the source will help prevent water pollution?

- All living things need water, and many kinds of wildlife live in water.

- People use water for drinking, bathing, cooking, landscaping, farming, industry, transportation, and recreation.

- Oceans hold 97 percent of Earth's water. The remaining 3 percent is freshwater on the surface, underground, and in ice caps.

- Creeks, rivers, ponds, lakes, swamps, and oceans hold Earth's surface water. Aquifers store groundwater, which enters from the surface through a recharge zone.

- Pollution in a watershed causes contaminants to enter bodies of water. All water resources downstream from the pollution will have contaminants.

- Wetlands and other aquatic ecosystems purify water and control floods.

- People manage water resources by building dams, reservoirs, and water treatment plants.

- Point-source pollution comes from a single source, such as a sewer pipe. Nonpoint-source pollution is collected from broad areas by runoff.

- Inorganic pollutants, such as lead, mercury, and arsenic, are poisonous to living things. Organic pollutants, such as animal wastes, contain disease-causing agents.

- Drip irrigation in agriculture and xeriscaping around homes and businesses help conserve water.

- Legislation passed in the 1970s led to many laws that protect water resources.

- Protecting watersheds and wetlands from pollution and development can help protect water resources.

Vocabulary

aquifer, 296	herbicide, 311	point-source pollution, 308	sewage treatment plant, 310
bioaccumulation, 312	impermeable, 297	purification, 303	sprinkler system, 302
cholera, 310	industry, 300	radioactive waste, 312	surface water, 294
depleted, 297	irrigate, 302	recharge, 297	thermal pollution, 312
divert, 302	landscaping, 302	recharge zone, 297	virus, 310
drip irrigation, 317	low-flow, 318	recreation, 294	water table, 296
drought, 300	nonpoint-source pollution, 309	reservoir, 304	water treatment, 301
dysentery, 310	organic waste, 311	runoff, 309	watershed, 295
eutrophication, 311	pathogen, 301	scarcity, 298	well, 297
fertilizer, 311	permeable, 297	seep, 296	xeriscaping, 318
gray water, 318		sewage, 310	
hepatitis, 310			

Chapter 8 R E V I E W

Word Bank

cholera

drip irrigation

gray water

impermeable

irrigate

organic waste

permeable

recharge zone

recreation

runoff

sewage treatment plant

thermal pollution

water table

water treatment

watersheds

xeriscaping

Vocabulary Review

On a sheet of paper, write the word or words from the Word Bank that complete each sentence correctly.

1. Surface water drains into rivers and lakes from their _____.

2. A type of irrigation that helps conserve water is _____.

3. A _____ is an area of land where water enters an aquifer.

4. Hot water from power plant cooling towers causes _____.

5. A method of gardening that is designed to conserve water is _____.

6. The process of _____ makes drinking water safe.

7. Waterborne diseases include _____, dysentery, and hepatitis.

8. A _____ releases cleaned wastewater into surface water.

9. To conserve freshwater, some communities are using _____ to water lawns.

10. Aquifers are found in _____ layers of rock.

11. People use many bodies of water for boating and other forms of _____.

12. A well must be dug below the _____, or it will go dry if the water level drops.

13. Farmers must often _____ crops to help them grow.

14. Nonpoint-source pollution is carried into freshwater sources by _____.

15. Layers of rock that water cannot flow through are said to be _____.

16. Much of the material in sewage is _____, or waste from living organisms.

Continued on next page

Concept Review

On a sheet of paper, write the letter of the answer that completes each sentence correctly.

17. The Clean Water Act was passed after a _____ caught fire.

    A building   **C** river

    B farm field   **D** chemical plant

18. Much of the water in the Ogallala Aquifer came from _____.

    A the Colorado River   **C** heavy rainfall

    B the Red River   **D** melting glaciers

19. Some toxins accumulate in living things. These toxins are most concentrated in the _____ levels of food chains.

    A highest   **C** middle

    B lowest   **D** second

20. People in the United States use an average of _____ liters of water daily.

    A 16   **C** 100

    B 40   **D** 379

21. Most large cities of the world developed in areas with nearby sources of _____.

    A groundwater   **C** recreation

    B surface water   **D** water treatment

Critical Thinking

On a sheet of paper, write the answers to the following questions. Use complete sentences.

22. Caves and sinkholes serve as points of recharge for many major aquifers. Evaluate the practice of using caves and sinkholes as trash dumps.

23. Many desert cities, such as Las Vegas, are growing very quickly. What effects could this have on local and regional water resources?

24. How do organic wastes both benefit and hurt the environment?

25. Water quality has improved in many ways over the years. What still needs to be done to protect the quality of water?

Test-Taking Tip Do not wait until the night before a test to study. Plan your study time so that you can get a good night's sleep before a test.

Air Pollution

It is difficult to see the buildings in this photo of Vancouver, British Columbia. Sometimes, the buildings and the hills around this Canadian city cannot be seen at all. This is due to a haze called smog. Smog is caused by air pollution that results from human activities. Air pollution can also cause health problems in people, as well as environmental problems. In Chapter 9, you will learn about the causes and effects of air pollution. You will find out how heat, noise, and light can be forms of pollution. You will read about how Earth's climate is changing. Finally, you will learn about ways to reduce air pollution.

Organize Your Thoughts

Air pollution

- Smog
- Noise pollution
- Light pollution
- Heat

• Industrial smog
• Photochemical smog

• Urban heat island effect

Goals for Learning

◆ To explain what air pollutants are and where they come from

◆ To describe four major forms of urban air pollution

◆ To explain how acid rain forms and what effect it has

◆ To describe global warming and climate change

◆ To explain some of the ways to reduce air pollution

327

Objectives

After reading this lesson, you should be able to

◆ define air pollution

◆ give examples of natural and human sources of air pollution

◆ describe how air pollutants get into and out of the atmosphere

Particulate matter

Liquid or solid particles in the air

Air pollutant

A material in the air that harms living things and nonliving materials

Air pollution

Pollution in the air

What Is in the Air?

Stand outside of your school and take a deep breath. That breath of air is made up mostly of oxygen and nitrogen. Without those elements, you could not survive.

The air you breathe contains small amounts of other things, too. It contains carbon dioxide, argon, and other gases. Can you feel any humidity in the air? Tiny droplets of water are part of every breath you take. Have you ever noticed the wind stirring up dirt on a road or baseball field? The air contains particles of dust and other solids, too.

The air picks up these and other materials as it moves over the earth. A spring wind blows pollen out from a tree. Warm air absorbs water from a stream. Air over a busy street becomes filled with car exhaust. These chemicals will be most dense in the air near their source. Then, as the air circulates, it will carry them vertically and horizontally through the atmosphere.

Bits of solids and liquids in the air are called **particulate matter.** Eventually, all particulate matter will fall to the ground. It can be pulled down by gravity. It can also be washed down from the air by precipitation. How long particulate matter stays in the air depends on its size and on the climate. The largest particles may settle in minutes or hours. The smallest particles can stay in the troposphere for one to two weeks.

Air Pollutants

Sometimes the materials in the air can harm people, wildlife, plants, and even nonliving materials. These damaging substances are known as **air pollutants.** They cause different types of **air pollution.**

Air pollutants can come from natural sources, such as volcanoes and forest fires. Ash, pollen, and wind-blown dirt are all natural air pollutants. Natural air pollutants are not usually concentrated enough to harm living things.

Primary air pollutant

A harmful chemical that enters the air directly

Secondary air pollutant

A harmful chemical that forms as a reaction between other chemicals in the air

Outdoor air pollution

Pollution that is found and measured in outdoor air

Indoor air pollution

Pollution that is found and measured indoors

Link to ➤➤➤

Physics

Air a mile up in the atmosphere is less dense than air at sea level. This causes baseballs hit in Denver to travel farther than baseballs hit in other cities. The thinner air of Denver has fewer air particles. Therefore, a moving object encounters less air resistance.

Most damaging air pollutants come from human activities. Paint fumes, for example, spread harmful chemicals into the air. The use of pesticide sprays does, too. Smoke from wood-burning stoves, cement dust, and mining dust are other human sources of air pollution. Most air pollution, though, comes from just one activity: burning fossil fuels. Factories, power plants, and motor vehicles create 90 percent of the air pollution in the United States.

Scientists group air pollutants into two categories. The first category is **primary air pollutants.** These pollutants are released directly by human or natural sources. Other pollutants form from a chemical reaction between substances in the air. These are called **secondary air pollutants.**

When people talk about air pollution, they usually mean **outdoor air pollution.** Outdoor air pollution is found and measured outdoors. Yet air quality indoors can often be worse than air quality outdoors. That is because additional pollutants tend to be added to the air inside buildings. **Indoor air pollution** includes chemicals released from carpets, cleaning products, insect spray, and tobacco smoke. Because they are contained in a small space, indoor air pollutants can reach dangerous levels. Also, people in industrialized countries spend about 90 percent of their time indoors. Babies, older adults, and sick people often spend even more time indoors. For all these reasons, indoor air pollution can be a very serious health issue.

Technology and Society

Research labs and medical labs depend on having clean air. Pollutants or microbes can ruin laboratory tests. High Efficiency Particulate Air (HEPA) filters are regularly used in such places that require clean, sterile air. These high-tech filters remove even the smallest particles, including viruses, from the air.

Impacts and Solutions

Air pollution affects human health in many ways. It can make people's eyes and throats burn. It can cause heart problems and lung cancer. Asthma and emphysema are two types of **respiratory,** or breathing, illnesses. Both are made worse by breathing polluted air. Each year, more than 600,000 people worldwide die earlier than they normally would have because of air pollution.

Air pollution affects other kinds of living things, too. For example, air pollutants can wash into waterways and harm aquatic wildlife. They can make it harder for plants to grow. Air pollution can even damage statues and buildings.

It can be very difficult to clean polluted air. For this reason, most experts try to tackle air pollution at the source. They try to reduce **emissions** of pollutants from factories, vehicles, and other sources. They research and support new products and alternative forms of energy that produce less pollution. They try to educate the public about how to reduce their contribution to air pollution.

Science in Your Life

Technology: Radon Gas

One source of indoor air pollution is radon gas. Radon is a radioactive gas that seeps up through the soil. Radon gas is only a problem indoors because it builds up and becomes concentrated. It is second only to smoking as a cause of lung cancer.

Radon is produced by the breakdown of small amounts of uranium in the soil. The gas seeps up into a home through pores and cracks in the foundation. It has no smell or taste, so it is not noticeable. Kits are available to test for radon, however. These kits are inexpensive and easy to use. You can find them at a local hardware store.

If radon is detected in a home, a removal system can be installed. It vents the radon gas outside where it disperses harmlessly. Newer homes are built with technology that keeps radon out. All homes should be tested for radon, regardless of whether they are old or new.

1. How does radon gas get into homes?

2. What can you do to make sure there is no radon gas in your home?

Addressing air pollution is complicated because air moves. Communities affected by air pollution are often far from those that create it. For this reason, communities, states, and even nations must work together to address air pollution.

The U.S. government addresses air pollution through the Clean Air Act. The Clean Air Act is a law that sets national standards for air quality. This act is sometimes changed to address new air pollution problems.

Through laws and new technologies, people have already made improvements in air quality. For example, gasoline in the United States used to have lead in it. This helped engines run. However, burning leaded gasoline released lead into the air. Lead in the environment can poison people and cause developmental problems in children. In 1970, the Clean Air Act required gasoline to be lead-free by the mid-1980s. Even by 1980, the level of lead in people's blood had dropped by 50 percent.

In the following lessons, you will learn more about the major forms of air pollution. You will also learn more about how people are working to control them.

Express Lab 9

Materials
◆ air freshener or perfume spray

Procedure
1. Remain seated as your teacher sprays the air freshener or perfume.

2. Raise your hand as soon as you can smell the spray.

3. Compare the smell each person experienced.

Analysis
1. How far away was the spray smelled?

2. How does the spray move through the air?

Word Bank

air pollutants

emissions

indoor

On a sheet of paper, write the word or words from the Word Bank that complete each sentence correctly.

1. Materials in the air that can harm living things are called _____.

2. Pollution found inside a building is called _____ air pollution.

3. Releases of pollutants into the environment are called _____.

On a sheet of paper, write the letter of the answer that completes each sentence correctly.

4. Two or more substances in the air can react to form a _____ air pollutant.

    A particle   **B** primary   **C** secondary   **D** particulate

5. Air pollution causes _____ difficulties for many people.

    A eating   **B** sleeping   **C** walking   **D** breathing

6. Most air pollution comes from _____.

    A natural sources   **C** fires
    B burning fossil fuels   **D** paint

Critical Thinking

On a sheet of paper, write the answers to the following questions. Use complete sentences.

7. How has the Clean Air Act improved people's health?

8. What is the biggest difference between indoor and outdoor air pollution?

9. Why is controlling emissions important for the reduction of air pollution?

10. What are two examples of air pollution that do not come from humans?

INVESTIGATION 9

Materials

- cardboard
- scissors
- aluminum foil
- masking tape
- string
- petroleum jelly
- paper towel
- magnifying glass or microscope

What Is in the Air?

Although you usually cannot feel or see air, it is a substance. Air has mass. Air is filled with many different particles, most of which you do not notice. How can you tell what particles are in the air? Is there a way to capture them and find out? This lab will show you one way to do exactly that.

Procedure

1. Cut a 4 cm x 4 cm square from the cardboard.

2. Completely cover the cardboard square with aluminum foil. Make sure that the foil is flat and smooth.

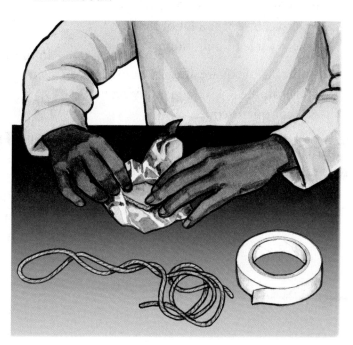

Continued on next page

3. Use tape to attach one end of a piece of string to your square.

4. Using a paper towel, cover both sides of the square with a thin, even layer of petroleum jelly. Wipe your hands immediately after using the petroleum jelly. **Safety Alert: Keep the petroleum jelly away from your eyes, nose, and mouth.**

5. Use the string to hang your square in an indoor or outdoor location. Record the specific location. Make notes about the surroundings. For example, is it near a lot of traffic or other source of pollution?

6. Collect your square after 24 hours and examine it with a magnifying glass or microscope.

Cleanup/Disposal
Return the materials and make sure your area is clean before you leave the lab. Wash your hands thoroughly.

Analysis
1. What did you find on your square? Make a list of the things you observed.

2. Where do you think these particles come from? Add these notes to your list.

Conclusions
1. Compare the types of things found on the squares that were hung outside with the squares that were hung inside. How were they different?

2. What do you think you would find in the air of the house of someone who smokes?

3. How do air particles affect you?

Explore Further
Work with a partner to prepare a presentation of the investigation results. Gather data from all indoor and outdoor squares. Create a visual presentation of the combined results.

Objectives

After reading this lesson, you should be able to

◆ describe what smog is and where it occurs

◆ explain what an urban heat island is

◆ explain how noise can be a type of pollution

◆ give examples of how light can pollute

Smog
A haze that forms as a result of vehicle and industry emissions

Industrial smog
A form of smog produced by burning coal and oil

In 1970, Chattanooga, Tennessee, had serious air pollution problems. Some days were so dark from pollution that people had to drive with headlights on. Pollutants in the air could destroy a woman's nylon stockings as she walked down the street.

Chattanooga has much cleaner air now, thanks to laws and community efforts. Yet urban areas around the world continue to have many air pollution problems. Four forms of air pollution, in particular, occur most often in urban environments.

Smog

You may have noticed a dark haze on the horizon of certain cities. That haze is called **smog.** Some people think of it as a combination of smoke and fog. Yet smog is not quite that simple.

There are actually two types of smog. **Industrial smog** is smog caused by burning coal and oil. It became severe in many big cities after the start of the Industrial Revolution. That is when people began burning huge amounts of coal for power. Burning coal and oil releases sulfur dioxide (SO_2) into the air. It also releases liquid and solid particulate matter. Together, these chemicals form a grayish haze. Normally, industrial smog breaks up from day to day. Certain weather patterns, though, can cause industrial smog to remain for extended periods. In 1952, an estimated 12,000 London residents died from five days of concentrated smog. This event caused London and other cities to take steps to reduce industrial smog. The most significant change was to make smokestacks taller so pollutants would blow up and away.

Research and Write

Find the air quality reports for your area and track them throughout the week. What pollutants are a problem in your area? Create a graph to track your data from day to day.

Today, **photochemical smog** is more common. Photochemical smog produces a brownish haze in the sky. It is most common in cities with warm, dry, sunny climates, such as Los Angeles and Denver. The source of photochemical smog is primarily cars and other motor vehicles. As they burn gasoline, these vehicles release nitrogen oxides (NO_x) into the air. These gases react with sunlight to form several harmful gases. One of these is nitrogen dioxide, a brownish gas with a terrible smell. Another is **ozone.** Ozone causes breathing difficulties, headaches, and fatigue. A third is called peroxyacetylnitrate, or PAN. PAN can make people's eyes water and sting.

Science Myth

Myth: The ozone layer is a layer of pollution.

Fact: There are two types of ozone. Atmospheric ozone is found in the ozone layer, which is high in the stratosphere. This ozone prevents high levels of radiation from reaching Earth. Ground-level ozone is a secondary air pollutant and exists in the air that people breathe. Ground-level ozone is unhealthy.

Map Skills: Ozone Levels

Ozone gas can form when pollutants react with sunlight. Ozone often builds up in climates that are hot, sunny, and have little wind. Ozone levels are monitored so that people can be warned when levels are high. You should avoid outdoor activities on high ozone days.

This map shows the ozone levels in the Los Angeles area for August 28, 2005. In January 2005, this same area map was all green. Use the map to answer the questions below.

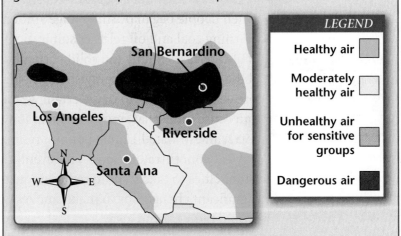

1. In what color area is the city of Los Angeles?
2. What times of the year are more likely to have dangerous levels of ozone?
3. Why do you think the areas along the coast are green?

Catalytic converter

A device designed to reduce emissions of air pollutants from vehicle exhaust

Urban heat island effect

Increased temperatures in urban areas caused by human development and activity

Link to ➤➤➤

Health

Air quality levels depend on the physical features of land. For example, Los Angeles lies in a large basin, or valley. Since less air moves through this basin than over flat land, pollutants are trapped. This pollution has been linked to increased occurrences of asthma, heart attacks, and strokes.

To help reduce photochemical smog, the U.S. government requires car makers to install **catalytic converters** on all vehicles. Catalytic converters are devices that reduce emissions of air pollutants from cars' exhaust systems. These devices have greatly reduced each car's pollution emissions since the 1970s and 1980s. However, people today drive many more miles each year than they did then. As a result, automobile emissions remain high overall and photochemical smog is still common.

Heat Islands

Leaving the city on a hot day, you may notice that the temperature decreases. Urban areas are usually 1°C to 5.5°C hotter than surrounding areas. Scientists call this the **urban heat island effect.**

What causes cities to be hotter than surrounding areas? First, activities that use energy give off waste energy as heat. More of these activities are concentrated in urban areas, increasing this heat load. Also, as cities develop, natural vegetation is lost. Before, this vegetation provided shade from the sun and decreased the air temperature. Finally, urban building materials such as asphalt and brick are dark in color. They absorb a lot of heat and release it slowly into the air.

Heat in the air is not a form of air pollution. However, increased urban temperatures in summer months can increase energy use for cooling. More energy use generally means more pollution. Also, heated air above cities tends to trap more pollutants.

There are two main solutions to the heat island effect. One is to plant more trees and other vegetation. Another is to turn dark surfaces into light surfaces. When a building's roof is light colored, it uses 40 percent less energy for cooling.

Noise Pollution

Noise pollution is defined as noise that interrupts daily life. It is not a typical form of air pollution. It is caused by sounds, not pollutants, that travel through the air. This noise comes from air, rail, and car transportation. It comes from construction and industry. Sometimes it even comes from recreational activities. All of these activities tend to be concentrated in urban areas. High noise levels can make it harder for people to sleep and work. They can raise stress levels. They can disrupt the activities of wildlife. They can even damage hearing over time.

Noise pollution is very hard to control. Yet many cities have taken steps to reduce noise pollution. For example, some cities construct walls to block highway noise. Others restrict airplane landings and takeoffs at night.

Light Pollution

In photographs of North America taken at night, major urban areas glow with light. Some people believe there is too much light in developed areas. They call this **light pollution.** Light pollution results from three things. The first is having more lights than are necessary for safety. The second is having lights that are brighter than necessary. The third is allowing the light to spread up and out.

Light pollution causes a number of problems. It can prevent people from seeing the stars or even keep people awake at night. It can also create a glare that makes it hard for some people to see and drive. Last, light pollution can disrupt the movement of wildlife. For example, newly hatched sea turtles follow the moon's light to get to sea. In some places, though, they accidentally crawl toward the lights of nearby towns. Careful placement of lights and control of light angles, however, can minimize light pollution.

Smog, the heat island effect, noise pollution, and light pollution are most common in cities. Still, even small towns can have problems such as loud noises and bright lights. The following lessons describe air pollution problems that affect everything from cities to wilderness.

Noise pollution

Noise that interrupts daily life

Light pollution

Bothersome brightness or glare caused by human-made lights

Link to >>>

Physics

A decibel (dB) is a unit used to measure loudness. Zero dB is the quietest noise a human ear can hear. With each increase of 10 dB, the intensity of the sound increases by 10 times. For example, 30 dB is 10 times the intensity of 20 dB, and 100 times the intensity of 10 dB. Long exposure to sounds of 120 dB or higher can lead to deafness.

Lesson 2   R E V I E W

Word Bank

heat island

noise

smog

On a sheet of paper, write the word or words from the Word Bank that complete each sentence correctly.

1. A dark haze called _____ hovers over many cities.

2. A jackhammer and a loud truck can both contribute to _____ pollution.

3. The urban _____ effect refers to the higher temperatures found in urban areas.

Critical Thinking

On a sheet of paper, write the answers to the following questions. Use complete sentences.

4. How are the two types of smog different?

5. Why is light considered to be a form of pollution?

★ ★

Achievements in Science

The Discovery of the Hole in the Ozone Layer

The ozone layer blocks 95 percent of the sun's harmful ultraviolet radiation. Without this protection, more humans would develop skin cancer. Other harmful results would include the destruction of some farm crops and marine organisms.

Scientists at the British Antarctic Survey began measuring the ozone layer in the late 1970s. In 1985, they reported that there was a "hole" in the layer directly above Antarctica. This hole is actually where the ozone layer is very thin, allowing radiation to come through. The scientists also concluded that the hole was growing.

Around the same time, chemists discovered that chemicals called CFCs were destroying atmospheric ozone. CFC stands for "chlorofluorocarbon." CFCs were released by using aerosol sprays and fire extinguishers. They were also used as a coolant in refrigerators and air conditioners. Since 1987, many countries have signed the Montreal Protocol, which bans the use of CFCs. Scientists think the ozone layer will recover if CFCs are kept out of the atmosphere.

Materials

- colored ceramic tiles or paint chips
- 2 clear drinking glasses or plastic cups
- 2 thermometers
- stopwatch, or clock with a second hand
- heat lamp or strong sunlight

Colors and Heat

The colors of building materials can contribute to the urban heat island effect. How much does color affect the amount of heat that is absorbed? Which colors absorb more heat? You will find out in this lab.

Procedure

1. In a small group, select two colors of the same material, such as ceramic tiles or paint chips. Choose a very dark color and a very light color.

2. Write a hypothesis about the amount of heat each item will absorb.

3. Write a procedure and Safety Alerts for your experiment, using the materials listed.

4. Have your hypothesis, Safety Alerts, and procedure approved by your teacher. Then perform your experiment.

5. Collect and record data. Use your data to create a graph that shows the temperatures of the different colored materials at different time intervals.

Cleanup/Disposal

Return the materials and make sure your area is clean before you leave the lab.

Analysis

1. Was your hypothesis correct? Explain why or why not.

2. What color absorbed the most heat? Explain.

3. What color absorbed the least heat? Explain.

Conclusions

1. What color would be good to use on a house in a cold climate? Explain your answer.

2. What color would be good to use on a house in a hot climate? Explain your answer.

3. Contrast how light- and dark-colored materials interact with energy from the lamp or the sun.

Explore Further

Take the paint chip that, according to your data, absorbed the most heat. Cut pieces of another color and glue these pieces to the paint chip. How do you think this will affect the original paint chip's ability to absorb heat? Write a hypothesis and test it.

Objectives

After reading this lesson, you should be able to

◆ describe the major sources of acid rain

◆ explain why acid rain affects places far from its sources

◆ describe problems with and solutions to acid rain

Acid

A sour-tasting substance that reacts with metals to produce hydrogen

Acid rain

Precipitation with high levels of acidity

Acid deposition

Another term for acid rain

Dry deposition

Acid pollutants that settle on the earth as solids

Wet deposition

Acid pollutants that reach the earth in precipitation

In the 1960s, scientists became concerned about the health of certain freshwater lakes and forests. Biodiversity was declining in the lakes. Many of the trees in the forests were dying. The scientists studied the conditions in these ecosystems to discover the cause. They found that the lakes' water and the forests' soils were very acidic. This meant they had a high concentration of **acid.** This acid was harming plants and animals. But where did the acid come from?

The scientists soon discovered that the acid was coming from the air. This form of pollution is known as **acid rain** or **acid deposition.** Acid rain begins with the emission of sulfur dioxide (SO_2) and nitrogen oxides (NO_x) into the air. Most of the sulfur dioxide emissions come from coal-burning power plants. Most of the nitrogen oxides emissions come from power plants and motor vehicles.

Once in the atmosphere, sulfur dioxide and nitrogen oxides react with water, oxygen, and other chemicals. They form secondary pollutants, such as sulfuric acid and nitric acid. These pollutants sometimes settle as solids on trees, buildings, water, and land. This is called **dry deposition.** Other times, they are carried to the ground by precipitation. This is called **wet deposition.** Wet deposition is not just rain. It can also be snow, sleet, fog, and dew with these acids in it.

Understanding Acids

Acids are sour-tasting substances. They react with metals to produce hydrogen. A mild acid can be found in oranges and lemons. A much stronger acid helps break down food in your stomach.

The opposite of acids are a group of substances known as **bases.** These substances taste bitter and feel slippery. They contain something called the hydroxyl (OH) radical. A **radical** is a group of two or more atoms that acts like one atom. Soap, deodorants, and antacid medications all contain bases.

A substance's **pH** determines whether something is an acid or a base. The pH scale runs from 0 to 14. Anything below 7 is an acid. Anything above 7 is a base. A pH of exactly 7 means that a substance is neither an acid nor a base. It is **neutral.** Pure water is neutral. Vinegar is an acid with a pH of about 4. Many household cleaners are bases with a pH of around 10. More materials and their pHs can be seen in Table 9.3.1, below.

Acids in the Environment

Acidity levels in ecosystems can vary. Natural precipitation has a pH of about 5.6. This slight acidity helps dissolve minerals that plants and animals need.

When pH levels fall below 5.5, however, the acidity can cause many problems. The acidity can kill fish, microorganisms, and aquatic plants. It can take nutrients out of the soil. In combination with other pollutants, it can harm trees, crops, and other plants.

Table 9.3.1 *The pH Scale of Some Common Substances*

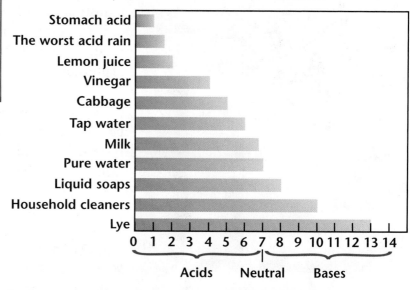

Link to >>>

Arts

One of China's most treasured archaeological artifacts is the army of terra-cotta warriors. These statues were discovered near the city of Xi'an in 1974. Unfortunately, this work of art is being destroyed by air pollution. Features on the life-size warriors are turning gray and may eventually break apart.

The impacts of acid rain depend on the ecosystems and species involved. When rain falls, only a small portion falls directly into lakes and streams. The rest falls on land and flows through the soil. Then it drains into lakes and streams. The soils in some regions contain a lot of limestone and other substances that are bases. When acid rain flows through these soils, the bases react with it and neutralize it. The water that reaches lakes and streams is no longer acidic.

Some places, though, have thin, acidic soils. As acid rain passes through these soils, it becomes even more acidic. It flows into local lakes and streams and raises acidity levels even higher.

Ecosystems with high acidity lose biodiversity. Yet not all species react in the same way. For example, snails, crayfish, salmon, and trout die when water becomes too acidic. Other species, such as water beetles, bloodworms, and eels, do well in acidic waters.

Acid rain also affects humans and their communities. It can damage buildings and statues. It can create a haze similar to smog that makes it harder to see. It can also contribute to health problems for people with breathing difficulties.

The Geography of Acid Rain

In Lesson 2, you learned that burning fossil fuels in power plants can cause industrial smog. The local impacts of these power plants are no longer so great, however. That is because power plants now use very tall smokestacks, like the ones in Figure 9.3.1. When these smokestacks are tall enough, pollutants are not trapped above a city. Instead, the wind carries them away from their source.

Figure 9.3.1 *Using taller smokestacks helps to disperse pollutants.*

Tall smokestacks have disadvantages, though. Their pollutants do not go away completely. Instead, they blow to other places. They also have a chance to react and form secondary pollutants, such as those in acid rain.

Acid rain is a major problem in many parts of the world. These include parts of Europe, Scandinavia, China, southeastern Canada, and the northeastern United States. The pollution that causes acid rain in these regions comes mostly from other places. For example, more than half of Canada's acid rain comes from the United States. Much of the acid rain in the northeastern United States comes from the upper Midwest.

Addressing Acid Rain

The effects of acid rain are visible all over the world. Sugar maples are dying in Vermont. More than 4,000 lakes in Sweden contain no fish. One-quarter of the lakes in New York's Adirondack Mountains are considered biologically dead. These lakes were once full of otters, loons, and trout.

In the 1970s, scientists and others began working to reduce acid rain. That required reducing emissions of the pollutants that cause it. The Clean Air Act requires power plants to reduce their emissions of sulfur dioxide and nitrogen oxides. In general, they can do this by burning low-sulfur coal or by installing **scrubbers.** Scrubbers are devices that remove sulfur from smokestack emissions before they reach the air.

These requirements have been partly successful. Between 1990 and 1998, sulfur dioxide emissions decreased by 17 percent. Yet nitrogen oxides continue to be emitted at the same rate. Moreover, acid levels remain dangerously high in many parts of the country and the world. Solving these pollution problems is still a major concern for scientists.

Lesson 3   REVIEW

On a sheet of paper, write the word from the Word Bank that completes each sentence correctly.

1. Another term for acid rain is acid _____.

2. A _____ substance is neither an acid nor a base.

3. Devices that clean sulfur from smokestacks are called _____.

On a sheet of paper, write the letter of the answer that completes each sentence correctly.

4. Substances with a pH higher than 7 are _____.

    A acids   **B** bases   **C** neutral   **D** radicals

5. An ecosystem with high acidity loses _____.

    A water   **B** soil   **C** sunlight   **D** biodiversity

6. Sulfuric acid and nitric acid are examples of _____ pollutants.

    A safe   **B** secondary   **C** stationary   **D** primary

Critical Thinking

On a sheet of paper, write the answers to the following questions. Use complete sentences.

7. What can you guess about the pH of medicine used to treat an acidic stomach? Explain your answer.

8. How does acid rain form?

9. What kind of damage would you expect to find in a city that receives acid rain?

10. How can acid rain fall in areas where there is no industry?

Objectives

After reading this lesson, you should be able to

◆ define global warming and climate change

◆ describe the greenhouse effect and how it contributes to global warming

◆ name several impacts of climate change on people and ecosystems

Climate change

A change in Earth's climate associated with global warming

Montana's Glacier National Park is named for its many enormous glaciers. Today, though, these glaciers are melting and shrinking. Many scientists believe that by 2030, Glacier National Park will no longer have glaciers. The reason is that temperatures are getting warmer each year. Since 1900, average summer temperatures at the park have risen by 1°C. This trend is happening all over the world.

Figure 9.4.1 *The glaciers of Glacier National Park in Montana are slowly shrinking.*

A Changing Climate

Global temperatures have been accurately recorded since the late 1800s. Since that time, average temperatures worldwide have risen from between 0.4°C and 0.8°C. As you learned in Chapter 1, this is called global warming. Current data suggest that temperatures are still rising. The 10 hottest years of the 1900s occurred in that century's last 15 years. The first five years of the 2000s had four of the five hottest years on record.

These increases in Earth's temperature affect the climate in other ways. They affect wind patterns, precipitation patterns, and hurricane intensity. These changes are referred to as global **climate change.** Sometimes "global warming" and "climate change" are used to mean the same thing. In general, though, climate change refers to more than just rising temperatures.

The Greenhouse Effect

You may recall that Earth's climate has always been changing. Ice ages have been followed by periods of warming. Short-term changes in temperature and precipitation have also occurred. Such natural changes in the climate are still going on. Yet most scientists believe that current climatic changes are largely caused by human activities.

Over the last 200 years, the makeup of the atmosphere has been changing. Since the Industrial Revolution began, the amount of carbon dioxide has increased by almost one-third. The amount of methane has more than doubled. Nitrogen oxides have also increased. These gases are referred to as **greenhouse gases.** They normally help trap heat around the Earth. This is known as the **greenhouse effect.** Now they are increasing in the atmosphere and trapping even more heat. The result is higher temperatures at Earth's surface.

Most scientists believe that human activities are causing this increase of greenhouse gases. The main cause is the burning of fossil fuels. About 98 percent of U.S. carbon dioxide emissions come from burning fossil fuels. Burning fossil fuels also contributes about one-fourth of methane emissions and 18 percent of nitrogen oxides emissions. The rest of these emissions come from cutting down forests, mining, and other activities. The United States contributes about one-fifth of all the greenhouse gases emitted worldwide.

Science Myth

Myth: The greenhouse effect is bad for life on Earth.

Fact: The greenhouse effect is one reason that life can exist on Earth. The gases trap enough heat against the planet for humans and other living things to survive. However, pollution has caused an increase in the greenhouse effect. This increase may lead to global warming and other problems.

Research and Write

Some scientists believe that global warming is due to the buildup of greenhouse gases. Other scientists believe that Earth is going through a natural warming period. Research both sides of the issue and pick a point of view. Write a paper that explains why you chose the position that you did.

Impacts of Climate Change

Scientists agree that global warming is occurring. Yet some uncertainty surrounds exactly how Earth's climate will change. Past changes in greenhouse gas concentrations have caused big changes in temperature, rainfall, and sea level. These past changes can be used to develop tools to predict future changes.

Among the most useful tools for predicting future climate changes are computer models. These models simulate the buildup of greenhouse gases in the atmosphere. They calculate average temperatures in the air and in the seas. They also calculate how climate change will affect the polar ice caps, glaciers, and wildlife habitats. Scientists can get a sense of how accurate their models are. They enter past data and see how well their models "predict" what happened next.

Scientists now predict that by 2050, Earth's average temperatures could rise by another 0.6°C to 2.5°C. They predict a rise of 1.2°C to 5.6°C by 2100. That may not sound like a major increase in temperature. Yet only a 5°C to 8°C decrease in average temperatures caused the last ice age.

Scientists believe that rising temperatures will change many aspects of life on Earth. Warming seas and melting polar ice have already caused sea levels to rise. These levels could rise by 80 cm by 2100. This would flood many coastal communities around the world. Cities near or below sea level, such as New Orleans, Louisiana, are especially at risk.

Global warming is expected to increase precipitation and extreme weather. Disastrous floods, storms, and droughts are already becoming common. For example, global warming is believed to increase the intensity of hurricanes. The related change in climate is also likely to increase the spread of human diseases. Warmer, wetter climates encourage disease-carrying insects. Climate change could also reduce water supplies and the amount of food grown. This is due to shifts in patterns of rainfall and changes in temperature. Both of these factors affect what crops can be grown where.

Rising temperatures on land and at sea will change and destroy wildlife habitat. During past climate changes, some species migrated north and south to find more suitable habitats. Now human development and the speed of climate change might make this impossible. Some mountain species are already dying out as their high-elevation retreats become too warm.

Global warming affects wildlife in other ways, too. For example, Arctic ice has been forming later and melting earlier in recent years. Polar bears, like the one in Figure 9.4.2, depend on this ice for hunting seals. Now many polar bears are becoming too thin to reproduce, and some are starving and even drowning.

Figure 9.4.2 *Polar bears are one of many wild species affected by global warming.*

Addressing Climate Change

One way to combat climate change is to reduce greenhouse gas emissions. However, not all countries have agreed on a plan to reduce emissions of greenhouse gases. Still, some nations, cities, and companies have pledged to reduce their emissions. This can be achieved in part by reducing fossil fuel use and turning to alternative forms of energy.

Carbon sequestration

The long-term storage of carbon in forests, soils, oceans, and underground

Carbon sink

A place where carbon builds up and is stored

Some scientists are also researching ways to store excess carbon emitted by human activity. This is called **carbon sequestration.** Earth is already filled with natural **carbon sinks.** Carbon sinks are places that absorb and store carbon dioxide. Oceans, forests, and soils are all carbon sinks. Scientists estimate that carbon sinks on U.S. land absorb 300 to 600 million metric tons of carbon. Yet the United States emits between 4.5 and 5.5 billion metric tons each year. Some scientists believe that by maintaining and improving natural processes, they can increase carbon sequestration. This means protecting tropical forests and other large carbon sinks. New methods, such as injecting carbon deep into the earth, could also help.

No one knows for sure how climate change should be addressed. Yet most experts agree it is one of the world's greatest environmental challenges.

Science at Work

Climatologist

Monitoring Earth's climate is an important job. This work is done all over the world by climatologists. Climatologists work mostly with state and federal government agencies to determine a climate's impact on humans. A climatologist collects weather data to create a complete picture of Earth's climate. This data includes daily temperature ranges and amounts of precipitation. A climatologist also studies hurricanes, blizzards, tornadoes, droughts, heat waves, and other extreme weather. Climatologists also make predictions about future climate changes.

A climatologist must have a bachelor's degree in meteorology or atmospheric science. A strong background in math and science is also recommended. Climatologists must also have good communication skills and be able to use databases and computer modeling programs.

Lesson 4   R E V I E W

Word Bank

climate change
global warming
greenhouse effect

On a sheet of paper, write the words from the Word Bank that complete each sentence correctly.

1. The rise in average temperatures around the globe is known as _____.

2. The global change in patterns of temperature and precipitation is known as _____.

3. The way certain gases in the atmosphere trap heat against the earth is called the _____.

On a sheet of paper, write the letter of the answer that completes each sentence correctly.

4. The buildup of greenhouse gases in the atmosphere is believed to be mostly caused by _____.

   A burning fossil fuels   **C** volcanic activity
   B mining   **D** forest clearing

5. Forests and oceans store carbon and are known as _____.

   A storehouses   **C** carbon sinks
   B greenhouses   **D** carbon copies

6. Climate change is expected to reduce _____.

   A sea levels   **C** extreme weather
   B disease   **D** wildlife habitat

Critical Thinking

On a sheet of paper, write the answers to the following questions. Use complete sentences.

7. Does a week of record-breaking cold weather mean global warming is not occurring? Explain.

8. How could climate change could affect human life? Give examples.

9. What is carbon sequestration?

10. How are the current changes in climate different from the global coolings and warmings that have occurred before?

Artificial Trees and Carbon Pollution

Burning fossil fuels releases carbon dioxide into the atmosphere. This creates pollution and may contribute to global warming. Until now, the only strategy to reduce carbon emissions has been to cut down on fossil fuels and develop new energy sources. But as the planet's population grows and energy needs increase, it becomes more difficult to reduce the use of fossil fuels. However, scientists are working on other methods of reducing carbon pollution.

One possible method involves devices that will collect and store carbon in the same way trees and other plants do. Scientists are trying to develop these synthetic "trees" to absorb carbon from the air. That would greatly improve air quality.

The synthetic trees look like football goalposts with rows of flat shutters. The shutters would hold sodium hydroxide and expose it to the air. Sodium hydroxide would combine with carbon dioxide in the air to create sodium carbonate. Sodium carbonate can be treated to remove the carbon in a mineral form. This form of carbon could be stored or buried. The sodium hydroxide is then ready to be used again to capture more carbon dioxide.

Scientists are currently testing this method in hopes of creating an efficient machine. Someday, we may be able to reduce carbon pollution two ways: by cutting back on emissions and by removing some of what is already in the air.

1. Describe how a synthetic tree could be used to remove carbon from the atmosphere.

2. What happens to the carbon after it is removed?

3. Where do you think might be a good place to "plant" these artificial forests? Explain your answer.

- Most air pollution comes from human activities, especially burning fossil fuels.

- Air pollutants can be released directly into the air (primary pollutants) or can form as a reaction between substances in the air (secondary pollutants).

- The Clean Air Act is a piece of legislation designed to maintain air quality in the United States.

- Certain forms of air pollution are most common in urban areas: smog, the urban heat island effect, noise pollution, and light pollution.

- Smog can come from industrial activity (industrial smog) and from vehicle emissions (photochemical smog).

- Acid rain can harm wildlife, people, and nonliving materials.

- When the pH of ecosystems falls below 5.5, many plants and animals will die.

- Global temperatures are rising, which in turn is causing global climate change.

- Most scientists believe that global warming is caused by increased levels of greenhouse gases in the atmosphere.

- Rising temperatures will cause a variety of changes on Earth, including rising sea levels, extreme weather, widespread diseases, and reduced wildlife habitat.

- Reducing greenhouse gas emissions and preserving carbon sinks are two ways people are working to address climate change.

Vocabulary

acid, 342
acid deposition, 342
acid rain, 342
air pollutant, 328
air pollution, 328
base, 343
carbon sequestration, 351
carbon sink, 351
catalytic converter, 337

climate change, 347
dry deposition, 342
emission, 330
greenhouse effect, 348
greenhouse gas, 348
indoor air pollution, 329
industrial smog, 335
light pollution, 338

neutral, 343
noise pollution, 338
outdoor air pollution, 329
ozone, 336
particulate matter, 328
pH, 343
photochemical smog, 336
primary air pollutant, 329

radical, 343
respiratory, 330
scrubber, 345
secondary air pollutant, 329
smog, 335
urban heat island effect, 337
wet deposition, 342

Chapter 9 R E V I E W

Word Bank

acid rain

acids

air pollutants

carbon sinks

climate change

emissions

greenhouse gases

indoor air pollution

neutral

noise pollution

particulate matter

pH

respiratory

scrubbers

secondary air
  pollutant

smog

urban heat island
  effect

Vocabulary Review

On a sheet of paper, write the word or words from the Word Bank that complete each sentence correctly.

1. Materials in the air that can harm living and nonliving things are called _____.

2. Bits of solids and liquids in the air are known as _____.

3. A(n) _____ forms as a reaction between two or more substances in the air.

4. Pollution found inside buildings is called _____.

5. Releases of chemicals into the environment are called _____.

6. Urban haze caused by traffic or industrial activity is called _____.

7. The _____ is an increase in city temperatures caused by human development and activity.

8. Heavy trucks, car alarms, and jackhammers can all cause _____.

9. Acidic pollution that falls from the air is called _____.

10. Substances that are sour-tasting and react with metals to produce hydrogen are called _____.

11. The _____ scale measures whether something is an acid or a base.

12. A(n) _____ substance is neither an acid nor a base.

13. Devices called _____ can remove sulfur dioxide from smokestack emissions.

14. Air pollution can cause many _____ problems in both children and adults.

Continued on next page

15. A global shift in climate caused by rising temperatures is called _____.

16. Carbon dioxide and other atmospheric gases that trap heat are called _____.

17. Places that absorb and store carbon dioxide are called _____.

Concept Review

On a sheet of paper, write the letter of the correct answer.

18. What is the primary cause of air pollution worldwide?

   A forest fires   **C** paint fumes
   B mining   **D** fossil fuel burning

19. Which of the following is a secondary air pollutant?

   A sulfur dioxide   **C** ozone
   B cigarette smoke   **D** ash

20. Which of the following reduced local smog but increased acid rain?

   A tall smokestacks   **C** wind power
   B catalytic converters **D** scrubbers

21. Which of the following is **not** associated with global climate change?

   A melting glaciers   **C** volcanic activity
   B rising sea levels   **D** species decline

Critical Thinking

On a sheet of paper, write the answer to each of the following questions. Use complete sentences.

22. Which members of the population tend to spend the most time indoors? How does this increase the harmfulness of indoor air pollution?

23. Describe some characteristics of air pollutants that make them easier to stop at the source than clean up later.

24. What are two ways in which burning a tropical forest contributes to global warming?

25. Some people once doubted that global warming existed. They pointed out that world temperatures were generally measured near cities. Why would this affect the results?

Test-Taking Tip To answer a multiple-choice question, read every choice before you answer the question. Cross out the choices you know are wrong. Then choose the best answer from the remaining choices.

Chapter

10

Solid and Hazardous Waste

A mountain of garbage is growing in the tropical forest shown in this photo. This method of waste disposal is used by many developing nations. Once common in North America, open dumps and open dumping are now banned by federal laws. However, the practice continues in rural and wilderness areas. The result is land pollution. Plus, water trickling over and through the garbage causes water pollution. In Chapter 10, you will learn about sources of land pollution and its effect on the environment. You will learn about hazardous waste and how it is disposed of. You will also learn about ways to control this growing problem.

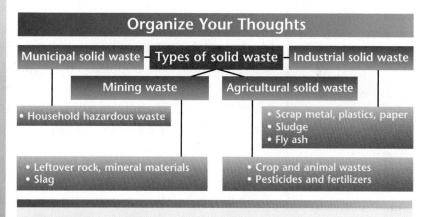

Organize Your Thoughts

Municipal solid waste — Types of solid waste — Industrial solid waste

Mining waste — Agricultural solid waste

• Household hazardous waste

• Scrap metal, plastics, paper
• Sludge
• Fly ash

• Leftover rock, mineral materials
• Slag

• Crop and animal wastes
• Pesticides and fertilizers

Goals for Learning

◆ To describe the major types of solid waste

◆ To explain four ways solid waste is managed

◆ To describe the major types of hazardous waste

◆ To understand several ways to prevent and control solid waste

After reading this lesson, you should be able to

◆ define solid waste

◆ give examples of different types of solid waste

◆ describe the difference between biodegradable and nonbiodegradable waste

Solid waste

Solid materials such as paper, metals, and yard waste that are thrown away

Waste stream

The creation, collection, and disposal of waste

Hazardous waste

Waste that is very dangerous to living things and the environment

What Is Solid Waste?

Think about everything you threw away today. Did you throw away any writing paper? Plastic bottles? A banana peel or an apple core? An old cell phone? Every person on Earth creates waste. In the United States, each person produces more than 2 kilograms of **solid waste** each day. Solid waste is garbage that is in a solid or semisolid state. It can also include liquids that are stored in containers. Solid waste includes trash from homes, such as old furniture and food scraps. It also includes all the waste that is produced by industry and farming. In the United States, this adds up to more than 10 billion metric tons of waste each year.

All of the garbage that people throw away becomes part of the **waste stream.** The waste stream is the flow of waste through society. It includes how waste is created, collected, and disposed of. The waste stream always starts with people. People use resources and other products and then throw away the waste that results.

Since 1960, the amount of waste generated in the United States has more than doubled. This increase in solid waste has created serious health and environmental problems around the country. Many areas have run out of places to put the waste. Many types of waste are also very difficult to dispose of safely.

About 10 to 15 percent of what people throw away is classified as **hazardous waste.** This is waste that is very dangerous to living things and the environment. Most hazardous waste is generated by the chemical industry. The chemical industry creates chemicals for use in many areas, including industry and daily life. However, other businesses produce large amounts of toxic materials as well. Many households also throw away hazardous materials that end up in the waste stream. You will learn more about hazardous waste in Lesson 3.

Link to ➤➤➤

Social Studies

Throughout most of history, city living was relatively unhealthy. Until the mid-1800s, cities lacked systems for the safe disposal of solid waste. Animal waste and garbage littered the streets. Diseases spread rapidly because of these conditions.

Biodegradable and Nonbiodegradable Waste

Solid waste is divided into two categories: **biodegradable** waste and **nonbiodegradable** waste. Biodegradable waste can be broken down by living things. Most animal and plant waste is biodegradable. If you throw away a piece of fruit, for example, decomposers can break it down. Bacteria, fungi, and even insects help with this process. Over time, biodegradable waste will be absorbed into the soil. Once plant and animal materials have been decomposed, other organisms can use their nutrients. Other examples of biodegradable waste include food scraps, paper, and wood.

Waste that is nonbiodegradable cannot be broken down by living things. Many products people use are made of **synthetic,** or human-made, materials that are nonbiodegradable. Scientists create synthetic materials by combining chemicals to form new compounds. Although they might contain carbon, these compounds do not behave the way natural materials behave. Bacteria, insects, and other decomposers cannot break them into simpler substances. Plastic bottles, nylon cloth, tin cans, and many types of industrial wastes are nonbiodegradable.

Nonbiodegradable waste can last for hundreds or thousands of years. If you throw away a plastic bottle, it would not be broken down by decomposers. However, it may eventually be broken down by physical wear. Table 10.1.1 shows how long it takes for some common materials to break down.

Table 10.1.1 Time to Break Down Common Materials	
Item	Time
Orange and banana peels	up to 2 years
Cotton cloth	6 months to 2 years
Cigarette butts	1 to 5 years
Nylon cloth	30 to 40 years
Plastic bottles	indefinitely
Glass bottles	up to 1 million years
Rope	1 year
Tin cans	50 to more than 100 years
Plastic bags	between 20 and 1,000 years

Sources of Solid Waste

Municipal solid waste

Garbage generated by homes, businesses, and institutions

Household hazardous waste

Harmful wastes, such as batteries, bleach, and paint, that are generated by households

Smelting

The process of removing metals from rocks through melting

Ore

A mineral that contains metal

Slag

The waste leftover from smelting

What people throw away every day is called **municipal solid waste,** or MSW. Municipal solid waste is also called garbage, trash, and rubbish. It consists of waste that is generated by households. It also includes wastes from businesses and institutions such as schools. The most common type of municipal solid waste is paper, including newspapers, packaging, and cardboard.

A number of common household items are considered **household hazardous waste.** They include materials such as nail polish, batteries, bleach, oil-based paint, and lawn and garden pesticides. Like other hazardous waste, household hazardous waste directly harms the environment. Some states do require hazardous waste to be collected separately. However, these materials are generated in small amounts. Therefore, they often are not separated out from the larger waste stream.

Municipal solid waste makes up less than 3 percent of the total waste in the United States. The rest of the waste in this country comes from mining, agriculture, and manufacturing.

Waste from mining operations makes up about 75 percent of U.S. solid waste. The type of waste depends on which materials are being mined. Most of the waste includes leftover rock and mineral materials. This waste can wash into both marine and freshwater systems, harming aquatic life. It can also pollute the soil and create acid runoff. Many mining operations also have **smelting** operations near the mine. Smelting is the process of separating out metals from **ores.** In smelting, the ores are heated to high temperatures to remove any impurities. The leftover waste is called **slag.** Slag can contain hazardous materials and often creates water and soil pollution problems.

Mining waste 75%

Municipal solid waste 3%

Industrial solid waste 9%

Agricultural solid waste 13%

Table 10.1.2 *The sources of solid waste in the United States include homes, mines, farms, and industry.*

362 *Chapter 10 Solid and Hazardous Waste*

Agricultural solid waste

Crop and animal waste

Industrial solid waste

Waste from manufacturing and other industrial processes

Sludge

The semisolid leftovers from sewage treatment processes

Fly ash

Waste ash from coal-burning electrical power plants

Agricultural solid waste makes up about 13 percent of U.S. solid waste. It is mostly crop and animal waste. Most of this waste is plowed back into the soil or used as a fertilizer. However, the pesticides and fertilizers mixed in with the waste can cause serious problems. They often wash into freshwater systems and seep into groundwater.

Industrial solid waste from industry and manufacturing is about 9 percent of the total. This type of waste includes scrap metal, plastics, paper, and **sludge** from sewage treatment plants. Sludge is the leftover, semisolid material from waste water treatment processes. **Fly ash** is also considered industrial solid waste. Fly ash comes from electrical power plants that are powered by burning coal.

All types of solid waste can create pollution. In Lessons 2 and 3, you will learn more about how people dispose of solid waste. In Lesson 4, you will learn how people are reducing the amount of solid waste entering the waste stream.

Express Lab 10

Materials
◆ latex gloves
◆ 2 clean, wide-mouthed glass jars
◆ 2 plastic bags
◆ masking tape
◆ 2 pieces of garbage

Procedure
1. Put on the latex gloves.
2. Select a piece of garbage you think is biodegradable.
3. Select a piece you think is not biodegradable.
4. Place one piece of garbage in each jar.
5. Place a plastic bag over each jar, and seal the bag with tape.
6. Observe both jars over the next two days.

Analysis
1. Describe any differences in how each bag looks.
2. Which material do you think is biodegradable? How can you tell?

Lesson 1   R E V I E W

Word Bank

agricultural

municipal

solid waste

On a sheet of paper, write the word or words from the Word Bank that complete each sentence correctly.

1. Anything solid or semisolid that people throw away is _____.

2. Animal manure, dead crop plants, and pesticides are all examples of _____ waste.

3. Waste from homes, libraries, businesses, hospitals, schools, and restaurants is called _____ solid waste.

On a sheet of paper, write the letter of the answer that completes each sentence correctly.

4. _____ waste can be broken down by living things.

   A Nonbiodegradable   **C** Biodegradable
   B Glass   **D** Hazardous

5. Examples of nonbiodegradable waste include plastic, _____, and radioactive waste.

   A nylon   **C** newspaper
   B banana peels   **D** yard waste

6. _____ solid waste makes up the smallest portion of all the solid waste produced.

   A Agricultural   **B** Industrial   **C** Municipal   **D** Mining

Critical Thinking

On a sheet of paper, write the answer to each of the following questions. Use complete sentences.

7. What are the three main parts of the solid waste stream?

8. What are three ways that you could reduce the amount of solid waste you produce?

9. Why are plastics nonbiodegradable?

10. Why do humans produce more waste today than they did 50 years ago?

Objectives

After reading this lesson, you should be able to

◆ describe three main ways waste is managed

◆ explain the pros and cons of burying trash and burning it

◆ explain how recycling, composting, and incineration reduce the amount of waste in landfills

Open dump

A place where garbage is dumped without environmental controls

Sanitary landfill

A site for disposing of solid waste on land

What happens to your waste once you throw it in the garbage can? The answer depends on the type of waste. Most waste is either dumped, burned, recycled, or composted.

Open Dumps

The first garbage dumps were created by the early Greeks more than 5,000 years ago. People once dumped their garbage in the streets or into oceans or rivers. This created serious health problems. Many cities passed laws that required garbage to be taken outside of the city.

These dumps, called **open dumps,** were very unhealthy. Rats, flies, cockroaches, and bacteria thrived in these dumps. Many caught on fire or gave off strong odors. Liquid from containers and decomposed trash seeped into the soil and ran into water systems.

Sanitary Landfills

Today, open dumps are illegal in most countries. Communities have replaced them with **sanitary landfills.** Sanitary landfills are a type of dump. In a sanitary landfill, however, the waste does not sit on top of the ground. Instead, it is spread into a hole about three meters deep and then compacted by bulldozers. Soil is added on top of the waste and compacted again. The layers of soil help prevent odors and reduce the number of rats and flies. When the sanitary landfill becomes full, grass can be planted on top. Many of these areas are turned into playgrounds and parks.

Science Myth

Myth: Processed foods produce more waste than fresh foods.

Fact: The processed food industry produces different types of waste than fresh food production. Processed food production creates more packaging waste. Fresh food production creates more organic waste. Packaging can often be recycled, while organic waste can be composted.

Leachate

Contaminated water that leaks from a dump or landfill

Heavy metal

A metallic element that can damage living things, such as mercury, arsenic, or lead

Aerobic decomposition

The natural breakdown of organic matter that requires water and oxygen

Research and Write

Anthropologist William Rathje discovered that newspapers left in landfills for 50 years could still be read. Research the work of William Rathje to learn some of his other discoveries about trash. Summarize your findings with a poster presentation.

Figure 10.2.1 shows how a sanitary landfill is laid out. Sanitary landfills create less pollution than open dumps. That is because the bottom of the landfill must be covered by compacted clay and plastic sheets. This prevents liquids from leaking into the groundwater or into nearby streams and rivers. Some landfills also have systems that collect contaminated water, called **leachate,** before it leaks out. They may also have systems to help collect methane. This gas builds up due to all the decomposition taking place in a landfill. If the gas that builds up is not collected, it can cause explosions. If the methane is released into the atmosphere, it can also contribute to global warming.

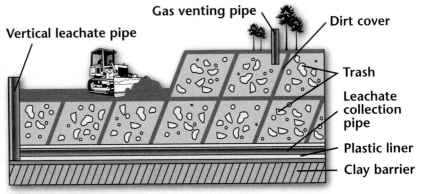

Figure 10.2.1 *A sanitary landfill is composed of layers of compacted trash.*

Problems with Sanitary Landfills

More than 50 percent of the solid waste in North America ends up in sanitary landfills. Although they are more environmentally friendly than dumps, landfills still cause some problems. Some leachate does seep into the groundwater. This can cause serious problems if people have thrown out household hazardous waste with their trash. For example, bacteria in the soil can break down the metal casings of batteries. This allows the **heavy metals** inside to leak out and cause damage to living things. In many landfills, even biodegradable materials do not break down very quickly. That is because the garbage is compacted, so there is little oxygen in sanitary landfills. **Aerobic decomposition** is the natural breakdown of organic matter. This happens much more slowly in a landfill because it requires oxygen and water.

It can sometimes be difficult to find a good location for new sanitary landfill sites. Soil, climate, geology, and water systems all help determine where a sanitary landfill can be built. They are usually built outside of cities, since no one wants to live near sanitary landfills. Even though landfills are covered with soil, they still produce a very strong odor. Landfills also need to be accessible. Garbage trucks need to be able to get to the site easily.

Map Skills: Topographic Maps

A topographic map shows the shape of the surface of the land. Lines called contours or contour lines connect points with the same elevation above sea level. Lines that form closed circles indicate a hill. Lines that are close together show steep slopes. Lines that are far apart show relatively flat land. The contour interval in the legend gives the vertical distance between any two contour lines next to each other. The elevation of every third contour is marked. The exact elevation of a hilltop also is marked.

Solid waste managers and city planners use topographic maps to choose sites for landfills. They must find areas that are large enough and can be reached easily by garbage trucks. They must also find places where pollution is not likely to reach a water source.

Use the map and its legend to answer the following questions.

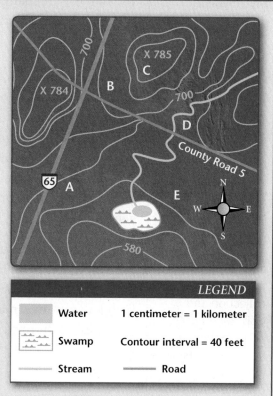

LEGEND

Water — 1 centimeter = 1 kilometer

Swamp — Contour interval = 40 feet

Stream — Road

1. Which letter is near the top of a hill?

2. What is the change in elevation from the pond to the top of the highest hill?

3. Which letter shows the best place to build a landfill? Give reasons for your answer.

4. What makes each of the other locations unsuitable for a landfill?

Science Myth

Myth: Waste disposal costs less than recycling.

Fact: Good recycling programs cost about the same as waste disposal by other methods. In communities that recycle a high percentage of solid waste, recycling costs less. Many cities have added recycling to existing waste collection and disposal services at no extra cost. Improvements in the recovery of materials from recycled trash will make recycling more cost-effective.

Solid waste managers also need to make sure landfills do not harm important habitats. In the past, many wetlands became landfill sites. People thought this was a good way to use the land. Unfortunately, the trash interrupted important wetland functions, such as controlling floods and filtering out silt and other pollutants. In some cases, the amount of leachate increased because the soil was always so wet. Landfills also decreased biodiversity by decreasing the amount of habitat.

Today, there are many laws that regulate how to design a landfill and where a landfill can be located. There are also laws to protect people from having a landfill located too close to where they live.

Incinerators

More than 15 percent of U.S. solid waste produced is burned in **incinerators.** Incinerators are furnaces that heat the waste to very high temperatures. They can reduce the volume of solid waste by more than 90 percent. That means much less solid waste ends up in a landfill. Incinerators also produce heat. This heat can be used to produce steam that heats buildings and generates electricity.

Incinerators have a number of disadvantages, however. They are very expensive to build and operate. Also, incineration can create serious air pollution problems. The leftover ash can contain high levels of toxic materials, making it hazardous waste. Much of this ash is dumped in landfills or disposed of illegally. If it is dumped in landfills, the ash can leak into groundwater or wash into surface water.

❋❋❋❋❋❋❋❋❋❋❋❋❋❋❋❋❋❋❋❋❋❋❋❋❋❋❋❋❋❋

Technology and Society

Technology companies are working to develop reusable paper, or e-paper. This material is made of two thin plastic sheets with tiny, round beads between the sheets. Each bead is two colors. One half might be white and the other half black. A special pencil produces an electric charge that turns the beads black. E-paper can be erased and used thousands of times.

Recycling and Composting

The amount of waste that is recycled in the United States has increased steadily since the 1960s. Today, about 23 percent of municipal solid waste is recycled compared to less than 7 percent in 1960. Recycling is a process that is designed to recover value from waste. In some cases, waste is reused as energy. In other cases, waste is reprocessed to create materials that can be used again.

Composting is another way that materials are removed from the waste stream. Composting converts organic waste into fertilizer for gardens, landscaping, and parks. In some areas, composting centers collect crop waste, slaughterhouse waste, and animal manure. It is then mixed with soil to create compost. The compost is bagged and sold as a soil conditioner and as a natural fertilizer. Almost no waste was composted in the 1960s. Today, some experts estimate that more than 30 percent of biodegradable materials are composted or recycled. Composting and recycling keep materials out of the solid waste stream and out of landfills.

Achievements in Science

Trash or Treasure?

You may have heard the saying, "One man's trash is another man's treasure." This usually means that what one person finds useless, another person finds useful. But in the science of archaeology, this saying can be taken literally. The trash of ancient humans can become treasures in a museum.

Archaeology is the study of past human life. Archaeologists often study the remains of buildings and artwork left by ancient cultures. Archaeologists can also learn much about ancient peoples by studying their trash.

Early groups of humans left waste and broken items in caves and in open dumps. These sites are known as middens. Studying middens enables archaeologists to learn about what early humans ate and how they lived. Middens might contain shells and bones from animals that people ate. These ancient dumps might have remains of charcoal and burnt stones that were used to cook food. Some middens also contain broken pottery and broken or worn-out tools. All these items are clues to what day-to-day life was like in the past. They also provide clues to past environments and human health.

Lesson 2   R E V I E W

On a sheet of paper, write the word from the Word Bank that completes each sentence correctly.

Word Bank

compost

dumps

landfills

1. Sanitary _____ are a special type of dump where waste is put in a pit, compacted, and covered with soil.

2. In many places, _____ is used as a fertilizer or to condition the soil.

3. Rats, flies, cockroaches, and other disease-carrying organisms are often found in open _____.

On a sheet of paper, write the letter of the answer that completes each sentence correctly.

4. The amount of waste that is recycled and composted has _____ since the 1960s.

   A increased   **C** decreased
   B stayed the same   **D** increased, then decreased

5. Most municipal solid waste ends up _____.

   A as compost   **C** in a sanitary landfill
   B in an open dump   **D** being burned in an incinerator

6. Contaminated water that leaks from a landfill is called _____.

   A sludge   **B** leachate   **C** methane   **D** sewage

Critical Thinking

On a sheet of paper, write the answer to each of the following questions. Use complete sentences.

7. What is a disadvantage of burning solid waste instead of burying it?

8. How are sanitary landfills an improvement over open dumps?

9. What is the connection between biodegradable waste and compost?

10. How is composting similar to recycling?

INVESTIGATION 10

Materials

- safety goggles
- lab coat or apron
- several sheets of printed copier paper
- plastic bowl
- hand-operated mixer
- hot tap water
- eyedropper
- dish detergent
- plastic tray
- spoon
- drinking straws
- several sheets of filter paper
- magnifying glass

De-inking Paper

Before printed paper can be made into recycled paper, it must pass through several steps. First, the paper must be ground into a pulp. Then the ink must be removed. This process is called de-inking. Several steps are needed to de-ink paper. In this lab, you will turn printed paper into pulp and begin to de-ink it.

Procedure

1. In a group, make a data table like the one shown below.

Sample	Description
1	
2	
3	
4	

2. Put on safety goggles and a lab coat or apron.

3. Tear printed copier paper into 4-cm squares. Place the squares in a bowl.

4. Add 1 liter of hot tap water to the bowl. Place the bowl on a plastic tray. Then use the eyedropper to add 5–10 drops of detergent to the bowl. Use the hand-operated mixer to mix for three minutes.

5. Scoop out half a spoonful of the paper mixture, called pulp, onto a piece of filter paper. Label this Sample 1 and set it aside to dry.

Continued on next page

6. Have each group member hold a separate straw in the mixture and blow through the straw. Continue blowing for 5 minutes, taking breaths every 15 seconds or as often as necessary. **Safety Alert: Be careful not to suck up the paper mixture through the straw. If you feel dizzy, stop blowing and breathe normally. Keep track of which straw is yours. Do not share straws.**

7. As you blow, bubbles will form. Use the spoon to scoop the bubbles onto the tray.

8. Repeat Step 5 and label it Sample 2. Make sure you scoop out the pulp, not the foamy bubbles.

9. Examine both samples of pulp with a magnifying glass. Record your observations.

10. Repeat Steps 6–9 two more times.

Cleanup/Disposal

Before you leave the lab, clean your work area and wash your hands.

Analysis

1. Summarize the appearance of each sample of paper pulp.

2. During what part of the investigation is the ink removed?

Conclusions

1. Which sample of pulp would be best for making recycled copier paper?

2. What other steps may be needed to make sure all the ink color is gone?

Explore Further

Repeat the experiment using different types of paper or detergent.

Objectives

After reading this lesson, you should be able to

◆ describe three characteristics of hazardous waste

◆ describe three types of hazardous waste

◆ identify three examples of household and industrial hazardous waste

In 1955, the *New York Times* ran an article about the origin of the saying "mad as a hatter." The story focused on a 1941 ban preventing the use of mercury in the hat industry. For many years, people who made hats got very sick. That is because mercury was used to condition the fur used to make hats. The hatters were exposed to mercury through their skin and their lungs. Victims suffered from twitching limbs and confused speech. Many appeared to be crazy. This condition became known as mad hatter syndrome.

Today people know that mercury can cause kidney and brain damage. Although people knew that mercury was toxic, it was not banned until 1941. This was many years after it was first used.

In addition to mercury, hundreds of other toxic chemicals are used to make products today. Many manufacturing processes also produce hazardous waste. Scientists estimate that industries in the United States use more than 80,000 different chemicals. Many of these chemicals are not tested before they are used in products.

Figure 10.3.1 *Hazardous waste is dangerous to living things.*

Many of the products people use create hazardous waste when they are disposed of. Hazardous waste can create problems if it is not treated, stored, transported, or disposed of correctly. It requires special methods of disposal so that it becomes less dangerous.

Hazardous waste comes in many different forms. It can be a solid, liquid, or gas. It can be stored in barrels or canisters. Most of the country's hazardous waste is generated by the chemical industry. Still, small businesses and homes also produce an enormous amount each year.

Types of Hazardous Waste

Ignitable waste

Waste that catches on fire easily

Corrosive waste

Waste that eats or wears away material by chemical action

Reactive waste

Unstable waste that can explode or give off toxic fumes

PCBs

A group of toxic industrial chemicals that were once used in making paint, electrical equipment, and other products

There are several types of hazardous waste. One category includes **ignitable waste,** which catches on fire easily. Another includes waste that contains toxic chemicals. **Corrosive waste,** which eats or wears away materials by chemical action, is considered hazardous. Radioactive waste, a by-product of nuclear reactions, is also hazardous. It gives off harmful radiation that can affect all living things. Some materials are also **reactive waste.** This means they can explode or give off toxic fumes under certain conditions. The U.S. EPA oversees the disposal of all of these categories of hazardous waste.

Many types of industrial waste are hazardous. **PCBs** are one example. PCB is an abbreviation for polychlorinated biphenyl. PCBs include a group of chemicals used in industry. From the 1930s until the 1970s, these chemicals were used to make electrical equipment, inks, and pesticides. Health officials first became concerned when some rice oil became contaminated with PCBs. People who ate the rice oil suffered from liver and kidney damage. In further testing, PCBs were shown to cause a variety of health problems.

Though most PCBs were banned in the late 1970s, they are still a threat today. That is because many were dumped into landfills, fields, and sewers. Equipment and supplies that contained PCBs were also dumped. Over time, the PCBs have started leaking out. They build up in the fatty tissues of people and other animals and cause illness. PCBs show how important it is to test chemicals before they enter the waste stream. They also show how important it is to make sure hazardous materials are disposed of safely.

Link to ➤➤➤

Biology

Worldwide, millions of pets and wild animals die each year due to human trash. Plastic bags, plastic six-pack holders, and open jars are among the biggest offenders. Animals become tangled in six-pack holders or swallow pieces of plastic. Causes of death include choking, drowning, and starvation.

Infectious waste

Waste that can cause diseases

There are many other types of industrial hazardous waste. Acids can leak from a variety of sources, including power plants and incinerators. Cyanide, a poisonous chemical, is often a waste product of gold and silver mining operations. Many heavy metals, including lead, mercury, arsenic, and copper, can come from common products. Batteries, paints, stains, TV picture tubes, household cleaners, and medicines can all contain heavy metals. Most are very toxic, even in low doses. Hospitals and scientific labs often throw away **infectious wastes.** These wastes include body parts, tissues, and other materials that can cause diseases.

Household Hazardous Waste

In Lesson 1, you learned that many household products are considered hazardous waste. Many cities and towns have collection sites where people can bring their hazardous wastes. These collection sites help reduce the amount of toxic material in the waste stream. They are also designed to make sure the materials do not harm people or the environment. Table 10.3.1 below shows some types of hazardous wastes you might find in your house.

If household hazardous waste is dumped directly into the garbage, it can create serious problems. In some cases, people who collect garbage can be harmed. Some materials can burn the skin or release harmful fumes. In other cases, products can catch on fire in dumps. Some toxic chemicals can leak out of landfills and pollute groundwater and surface water.

Table 10.3.1 Types of Household Hazardous Waste	
Paint and paint products	oil-based paints, some types of preservatives, paint removers, paint thinners, stains, and wood sealers
Cleaning products	bleach and ammonia-based products
Garden and pest control	insecticides, insect repellents, mothballs, flea collars, herbicides, fungicides, rodent poisons, ant poisons, and chemical fertilizers
Car parts and products	used motor oil, gasoline, antifreeze, transmission and brake fluid, car wax and polish, and lead acid batteries
Other	nail polish and nail polish remover, some hair products, art and hobby supplies, some types of batteries, cell phones, computer equipment, expired medicine, pool chemicals, lighter fluid, and ammunition

Link to >>>

Health

Substances that cause cancer are known as carcinogens. Carcinogens cause cancer by altering the DNA in cells, which changes their programming. As a result, the cells begin to divide rapidly. This uncontrolled division can cause tumors or interfere with the functioning of other organs. Many hazardous wastes are carcinogens, including asbestos and benzene.

Managing Hazardous Waste

In the 1940s and 1950s, a chemical company buried toxic waste in an unused canal. Love Canal, near Niagara Falls, New York, later became the site of a housing development. In the 1970s, people living there began to get very sick. Tests showed that the air, water, and soil were heavily contaminated with toxic chemicals. Everyone was ordered to leave their homes. In 1980, Love Canal was declared a federal disaster area.

Today, there are several important laws that help protect people from hazardous waste. The Resource Conservation and Recovery Act (RCRA), passed in 1976, established guidelines for managing hazardous waste. It requires the EPA to identify which wastes are hazardous. It also requires the EPA to provide guidelines for safely managing and recycling hazardous wastes.

The second important federal law is called the Superfund Act. This was established in 1980 to help clean up uncontrolled and abandoned toxic waste sites. The U.S. government estimates that there are more than 400,000 hazardous waste sites. These sites include industrial areas, landfills, and military bases. The Superfund Act also supports research into cleaning up mining waste. The government has created a list of the most critical sites to clean up. So far, it estimates that it has cleaned up more than 880 of the worst sites. However, there are still thousands more to go.

The Resource Conservation and Recovery Act and the Superfund Act both help to manage hazardous waste. However, many experts believe that much more needs to be done. People must first reduce the amount of hazardous waste that is produced. You will learn more about this in Lesson 4.

Figure 10.3.2 *The problems at Love Canal helped make people aware of the dangers of hazardous wastes.*

Lesson 3 R E V I E W

On a sheet of paper, write the word from the Word Bank that completes each sentence correctly.

Word Bank
household
mercury
PCBs

1. Heavy metals, acids, pesticides, and _____ are examples of hazardous waste.

2. "Mad as a hatter" is a saying that is linked to poisonous fumes from _____.

3. In many communities, _____ hazardous waste is collected at special sites and disposed of separately.

On a sheet of paper, write the letter of the answer that completes each sentence correctly.

4. Household hazardous waste includes batteries and _____.

   A nail polish   C food waste
   B radioactive waste   D leachate

5. The Superfund Act authorizes the EPA to clean up _____ sites.

   A agricultural   C water pollution
   B toxic waste   D open burning

6. _____ wastes are materials that easily catch fire.

   A Hazardous   B Household   C Industrial   D Ignitable

Critical Thinking

On a sheet of paper, write the answer to each of the following questions. Use complete sentences.

7. What are three reasons that PCBs are considered to be hazardous?

8. What is the difference between toxic and infectious wastes?

9. How should household hazardous waste be handled to protect the environment?

10. Why has the Superfund Act not been able to get rid of all toxic waste sites?

Objectives

After reading this lesson, you should be able to

◆ describe integrated waste management

◆ define source reduction

◆ list two challenges to disposing of hazardous waste

◆ explain three things people are doing to help address solid waste problems

Integrated waste management

Controlling solid waste by using a combination of approaches, including source reduction and recycling

Managing solid waste is a huge challenge for societies everywhere. As you have discovered, many types of waste pollute the environment and affect human health. Producing and disposing of waste also costs a lot of money. With the world population increasing, experts agree that the amount of waste will also increase. How can society best deal with the solid waste problem? In this lesson, you will learn about some creative waste management solutions. You will also learn about actions that everyone can take to responsibly manage waste.

Integrated Waste Management

People have come a long way from tossing trash into the streets. Today, most waste experts recommend using an integrated approach to waste management. **Integrated waste management** is the use of a combination of practices. Each type of waste is managed in the way that is best for people and the environment. Integrated waste management is designed to help waste managers meet environmental regulations and reduce costs. Above all, it is designed to make waste management as safe as possible. This benefits people, wildlife, and ecosystems.

Some people use "the three Rs" as a way to think about waste prevention. This stands for "Reduce, Reuse, and Recycle." Integrated waste management incorporates these three strategies in several ways.

Link to ➤➤➤

Cultures

The United States and European countries are developed nations. However, they differ in the production of solid waste. Each U.S. citizen produces about 2 kilograms of waste per day. The European average is between 1 and 1.5 kilograms per day.

Source Reduction

Source reduction is the most effective waste management strategy. Source reduction simply means generating less waste in the first place. This can be done with changes in the design, manufacturing process, or use of materials. In this way, manufacturers can play a role in reducing waste. When consumers buy products that have less packaging, they also produce less waste. Products that last longer or can be reused also cut down on the amount of waste. For example, if you buy rechargeable batteries, you can help reduce battery waste. Source reduction strategies decrease the amount of waste that ends up in landfills.

Recycling and Composting

After source reduction, recycling and composting are considered the best ways to reduce waste. Composting produces free fertilizer. Recycling helps recover valuable materials from the waste stream. Making products from recycled materials can save both money and natural resources. For example, it takes about 60 percent less energy to make paper from recycled paper than from trees. In addition, using recycled paper can reduce the amount of habitat lost due to logging.

Many experts believe that people can double the amount of waste that is recycled or composted in the next decade. New technologies are being created every year that help make new products from old products. Many companies are also looking at redesigning their products to make them easier to recycle.

Technology and Society

The use of durable goods is one kind of source reduction. Durable goods are manufactured products that are expected to last three years or more. Because they last longer, they take longer to reach the waste stream. The Internet has turned reselling and reusing durable goods into a growing business.

Incineration and Landfills

No matter how much waste is recycled, some will always need to be burned or buried in landfills. Experts are exploring new ways to reduce the risks of dumping and burning waste. For example, new computerized systems can better measure and control the amount of leachate and methane gas produced in landfills. New incineration methods are helping to reduce the amount of toxic materials released into the air.

Disposing of Hazardous Waste

Getting rid of hazardous waste safely is a special challenge. Currently, there are three different ways that hazardous waste can be dealt with. First, the total amount of hazardous waste produced can be reduced. This can be accomplished by finding less hazardous replacements for currently used materials. It can also occur by reusing and recycling hazardous wastes.

The second way to deal with hazardous waste is to change it into something less toxic. Some materials can be spread out on the land. Over time, they will decompose into less harmful materials. Some can be treated chemically or physically to become less hazardous. Still others can be burned in incinerators with special pollution control devices.

The third option for handling hazardous waste is to store it permanently in very secure sites. These sites must not have any leaks. They must be safe from earthquake damage and other disturbances.

Most experts agree that the best options for dealing with hazardous wastes are the first two mentioned above. However, most hazardous waste produced in the U.S. is placed in permanent storage sites. Very few of these sites are considered environmentally safe and secure.

New technologies also hold promise for containing these wastes. For example, burning fabric from old car seats can release toxic materials into the air. The auto industry is now experimenting with ways to dispose of these toxic materials before burning. One method is to use **solvents** that wash out the toxic materials. Solvents are chemicals that dissolve other materials. This makes incineration of these materials safer. It also captures the toxic materials and allows them to be recycled.

Many companies are also selling their hazardous waste to other companies. In some cases, the buyer can use the hazardous waste to make new products or materials. For example, many medical products still contain mercury. Some companies now try to capture the mercury and reuse it. This reduces the amount of mercury that ends up in a landfill.

Science at Work

Environmental Compliance Specialist

Environmental compliance specialists make sure that waste disposal and treatment plants follow laws and guidelines. They observe procedures to assure the safety of the workers and the environment.

Environmental compliance specialists must be skilled in communicating and using computers. They must have critical thinking skills and the ability to do research. Most specialists have a bachelor's degree in engineering, environmental studies, or science. A master's degree or a Ph.D. is required for senior positions.

Environmental compliance specialists work for many different kinds of employers. These include government agencies, private waste-disposal companies, industrial plants, and environmental consulting firms.

Deep-well injection

A process where toxic liquids are pumped into cracks in underground rock layers

Secure chemical landfill

A dump designed specifically for hazardous waste

Many research labs are also looking for new ways to make hazardous waste less toxic. One method they are using is to burn the materials at very high temperatures.

Some waste is considered too toxic to dump in landfills or burn. Many industries use something called **deep-well injection** to get rid of these wastes. The toxic liquids are injected or pumped into cracks and crevices in underground rocks. Although the waste is stored below aquifers, many people are concerned that the waste can leak into water systems. They also worry that this waste can affect the soil.

Secure chemical landfills are another way hazardous waste is stored. These landfills are built in areas where the bedrock is solid. They are lined with special materials and covered with clay to keep water out. They are also monitored to capture any waste before it can leak into the groundwater.

All of these methods have risks. The most important thing that people can do to help manage hazardous waste is to use fewer toxic materials. People can demand that companies use fewer toxic chemicals. Homeowners can also reduce the amount of toxic materials they buy and use.

Research and Write

The EPA created an Office of Environmental Justice in 1992 to help address environmental justice concerns. The environmental justice movement promotes the fair treatment of people of all races, cultures, and incomes regarding environmental policies and regulations. Research this movement and report on some events in its history.

Looking Ahead

There is no perfect solution to the solid waste problem. Integrated waste management is considered the best approach. By relying on the three Rs (Reduce, Reuse, and Recycle), the amount of waste that ends up in the environment can be reduced drastically. Educating the public about the issues is also critical. By encouraging people to buy products that are environmentally friendly, communities can reduce their solid waste problems. In addition, it is important to increase demand for recycled and less toxic materials. Consumers can influence industry to produce safer and less wasteful products.

Science in Your Life

Technology: E-Waste

How many electronic devices do you own? What do you do with the devices and batteries that do not work anymore? Do you just throw them away? If so, you may be polluting the environment with hazardous waste. Electronic devices, large and small, contain a variety of toxic substances. These include heavy metals such as lead and cadmium and organic substances such as PCBs. The older a device is, the greater the potential for danger. With so many electronic devices in the waste stream, they now have their own category: e-waste.

E-waste needs special attention to protect the health of people and the environment. Many countries have passed laws that require the use of safer materials in electronics. New laws have been proposed that require electronics companies to handle e-waste from their products.

Many recycling programs for electronic devices have also been established. Fortunately, many electronic components can be reused when electronic devices are recycled.

1. How do electronic devices pollute the environment?

2. What is a responsible thing to do with electronic devices that no longer work?

Lesson 4   R E V I E W

Word Bank

integrated waste
  management

reuse

source reduction

On a sheet of paper, write the word or words from the Word Bank that complete each sentence correctly.

1. Reducing the amount of waste that enters the waste stream is called _____.

2. The use of a combination of practices to safely handle solid waste is called _____.

3. "Reduce, _____, and recycle" are often called the three Rs of waste prevention.

On a sheet of paper, write the letter of the answer that completes each sentence correctly.

4. All of the following are used in integrated waste management except _____.

    A recycling   **B** composting **C** logging   **D** incineration

5. Deep-well injection is most likely to pollute _____ if the hazardous waste escapes from storage.

    A oceans   **B** food   **C** the air   **D** groundwater

6. Recycling, composting, and source reduction are designed to _____ the amount of waste entering landfills.

    A increase   **B** decrease   **C** report   **D** measure

Critical Thinking

On a sheet of paper, write the answer to each of the following questions. Use complete sentences.

7. If household solid waste is only a small percent of the total waste stream, why should people be concerned about it?

8. List three ways that solid waste disposal could affect you in the next 10 years.

9. Describe two ways that solid waste disposal affects wildlife.

10. Describe three ways that people are working to address solid waste issues.

Materials

- safety goggles
- lab coat or apron
- two 2-liter plastic bottles
- scissors
- gravel
- blue sponge
- plastic grocery bag
- soil
- yellow sponge
- water
- red or green food coloring
- plastic cup

Landfill Design

Modern sanitary landfills are designed to hold garbage safely. A landfill site is designed to help prevent water pollution. Still, some liquids leak from landfills. How? Explore some possible answers by designing and building a model landfill.

Procedure

1. Cut the top one-third off of a plastic bottle. Cut the bottom one-third off of the other plastic bottle. **Safety Alert: Be extremely careful when cutting the plastic bottles with the scissors.** You should be able to assemble the pieces as shown.

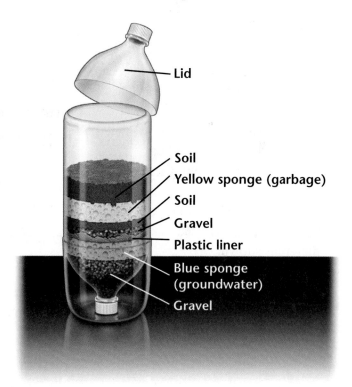

Lid

Soil
Yellow sponge (garbage)
Soil
Gravel
Plastic liner
Blue sponge (groundwater)
Gravel

Continued on next page

2. Cut the sponges to make circular disks that will fit snuggly in a plastic bottle. The yellow sponge stands for garbage and the blue sponge stands for groundwater. From the grocery bag, cut a circle of plastic slightly larger than a bottle's diameter. This stands for a plastic liner in a landfill.

3. Gather the remainder of the materials. Use the diagram of a plastic bottle landfill on page 385 as a guide for making your own model. You can vary the placement and amount of materials. You do not have to use all of the materials.

4. In your lab group, discuss the features of a landfill and their purposes. Speculate about how a landfill could pollute groundwater, as well as ways this could be prevented. Write a hypothesis about how well landfills prevent leachate from escaping that could be tested with an experiment that uses the materials shown.

5. Write a procedure for your experiment. Include Safety Alerts.

6. Have your hypothesis, procedure, and Safety Alerts approved by your teacher. Then carry out your experiment. Record your results.

Cleanup/Disposal
Put away all materials and clean your work area before leaving the lab.

Analysis
1. What were the important differences between your group's landfill models and those of other groups?

2. Compare the leaked liquid that came from each model.

Conclusions
1. Which features of a sanitary landfill help prevent pollution?

2. Why must the leachate from landfills be monitored for many years?

Explore Further
Repeat the experiment using coffee grounds to represent garbage instead of a yellow sponge.

Living with Mining

Mining is one of the largest industries in the United States. It also can be very destructive to the environment. Mining destroys habitats and pollutes the air and water. It also creates almost three-fourths of U.S. solid waste. A large amount of this waste is hazardous waste. Mining releases close to half of all the toxic emissions in some countries. Leftover rock and unusable minerals, called mine tailings, clog and pollute streams and groundwater resources.

There is another side to this issue, however. Almost everything people use contains materials that came from a mine. This includes all metals, all materials for concrete, and all coal used for electricity. Even the food people eat contains minerals that came from a mine. Some of these minerals came from fertilizers used on crops. Others were added to processed foods to make them more nutritious. People's way of life depends on the mining industry. The question then is not whether to mine but how to mine.

Mining companies and the government are working to make mining processes less dangerous and destructive. More than three dozen federal laws and regulations control how minerals are mined and processed. These include the Clean Water Act, Clean Air Act, Endangered Species Act, and RCRA. Mining engineers are developing ways to safely contain hazardous wastes. They are also working with biologists to reclaim land that has been damaged by mining. The photo above is an example of a reclaimed mining site. Recyclers are developing ways to recover and reuse rare and valuable metals. You can help reduce the environmental impact of mining by recycling products that contain useful metals.

1. Why is mining an important industry?

2. What is being done to reduce the impact of mining on the environment?

3. What parts of your life depend the most on mining? Explain.

- Solid wastes are produced by agriculture, industry, mining, and municipal activities.

- The solid waste stream is the flow of waste in society. It includes how waste is created, collected, and disposed of.

- Most solid waste in the United States comes from agricultural, mining, and industrial activities.

- Hazardous waste includes materials that are ignitable, reactive, radioactive, toxic, infectious, and corrosive.

- Solid-waste and hazardous-waste disposal can cause serious problems for human health and the environment.

- Sanitary landfills are more environmentally friendly than open dumps but still take up space. Also, they can contaminate soil and water and harm ecosystems and wildlife.

- Incineration greatly reduces the volume of solid waste. However, it can create serious air pollution problems.

- The Superfund Act was designed to clean up hazardous waste sites across the country. The Resource Conservation and Recovery Act was designed to help manage hazardous and municipal solid waste.

- Recycling and composting remove waste from the waste stream and recover value from waste.

- Three major goals of waste prevention are to reduce, reuse, and recycle.

Vocabulary

aerobic decomposition, 366	household hazardous waste, 362	municipal solid waste, 362	slag, 362
agricultural solid waste, 363	ignitable waste, 374	nonbiodegradable, 361	sludge, 363
biodegradable, 361	incinerator, 368	open dump, 365	smelting, 362
corrosive waste, 374	industrial solid waste, 363	ore, 362	solid waste, 360
deep-well injection, 382	infectious waste, 375	PCBs, 374	solvent, 380
fly ash, 363	integrated waste management, 378	reactive waste, 374	source reduction, 379
hazardous waste, 360	leachate, 366	sanitary landfill, 365	synthetic, 361
heavy metal, 366		secure chemical landfill, 382	waste stream, 360

Word Bank

- aerobic decomposition
- agricultural solid waste
- deep-well injection
- hazardous waste
- heavy metals
- household hazardous waste
- incinerator
- integrated waste management
- leachate
- municipal solid waste
- nonbiodegradable
- open dump
- radioactive waste
- sludge
- smelting
- solid waste
- source reduction
- synthetic

Vocabulary Review

On a sheet of paper, write the word or words from the Word Bank that complete each sentence correctly.

1. In _____, toxic materials are pumped deep underground for storage.

2. Any waste that is harmful to people, living things, and the environment is called _____.

3. Less than 3 percent of the solid waste stream is made up of _____.

4. Nail polish, pesticides, paint thinner, and bleach are all examples of _____.

5. Mining operations use _____ plants to heat metal ores and remove the impurities.

6. A(n) _____ can be used to generate electricity by burning trash.

7. The liquid waste that can seep out from sanitary landfills is called _____.

8. Animal manure, leftover crops, and pesticides are some of the major types of _____.

9. Solid waste from sewage treatment plants is called _____.

10. In a(n) _____, waste is dumped without environmental controls.

11. A product of nuclear reactions called _____ is hazardous to all living things.

12. Decomposition that takes place with oxygen is called _____.

13. The three Rs of _____ prevention stand for "Reduce, Reuse, and Recycle."

14. Mercury, lead, copper, and arsenic are all examples of _____.

Continued on next page

15. Using a variety of approaches to manage solid waste, including recycling, composting, and source reduction, is called _____.

16. The most effective way to reduce the amount of waste in the solid waste stream is through _____.

17. Living things cannot break down plastic bottles, synthetic clothing and material, or aluminum cans. Therefore, these items are all examples of _____ waste.

18. Materials that are _____ are created by humans.

Concept Review

On a sheet of paper, write the letter of the answer that completes each sentence correctly.

19. Incineration greatly reduces the _____ of solid waste.

   A chemical content   **B** cost   **C** types   **D** volume

20. All of the following are considered a type of solid waste except _____.

   A food scraps and nail polish
   B cigarette smoke and ozone
   C cardboard boxes and soda cans
   D newspapers and old furniture

21. Most of the municipal solid waste produced in the United States is disposed of by _____.

   A burning   **C** burying in landfills
   B recycling   **D** dumping in the ocean

22. If your pants are made of 50 percent cotton, 40 percent polyester, and 10 percent nylon, the percentage of biodegradable materials is _____.

   A 10 percent   **C** 50 percent
   B 40 percent   **D** 60 percent

Critical Thinking

On a sheet of paper, write the answer to each of the following questions. Use complete sentences.

23. How could your shopping habits now affect the quality of the environment 50 years from now?

24. Describe the benefits of buying a recycled product over a product made from raw materials.

25. Recall the issue of environmental justice, discussed in Chapter 1. Explain how solid waste disposal can be an environmental justice issue.

Test-Taking Tip Answer all questions you are sure of first. Then go back and answer the others.

Chapter

11 Feeding the World

The colorful Indian corn seen here was a staple food of American pioneers. Like wheat and rice, corn is the fruit of a grasslike plant. All three are nutritious grains. In fact, corn, wheat, and rice are the most important food crops in the world. Corn and wheat are also fed to livestock grown for meat and milk. In Chapter 11, you will learn how modern agriculture and aquaculture help feed the world. You will also learn how agricultural practices can harm the environment. Finally, you will learn about current sustainable agricultural practices.

Organize Your Thoughts

Agriculture

Industrialized agriculture
- Plantation agriculture
- Feedlot
- Rangeland

Sustainable agriculture
- Organic farming
- Local agriculture
- Shade-grown coffee
- Sustainable animal production

Goals for Learning

◆ To understand the environmental impacts of agriculture

◆ To describe the causes and impacts of soil erosion

◆ To explain how the world food supply is distributed and some problems this causes

◆ To describe sustainable approaches to agriculture

◆ To describe current trends in world fisheries

393

Draft animal

A horse or other large animal that pulls farm equipment

Origins of Agriculture

As you learned in Chapter 1, humans were hunter-gatherers for thousands of years. They hunted animals for meat. They gathered fruits, nuts, and plants. They moved with the seasons to follow their sources of food. These practices changed with the beginning of agriculture about 11,000 years ago.

From the beginning, agriculture changed the natural environment. People needed space for growing crops. As a result, they burned or cut down trees and other native plants. The animals they raised, or livestock, also needed space and food. Soon livestock were using many areas once dominated by wildlife.

Agriculture also changed how people lived. They could now settle in permanent or semipermanent communities. Human populations quickly increased in size.

Subsistence Agriculture

Two major forms of agriculture are practiced around the globe. The first is called subsistence agriculture. As you learned in Chapter 6, subsistence agriculture means growing enough food to meet a family's immediate needs. Subsistence agriculture has changed very little for thousands of years. Farmers use the sun, their own labor, and **draft animals** to grow food. Draft animals are horses, oxen, and other large animals that can pull farming equipment.

Subsistence agriculture is the main type of agriculture practiced in developing nations. In some places, its impact on the environment is small. In other places, subsistence agriculture threatens rare habitats and species. For example, villagers in the tropics may cut down valuable forests when they need more farmland.

Subsistence agriculture often includes raising livestock. In some places, livestock may compete with wild animals for food. Wild goats and sheep in Tibet are threatened by competition from **domesticated** goats and sheep. Domesticated animals have been bred for human use. Snow leopards and other local predators are also threatened by this competition. As their usual prey declines, they will often prey on domesticated animals. Ranchers may then kill these predators to protect their livestock. In these and other ways, subsistence agriculture can reduce biodiversity.

Industrialized Agriculture

The second kind of agriculture, **industrialized agriculture,** is most common in industrialized nations. Industrialized agriculture uses machinery such as tractors and plows. This consumes fossil fuel energy in addition to energy from people, animals, and the sun. Industrialized agriculture also makes use of other materials and methods. These include fertilizers, pesticides, and irrigation.

Industrialized agriculture is very efficient. It greatly increases the size of a harvest, or **crop yield.** Fewer farm workers and less land are needed to grow more food. About 11 percent of the earth's land area is used for farming. An additional 25 percent is used for **pasture,** where livestock can graze. These numbers would be higher without advances in agricultural efficiency.

Still, industrialized agriculture has many environmental impacts. It uses huge amounts of fossil fuels. The energy you receive from the food you eat requires 10 times more energy to produce. This fossil fuel use causes air, water, and land pollution.

Industrialized agriculture also requires large amounts of water. More than 80 percent of the water consumed in the United States is used for agriculture. Heavy water use can reduce surface water and groundwater supplies.

Chemical fertilizers and pesticides also present many threats to people and wildlife. They can cause health problems for the farm workers who use them. They can also run off into local water supplies, causing pollution and harming wildlife. For example, agricultural runoff has caused huge **dead zones** in the Gulf of Mexico. A dead zone is an area of water with almost no living organisms. These dead zones are caused by fertilizers flowing down the Mississippi River. The fertilizers cause an overgrowth of algae. When the algae die, they are broken down by bacteria. In the process, the bacteria consume most of the available oxygen. Fish swim away. Organisms that cannot move will die. In 2001, scientists found that the dead zone in the Gulf was about the size of Massachusetts. You can see the extent of this dead zone in Figure 11.1.1.

Figure 11.1.1 *The dead zone in the Gulf of Mexico is an area where marine organisms cannot survive.*

Another part of industrialized agriculture is **plantation agriculture.** In plantation agriculture, single crops are grown on a large scale to export to industrialized nations. The bananas, coffee, and cocoa consumed by your family probably came from tropical plantations. These plantations have often replaced tropical forests. They generate pollution that reaches freshwater and marine ecosystems. Chemicals used on banana plantations, for example, can end up causing problems for nearby coral reefs.

Feedlot

A small area where large numbers of livestock are raised together

Rangeland

Grass-covered land that animals can graze on

Soil erosion

The movement of soil from one place to another

Industrial Animal Production

Part of industrialized agriculture includes raising large numbers of animals for food. In many cases, thousands of animals are raised together in small areas called **feedlots.** These feedlots create a lot of pollution. North Carolina, for example, has many large-scale hog farms. Together, these hogs produce over 45,000 metric tons of waste a year. This waste can pollute local rivers, wetlands, and coastal areas.

Other times, animals graze on **rangeland.** Rangeland is fenced or unfenced land where livestock feed on native grasses. In some parts of the world, heavy grazing by livestock has damaged native vegetation. It has also caused severe **soil erosion,** especially around rivers and streams where the animals drink. Soil erosion is the movement of soils. You will learn more about soils and soil erosion in Lesson 2.

Achievements in Science

Industrialized Agriculture

Throughout most of human history, farming depended on the work of the farmer, and perhaps some animals, to power the efforts. That all changed in the early 1800s. During this time, the Industrial Revolution spread into farming. New machines were invented to help farmers plant and harvest crops.

For example, in the 1830s, Cyrus McCormick invented the McCormick reaper. This machine allowed two workers to harvest more grain than a crew of 10 workers could by hand. Improvements on the McCormick reaper allowed farmers to continue to increase their crop yields with less work. Modern versions of the McCormick reaper can cut and process 50 acres of grain in a day.

Word Bank

dead zone

feedlot

rangeland

On a sheet of paper, write the word or words from the Word Bank that complete each sentence correctly.

1. A _____ is an area in the ocean that contains no life.

2. Some animals graze on native grasses on _____, which can be fenced or unfenced.

3. A small area where many animals are raised is called a _____.

On a sheet of paper, write the letter of the answer that completes each sentence correctly.

4. _____ agriculture makes use of machines and fossil fuels.

    A Solar   **B** Industrialized   **C** Subsistence   **D** Animal

5. A(n) _____ is an example of a draft animal.

    A rabbit   **B** grasshopper   **C** hawk   **D** ox

6. Heavy grazing by animals can cause _____.

    A dead zones   **C** crop yields

    B soil erosion   **D** subsistence agriculture

Critical Thinking

On a sheet of paper, write your answers to the following questions. Use complete sentences.

7. What are the advantages and disadvantages of industrialized agriculture?

8. A classmate says that fertilizers should not cause dead zones in oceans, since fertilizers help plants grow. How would you explain the cause of dead zones to this person?

9. Describe how early agriculture affected the environment.

10. Compare and contrast the impact that feedlots and rangelands have on the environment. Which do you think is less damaging?

After reading this lesson, you should be able to

◆ explain how soil forms

◆ describe soil erosion and its environmental impacts

◆ name several ways to reduce soil erosion

Parent material

The material from which soil first forms

Bedrock

The solid layer of rock beneath soil and other loose materials

Weathering

The process by which bedrock is broken down into small particles

Between 1890 and 1934, several major droughts struck the midwestern United States. The ground became dry and dusty. During previous droughts, native grasses had helped hold the soil in place. Now, though, many areas had been cleared for farming or grazed heavily by livestock. Strong winds blew the dry soil off the land and into the air. Enormous dust clouds darkened the sky. This period became known as the Dust Bowl. Winds carried the dirt so far east it landed on ships in the Atlantic Ocean. Concern grew over how much soil was blowing off the land. Soil erosion has been a major concern ever since. It affects both agricultural productivity and the health of Earth's ecosystems.

What Is Soil?

You have probably walked across a dirt field or muddy path. Have you ever thought about what you are walking on? Soil forms the topmost layer of the earth. It is about one to two meters thick and consists of many things. It contains inorganic materials such as clay, silt, and sand. It contains decaying organic matter. It contains water and air. Finally, it contains living organisms such as earthworms, insects, and microorganisms.

It takes a very long time for soil to form. This process begins with **parent material.** Parent material can consist of **bedrock,** the solid layer of rock beneath the soil. It can also consist of deposits from volcanoes, glaciers, and other sources. Over time, this parent material breaks down into smaller particles. This is called **weathering.** As you learned in Chapter 3, dead plants and animals also decay into the soil. This process adds nutrient-rich organic material to the mix. Living animals, such as bacteria, fungi, and moles, are also important in soil formation. They help mix and enrich the soil.

Horizon
A layer of soil

O horizon
The topmost layer of soil; also called humus

A horizon
The second layer of soil, made up of decaying organic material, living things, and inorganic particles; also called topsoil

Porosity
The percentage of a volume of soil that is empty space

Loam
A soil made up of clay, silt, and sand; considered best for growing crops

Scientists divide soil into several layers, called **horizons.** The top layer is called the **O horizon.** It contains newly fallen and partially decayed leaves, twigs, and other organic waste. If you raked a forest floor, you would pull up parts of the O horizon. The O horizon is mostly humus. The next layer is called the **A horizon,** or topsoil. Topsoil is a mixture of living organisms, inorganic mineral particles, and humus. Humus is rich in nutrients that can be taken up by plants. That is why the roots of most plants grow in the O and A horizons.

Below the O and A horizons lie the E, B, and C horizons. These layers have more minerals and less organic material than the O and A layers. The final soil layer goes by the letter R. It is the solid layer of bedrock underneath all soils. As you know, parts of this bedrock layer are always weathering into new soil. See Figure 11.2.1 for a diagram of these different layers of soil.

Healthy, nutrient-rich soils are the best for growing crops. These fertile soils usually have a thick layer of topsoil with lots of humus. They are usually dark brown or black in color. The prairie regions of the United States have dark soils. Less fertile soils are often yellow, gray, or red.

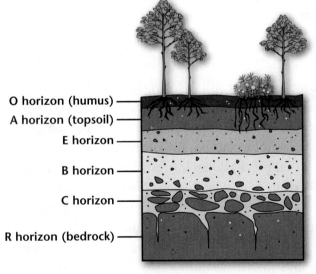

O horizon (humus)
A horizon (topsoil)
E horizon
B horizon
C horizon
R horizon (bedrock)

Figure 11.2.1 *Soil is divided into six different layers, called horizons.*

Different soils vary in depth. They have different levels of acidity. They also have different levels of **porosity.** Porosity is the percentage of a volume of soil that is empty space. Medium porous soils, called **loams,** are best for growing crops. The spaces between the particles can hold good amounts of water and air. If the spaces were larger, the water would drain out. If the spaces were smaller, the water and air could not get in.

Soil Erosion

Soil moves all the time, mostly because of the action of wind and water. Wind blows dry topsoil off a field. A heavy rain washes soil down a hillside. Any movement of soil can be defined as soil erosion. Certain conditions, though, make soil erosion worse. For example, wind erosion is especially bad on flat, sandy land. Wind and water erosion can be severe on steep slopes. That is why many mountain regions have thin, rocky soils. Soil erosion is also worse where vegetation has been cleared. Normally, plants help hold soil in place. When plants are removed, soil moves more easily.

Map Skills: Soil Types

Soil is not the same everywhere. For example, the red clay soil of Georgia is very different from the dark brown soil of Wisconsin. However, soils can differ greatly even within a state.

The map below shows the different types of soil that have been classified in the United States. To classify the soils, scientists first take samples. Then they examine the particle sizes, amount and type of organic materials, and the characteristics of each layer of the soil. These characteristics help determine the type of soil. These soils are grouped into orders. The names of the orders of soil are found in the legend.

LEGEND			
Alfisols	Entisols	Mollisols	Utisols
Aridsols	Inceptisols	Spodosols	Mountains

1. How many different types of soil classifications are recognized in the United States?

2. Name two states with similar soils.

3. Why do you think that soils with the same classification are grouped together in one large area?

Siltation

The buildup of soil in aquatic ecosystems

No-till farming

Leaving the soil undisturbed as a new crop is planted

Till

To plow up the soil

Contour farming

Planting crops around the contours of the land rather than in straight rows

Shelterbelt

A row of trees planted to help block wind

Link to ≻≻≻

Arts

Ancient human cultures used different soils to make pigments for paints. Many artists still use soils as art material.

Soil washes off the land and builds up in freshwater and marine ecosystems. This is called **siltation.** Siltation makes water less clear. It can make it difficult for aquatic animals to get oxygen. It can make it harder for some aquatic plants to grow.

Loss of topsoil is also a major concern for agriculture. It can take thousands of years for a few centimeters of topsoil to form. Yet many areas are losing a few centimeters of topsoil every 10 years or less. Without thick layers of nutrient-rich soils, it is much harder to grow crops. Irrigation and fertilizers can help grow crops in places that have lost topsoil. Yet many people believe this is not a good long-term solution to soil erosion.

Soil erosion is a big problem where forests have been cleared. From mountain slopes to tropical forests, large-scale deforestation can leave soils unstable and less fertile. Mud slides are also more common where hillsides have been cleared of trees and other vegetation.

Reducing Soil Erosion

Ever since the Dust Bowl, farmers have taken steps to reduce soil erosion. For example, some farmers use **no-till farming** to preserve topsoil. Most farmers **till** the soil, or plow it up before planting. However, tilling makes soil more likely to erode. No-till farming leaves the soil undisturbed as a new crop is planted. In **contour farming,** crops are not planted in straight rows. Instead, the rows curve around the contours of the land. This reduces soil erosion, keeps the soil more fertile, and prevents water waste. Farmers can also plant rows of trees, called **shelterbelts,** to cut down on wind erosion.

Farmers are not the only people who can help prevent soil erosion. For example, foresters and landowners can avoid cutting down trees on steep slopes. Property owners can maintain plants along lakes and streams to stabilize soils.

The condition of soils affects the health of ecosystems and the success of food production. In Lesson 4, you will learn more about agricultural practices designed to maintain healthy and stable soils.

Word Bank

horizon

porosity

weathering

On a sheet of paper, write the word from the Word Bank that completes each sentence correctly.

1. The percentage of empty space in a volume of soil is known as _____.

2. Soil is divided into layers, each called a _____.

3. When _____ occurs, organic and inorganic materials break down into smaller particles.

Critical Thinking

On a sheet of paper, write your answers to the following questions. Use complete sentences.

4. List the soil horizons in order from the surface to the deepest. Then write a short description of each horizon.

5. What recommendations would you give a farmer for reducing soil erosion?

Express Lab 11

Materials

◆ tray

◆ soil

◆ pencil

◆ watering can

Procedure

1. Create two mounds of soil in the tray. Make sure the mounds are as similar as possible, with the same height and the same slope.

2. Use the pencil to "plow" rows on each pile. On the first mound, make rows that are parallel to the slope, following the contours of the mound. On the second mound, make rows that are perpendicular to the slope.

3. Sprinkle both slopes with the same amount of water from the watering can. Observe the soil that collects at the bottom of each mound.

Analysis

1. Which mound eroded the most?

2. How does contour farming help reduce erosion?

INVESTIGATION 11

Materials

- safety goggles
- lab coat or apron
- sandy soil
- clay soil
- potting soil
- variety of soil sifters
- magnifying glass
- paper towels
- plastic tray

How Are Soils Different?

You probably do not think about the soil under your feet very often. However, soil is a very important resource. We grow our food in it and plant trees and flowers in it. Are soils really that different from place to place? What different properties do they have? In this lab, you will find out.

Procedure

1. Put on safety goggles and a lab coat or apron. **Safety Alert: Do not rub your eyes if your fingers are dirty.**

2. Get a cup of the sandy soil.

3. Pass the soil through the coarsest sifter (the one with the largest holes). Be sure to put a paper towel underneath to catch the soil that passes through.

4. Place what the sifter keeps in a pile on the tray.

5. Use the soil that passed through the sifter and pass it through the next finer sifter. Again, place what the sifter keeps in a pile on the tray.

6. Repeat Step 5 using the next finest sifter. You should have several piles of soil sorted by particle size.

7. Examine the particles in each pile. Record your observations.

8. Repeat Steps 3–7 for the clay soil and the potting soil. Make notes on what you observe in each sample, as well as the amount of soil that sifts out at different sizes.

Cleanup/Disposal

Dispose of your soil samples according to your teacher's instructions. Make sure your work surface is clean.

Analysis

1. How did the particle size of the potting soil compare to the particle sizes of the sandy soil and the clay soil?

2. What other differences did you observe between the soils?

Conclusions

1. What relationship did you find between the size and type of soil particles and how well plants grow in the soil?

2. How easy would it be for water to move through the different types of soil? How might that affect what plants can grow in each type of soil?

Explore Further

Collect a soil sample from your yard or outside your school. Run your sample through the soil sifters and examine it with the magnifying glass. Which type of soil does it most closely resemble?

World food supply

The amount of food available for the world's population

Edible

Able to be safely eaten

Green Revolution

A large increase in crop yields achieved by developing new varieties of plants

World Food Supply

How much food is there in the world? What kind of food is it? Does it meet the nutritional needs of the world's people? These are all questions people ask about the **world food supply.** The world food supply is the amount of food available for Earth's human inhabitants.

There are more than 80,000 species of **edible** plants. Edible means that something can be safely eaten. Yet just four crops supply most of the food people eat. These crops are corn, wheat, rice, and potatoes. The rest of the foods people eat include fish, shellfish, meat, and animal products. Eggs, milk, butter, and cheese are all examples of animal products.

You might think that there simply is not enough food to feed Earth's growing population. This is not the case. Advances in agriculture have helped food production keep up with population growth.

One of these advances was called the **Green Revolution.** The Green Revolution was a big increase in crop yields mostly due to breeding new plant varieties. Botanists would breed one crop plant with a closely related wild plant. They tried to develop traits that would make the plants grow better under local conditions. This led to huge increases in crop yields in Mexico and the United States between 1950 and 1970.

In 1967, the Green Revolution spread throughout the developing world. Special varieties of rice and wheat were introduced to many tropical countries. These varieties could produce crop yields three to five times higher than traditional varieties.

Many people believe these advances in agriculture are some of human society's greatest achievements. The world's population has grown exponentially. Yet food production has, too. Imagine that all the world's food were divided equally among its people. If it were, everyone would receive more than enough food to stay alive.

Kilocalorie

1,000 calories; referred to as a calorie in everyday usage

Calorie

The unit of heat needed to raise one gram of water one degree Celsius

Protein

A chemical used by cells to grow and work

Fat

A chemical that stores large amounts of energy

Carbohydrate

A sugar or starch that living things use for energy

Iron

A mineral that helps move oxygen through the bloodstream

Calcium

A mineral important for teeth, muscles, and bone growth

Vitamin C

A vitamin that supports health and growth

Food is not evenly distributed among the people on Earth, however. For this reason, millions of people are hungry. Worldwide, about one person in seven does not get enough food to be healthy.

Dietary Requirements

Human beings need to eat a certain amount and quality of food to stay healthy. How much food they need depends on their size and activity level. On average, adults need to eat about 2,200 **kilocalories** (kcals) a day. In science, a **calorie** is a unit of heat. It is the amount of heat needed to raise a gram of water one degree Celsius. A kilocalorie equals 1,000 of these small calories. You have probably heard people talk about the calories in the food they eat. What they are really talking about are kilocalories.

In addition to water, people need three main forms of foods in their diets. These are **proteins, fats,** and **carbohydrates.** Proteins are chemicals largely found in meat and meat products. They are considered the building blocks of the human body. Fats are chemicals that store a lot of energy. They also help transport certain vitamins through the body. Food sources with fats include animal fats such as butter, as well as vegetable oils. Carbohydrates are sugars and starches found in breads, cereals, fruits, and vegetables.

People also need nutrients, such as **iron, calcium,** and **vitamin C.** The mineral iron helps move oxygen through the blood. Calcium is a mineral important for teeth, muscles, and bone growth. Vitamin C is one of many vitamins that help support health and growth. All these nutrients are found in different kinds of food.

Science Myth

Myth: Eating fats will make you fat.

Fact: Fats are essential to a healthy diet. However, fats do contain more calories than proteins and carbohydrates. This means you should limit how much fat you eat.

Nutritional needs can be different for everyone. Visit the U.S. Department of Agriculture's MyPyramid online to determine how much of each type of food you should be eating.

Malnutrition

Many people do not get enough food or nutrients to meet their daily needs. As you learned in Chapter 6, this is called malnutrition. When human bodies suffer from malnutrition, they slow down. They are also more likely to get diseases. The most basic form of malnutrition is **protein-calorie malnutrition.** That means that someone is not getting enough fats, proteins, or carbohydrates.

Science in Your Life

Consumer Choices: Types of Fats

Fats can contribute to obesity, high cholesterol, and heart disease. Cholesterol is a fatlike substance that can build up in arteries and slow or stop the flow of blood. However, some fats are not as damaging. Many fats are even healthy for you. Fats are classified into three categories:

• **Saturated fats** are the most harmful. They are usually found in meats and baked items such as cookies and cakes. Coconut oil and palm oil are also saturated fats. You should limit the amount of saturated fats in your diet as much as possible. They can raise your level of cholesterol and lead to health problems.

• **Polyunsaturated fats** are found in plants and fish. They are generally good for your body and can help reduce your cholesterol level. Foods that contain polyunsaturated fats include fish, walnuts, almonds, and corn and sunflower oils.

• **Monounsaturated fats** also come from plants. They can help your body by raising the levels of HDL, or good cholesterol. This helps rid your body of LDL, the cholesterol that can damage your body. Monounsaturated fats are found in foods such as olives, peanuts, and canola oil.

1. How are saturated fats different from monounsaturated fats?

2. List foods you have eaten in the past few days that contained saturated fats, polyunsaturated fats, or monounsaturated fats.

Anemia

A blood condition that can result from lack of iron

Overnutrition

Eating too many calories, especially fats and sugars

Famine

When large numbers of people in an area are hungry due to a natural disaster or war

Link to >>>

Physics

The mineral iron listed on an iron-fortified box of cereal is the same metal iron that is used to make automobiles. Iron is added as tiny, thin flakes to food. You can actually attract the iron in a bowl of breakfast cereal by breaking the cereal into fine bits and slowly swirling a magnet through it.

Other forms of malnutrition are actually more common than protein-calorie malnutrition. Iron deficiency is the most common form of malnutrition. **Anemia** is a blood condition that can result from not getting enough iron. People with anemia are usually tired. Anemia can also harm children's mental development. Another common form of malnutrition is vitamin A deficiency. Vitamin A deficiency makes someone more likely to get sick. It also leads to blindness in many children.

Malnutrition causes about 10 million deaths each year. Malnourished people die from hunger or illnesses made worse by hunger. About half of these are children under the age of five.

Most people suffering from malnutrition live in developing nations. A more common problem in industrialized nations is **overnutrition.** Overnutrition means eating too many calories, especially fats and sugars. Overnutrition leads to obesity, which you learned about in Chapter 6. People with obesity experience higher rates of many diseases, as well. These include heart disease, diabetes, and high blood pressure.

In recent years, overnutrition has begun to affect as many people worldwide as malnutrition. In the United States, more than 64 percent of adults are overweight or obese. Obesity now affects nearly one-third of all Americans.

Fighting Hunger

Some people suffering from malnutrition are living through a **famine.** During a famine, large numbers of people in a particular place do not have enough food. Famines result from natural disasters, such as droughts, or from war. When a famine occurs, aid organizations respond with donations of food. Food aid is one solution to a short-term problem.

Most hungry people around the world are not experiencing a famine. Their hunger is a long-term problem caused by poverty. Increasing food production helps address it. Yet this does not solve unequal access to food. For this reason, addressing world hunger requires the input of political leaders, scientists, economists, and many others.

Lesson 3   R E V I E W

Word Bank
calcium
calorie
famine

On a sheet of paper, write the word from the Word Bank that completes each sentence correctly.

1. A _____ is the unit of heat needed to raise a gram of water one degree Celsius.

2. During a _____, many people in an area are unable to get enough food because of a natural disaster or war.

3. Bone growth requires the mineral _____.

On a sheet of paper, write the letter of the answer that completes each sentence correctly.

4. Sugars and starches are the main kinds of _____.

   A fats   **C** proteins
   B carbohydrates   **D** nutrients

5. Lack of iron causes a condition called _____.

   A anemia   **B** blindness   **C** gout   **D** starvation

6. People whose diets contain too many calories experience _____.

   A hunger   **B** malnutrition   **C** anemia   **D** overnutrition

Critical Thinking

On a sheet of paper, write your answers to the following questions. Use complete sentences.

7. What was the Green Revolution?

8. Name one food source for each of the following: protein, fat, carbohydrate.

9. What are some of the health risks associated with overnutrition?

10. Why is hunger a problem that involves politicians and other people besides scientists?

Materials

◆ paper and pencil
◆ variety of food labels

Using Food Labels for Better Nutrition

How do you know exactly what you are eating? Read the labels. Almost every food product you buy has a nutrition label on the package that tells you what it contains. How can you use food labels to monitor your diet and maintain good health? You can design a lab to find out.

Procedure

1. Examine several food labels. In your lab group, discuss the different parts of the labels. Include the list of ingredients, the nutrition information, and the calories per serving.

Nutrition Facts

Serving Size 2 bars (42g)
Servings Per Container 6

Amount Per Serving	2 bars		1 bar	
Calories	180		90	
Calories from Fat	50		25	
		% DV*		% DV*
Total Fat	6g	9%	3g	5%
Saturated Fat	0.5g	3%	0g	0%
Cholesterol	0mg	0%	0mg	0%
Sodium	160mg	7%	80mg	3%
Total Carbohydrate	29g	10%	15g	5%
Dietary Fiber	2g	8%	1g	4%
Sugars	11g		6g	
Protein	4g		2g	
Iron		6%		2%

Not a significant source of vitamin A, vitamin C and calcium.

*Percent Daily Values are based on a 2,000 calorie diet. Your daily values may be higher or lower depending on your calorie needs:

	Calories:	2,000	2,500
Total Fat	Less than	65g	80g
Sat Fat	Less than	20g	25g
Cholesterol	Less than	300mg	300mg
Sodium	Less than	2,400mg	2,400mg
Total Carbohydrate		300g	375g
Dietary Fiber		25g	30g

Continued on next page

2. Write a hypothesis about how you can use food labels and other nutrition information to improve your nutrition.

3. Write a procedure to test your hypothesis. You may want to carry out your procedure over a week as you track the nutrition of your diet. Have your hypothesis, procedure, and any Safety Alerts approved by your teacher.

4. Carry out your procedure. Record your results.

Cleanup/Disposal

Return any packaged food and labels as directed by your teacher.

Analysis

1. How many calories did you consume during the day? How many are recommended?

2. Make a data table or graph that shows how much protein, carbohydrates, fat, and fiber are recommended and how much you consumed.

3. What is likely to happen to someone who regularly eats more calories than is recommended? What is likely to happen to someone who regularly eats fewer calories than is recommended?

Conclusions

1. How did your diet compare to the recommended daily allowances?

2. What nutrients did you not get enough of in your daily diet?

3. In what ways could you improve your diet?

Explore Further

Write a description of three fast-food meals. Use the Internet or other research to obtain nutrition information about these foods. How would a daily diet of fast food compare to the daily recommended allowances?

Sustainable agriculture

Ways of producing food for current generations that do not deprive future generations

As you learned in Lesson 1, increases in food production have come with many costs. Many farming practices pollute the air and water. Many cause soil erosion. Many cause a loss of biodiversity. Industrialized agriculture also has social and economic costs. In the United States, many small family farms have gone out of business. Families have lost their sources of income and rural communities have lost a way of life.

Many people believe that today's farming practices are not sustainable. What happens when agriculture is not sustainable? History offers some examples. Experts believe that several ancient civilizations collapsed because of agricultural practices. These practices damaged the natural environment. Eventually, people could no longer grow the food they needed to survive.

A Sustainable Approach

In recent years, the idea of **sustainable agriculture** has been gaining support. In Chapter 1, you learned about a sustainable society. Sustainable agriculture is part of that. Its goal is to produce food for current generations while leaving resources for future generations. It seeks to support three areas at once. They include environmental, economic, and social health. You will learn more about these areas in Chapter 13.

Sustainable agriculture also looks at the whole of agriculture instead of just individual parts. How is a farm affected by agricultural practices? How is the local ecosystem affected? How are human communities affected both locally and globally? Sustainable agriculture takes these questions into consideration.

Say a group of farmers was thinking about using a new pesticide. Their first question might be how that pesticide would help the crops. Thinking more broadly, they might ask whether the pesticide would affect local biodiversity. They might also consider how making, using, and disposing of the pesticide would affect people around the world.

Organic farming

Growing produce without the use of chemicals

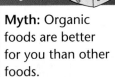
In sustainable agriculture, people try to use fewer resources, such as water and fossil fuels. They try to limit use of pesticides and other toxic chemicals. They try to prevent soil erosion. They also try to grow crops while still maintaining habitat for wildlife. The following four movements reflect all of these trends.

Organic Farming

Perhaps you have seen fruits or vegetables at the grocery store labeled "organic." **Organic farming** means the produce has been grown without chemicals. Organic growers treat the soil as a living organism. They do not want to damage it and then add chemicals to fix it. Instead, they try to keep it healthy. For example, a healthy soil has many insects. Predator insects keep pest insects from growing out of control. Organic farmers support predator populations instead of using pesticides. They may even bring in more ladybugs and other insects.

In general, growing food organically requires more work. Yet it is less damaging to natural ecosystems and may even produce healthier crops. In the United States, organic produce is becoming more and more popular. The U.S. government uses labels to let consumers know which products were grown organically.

Local Agriculture

Many people buy their food without ever seeing the farm where it came from. In fact, supermarkets carry food that has been imported from all over the world. Imported food usually provides much more variety than local food. New Yorkers, for example, can eat oranges in winter thanks to imports from Florida. Canadians can eat bananas thanks to imports from the tropics.

Research and Write

What guidelines must be met before food can be labeled as organic? Research what the government requires from organic growers. Find and describe some examples of how organic food is grown compared to regular food. If possible, provide examples of organic and nonorganic versions of the same food. Have a taste test.

Imported food has many benefits. Yet it also comes with certain costs. It can be very expensive to transport food long distances. The food must be carefully stored along the way. Often it must be kept cold or even frozen. Travel, storage, and cooling all require the use of fossil fuels. You can read more about these and other aspects of food transportation and production in Appendix D, found on pages 508 to 510.

For all these reasons, locally grown food is becoming more popular. Usually, this food comes from nearby farming communities. It is typically sold in local markets or **farmers markets.** Farmers markets are places where local farmers come together to sell their produce. The produce is fresher and often less expensive than store-bought food.

Other times, people obtain their food through **community-supported agriculture.** In community-supported agriculture, people sign up to receive deliveries of produce from local farms. They usually make a single payment each season. The farmer decides how much and what kind of food members receive. Sometimes members even volunteer on the farm. Community-supported agriculture gives farmers a dependable income each year. Members usually receive plenty of food. Still, they share the risks of a bad growing season with the farmer. In this way, they become more aware of local farming issues.

Getting food from nearby farms is not the only way to obtain locally grown produce. Many cities are turning unused lots into gardens for fruits and vegetables. These gardens allow city residents to grow their own food. They often give city residents access to fresher, healthier food than local markets supply.

Shade-Grown Coffee

In Lesson 1, you learned about plantation agriculture. Some people interested in sustainable agriculture are trying to address the problems of plantation agriculture. The effort to promote **shade-grown coffee** is one example of their work.

Until 1970, most coffee was shade-grown. This means it was grown in the shade of tropical trees. Then, pressure for greater production caused a switch to sun-grown coffee. Millions of square kilometers of tropical forest were cleared. Songbirds, monkeys, and many other animals lost their habitat. Sun-grown coffee also required many more pesticides and fertilizers. This threatened the health of workers and local ecosystems.

Concern about these issues has led to a renewed interest in shade-grown coffee. This method helps protect wildlife habitat. Soil quality is improved. Labels on shade-grown coffee allow consumers to choose it. Though often more expensive, shade-grown coffee provides many social and ecological benefits.

Science at Work

Farmer

No matter what you ate today, you can probably thank a farmer for it. Farmers grow almost all the food that people eat. Meat and milk products, too, are possible only because of the animal feed provided by farmers.

A farmer must work long hours and have many skills. Most farmers learn skills passed on from their family or others in the farming business. They must be knowledgeable in all areas of growing, harvesting, and preparing crops for transporting. They must also maintain their machinery.

As farms grow larger and larger, a farmer must be a skilled manager. Both a bachelor's degree in business and work experience can be useful to learn how to manage farm operations. Most farmers must manage a large staff of workers and equipment. They must also be able to work with suppliers and other business partners. Farmers are constantly learning new growing and cultivating methods. They typically work together with extension agents and other experts to ensure successful growing seasons.

Sustainable Animal Production

As you learned in Lesson 1, industrial agriculture raises large numbers of animals in a small space. Yet doing so can lead to overgrazing, soil erosion, and water pollution. Sustainable animal production looks closely at how animals affect the local ecosystem. Limiting the numbers of grazing animals can prevent damage to local vegetation. Raising animals outside of feedlots can make them healthier and reduce pollution.

Many people also believe more farms should raise both crops and animals together. Animal manure can then be used as a crop fertilizer instead of becoming a pollutant. Animal feed can also be grown on the farm instead of being transported long distances.

Impacts of Sustainable Agriculture

The above sections describe four efforts to make agriculture more sustainable. These approaches may appear to be less efficient than most industrialized agriculture. More labor, space, and money may be required. Yet by reducing environmental impacts, the total savings to society and the earth are great.

Link to ➤➤➤

Cultures

Fair-trade coffee is grown by small, family-owned farms in other countries. The workers who produced fair-trade coffee are paid a fair wage for their labor. Some of the profits are also returned to the local community.

Lesson 4   R E V I E W

Word Bank

imported

organic

sustainable

On a sheet of paper, write the word from the Word Bank that completes each sentence correctly.

1. Agriculture that is _____ does not use up resources over time.

2. Produce that is _____ has been grown without the use of chemicals.

3. Produce that is _____ has been brought in from other regions or countries.

On a sheet of paper, write the letter of the answer that completes each sentence correctly.

4. _____ coffee is grown without clearing trees and destroying forests.

    A Decaffeinated   **C** Shade-grown
    B Inorganic   **D** No-till

5. Animal manure can be used as a _____ for crops.

    A pesticide   **B** seed source   **C** water source   **D** fertilizer

6. A _____ is a place where local growers can sell their produce.

    A production center   **C** plantation
    B farmers market   **D** feedlot

Critical Thinking

On a sheet of paper, write your answers to the following questions. Use complete sentences.

7. How does community-supported agriculture work?

8. List some advantages of buying food at a farmers market.

9. Your neighbor wants to use pesticides to kill all of the insects in her garden. Why might this not be a good idea?

10. Why do you think organic food is often more expensive than the same food grown with the help of chemicals?

Objectives

After reading this lesson, you should be able to

◆ describe some environmental impacts of large-scale fishing methods

◆ describe the strengths and weaknesses of aquaculture

◆ give examples of sustainable fishing methods

Gill net

A net that traps a fish's head and gill covers

Drift net

A net that floats freely through the ocean

For thousands of years, fish have been a major part of humans' diets. Worldwide, fish and shellfish supply about 20 percent of all animal protein eaten by people. In some parts of the world, seafood amounts to as much as 90 percent of animal protein eaten. In the United States, fish consumption has been rising steadily since the 1960s. As you learned in Chapter 6, businesses called fisheries catch and sell fish to meet this demand.

Fishing Methods

For most of human history, fish were caught with simple tools. These included spears, baited hooks, and nets. Small-scale fishing still happens today. Yet more and more fishing these days takes place on huge boats. These boats are like factories. A typical boat can catch between 136,000 and 460,000 kilograms of fish in a single net.

Large-scale fishing boats use special equipment to increase their catches. Some use enormous nets called **gill nets.** The holes in these nets catch a fish's head so it cannot get free. Some gill nets are set at fixed points in the water. Others are allowed to float through the water. These are called **drift nets.** They are later hauled up, full of fish. Some boats set out more than 60 kilometers of drift net every day. You can see an example of fish nets in Figure 11.5.1.

Figure 11.5.1 *Gill nets, drift nets, and trawl nets help fisheries catch massive amounts of fish.*

Other nets used by many fishing boats are called **trawl nets.** Trawl nets are large nets hauled through the water by a moving boat. Sometimes they are pulled through open water. More often, they are dragged along the ocean floor. Fish swim into the opening of the trawl net. If they are small, they swim out the other side. Otherwise, they are caught inside the net and later hauled into the boat. Trawl nets are commonly used to catch shrimp.

Other fisheries use **longlines** to catch fish. Longlines are long cables that stretch more than 60 kilometers across the ocean. They have floats attached every few hundred meters and baited hooks every few meters. Longlines are commonly used to catch tuna and swordfish.

Many boats use technology to help them catch fish. They may use sonar and helicopter surveys to help them locate schools of fish. They may also use lights to attract fish. These technologies have greatly increased the number of fish caught around the world. Every year, about 3.6 million metric tons of fish are caught in the United States. About 77 million metric tons are caught worldwide.

Environmental Impacts

Improved technologies have greatly increased fish catches around the world. Yet these gains have come with environmental costs. For example, gill nets and longlines do not just catch the targeted fish. They also catch fish that are too young or small. They catch fish of the wrong species. They even catch other animals, such as turtles, dolphins, and whales. These unwanted animals are known as **bycatch.** In most cases, the bycatch is never used. Dead fish and other animals are thrown overboard. Experts estimate that about one-quarter of all animals caught are bycatch.

Sometimes fishing boats lose their lines and other gear. Lost drift nets can float through the ocean for years, catching fish and other animals. Fishing gear, lost and not, kills an estimated 308,000 whales, dolphins, and porpoises each year.

Another environmental problem associated with fishing is the destruction of marine habitats. Trawlers that drag their nets across the ocean floor scrape up every living thing they encounter. Some people have compared the effects of this to **clear-cutting** a forest.

Finally, modern fishing methods threaten the species they catch. Around the world, many species are being **overfished.** Overfishing means catching fish faster than they can reproduce. Too many fish are taken each season, including **immature** fish. Immature fish have not yet reached an age when they can reproduce. Catching immature fish reduces the chances for restoring the population in the future.

The United Nations estimates that 70 percent of global fisheries are overfishing, or close to it. Some fisheries are taking as many fish as they can. Others already take too many for the species to support. As a result, salmon populations in the northwestern United States have dropped. The amount of Atlantic cod, tuna, and swordfish has also greatly decreased in recent years. Atlantic cod fisheries once supported coastal communities of northern New England and Canada. Now they have closed and many people have been left without jobs. Many more have lost an important food source.

Fish Farming

Not all fish are caught in the wild. Some fish are now farmed. Fish farming is called **aquaculture.** Aquaculture has many benefits. Large numbers of fish can be raised directly for human consumption. About one-fourth of the fish eaten worldwide come from fish farms. This has been done without destroying the sea floor or creating lots of bycatch.

Still, aquaculture has its problems. Creating a fish farm often requires the destruction of a coastal habitat. For example, building shrimp farms in the Philippines has destroyed coastal mangrove forests. The biodiversity and ecological services of these forests are lost. Domestic fish can also escape from fish farms and mix with wild species. In the process, they can spread diseases. Fish farms often create significant environmental pollution. Fertilizers, medicines, fish food, and fish waste can reach surrounding ecosystems.

The Future of Fisheries

There are many present and future practices that can help sustain fisheries. For example, many people believe aquaculture can be better managed to minimize its environmental impacts. Farm-raised fish will not replace wild species. Instead, they will make it easier to conserve wild habitats and species.

Most people think that better research and management can also protect fish species. If careful limits are set on numbers of fish caught, species can be sustained.

Figure 11.5.2 *Sea turtles are one of many types of marine animals fisheries are working to protect.*

Wild fish can also be caught in ways that are much less destructive. For example, most trawl nets now carry devices called turtle excluder devices, or TEDs. TEDs help sea turtles like the one in Figure 11.5.2 on page 422 escape from a trawl net before they drown. Some fish are caught only with a hook and line so no bycatch is created. Trawl nets can be dragged through open water so they do not destroy sea floor habitat.

Ordinary consumers are becoming better educated about fishing methods. That helps them support fisheries with good practices. For example, tuna fishing once resulted in many dolphin deaths. Now consumers can choose to buy tuna that has been caught without harming dolphins.

Groups such as the Marine Stewardship Council and the Blue Ocean Institute can help consumers buy more wisely. The Marine Stewardship Council certifies fisheries that they believe practice sustainable fishing methods. Some grocery stores only sell fish from well-managed fisheries. When consumers support these fisheries, they help maintain fish populations for future generations.

Lesson 5   R E V I E W

On a sheet of paper, write the word from the Word Bank that completes each sentence correctly.

1. A _____ is a fish-catching business.

2. Catching fish faster than they can reproduce is called _____.

3. Fish farming is known as _____.

On a sheet of paper, write the letter of the word that completes each sentence correctly.

4. Sharks and dolphins caught on longlines meant for tuna are examples of _____.

    A targets   **B** bonuses   **C** bycatch   **D** intruders

5. _____ fish are not yet able to reproduce.

    A Immature   **B** Organic   **C** Unwanted **D** Farm-raised

6. A _____ floats in the water, catching everything it encounters.

    A trawl net   **B** longline   **C** drift net   **D** hook

Critical Thinking

On a sheet of paper, write your answers to the following questions. Use complete sentences.

7. Describe some fishing methods that create a lot of bycatch.

8. Why is bycatch a problem?

9. Describe some advantages and disadvantages of aquaculture.

10. Describe two ways to make fishing more sustainable.

Overfishing Threatens Fish Species

Fish is an important food in many people's diets. However, unwise fishing practices have brought some fish species to near extinction.

For example, orange roughy is a popular fish eaten as food. However, it grows slowly and can live for 100 years. It does not reproduce until it is 20 years old. If orange roughy are caught before they have reproduced, the population declines quickly. Fishery managers are now trying to reverse the effects of overfishing this species.

Part of the problem is the new technologies that allow fishing boats to capture more fish more easily. Fishing boats now use sonar, maps, and even global positioning satellite (GPS) devices to locate groups of fish. Also, fishing boats capture many small or immature fish that cannot be used for food. Instead of growing and reproducing, these small fish die in the fishing nets and are wasted.

Overfishing is already having a large impact on fish populations. Scientists estimate that many fish species have only 1 percent to 10 percent of their original populations remaining. Common fish such as Atlantic cod and bluefin tuna have been fished extensively as demand has increased. Some fish may be almost extinct.

Governments work to protect against overfishing by limiting how much of different species can be caught. This can cause difficulty for the fishing industry, though. It means that fishers may not be able to catch enough to make a living. However, allowing fish populations to grow provides future resources for fishers and consumers.

1. How has technology been partly responsible for some fish species becoming endangered?

2. How might restrictions on overfishing hurt the economy of a fishing village? How might it help the economy of that village?

Chapter 11 SUMMARY

- Subsistence agriculture sometimes threatens local biodiversity.

- Industrialized agriculture uses fossil fuels, as well as inputs of chemicals and water, to produce large crops.

- Soils are made of inorganic material such as silt and clay, decomposing organic material, water, air, and living organisms.

- It takes thousands of years for a few centimeters of soil to form. In some places, several centimeters of soil are eroding every year.

- Water and wind cause soil erosion, but steep slopes and lack of vegetation make it much worse.

- The Green Revolution was an increase in crop productivity caused mostly by breeding new varieties of plants.

- Worldwide, about one in seven people suffers from malnutrition. Almost an equal number of people experience overnutrition.

- Sustainable agriculture aims to meet food needs of current generations without depriving future generations. It also tries to protect biodiversity and reduce use of chemicals, water, and fossil fuels in agriculture.

- Fisheries use many methods to increase catches. Some methods cause bycatch. Others cause habitat destruction.

- Overfishing is affecting many fisheries worldwide by reducing the numbers of wild species.

- Aquaculture can be very efficient but can also produce pollution, cause habitat destruction, and weaken wild fish populations.

Vocabulary

A horizon, 400
anemia, 409
aquaculture, 421
bedrock, 399
bycatch, 420
calcium, 407
calorie, 407
carbohydrate, 407
clear-cutting, 421
community-supported agriculture, 415
contour farming, 402
crop yield, 395
dead zone, 396
domesticated, 395

draft animal, 394
drift net, 419
edible, 406
famine, 409
farmers market, 415
fat, 407
feedlot, 397
gill net, 419
Green Revolution, 406
horizon, 400
immature, 421
industrialized agriculture, 395
iron, 407
kilocalorie, 407

loam, 400
longline, 420
no-till farming, 402
O horizon, 400
organic farming, 414
overfishing, 421
overnutrition, 409
parent material, 399
pasture, 395
plantation agriculture, 396
porosity, 400
protein, 407
protein-calorie malnutrition, 408

rangeland, 397
shade-grown coffee, 415
shelterbelt, 402
siltation, 402
soil erosion, 397
sustainable agriculture, 413
till, 402
trawl net, 420
vitamin C, 407
weathering, 399
world food supply, 406

Chapter 11 R E V I E W

Word Bank

aquaculture

bycatch

calorie

carbohydrates

dead zones

fat

gill nets

Green Revolution

horizon

industrialized
  agriculture

organic farming

overnutrition

protein

siltation

sustainable
  agriculture

trawl nets

weathering

world food supply

Vocabulary Review

On a sheet of paper, write the word or words from the Word Bank that complete each sentence correctly.

1. Large-scale, mechanized agriculture is called _____.

2. A soil layer is called a _____.

3. Agricultural runoff can create areas called _____ in oceans, where no life can exist.

4. Some fishing boats use _____, which are large nets that are usually dragged along the ocean floor.

5. Meat, eggs, and milk all contain _____, which is used by your body's cells to grow and work.

6. Bedrock wears down into smaller pieces through a process called _____.

7. One method of catching fish is to use _____, which catch a fish's head so it cannot get free.

8. A nutrient that stores lots of energy for your body to use is _____.

9. The accumulation of soil in aquatic ecosystems is known as _____.

10. The _____ is the amount of food available for Earth's people.

11. The _____ was a large gain in the world food supply achieved by creating new varieties of plants.

12. A _____ is the unit of heat needed to raise a gram of water one degree Celsius.

13. Your body uses _____, such as starches and sugars, for energy.

Continued on next page

14. Ways of producing food for current generations that do not deprive future generations are known as _____.

15. Growing crops without the use of toxic chemicals is called _____.

16. Unwanted fish and other animals caught in fishing gear are called _____.

17. Eating too many calories causes _____.

18. Another word for fish farming is _____.

Concept Review

On a sheet of paper, write the letter of the correct answer.

19. Which of the following does not contribute to soil erosion?

   A wind   **C** vegetation
   B water flow   **D** tilling

20. What is the main cause of hunger around the world?

   A drought   **C** war
   B poverty   **D** floods

21. Which of the following is needed to grow produce in dry regions?

   A tractors   **C** plantations
   B draft animals **D** irrigation

Critical Thinking

On a sheet of paper, write your answers to the following questions. Use complete sentences.

22. How is a city garden a form of subsistence agriculture?

23. What is wrong with the saying, "An apple a day keeps the doctor away"?

24. Supporters of sustainable agriculture say that some land is not suitable for growing crops. What kinds of places might they be referring to?

25. How is aquaculture like agriculture?

Test-Taking Tip To choose the answer that correctly completes a sentence, read the sentence using each answer choice. Then choose the answer that makes the most sense when the entire sentence is read.

12 Protecting Biodiversity

The bald eagles shown in the photo are symbols of the United States. However, the bald eagle was once an endangered species. This was due to the effects of DDT, habitat loss, and people hunting the bald eagle for its feathers. Thanks to laws banning DDT and protecting habitat, the bald eagle has made a comeback. In Chapter 12, you will learn how the activities of humans affect other species on Earth. You will find out the main causes of the ongoing loss of biodiversity. You will also learn about what is being done to preserve biodiversity and save species from extinction.

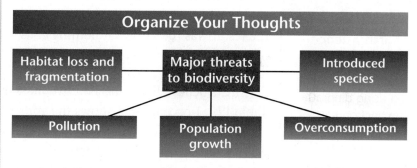

Organize Your Thoughts

- Habitat loss and fragmentation
- Major threats to biodiversity
- Introduced species
- Pollution
- Population growth
- Overconsumption

Goals for Learning

- ◆ To describe the major threats to biodiversity
- ◆ To explain the major causes of habitat destruction
- ◆ To explain how habitat loss is connected to species extinction
- ◆ To describe how nonnative species affect biodiversity
- ◆ To explain how wildlife trade affects biodiversity
- ◆ To describe strategies for preventing biodiversity loss

Asteroid

A rocky space object

More than 100 million years ago, the earth was a very different place. Dinosaurs bigger than school buses roamed the land. Dragonflies the size of birds buzzed in the air. Hot, humid swamps existed in places that are deserts today. All that changed about 65 million years ago when dinosaurs and many other organisms became extinct.

Disappearing Species

As you learned in Chapter 4, extinction is the loss of all members of a species. How could so many giant creatures disappear? No one is exactly sure what caused this mass extinction. Many scientists think the cause was some type of natural disaster. One of the most accepted theories is that a giant **asteroid** slammed into the earth. This would have raised a massive cloud of dust. The cloud would have blocked the sun long enough for many plants to die. This loss of plant species could have caused extinctions that slowly moved up the food chains. Although there are other theories about what happened, the result was the same. Something caused massive extinctions of dinosaurs, marine creatures, plants, and other living things.

Scientists believe Earth has had five mass extinctions in the past. Table 12.1.1 on page 433 shows the approximate time period of the extinctions and their possible causes. Each mass extinction was caused by some type of natural disaster or dramatic change on Earth. Today, many scientists believe that the earth is entering another period of major extinctions. Some scientists estimate that the earth is currently losing more than 30,000 species a year. That breaks down to about three species every hour. Scientists may disagree on this number, but most agree that Earth is facing a biodiversity crisis. Many are calling this the earth's sixth mass extinction.

Myth: Scientists disagree about whether Earth's biodiversity is decreasing.

Fact: Scientists disagree about the number of species that have been lost due to human activities. They do agree that species are becoming extinct at an unnatural rate.

Table 12.1.1 Five Major Mass Extinctions		
Event	Time period (approximate)	Possible causes
First mass extinction	439 million years ago	Change in sea level from glaciers forming and melting
Second mass extinction	364 million years ago	Unknown
Third mass extinction	250 million years ago	Asteroid impact, volcanoes
Fourth mass extinction	199 to 214 million years ago	Volcanoes
Fifth mass extinction	65 million years ago	Asteroid impact

The Biodiversity Crisis

Extinction is a natural process. As you read in Chapter 4, thousands of species become extinct every year. Many other species are endangered. In the past 3.5 billion years, more than 99 percent of all species have become extinct. As some species became extinct, others evolved to fill changing niches.

The mass extinction facing Earth today is very different from those in the past. Today's mass extinction is occurring much more rapidly. This is especially true for plant species. Another difference is that it will be harder for species and ecosystems to recover. That is because too much habitat and genetic diversity have already been lost. Unlike extinctions in the past, human activities are the major cause of current extinctions.

It is difficult to believe that humans can cause such major changes to the planet. More than one-half of the original wetlands in the United States have been lost. Many species, from mountain gorillas in Africa to giant pandas in Asia, are facing extinction. In the United States alone, more than 250 known species have become extinct during the past 200 years. Almost 1,000 species are currently on the Endangered Species List. This list is maintained by the U.S. Fish and Wildlife Service. It identifies those plants and animals that are in danger of becoming extinct.

HIPPO

An acronym that stands for the five major reasons for biodiversity loss

Acronym

A word formed from the first letters of other words

Habitat fragmentation

Breaking up large areas of habitat into smaller pieces

Introduced species

An organism brought into an area where it is not found naturally

Link to ➤➤➤

Biology

In summer, monarch butterflies breed across the United States and Canada. In winter, they gather on certain trees in one small area in Mexico. Loss of breeding sites and winter habitat both threaten monarch butterflies with extinction.

Main Causes of Biodiversity Loss

Biodiversity is decreasing for many reasons. The reasons for biodiversity loss can be grouped under five major categories. **HIPPO** is one way to remember these five threats. HIPPO is an **acronym.** That means that each letter stands for another word or phrase. In this case, each letter stands for a different cause of biodiversity loss:

Habitat loss and fragmentation
Introduced species
Pollution
Population growth
Overconsumption

Habitat Loss and Fragmentation. Habitat loss is the biggest threat to biodiversity worldwide. It is mainly caused by people clearing land for development. In the process, they destroy the natural systems of the habitat. Plants and animals are removed or killed. Development also causes **habitat fragmentation.** Habitat fragmentation is the breaking up of large areas of habitat into smaller pieces. This fragmentation makes it more difficult for animals to find food, water, and shelter. Cheetahs, discussed in Chapter 4, are one example of a species affected by habitat fragmentation.

Introduced Species. Species that end up in areas where they are not found naturally are called **introduced species.** They are also called invasive, alien, or exotic species. Some introduced species can cause problems in their new homes. For example, they often outcompete native species, using the local resources the native species would have used. Many introduced species do not have predators in their new homes. This can allow their populations to grow rapidly.

Pollution and Climate Change. As you have already learned, many types of pollution can cause problems for biodiversity. Air pollution can cause health problems for living things. It can also lead to global warming and climate change. Water pollution, soil erosion, and solid waste can also cause problems for biodiversity.

Population. In Chapter 6 you learned how the human population has grown over time. Many people say that human population growth is the main cause of biodiversity loss. More people put more pressure on the earth's natural resources.

Overconsumption. In addition to population growth, the increase in the amounts individuals consume is also fueling overconsumption. More people are consuming more fossil fuels, water, and other resources. People are also illegally buying and selling wildlife and products made from them. This is called illegal **wildlife trade.** All of these forms of overconsumption are contributing to biodiversity loss.

The following lessons in this chapter cover some of the major causes of biodiversity loss. They also explore many of the ways that people are working to protect biodiversity.

Express Lab 12

Materials
◆ sample of pond water
◆ eyedropper
◆ microscope slide
◆ cover slip
◆ microscope

Procedure
1. Use an eyedropper to get a small amount of a pond water sample.
2. Place one drop of the pond water in the center of a microscope slide.
3. Cover the drop with a cover slip.
4. Observe the pond water under low power of a microscope.
5. Switch to high power to get a closer view of any living things you find.

Analysis
1. How many different kinds of organisms did you observe?
2. Would you rate the biodiversity of the pond water as low, medium, or high? Explain your answer.

Lesson 1   R E V I E W

On a sheet of paper, write the word or words from the Word Bank that complete each sentence correctly.

1. HIPPO is a(n) _____ that lists the major causes of biodiversity loss.

2. Many scientists believe that a sixth _____ is happening right now.

3. Plants and animals that are brought into an area where they are not found naturally are called _____.

On a sheet of paper, write the letter of the answer that completes each sentence correctly.

4. _____ are not major causes of biodiversity loss.
   A Habitat loss and introduced species
   B Tornadoes and earthquakes
   C Overconsumption and population growth
   D Illegal wildlife trade and introduced species

5. The main cause of recent extinctions has been _____.
   A habitat loss and fragmentation   C overconsumption
   B global and local climate change   D introduced species

6. Some scientists think that Earth is losing three species every _____.
   A year   B month   C day   D hour

Critical Thinking

On a sheet of paper, write the answer to each of the following questions. Use complete sentences.

7. How do scientists know that mass extinctions have happened before?

8. What happens in ecosystems when species become extinct?

9. What makes many recent extinctions different from those in the past?

10. How could the Endangered Species List help save biodiversity?

Math Tip

The total area of the Amazon rain forest is about 4.1 million square kilometers. How many years will the forest last if its deforestation continues at the present rate? Divide 4.1 million by 25,000 to find out. The answer is about 164 years.

As you read this sentence, rain forests the size of two football fields are being destroyed. In a year, an area of rain forest the size of Poland is cut down. Many of these rain forests are being cleared for farmland and cattle grazing. Others are being cut for timber and other wood products. Some are lost to development as people build more roads, houses, schools, and stores. In the past 200 years, half of the world's rain forests have been cut down. Brazil alone lost more than 25,000 square km of rain forest in 2004.

Rain forests are not Earth's only threatened ecosystems. Wetlands, deserts, coastal communities, tundra, and many other ecosystems are also in trouble. All types of ecosystems are affected by human activities. When people develop land, they change the natural habitat of the species that live there. These changes can cause species to migrate to other places. Those living things that cannot move may die. Habitat changes can also damage many of the complicated relationships in different ecosystems.

Scientists estimate that more than 70 percent of all current extinctions are being caused by habitat loss. In many places, scientists are concerned that species are disappearing before they have been studied. This is especially true of insects and other invertebrates, along with fungi and microorganisms.

Deforestation

One of the most serious threats to biodiversity is deforestation. Think about all the ways you use wood and paper products in a day. Did you write in a notebook? Did you read a book or newspaper? Did you sit on furniture made from wood? People rely on wood for building supplies, fuel, paper, and other products. Unfortunately, the huge demand for wood is causing serious problems for the world's forests.

Scientists estimate that Indonesia's tropical lowland forests could disappear in the next few years. Indonesia's forests have some of the greatest plant diversity in the world. However, these forests are being cleared to sell lumber to Japan and other industrialized nations.

The Brazilian Amazon is one of the richest areas of biodiversity in the world. This area shelters more than one-third of Earth's total number of species. The Amazon contains about 2,500 different types of trees, or one-third of Earth's tropical tree species. The Amazon is also a refuge for jaguars, harpy eagles, and giant river otters. Much of the forest has been cleared for logging, planting soybeans, and ranching.

In North America, many native forests are also under threat. About half of all U.S. forests have been cleared since the first European colonists arrived. That was more than 400 years ago, and some forests have since made a comeback. However, despite efforts to protect North American forests, many are still being logged or developed.

In the Pacific Northwest, many people are concerned about logging mature and old-growth forests. Mature forests have trees that are more than 80 years old. Old-growth forests have trees that are more than 150 years old. These old-growth trees are often huge, both in diameter and height. Many conservationists feel it is important to protect old-growth forests, given their age and biodiversity.

Link to ➢➢➢

Social Studies

Europeans began settling in North America during the 1600s. At that time, the passenger pigeon was the most common bird species living there. Scientists estimate there were once more passenger pigeons on Earth than any other kind of bird. Human activities such as hunting and clearing forests for farming caused their extinction by 1914.

Although deforestation is a major challenge, there are many people working to find solutions. These solutions explore how to provide the world with wood while still protecting biodiversity. In Lesson 5, you will learn more about the creative ways people are conserving forests.

Map Skills: Terrestrial Biodiversity Map

The diversity of living things is not spread out evenly on Earth. The map below shows the variation in the amount of biodiversity, or number of species, in different countries. Only the biodiversity of the living things on land is shown.

Notice that each country is just one color. This means the map shows the total amount of biodiversity found within each country. Some variation exists within each country.

Different shades of color represent different numbers of species. Study the map and the legend. Then use them to answer the questions that follow.

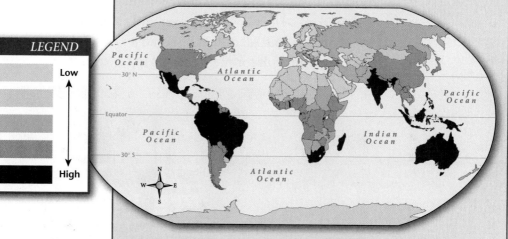

1. How does the amount of biodiversity in the United States compare with that of other countries?

2. Moving from the North Pole to the South Pole, how does biodiversity vary?

3. In general, where is most of the biodiversity on Earth found?

4. Why do you think North Africa has less biodiversity than you might expect in a tropical area?

Other Causes of Habitat Loss

Habitat can be lost for many reasons. Deforestation is one of the major causes. Development is another. Habitat loss is also caused by building dams to control a river or generate electricity. For example, in the Pacific Northwest, dams have caused a large decrease in salmon populations.

Other changes in the course or flow of a river can also affect habitat. The Aral Sea in Central Asia was the fourth-largest lake in the world. Then the two major rivers flowing into the lake were diverted for irrigation. Eventually, the Aral Sea shrank in size. Today, it is the eighth-largest lake. As you can see in Figure 12.2.2, old ships sit on land that used to be covered with water. They are reminders of how much the water level has dropped.

People can also destroy habitat in other ways. Off-road driving can damage alpine wildlife habitat. Underwater divers can break off chunks of coral when they are exploring coral reefs. Mining can strip away plant cover and allow toxic chemicals to seep into the soil. All of these human activities damage habitat, making it difficult for many species to survive.

Figure 12.2.2 *In the Aral Sea region, ships sit on land that used to be covered by water.*

Habitat Fragmentation

It is easy to understand how cutting down a forest can cause plants and animals to lose their homes. It is sometimes harder to see how breaking up an ecosystem into pieces can affect wildlife. In many parts of the world, habitat fragmentation makes it harder for species to survive.

If wildlife is not taken into account, development can create problems for many species. For example, some species will not cross a road. Species that do cross roads are likely to be killed by the traffic. Many species in highly developed areas live in small pieces, or fragments, of habitat. In some cases, they cannot find others of their kind. This can result in **inbreeding,** or breeding with relatives, and a loss of genetic diversity.

Habitat fragmentation can also change conditions in a habitat. If a road is cut through a forest, the habitat on each side of the road changes. Areas deep inside a forest are now exposed to wind, sunlight, and temperature changes. Animals living inside the forest would need to adapt to the new conditions or move. In some cases, there is not anywhere to move to. In other cases, such as with plants, species cannot move.

Hope for the Future

Slowing habitat loss is very important to conservationists. Many scientists are working to connect habitat fragments by setting aside land as **wildlife corridors.** These connecting corridors of habitat are designed to help species move from one area to another. Many countries are also setting aside more terrestrial, marine, and freshwater areas as parks. These protected areas can help preserve biodiversity.

Lesson 2   R E V I E W

Word Bank

habitat
    fragmentation

inbreeding

wildlife corridors

On a sheet of paper, write the word or words from the Word Bank that complete each sentence correctly.

1. Deforestation is one major cause of _____.

2. One way to fight habitat fragmentation is to establish _____.

3. Habitat fragmentation leads to _____, which decreases genetic diversity in a species.

On a sheet of paper, write the letter of the answer that completes each sentence correctly.

4. Using land for _____ is not a major cause of deforestation.

   A cattle grazing   **C** development

   B city parks   **D** farming

5. Trees in old-growth forests are more than _____ years old.

   A 50   **B** 80   **C** 150   **D** 300

6. Dams are often a serious problem for _____.

   A black bears   **C** Florida panthers

   B grasshoppers   **D** salmon

Critical Thinking

On a sheet of paper, write the answer to each of the following questions. Use complete sentences.

7. How does the demand for wood affect species in other parts of the world?

8. How do you think tourism and recreation could negatively impact biodiversity?

9. What can happen to local biodiversity when land is developed into shops, roads, and houses?

10. Why do you think some migrating birds that nest in North America and winter in South America are having a difficult time surviving?

Materials

- gloves
- roadside plants
- native plant key
- magnifying glass
- razor blade

Using an Identification Key

Have you noticed the many different kinds of flowering plants that grow along a roadside? Do you know what species they are? It is easy to find out if you know how to use an identification key. A key has sets of contrasting descriptions. A number or letter for another set follows each description. Sometimes, a species name follows a description. In this lab, you will use a key to identify the species a plant belongs to.

Procedure

1. Put on gloves.

2. Select a plant to identify.

3. Get an identification key from your teacher.

4. Observe the plant for general characteristics. Use the glossary of the key to find out what any unfamiliar terms mean.

5. Start with the first set (usually a pair) of descriptions.

6. Decide which description fits the plant. Record the number and/or letter at the end of that description.

7. Find the set of descriptions with the number/letter you wrote down.

Continued on next page

8. Repeat Steps 5 and 6 several times, if needed. When a scientific name follows a description you choose, you have identified the plant.

9. Read the description of that plant species to be sure you found the correct name. If the description does not fit, repeat Steps 4–7.

Cleanup/Disposal

Before you leave the lab, be sure your work area is clean. Return your identification key and plant sample to your teacher.

Analysis

1. Did you find the correct species name for your plant on the first try? Explain.

2. What should you do if the first name you find is incorrect?

3. Which of the words in the identification key did you find most difficult to understand?

Conclusions

1. What is the scientific name of the plant you identified?

2. Why must you work through the sets of descriptions in the order indicated?

Explore Further

Choose another plant and repeat the steps in the lab.

Examples of Identification Keys

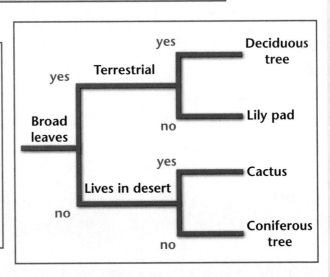

1. **Broad leaves**
   a. Yes...........Go to 2
   b. No ....Go to 3

2. **Terrestrial**
   a. Yes...........Deciduous tree
   b. No ....Lily pad

3. **Lives in desert**
   a. Yes...........Cactus
   b. No ....Coniferous tree

Objectives

After reading this lesson, you should be able to

◆ define introduced species

◆ explain how organisms are transported to new environments

◆ describe three ways that introduced species have contributed to biodiversity loss

Hatchery
A place where the eggs of fish are hatched

Populations of rainbow trout and other native fish have dropped in Montana and several other states. A microscopic parasite is responsible. This parasite causes whirling disease, which affects young fish. Some think the parasite was in fish shipped from Sweden. Eventually, the parasite got into fish **hatcheries** and infected young fish. Hatcheries are places where the eggs of fish are hatched. When the infected fish were shipped to other parts of the country, they carried the parasites with them. Over time, these parasites have infected many rivers and streams throughout the western United States.

This is one example of what can happen when a species enters a new environment. As you read in Lesson 1, an introduced species is a nonnative species that is introduced into a new ecosystem. These species are also called invasive, alien, or exotic species. They can be plants, animals, and microorganisms. Not all introduced species cause problems, however. Some die out quickly. Some prove to be harmless or even helpful. Yet a small percentage of these species cause major economic or environmental harm. They may also harm human health.

Where Do They Come From?

An introduced species can come from anywhere in the world. In many cases, species are transported by people. Sometimes natural events, such as hurricanes, transport species to a new part of the world.

Kudzu has pushed out native plants in many parts of the southern United States. It was originally imported from Japan in 1876. People brought it into the United States as an ornamental plant that could help prevent erosion. It had large leaves and sweet-smelling blossoms that attracted many gardeners. During the Great Depression of the 1930s, the government planted kudzu for erosion control. Farmers were paid to plant fields of the vines.

Over time, kudzu started growing out of control. The climate in the southeastern United States turned out to be perfect for the plant. In some places, the vines would grow as much as a foot a day during the summer. People started calling it "the mile-a-minute vine" and "the vine that ate the South." Kudzu does help prevent erosion, but it has also destroyed valuable forests. The vines prevented trees from getting sunlight. Today, the government is trying to control kudzu to protect native ecosystems.

Kudzu is an example of an introduced species that took over its new habitat. Its native insect predators were not imported, so it did not have natural controls in the United States. It is also very resistant to herbicides.

Introduced species have come from many other parts of the world. Zebra mussels from Europe and Asia have caused big problems in North American waters. They kill native clams by growing on top of them. They also clog water pipes and sink buoys. Before 1960, there were no zebra mussels in the United States. Today, these clamlike animals live in the Great Lakes and many other bodies of freshwater. Scientists think these mussels were brought to North America in the ballast tanks of large ships. You can see zebra mussels in Figure 12.3.1.

Figure 12.3.1 *The zebra mussel is an introduced species that kills native clams, clogs water pipes, and sinks buoys.*

The gypsy moth was imported to the United States from France. A man named E. Leopold Trouvelot imported these moths to try to raise them for silk production. The moths escaped from the cages he had in his backyard. Over time, these moths have become huge pests in North American forests.

How Nonnative Species Are Introduced

Species end up in new habitats for a number of reasons. Some are brought to a new place on purpose, like kudzu. In the United States, wheat, soybeans, and other agricultural plants were also introduced on purpose. These introduced species were brought to the United States to provide food. Some species are brought in to try to solve a problem. For example, dung beetles were introduced into Australia. As cattle ranching increased, the cow manure became a problem. Dung beetles helped control the waste.

Science in Your Life

Consumer Choices: Caring for Exotic Pets

Do you have an aquarium with tropical fish? How about a parakeet, a parrot, a boa constrictor, an iguana, or a guinea pig? If so, you have an exotic, or nonnative, pet. Most of these animals are from tropical areas. Responsible exotic pet owners buy from licensed dealers and care for their pets properly. Too often, however, owners of exotic pets release unwanted pets into the local environment.

Releasing a pet into the wild may seem like a kind thing to do. However, the consequences can be devastating. Exotic species are not adapted to the new environments and often die quickly. Sometimes, exotic pet species compete with the native species for food and living space.

When this happens, the native plants and animals may be harmed. If you can no longer care for an exotic pet, do not release it into the wild. There are a number of organizations that may be able to care for it if you cannot.

1. What is an exotic pet?

2. What can happen if an exotic pet is released into your local environment?

Sometimes, when one species is brought into an area, it brings other creatures along. The Pacific oyster was introduced to the state of Washington in the early 1900s. It was brought from Asia to help launch oyster fishing in the area. Unfortunately, the Japanese oyster drill and cordgrass, a marine plant, also came along. Both are causing big problems in the Pacific Northwest. The oyster drill is a snail that drills small holes through the shells of young oysters to feed on them. Cordgrass competes with other plants in the state of Washington.

Most introduced species are brought to new places accidentally. They can stick to people's shoes and clothing. They can escape from pet stores or people's houses. They can arrive with shipments of fruit and other foods. Many marine species are transported in or on ships or private boats.

Common animals, such as cats, pigs, and rats, can also create problems in new environments. These animals often escape from boats where they were kept as pets or food animals. When released, they can eat native species or compete with them for food and habitat. Introduced animals have hurt many native species of the Hawaiian Islands and Galápagos Islands.

How Introduced Species Affect Biodiversity

The good news is that most introduced species do not have much of an effect. A large percentage of introduced species do not survive in their new homes. That is because the habitat does not have the right conditions. If you tried to introduce a crab into the desert, it would probably not survive. That is because it needs water. Other species might survive but not create problems.

Research and Write

Use the Internet to research an introduced species affecting your area. Include where the species came from originally and how it was transported. Also include the effects the species has had on local ecosystems, as well as efforts to control the species and repair the damage. Report your findings to your class.

A small number of species do become serious pests. They can spread widely because they do not have native predators to control them. Some species are also quite aggressive. They can push out other species by taking over places to live. For example, purple loosestrife from Europe and Asia has taken hold in many wetland ecosystems. It is an aggressive plant that has caused the population of cattails to decrease. Once the cattails started disappearing, birds such as bitterns and rails also disappeared. That is because these birds depend on the cattails for food and shelter. A single purple loosestrife plant can produce up to 2.7 million seeds a year.

The most serious threat of introduced species is their ability to change entire ecosystems. Many scientists are worried that new species can change the relationships among living and nonliving things in an area. This harms all the living things in the ecosystem. It can make the ecosystem unstable. It can also damage the systems that provide many ecosystem services.

Many introduced species can also cause other species to become extinct. The small Indian mongoose has been introduced into island habitats to control rats and mice. Unfortunately, this animal has probably caused the extinction of more than 30 species worldwide. Plants such as yellow star thistle and cheatgrass have created big problems in the West. They have completely destroyed more than 13,000 hectares of native grassland. The rosy wolf snail is another pest. It was introduced in the Pacific Islands to control the giant African snail. The rosy wolf snail was not able to control the giant African snail. Instead, it caused the extinction of more than 50 native species of snails.

Introduced species are the second-greatest cause of biodiversity loss after habitat destruction. In Lesson 5, you will learn more about how people are addressing introduced species. You will also learn about ways that individuals can help, too.

On a sheet of paper, write the word from the Word Bank that completes each sentence correctly.

Word Bank
hatcheries
introduced
kudzu

1. Purple loosestrife, cordgrass, and _____ are all types of introduced plants.

2. The parasite that causes whirling disease may have moved from fish _____ to streams and rivers.

3. Another name for alien species is _____ species.

On a sheet of paper, write the letter of the answer that completes each sentence correctly.

4. _____ are the second major cause of biodiversity loss around the world.

   A Fish hatcheries   **C** Introduced species
   B Cattle   **D** Pollution

5. Gypsy moths, zebra mussels, and _____ were all introduced to North America by accident.

   A salmon   **B** dragonflies   **C** oyster drills   **D** maple trees

6. Introduced species can cause pollution, habitat changes, and _____ in the ecosystems where they are introduced.

   A extinctions   **C** earthquakes
   B climate change   **D** glaciers

Critical Thinking
On a sheet of paper, write the answer to each of the following questions. Use complete sentences.

7. Explain some of the ways that introduced species end up in new habitats.

8. Describe two examples of how introduced species have caused problems for other species.

9. How do introduced species threaten biodiversity?

10. Why do people call kudzu "the vine that ate the South"?

DISCOVERY INVESTIGATION **12**

Materials

- ◆ disposable gloves
- ◆ field notebook
- ◆ magnifying glass
- ◆ field guides and keys

Exploring Local Species Richness

How many different species of plants live on your school grounds? Species richness is one measure of biodiversity. You can estimate local species richness by identifying the number of different species in an area. This means identifying the species of each living thing you observe. How can you best do that? In this lab, you will explore the species richness of plants in your local area. You will use keys and field guides to help you identify species.

Procedure

1. In your lab group, discuss the idea of species richness and how it can be measured.

Continued on next page

2. Choose a specific area of your school grounds to investigate.

3. Decide how you will sample and record these different plant species in the area you have chosen.

4. Create a hypothesis about the amount of biodiversity in your area. Then write a procedure for your investigation. Include Safety Alerts.

5. Have your hypothesis, procedure, and Safety Alerts approved by your teacher. Then carry out your investigation. Record your results.

Cleanup/Disposal

Be sure to collect all your materials before returning to the lab.

Analysis

1. Summarize the results of your investigation.

2. How did your estimate of species richness compare with estimates made by other groups?

Conclusions

1. Was your hypothesis supported by the results of your experiment?

2. Do you think the animal species richness is similar to that of the plants in the area? Explain.

3. Suppose you continue your investigation and expand it to a wider area. How is your estimate of the area's species richness likely to change?

Explore Further

Estimate the species richness in other locations, such as your backyard or a local park.

After reading this lesson, you should be able to

◆ define wildlife trade

◆ explain how wildlife trade contributes to biodiversity loss

◆ describe how values and perceptions affect wildlife trade and other biodiversity issues

Every week, hundreds of animals and plants reach the Los Angeles International Airport. Some are wildlife products, such as crocodile-skin purses or jewelry made from coral. Others are cacti, lizards, snakes, tropical fish, monkeys, and other living things. Some of these products and wildlife are brought into the country legally. Others are brought into the country illegally. All are part of the worldwide trade in wildlife. This trade is a huge business, which is worth between 10 and 20 billion dollars a year.

What Is Wildlife Trade?

In Chapter 6, you learned more about how human consumption affects the environment. Wildlife trade is one type of consumption that directly affects biodiversity. As you learned in Lesson 1, wildlife trade is the buying or selling of wildlife or wildlife products. Wildlife trade can take place within one country or across international borders. It is illegal when it breaks state, national, or international laws and agreements.

The United States is the world's largest consumer of wildlife products. Every year, Americans import 10,000 primates, including apes, monkeys, and lemurs. They also import more than 5 million orchids, 450,000 live birds, and millions of tropical fish. Some of these plants and animals end up in botanical gardens and zoos. Others end up in people's homes as pets or decorations. Some are used in research. People and companies in the United States also import huge amounts of clothing, jewelry, and medicines made from wildlife. Japan, Europe, and other industrialized nations are also major consumers of wildlife.

Legal or Not?

Most wildlife trade is legal. Animals, plants, and wildlife products are sold in pet stores, department stores, and other markets. An example of a legal wildlife product can be seen in Figure 12.4.1. Trade is usually legal when a species population is not endangered. For example, in some countries, animals are raised to be sold. Examples include iguanas in Latin America, alligators in the United States, and tropical fish throughout the world.

Unfortunately, a growing amount of wildlife trade is illegal. This means people are hunting, buying, and selling endangered or threatened species. Illegal trade in wildlife has pushed many species to the point of extinction. Tigers have been hunted for their beautiful fur. Rhinoceroses have been hunted for their horns. Their horns are used to make traditional medicines that are used in many Asian countries. Elephants have been hunted for their valuable ivory tusks. People who hunt wildlife illegally are called **poachers.** When the demand for wildlife products is strong, prices rise. Poachers are more willing to break the law when they know they will be well paid.

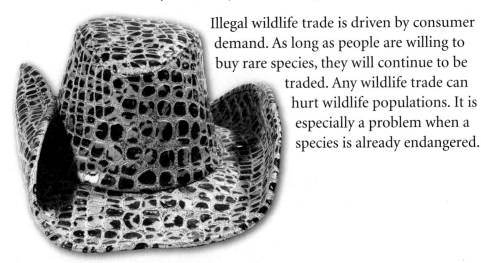

Illegal wildlife trade is driven by consumer demand. As long as people are willing to buy rare species, they will continue to be traded. Any wildlife trade can hurt wildlife populations. It is especially a problem when a species is already endangered.

Figure 12.4.1 *Wildlife products include alligator-skin boots, snakeskin belts, and hair clips made from tortoise shell. This hat is one example of a wildlife product.*

How Does Wildlife Trade Affect Biodiversity?

Wildlife trade can directly impact biodiversity by driving a species to extinction. Poachers have killed thousands of elephants. Elephant populations went from 1.3 million in 1979 to 625,000 ten years later. Rhinoceroses also have been killed extensively. Since the 1970s, black rhinoceros populations have decreased more than 90 percent.

Sometimes the effects of wildlife trade are hard to predict. For example, fruit bats living in tropical rain forests help pollinate trees and other plants. They also help disperse seeds. However, many of these bats have been hunted for food. As their numbers have dropped, the ecology of the rain forest has changed. Scientists say the overall health of the forests is threatened. The same thing is happening in areas where coral is being overharvested. Thousands of other species depend on coral. When coral reefs are damaged, all the species that live there are threatened.

There are hundreds of examples of chain reactions like these two. Some scientists think that overhunting frogs in Asia caused mosquito populations to increase. The frogs ate the mosquitoes, which can be carriers of **malaria.** Malaria is a disease that can cause chills, fever, and even death. People can get sick or die from malaria if they are bitten by these mosquitoes. As frog populations dropped, more pesticides were needed to control the mosquitoes. When selling frog legs became illegal, the mosquito populations decreased again. Then fewer pesticides were needed to control malaria.

Link to ➤➤➤

Cultures

One little-known part of wildlife trade is the sale of bushmeat. This term refers to wild animals eaten by humans. The sale of bushmeat contributes to the economies of many developing nations. It is one alternative to clearing tropical rain forests for agriculture. However, gorillas, chimpanzees, and elephants all are threatened by the bushmeat trade.

Ecological view

The opinion that it is important to protect biodiversity to preserve ecosystems and the services they provide

Utilitarian view

The opinion that it is important to protect biodiversity for the products it provides

Recreational view

The opinion that it is important to protect biodiversity because natural areas provide opportunities for outdoor activities

Spiritual view

The opinion that it is important to protect biodiversity because all species have a purpose for living

Valuing Wildlife and Biodiversity

Different people have different reasons to care or not care about wildlife and biodiversity. These views affect people's actions. They also help determine how people view wildlife trade and other biodiversity issues.

Many people hold an **ecological view** of the world. They are most concerned about how wildlife trade will affect biodiversity. They are worried that increasing trade in wildlife and wildlife products will hurt natural communities around the world.

Some people have a **utilitarian view** about wildlife and biodiversity. People with this view care about wildlife most when there is a direct benefit for people. For example, they value rain forests because of the medicine, wood, and other products they provide.

Many people have a **recreational view** about wildlife. They care about biodiversity because they enjoy being outdoors. They like to watch birds, hike, fish, or hunt.

Many people have a **spiritual view** about wildlife. They believe that every living thing has a purpose and needs to be protected.

❀ ❀

Technology and Society

Plants are the original source of the active ingredients in many medicines. Sometimes, a plant species is threatened with extinction because of its value as a medicine. This was the case with the Pacific yew, the source of the anticancer drug taxol. Now, when a plant with a useful compound is discovered, chemists figure out how to recreate the compound in the laboratory. That way, the plant can be protected.

Individual values and beliefs affect how people feel about wildlife trade issues. Of course, many people hold more than one view. It is important to remember that everyone has different ideas and opinions about wildlife and biodiversity. The challenge is to bring different points of view together to create workable solutions. You will learn more about how people are working together to protect biodiversity in Lesson 5.

Science at Work

Volunteer Coordinator

Volunteer coordinators recruit, train, and organize volunteers—also called docents—for public and private organizations. Volunteers play a very important role in protecting biodiversity. Almost every zoo, aquarium, wildlife refuge, park, museum, and wildlife rescue service relies on volunteers. The volunteers help with many different kinds of projects and assist in educating visitors.

Volunteer coordinators work with the staff of the institutions they work for and with the public. Some office work is required for planning, contacting people, and managing staff and volunteers. Often, volunteer coordinators for environmental organizations will spend much of their time working outdoors. Most volunteer coordinators in environmental science have a bachelor's degree in ecology, biology, or a related field.

Volunteer coordinators must enjoy working with a wide range of people from different backgrounds. Friendliness and enthusiasm for education, conservation, and helping people are important qualities.

Word Bank

fruit bats

poachers

wildlife trade

On a sheet of paper, write the word or words from the Word Bank that complete each sentence correctly.

1. Buying or selling wild animals and plants or products made from them is _____.

2. In recent decades, many elephants have been killed by _____ for their tusks.

3. Killing _____ for food threatens many tropical forests.

On a sheet of paper, write the letter of the answer that completes each sentence correctly.

4. The largest consumer of wildlife products is _____.

   A Japan   **C** Latin America
   B Europe   **D** the United States

5. Illegal trade in endangered and threatened wildlife is _____ around the world.

   A increasing   **C** staying the same
   B decreasing   **D** not a problem

6. People with a(n) _____ view of wildlife care about biodiversity because they enjoy the outdoors.

   A ecological   **B** recreational   **C** spiritual   **D** utilitarian

Critical Thinking

On a sheet of paper, write the answer to each of the following questions. Use complete sentences.

7. How is wildlife trade contributing to loss of biodiversity?

8. What drives illegal wildlife trade?

9. How does the ecological view of wildlife differ from the utilitarian view?

10. What must people do to solve the problems connected with wildlife trade?

Objectives

After reading this lesson, you should be able to

◆ describe four ways that people are helping to protect biodiversity

◆ describe how efforts to protect individual species compare to efforts to protect entire ecosystems

◆ describe how legislation helps protect biodiversity

Protecting biodiversity for the future is one of today's greatest challenges. An equally important challenge is how to also protect the quality of people's lives. There are many projects taking place to protect biodiversity. Some are focused on saving individual species. Others are looking at protecting entire ecosystems.

Setting Aside Land

One of the most important ways to protect biodiversity is to protect habitat. Setting aside land is the most effective way to save the most species in the short term. This is especially true for animals that need a lot of space to find food and mates. Setting aside large areas will also help protect the ecology of an area.

Many parks and protected areas support a variety of uses. Some allow recreational activities such as hiking, camping, and fishing. Others allow logging, grazing, and farming. Experts are looking at how to protect habitat, protect species, and provide for people's needs. This is especially true in parts of the world where people live directly off the land.

There are more than 7,000 protected areas worldwide, including about 1,500 national parks and wildlife preserves. However, this adds up to a very small percentage of the world's habitats. Many conservation groups and government agencies are working together to protect the most important habitats. They are also looking at how best to manage protected areas for people and wildlife.

Technology and Society

Many zoos take part in captive-breeding programs. The effort begins with developing a Species Survival Plan (SSP). SSPs contain information on breeding an animal and on its nutrition and living needs. Computer databases keep track of the genetic backgrounds of animals. Zoos avoid inbreeding by exchanging animals for breeding purposes. These programs return many offspring to the wild.

Restoring Habitats

In some places, so much original habitat has disappeared that **ecological restoration** is the only option. Ecological restoration is the process of returning a damaged ecosystem to its original condition. Although they can never be exactly the same, ecosystems can recover. In almost every part of the United States, some type of ecological restoration is taking place. In the Midwest, groups are working to restore parts of the original prairie ecosystem. Along the East Coast, efforts are under way to restore dunes and beach habitats.

One of the largest restoration projects in the country is taking place in the Everglades. The Everglades, shown in Figure 12.5.1, is a unique wetland in southern Florida that includes Everglades National Park. The Everglades is home to thousands of plants, insects, migrating birds, fish, and reptiles. Much of the water in the area has been drained to create land for development. Conservation groups, government agencies, and individuals are working together to restore the natural flow of water through the Everglades system.

Figure 12.5.1 *The Everglades in Florida is home to Everglades National Park.*

Captive Breeding and Saving Seeds

Another important strategy for protecting biodiversity is to protect individual species. This is especially true if a species is facing extinction. Zoos, aquariums, and botanical gardens play an important role in protecting threatened and endangered species. Some of these institutions are involved in **captive-breeding** programs. The animals they raise may be released to help rebuild wild populations.

Captive breeding is a last choice. It costs a lot of money and many efforts do not work. However, there have been some successes. California condors were saved from extinction, as were golden lion tamarins and whooping cranes. The most serious concern about captive breeding is that there is no guarantee that released species can survive over time.

One way to protect plant biodiversity for the future is through **seed banks.** Seed banks are large collections of seeds. The seeds are stored at low temperatures. They are safe from habitat destruction and climate change. These banks can store a large amount of genetic material in a very small space. Some seed banks have been able to restore an extinct plant species to the wild.

However, just like with captive breeding, there are many problems. Some plants do not have seeds that can be stored in a seed bank. For example, avocado and coconut seeds will not survive if they are dried and frozen. In addition, seeds in a seed bank stop evolving. If planted in the future, they might not be able to survive the new conditions.

Legal Action

Many countries have laws that protect biodiversity. The United States has some of the strongest. If enforced, or carried out, laws can be one of the most effective ways to protect species. The problem is that many countries do not have the resources to enforce the laws. In addition, many laws and regulations have strengths and weaknesses.

Here are three of the most important laws and treaties that protect biodiversity.

Endangered Species Act. This act was originally passed in 1973. It requires the U.S. Fish and Wildlife Service (FWS) to protect species in danger of becoming extinct. It also protects the ecosystems that these species depend on. The act requires the FWS to make a list of all U.S. species that are endangered and threatened. Today there are about 1,000 plants and animals on the Endangered Species List. The FWS has to design a recovery plan for each species listed. The FWS must also protect the listed species from human activities. Anyone who buys, sells, or hurts an animal or plant on the list is fined. Another part of the act prevents the government from carrying out projects that harm a listed species.

CITES. CITES stands for the Convention on International Trade in Endangered Species. This is an international treaty that protects endangered species. It is designed to make sure international trade does not threaten wild plants and animals. It bans hunting, capturing, and selling endangered or threatened species. More than 169 countries have signed the treaty, and it protects more than 30,000 species worldwide. CITES was drafted in 1963 at a meeting of the World Conservation Union. It was finally approved in 1973 and began to be enforced in 1975.

Treaty on Biological Diversity. In 1992, more than 100 world leaders met in Brazil for the first Earth Summit. It was an international effort to address some of the world's major environmental issues. One important result of the Summit was an international agreement called the Treaty on Biological Diversity. The treaty's goal was to protect biodiversity and support **sustainable development.** Sustainable development is development that balances the need for growth against the need to protect the natural environment. The treaty was also designed to protect genetic resources in countries around the world.

Other Conservation Efforts

There are many other efforts going on to protect biodiversity. Groups such as the World Conservation Union, the World Wildlife Fund, and Conservation International all work to protect habitats and species. All three organizations look for new ways to help people and nature live without conflict. The Nature Conservancy helps buy land to protect it for the future. These are only some of the many efforts taking place around the world.

In the final chapter of this book, you will learn more about what you can do to protect biodiversity. You will also find out how businesses, governments, communities, and consumers can take part in efforts to protect the environment for the future.

★ ★

Achievements in Science

Artificial Breeding

Artificial breeding, or artificial insemination, is a process that is used to breed many kinds of domesticated animals. Although artificial breeding is a high-tech process today, it is not new. The earliest known use of artificial breeding was by an Arabian horse breeder in the 1300s. In 1780, Italian Lazzaro Spallanzani used artificial insemination to breed dogs. In 1949, British scientist Chris Polge developed methods for freezing sperm, which carry a male's genetic material. This allowed breeders around the world to get sperm for livestock breeding.

Artificial breeding is also an important tool in captive-breeding programs. The numbers of animals in captivity are small compared with their numbers in the wild. Using only a few animals in a breeding program leads to inbreeding, which weakens a species. By using artificial breeding, however, zoos can breed animals that live in different parts of the world. By using frozen sperm, breeders can even breed animals that lived at different times.

Lesson 5 R E V I E W

Word Bank

CITES

Endangered
   Species Act

Treaty on Biological
   Diversity

On a sheet of paper, write the word or words from the Word Bank that complete each sentence correctly.

1. The _____ is a U.S. law that protects threatened and endangered species.

2. The international agreement that helps protect endangered species from wildlife trade is called _____.

3. In 1992, the _____ was created by leaders gathered at the first Earth Summit.

On a sheet of paper, write the letter of the answer that completes each sentence correctly.

4. One of the largest ecological wetland restoration projects is taking place in _____.

   A the city of Cincinnati   **C** the Grand Canyon
   B the Everglades   **D** South Dakota

5. The more than 100 _____ around the world are designed to protect the genetic diversity of plants.

   A national parks **B** zoos **C** aquariums **D** seed banks

6. _____ is not a group working to protect biodiversity.

   A Conservation International **C** The Red Cross
   B The World Wildlife Fund   **D** The Nature Conservancy

Critical Thinking

On a sheet of paper, write the answer to each of the following questions. Use complete sentences.

7. Give two examples of how laws and agreements help protect biodiversity.

8. Why do some scientists think protecting habitat is the most important way to protect species?

9. What are some of the problems with captive breeding?

10. What do you think will best protect biodiversity?

Urban Wildlife Management

Have you seen any wildlife in your neighborhood lately? Squirrels, raccoons, and opossums are common visitors. But have you found a deer, coyote, or bear in your backyard? These animals are becoming more common in cities, suburbs, and towns. Certain wildlife species have adapted well to urban areas. These urban areas provide them with food and water, protection from predators, and living space.

People and wildlife can coexist. However, problems can result when urban wildlife populations get too large. For example, squirrels can damage property by chewing on structures and wiring. Skunks and raccoons can carry diseases. Bears and coyotes have been known to prey on pets. Deer destroy gardens and are a serious danger to drivers. Flocks of geese leave droppings that can make parks and golf courses unusable.

Communities are working to solve problems caused by urban wildlife. One solution is to trap, relocate, and release animals away from urban areas. This is often done with small animals such as raccoons. Many police departments have animal control officers who perform these tasks. Relocating coyotes, bears, and moose often requires the assistance of licensed wildlife-rescue groups. These groups specialize in the safe handling of these large animals.

Some people think the best way to solve urban wildlife problems is to reduce the populations. Some communities organize special hunts to decrease the bear and deer populations in and around urban and suburban areas. These methods often cause much public debate. People argue that wildlife can be controlled by removing food sources instead. This can be done by bear-proofing dumpsters and garbage cans, taking in bird feeders at night, and not leaving pet food outside.

1. Why are so many wildlife species attracted to urban areas?

2. What are some reasons licensed professionals are needed to help with problems caused by wildlife?

Chapter 12 SUMMARY

- Many scientists think that the earth is in the midst of a sixth mass extinction caused mostly by human activities.

- Biodiversity is threatened by habitat loss, introduced species, population growth, pollution and climate change, overconsumption, and wildlife trade.

- Habitat loss and fragmentation are the most serious threats to biodiversity worldwide. Deforestation is the main cause of habitat loss.

- In addition to deforestation, dams, development, and off-road vehicles also cause habitat loss.

- Introduced species are a growing threat to biodiversity. These nonnative species can compete with native species and cause economic and environmental problems. Some also cause human health problems.

- Illegal wildlife trade can push species toward extinction, especially those species that are already vulnerable.

- Most conservation efforts today focus on protecting ecosystems, not individual species.

- To help protect individual species, many organizations use captive breeding.

- Seed banks are one way botanists are trying to protect plant diversity.

- Laws and agreements are an important way to protect biodiversity. Examples include the Endangered Species Act, CITES, and the Treaty on Biological Diversity.

- Many conservation groups around the world are working hard to protect biodiversity.

Vocabulary

acronym, 434
asteroid, 432
captive breeding, 461
ecological restoration, 460
ecological view, 456

habitat fragmentation, 434
hatchery, 445
HIPPO, 434
inbreeding, 441
introduced species, 434

malaria, 455
poacher, 454
recreational view, 456
seed bank, 461
spiritual view, 456

sustainable development, 462
utilitarian view, 456
wildlife corridor, 441
wildlife trade, 435

Chapter 12 REVIEW

Word Bank

acronym

asteroid

captive-breeding

ecological restoration

ecological view

habitat fragmentation

HIPPO

inbreeding

introduced species

malaria

poachers

recreational view

seed bank

spiritual view

utilitarian view

wildlife corridors

wildlife trade

Vocabulary Review

On a sheet of paper, write the word or words from the Word Bank that complete each sentence correctly.

1. A large _____ project is taking place in the Everglades.

2. Development that breaks a habitat into small, isolated pieces is an example of _____.

3. Reproduction that occurs between two closely related individuals is called _____.

4. Someone who thinks all species have a right to exist has a(n) _____ of the world.

5. A person with a(n) _____ of the world is interested in how wildlife can be used.

6. Connected patches of similar habitat form _____.

7. People who illegally hunt and kill endangered and threatened wildlife are called _____.

8. An acronym for the five major causes of biodiversity loss is _____.

9. Purple loosestrife, gypsy moths, and kudzu are examples of _____.

10. Buying and selling endangered or threatened species is an example of illegal _____.

11. People who want to protect wildlife for the good of an ecosystem have a(n) _____.

12. Diseases such as _____ can increase due to a loss of biodiversity.

13. People who enjoy the outdoors often have a(n) _____ of wildlife.

14. Many _____ programs have a difficult time reintroducing species to the wild.

Continued on next page

15. Many people believe dinosaurs became extinct due to a(n) _____ striking the earth.

16. A(n) _____ is a place where the genetic material of plants is stored for the future.

17. CITES is a(n) _____ for the name of an international agreement that helps prevent illegal trade in wildlife and wildlife products.

Concept Review

On a sheet of paper, write the letter that completes each sentence correctly.

18. The Endangered Species Acts requires the _____ to complete a recovery plan for each species listed as endangered.

    A U.S. Forest Service
    B U.S. Fish and Wildlife Service
    C U.S. Environmental Protection Agency
    D U.S. Department of Commerce

19. Development that meets the needs of the present without compromising the future is called _____ development.

    A ecological   **C** sustainable
    B invasive   **D** utilitarian

20. One way introduced species can cause problems in their new habitats is by _____.

    A mating with different species
    B increasing biodiversity
    C increasing wildlife trade
    D competing with native species

21. _____ can create serious problems for aquatic ecosystems by reducing the flow of water.

    A Dams   **B** Bridges   **C** Roads   **D** Off-road vehicles

Critical Thinking

On a sheet of paper, write the answer to each of the following questions. Use complete sentences.

22. Why is biodiversity more threatened today than it was during the time of the dinosaurs?

23. Why do some experts say the biggest challenge facing society is the loss of biodiversity?

24. How do you think that the pet trade contributes to biodiversity loss around the world?

25. Explain how human population growth affects all the other threats to biodiversity.

Test-Taking Tip When you are reading a test question, pay attention to words that are in bold type or capital letters. Those words will help you decide how to answer the question.

13 A Sustainable World

The photo shows land being prepared for development. With powerful machines like this, new housing developments can be built in a few months. The houses may be affordable for many people, but natural ecosystems are destroyed in the process. Some of the ecosystem services they provide will be lost. The natural resources used to build these houses may not be available for future generations. In other words, such practices may not be sustainable. In Chapter 13, you will learn more about what it takes to make a sustainable world. You will learn how governments, scientists, businesses, and citizens can work together to achieve sustainability.

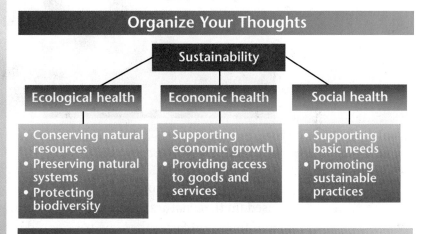

Organize Your Thoughts

Sustainability

Ecological health
- Conserving natural resources
- Preserving natural systems
- Protecting biodiversity

Economic health
- Supporting economic growth
- Providing access to goods and services

Social health
- Supporting basic needs
- Promoting sustainable practices

Goals for Learning

◆ To define sustainability and its application to natural resources

◆ To describe elements of a sustainable global economy

◆ To describe features of sustainable communities

◆ To explain the roles of government, science, business, and citizens in creating a more sustainable world

An entire civilization once existed on Easter Island in the South Pacific. These people fished, hunted, and raised crops. They also carved enormous rock statues that lined the hillsides of their island. You can see some of these statues in Figure 13.1.1. Then the civilization of Easter Island vanished.

For years, no one knew what happened to the people of Easter Island. Then scientists took a closer look at certain clues. They read journals from European visitors to the island. They studied bones and other waste. They looked at pollen grains buried deep in the ground.

Figure 13.1.1 *The people of Easter Island carved these enormous statues before they disappeared.*

Together, this evidence suggests that the people of Easter Island used up their natural resources. They cut down trees for canoes and fuelwood faster than the trees could grow back. Eventually, the island was completely deforested. Without trees for boats, the people could no longer fish. They had to burn grass and other materials for heat.

The Easter Islanders also hunted seals, birds, and other animals that lived on the island. They hunted them faster than they could reproduce. Soon the animals disappeared. The Easter Islanders planted crops. In time, though, the soils became too depleted to grow more food.

Link to >>>

Earth Science

Easter Island is located 3,700 km west of Chile. The island has three extinct volcanoes, one at each corner, which caused its formation. Volcanic rock is scattered across the landscape. The people of Easter Island used this rock to carve the giant statues found there.

Late in their existence, the people of Easter Island may have eaten other humans. It is believed that they formed tribes that fought one another for resources.

The story of Easter Island presents an example of an unsustainable society. Here was a place once full of natural resources. Yet the islanders used those resources faster than they could be restored. They left future generations without the opportunity to live well. They did not even have the resources to leave the island.

A Sustainable Approach

In some ways, Earth is also an island. It is full of natural resources, including air, freshwater, minerals, and healthy soils. As you have learned in this textbook, however, many of these resources are being used up. Fish populations are decreasing. Deforestation is occurring throughout the world. Pollution is damaging air, water, and land. Many plants and animals are becoming extinct.

Some people argue that these are small problems or that they can be fixed in the future. Others believe that people cannot wait to address these problems. As the example of Easter Island shows, unsustainable ways of life can have devastating results. The people of Easter Island may not have noticed the disappearance of plants and animals. Or maybe they were not concerned. In any case, they waited too long to address these problems. They reached the point where there was no way to recover.

People from many disciplines, backgrounds, and nations are working to prevent this result. They point out that people today have an advantage that Easter Islanders did not. They have written histories, records that help them see what is happening to the planet. They have the tools and creativity to act on this information. These advantages can help to create a more sustainable future.

Indicator

A measure of change

Quantify

To express something as a number

More than 178 countries voted to adopt Agenda 21 in 1992. At the World Summit on Sustainable Development in 2002, plans were made to put this agenda into action.

Agenda 21

As you learned in Chapter 12, the Treaty on Biological Diversity was written during the first Earth Summit in 1992. The world leaders who attended the Summit also created an agenda, or plan of action, called Agenda 21. This agenda was for both developing and industrialized nations. It describes what can be done to reduce consumption, fight poverty, and protect natural resources. Agenda 21 makes suggestions for individuals, businesses, and governments. Some of these ideas are discussed in Lesson 4. One of its basic ideas is that global cooperation is necessary for a sustainable future.

Measuring Sustainability

There are three main goals of sustainability. The first goal is ecological health. This includes conserving natural resources, preserving natural systems, and protecting biodiversity. The second goal is economic health, which includes economic stability or growth. It also includes widespread access to necessary goods and services. The third goal is social health. This includes supporting basic human needs as well as sustainable practices in the community.

You might wonder how people know if they are making progress toward sustainability. Most people use something known as sustainability **indicators.** Indicators are measures of specific kinds of information. The most useful indicators can be **quantified,** or expressed in numbers. Say you wanted to measure the activity level of your classmates. A good indicator might be the number of hours they exercised in a week.

Indicators of sustainability measure changes in ecological, social, and economic areas. One sustainability indicator might be the number of butterfly species in an area. Another might be the kilograms of greenhouse gases emitted by an industry. Another might be the number of malnourished people in the world. Indicators of any kind reflect the values of the people who use them. Together, they help measure people's success in meeting the goals of sustainability.

Lesson 1   R E V I E W

Word Bank

Agenda 21

indicators

quantified

On a sheet of paper, write the word or words from the Word Bank that complete each sentence correctly.

1. Measures of change in a given area are called _____.

2. Something that can be expressed in numbers can be _____.

3. A global plan called _____ describes how all nations need to cooperate to ensure a sustainable future.

Critical Thinking

On a sheet of paper, write the answers to the following questions. Use complete sentences.

4. How did deforestation contribute to a loss of food for Easter Islanders?

5. Why do you think sustainability needs to be a global goal?

Map Skills: Access to Clean Water

The availability of clean water is one indicator of sustainability. Much of the world's water is either not suitable for drinking or has become polluted. Also, there has been large population growth and many people live far from water sources. The map highlights the populations in several countries. The legend tells what percentage of each population has access to clean water. Use the map to answer the questions below.

Less than 50 percent

50–69 percent

70 percent or more

No data

1. Most of the countries where less than 50 percent of the population has access to clean water are on which continent?

2. Name two countries where more than 70 percent of the population has access to clean water.

3. What does the map tell you about the United States?

4. Does Africa or Australia have a better chance of achieving sustainability? Explain your answer.

Gross domestic product (GDP)

The total value of all goods and services produced in a country in a given period of time

One of the three major goals of sustainability is to achieve economic strength. People already associate economic growth with progress. Economic growth can give people jobs, help fight poverty, and increase people's well-being. It may also create funds for cleaning up the environment.

The most common indicator of economic growth is called the **gross domestic product,** or GDP. The GDP is the total value of all goods and services produced in a country in a year. Sometimes the GDP is divided by the population. This results in the average GDP per capita, or per person. The average per capita GDP makes it possible to compare GDPs between countries. For example, the average per capita GDP in the United States in 2004 was $40,100. The average per capita GDP in Guatemala was $4,200.

For people interested in sustainability, the GDP is not a very good indicator of progress. That is because it assumes that all economic activity is good. Imagine that a major oil spill occurs and many jobs are created to clean it up. This would make the GDP greater. Or imagine that a certain kind of edible flower was found to help fight colds. If people bought lots of these flowers, that would also boost the GDP. It would not matter if the flowers became extinct over time. Or suppose that only a few people in a country benefited from a stronger economy. Even if more people became poor or malnourished, the GDP would still show improvement.

Link to ≫≫≫

Mathematics

The equation for gross domestic product is $GDP = C + G + I + NX$. Private consumption (C) includes household expenses. Government (G) includes government expenses. Investments (I) include all business investments. Net exports (NX) include exports minus imports.

Genuine progress indicator (GPI)

A measure of progress that includes economic, social, and environmental factors

Research and Write

Research the most recent GDP and GPI numbers of several countries around the world. Create a map that shows the countries you studied, including their GDP and GPI. Write a short piece explaining what might cause differences between these two numbers. Provide examples.

For these reasons, the GDP does not reflect social and ecological losses. Ignoring these problems can eventually create economic problems. A tropical nation might become wealthy by rapidly cutting down and selling its forests. For a while, its GDP would rise. In time, though, the forests would disappear and the economy would suffer.

New Measures of Progress

Due to these concerns, many people are trying to develop new measures of economic progress. Like sustainability indicators, these measures try to reflect economic, social, and ecological impacts.

A group called Redefining Progress has developed an alternative to the GDP. It is called the **genuine progress indicator,** or GPI. The GPI is a measure of progress that includes economic, environmental, and social factors. It begins with the same economic information as the GDP. However, it also includes things such as housework and volunteering as gains. Then it subtracts numbers that show a decrease in national progress. Indicators of a decrease in progress include crime, overuse of natural resources, and loss of free time.

The GPI paints a very different picture of economic health than the GDP. According to the GDP, the U.S. economy grew by 2.64 percent between January 2000 and January 2003. This adds up to $180 more per person. According to the GPI, however, the U.S. economy grew by only 0.12 percent during this time. It calculates that the economy lost $212 per person during this period.

Some people are critical of the new indicators of economic growth. They say they are too subjective. Supporters of these new indicators argue that they are better measures of progress. They include many factors that the GDP and other traditional indicators ignore.

Science Myth

Myth: Sustainable economics is a charity or nonprofit effort.

Fact: One goal of sustainable economics is for businesses to care for people and nature first. However, businesses must make a profit for the economy to remain stable or grow. This is also an important part of sustainable economics.

Valuing Natural Resources

Do you value knowing that polar bears exist? Do you value having forests that help clean the air? Do you value clean oceans? Many people value these and other parts of the natural world. However, people are not required to pay for them. Because of that, according to traditional economics, they have no value. People who study economics are called **economists.** **Environmental economists** argue that traditional economics ignores the ways that natural resources benefit the economy.

Traditional economics stresses the importance of **financial capital.** This is wealth that can be used to create more wealth. Environmental economics stresses the importance of **natural capital.** This is a region's reserve of natural resources. Maintaining this reserve can be as essential for future economic health as maintaining financial capital.

One way to help people understand is to put a price tag on nature. Consider the plan to reintroduce wolves, like the wolf in Figure 13.2.1, to Yellowstone National Park. Many people argued for the wolves' ecological, historic, and emotional value. Environmental economists took a different approach by calculating the economic benefits of the wolves. Tourists would stay longer and spend more money if they could hear wolves. Wolves would boost big game populations, resulting in more money from hunting licenses. Even accounting for losses of nearby livestock, wolves could generate 110 million dollars in 20 years. Expressing the wolves' value in economic terms made many people take notice.

Figure 13.2.1 *Environmental economists calculated the economic benefit of wolves like this one.*

Others have used similar methods to calculate the value of the ecosystem services different species provide. Another researcher has calculated the value of the wild bees that pollinate blueberry plants. Each bee pollinates 15 to 19 liters of blueberries, making them "flying $50 bills." A team of economists has calculated the value of all services provided by world ecosystems. The total adds up to about $33 trillion per year. By comparison, the value of all human-produced goods and services is about $18 trillion per year.

All of these new ways of thinking about economics are ways of creating a more **sustainable global economy.** A sustainable global economy recognizes the value of natural capital. It encourages businesses that support human and environmental health. It discourages industries that do not conserve or protect resources. Finally, it tries for a more fair distribution of wealth. Together, these trends help to promote a more sustainable society.

Achievements in Science

Biosphere 2

In the late 1980s, scientists and engineers wanted to see if humans could create a completely sustainable environment. They built a large laboratory community on 3.15 acres in Arizona. It cost over $150 million to build. The laboratory was completely sealed off from the outside environment. There were rain forest, ocean, desert, savanna, and agricultural ecosystems. Since Earth is really the first biosphere, they named the laboratory Biosphere 2.

Four women and four men from different countries were recruited to live in Biosphere 2. They lived there for two years, starting in 1991. Although they had some problems, they were able to live using only the resources in the lab. They grew all their own food and recycled all materials, including water and waste. Some scientists felt that Biosphere 2 could be used for making controlled studies of the natural world. However, the project also showed how difficult it is to recreate the natural capital of Earth. Biosphere 2 barely supported eight lives, yet Earth's biosphere supports billions of lives.

Lesson 2   R E V I E W

Word Bank

gross domestic
    product

natural capital

sustainable global
    economy

On a sheet of paper, write the words from the Word Bank that complete each sentence correctly.

1. A _____ encourages businesses that protect natural resources and support human and environmental health.

2. The _____ measures the value of all goods and services produced in a country in one year.

3. Natural resources that one depends on for wealth are referred to as _____.

Critical Thinking

On a sheet of paper, write your answers to the following questions. Use complete sentences.

4. Explain two criticisms of the gross domestic product as a measure of progress.

5. How do environmental economists determine a "price tag" for things in nature that are usually free?

Express Lab 13

Materials

◆ map or photo of a local park or wildlife preserve

Procedure

1. Discuss the different things that the park or preserve provides to the community.

2. Create a data table. Include the name of each resource and its estimated value. If you cannot describe the value in dollars, write a description of what the resource provides.

Analysis

1. What types of things could you not estimate a value for in dollars?

2. How else could you measure the value of these things?

Commuter train

A train that provides transportation from suburbs or other locations to business areas

Sustainable community

A community built around the idea of sustainability

Suburb

A community that surrounds a city

Sprawl

Low-density, unplanned suburban development

Think for a moment about the place where you live. How far do you have to go to buy a loaf of bread? Does your community have buses or **commuter trains?** How many parks do you have? How clean is the air? These are the sorts of questions people might ask to find ways to make a community more sustainable. Used here, a *community* is a place and the people and other organisms that live there. A community might mean a neighborhood, a city, or even a region.

Sustainable communities are communities that are built around the ideas of sustainability. They try to meet the needs of people who live there now. They also try to make sure people can meet their needs in the future. Sustainable communities try to maintain ecological, economic, and social health. Meeting the goals of sustainability requires addressing many kinds of community issues. The following sections describe some of the main areas.

Development Patterns

Wherever people live, they create a built environment. How this development is laid out across the land affects sustainability. Many people in the United States live in **suburbs,** which surround a large city. The newest suburban growth is spread out across large areas with little planning. This is sometimes called **sprawl.** Sprawl claims forests, fields, deserts, and other wildlife habitat. It also uses land once available for farming. Sprawl replaced more than 45 acres of farmland every hour between 1982 and 1992. Sprawl also leads to more travel, which uses more fossil fuels and other natural resources.

Link to ≻≻≻

Language Arts

The word *suburb* is from the Latin word *suburbiam*. This can be broken down into *sub*, or "under," and *urbs*, or "city." The combination refers to an area "under," or just outside of, a city.

Urban growth boundary

A line around a city past which new development cannot occur

Public transportation

Buses, subways, and other forms of transportation shared by the public

Sustainability experts have many ideas for containing suburban sprawl. Portland, Oregon, created an **urban growth boundary** around the city to contain sprawl. New development cannot occur outside this boundary. In other places, suburban neighborhoods have been built around or near a community farm. Residents get much of their food from the farm, helping it stay in business. More suburban areas are building homes near businesses to save on land and travel.

Cities are gaining new attention as models for sustainability. Most cities fit more people onto less land. More compact housing saves on resources, such as building materials and energy.

Transportation

Transportation is another important feature of communities. In many communities today, people travel mostly in cars. This leads to increased air and water pollution, traffic congestion, and road building.

Communities interested in sustainability often support wider use of **public transportation,** such as buses and subways. These kinds of transportation are most often government-run or government-supported. They can be used by the public, which is the whole population of the community. By carrying many people at once, they can cut down on fuel use and traffic. They can be used by people who have handicaps and those too young or old to drive. They can also be used by people of every income.

Walking and biking are two other good options for reducing pollution and automobile traffic. Communities can encourage these choices by building sidewalks and bike paths.

Technology and Society

The Institute for Appropriate Technology works to develop and promote new technology that can contribute to sustainable communities. The institute has produced such items as a solar-powered car, soy-based foods, and live-in tree houses.

Jobs

Making sure that residents have jobs is an important part of sustainable communities. Jobs that are unsafe for workers or damage the environment are not sustainable. In Vermont, new jobs were created turning food, yard, and farm waste into compost. The compost has also helped restore local farmland. The Bronx Community Paper Mill, which makes recycled paper from newsprint, created over 600 jobs. The workers came from the poorest part of the city. Their work has reduced city waste and saved thousands of acres of trees.

Natural Resources

How a community uses and disposes of resources is a big part of sustainability. Las Vegas, Phoenix, and other desert cities use more water than is available locally. Encouraging water conservation can help reduce water use. For example, people can grow native cacti instead of water-demanding grass in their yards.

Science in Your Life

Consumer Choices: Fair-Trade Products

Part of creating a sustainable community is making sure that people can support themselves. Farmers and laborers in many countries struggle to earn enough money to survive. Many fall below the poverty level, even though they work long hours.

Fair-trade wholesalers work with local farmers to buy their products directly at a fair price. Wholesalers are companies that sell products to other companies rather than to consumers. These wholesalers allow the farmers to make a living wage. Also, the farmers do not need to cut down or burn more forests. This is because they already have enough land to support themselves. Sustainable agricultural practices help the land stay fertile.

You can find fair-trade products online or at organic food stores. Fair-trade products include coffee, tea, hot chocolate, nuts, honey, chocolate bars, salsa, and syrup.

1. Sustainable economies and communities strive to maintain ecological, economic, and social health. How does fair trade help these goals?

2. How do people help to preserve land when they buy fair-trade products?

Some communities have decided to support more renewable forms of energy. They are building wind farms or encouraging the use of solar panels on government buildings. Many communities have also developed city recycling programs. Others have creative ways of treating wastewater without strong chemicals. In Devil's Lake, North Dakota, wastewater is treated in a facility full of aquatic plants. These plants absorb pollutants. The water that is released is clean enough to return to local water supplies.

Wildlife Habitat

By definition, the built environment changes native habitat. Many species have a difficult time living near humans. If human communities are more contained, though, more space can be saved for parks and wilderness.

At the same time, many wildlife species can and do live in and around human communities. In the early 1980s, a colony of Mexican free-tailed bats moved into spaces under a rebuilt bridge in Austin, Texas. Many people wanted them killed. Now, though, attitudes have changed. These bats provide free mosquito control. They also provide entertainment. People watch the estimated 1.5 million bats fly out from the bridge each night. You can see these bats in Figure 13.3.2. Austin earns about 8 million dollars each year from these bat watchers visiting the city.

Figure 13.3.2 *People gather on this Austin, Texas, bridge at dusk to watch the bats.*

Providing city spaces for wildlife can benefit people in many ways. Peregrine falcons, for example, have been introduced to some big cities. Used to hunting between steep cliffs, the peregrines now hunt pigeons between skyscrapers.

Communities can take steps to support wildlife. New York City, Washington, D.C., and other large cities maintain large urban parks that harbor surprising biological diversity. As mentioned in Chapter 12, wildlife corridors give wildlife opportunities to move through human communities. These corridors can be passages on both land and water.

Community Indicators

Building better communities requires work and new ideas in many areas. Sustainability indicators are now being used widely on a community level. These indicators measure progress in areas including education, employment, air quality, and wildlife protection. Jacksonville, Florida, tracks lung cancer deaths. Seattle, Washington, tracks the number of wild salmon swimming in nearby rivers. Creating these indicators can be a community-building process.

▼◄▲▼◄▲▼◄▲▼◄▲▼◄▲▼◄▲▼◄▲▼◄▲▼◄▲▼◄▲▼◄▲▼◄▲▼◄▲▼◄▲▼◄▲▼◄▲▼

Science at Work

Community Planner

Community planners help cities and other community areas grow and function. The goal of community planners is to create a community that serves the people efficiently. They work with elected leaders to meet the economic, social, and environmental needs of the community. They deal with all aspects of how people live, including pollution, public transportation, schools, recreation areas, and business centers.

Community planners must make the best use of the community's resources, including land. They conduct field studies, surveys, and other research to determine the best course of action.

Community planners may meet with experts or hold public meetings to get feedback on their plans.

Community planners must be good communicators. They may use computer models and data to make recommendations. Most community planning jobs require a master's degree in urban or regional planning.

Word Bank

community

sprawl

urban growth
  boundary

On a sheet of paper, write the word or words from the Word Bank that complete each sentence correctly.

1. The line around a city past which no new development can occur is a(n) _____.

2. A particular place and the people and other living things that live there are called a(n) _____.

3. Unplanned, low-density growth is known as _____.

On a sheet of paper, write the letter of the word that completes each sentence correctly.

4. Subways, buses, and commuter trains are examples of _____.

   A private transportation   **C** public transportation
   B cars   **D** hybrid vehicles

5. Communities that lie just outside cities are called _____.

   A urban centers **B** sprawl   **C** country   **D** suburbs

6. A long city park that stretches between two habitats is an example of a _____.

   A corridor   **B** ladder   **C** highway   **D** cage

Critical Thinking

On a sheet of paper, write the answers to the following questions. Use complete sentences.

7. How might encouraging people to live in cities help protect wilderness?

8. Describe some jobs that contribute to sustainable communities.

9. How can communities help, and be helped by, local wildlife?

10. Name three indicators you would use to measure the sustainability of your community.

Materials

◆ Internet and library reference materials
◆ materials to create a poster or presentation

Creating Sustainable Communities

Sustainable communities must find the resources they need while maintaining the health of the environment. They must also deal with issues such as transportation, community planning, pollution, and economic health. In this lab, you will work to plan a sustainable community.

Procedure

1. In a small group, discuss what characteristics are necessary in a sustainable community. Have someone be the recorder and write down the characteristics of this imaginary community.

2. Determine the size of your community. The population can vary. It may have 20 or 30 people. It may also be a large city with a million people.

Continued on next page

3. Determine where your community exists, what surrounds it, and what natural resources are available.

4. You might also consider some of the following aspects when planning your sustainable community:
   • What jobs are needed?
   • How will you get resources?
   • How will you deal with waste and pollution?
   • What are your needs for public transportation, health, etc.?
   • What indicators will you monitor to determine success and failure?

5. Present your plan to the class as a poster or presentation. Include a drawing of your imaginary community.

6. Compare your plans with those of other groups in your class.

Cleanup/Disposal

Return any materials and make sure your area is clean.

Analysis

1. Which ideas did your group have that were unique?

2. Which ideas were used by more than one group?

3. What decisions did your group face as you created the plan for your sustainable community?

Conclusions

1. How are the needs and concerns of a small community different from those of a large community?

2. Why is it important to be able to publicly discuss sustainable policies and actions?

Explore Further

Research one or more of the sustainable community projects currently going on in the United States. Compare these communities to the one you created.

Objectives

After reading this lesson, you should be able to

◆ explain how governments can help protect the environment

◆ define corporate social responsibility and explain what businesses are doing to create a more sustainable society

◆ describe the role scientists play in affecting environmental policies

◆ list four ways that individuals can help address environmental problems

When Hurricane Katrina smashed into New Orleans in 2005, all levels of society sprang into action. Government programs moved to help the victims. You can see an example of this in Figure 13.4.1. Businesses helped to fund restoration projects and rebuild towns. Scientists studied links between the hurricane's strength and global warming. They also looked at the role wetlands play in reducing storm damage. Many local citizens gave money and volunteered their time to help the newly homeless.

That same combination of forces is needed to help create a more sustainable society. Businesses, scientists, governments, and individuals can work together. As a group, they can help protect the environment while meeting human needs.

Figure 13.4.1 *A military helicopter transports sand bags to help repair the break in the New Orleans levee.*

Research and Write

Use the Internet or your library to find a community that is promoting sustainability. Write a brief description of the community's goals and how members are working to achieve those goals. Include a list of the indicators used to track the community's progress.

The Role of Government

As you have learned, many governments help protect the environment through laws. Every year, the U.S. government spends billions of federal tax dollars on environmental protection. Much of that money goes to enforce **regulations** and to manage the country's natural resources. Regulations are rules enforced by government agencies. Many federal agencies are involved in environmental protection. They include

- the U.S. Fish and Wildlife Service

- the National Park Service

- the U.S. Forest Service

- the U.S. Environmental Protection Agency

Since the first Earth Day in 1970, lawmakers have introduced many laws and **policies** designed to protect the environment. You may recall from Chapter 1 that Congress established the EPA in 1970. Its job is to oversee the country's environmental protection strategy. The EPA is a **regulatory agency,** which means it helps enforce environmental laws and regulations. These laws include acts such as

- the Clean Water Act

- the Clean Air Act

- the Resource Conservation and Recovery Act

- the Superfund Act

Government agencies at the state and local level are also working to protect the environment. These local efforts can support the national laws. In some cases, states have passed laws that require more protection than national laws. For example, California's clean air laws are stricter than the federal Clean Air Act. Many local agencies hold public meetings that allow citizens to voice their opinions about environmental issues.

The Role of Science

Science plays an important role in protecting the environment. Most experts believe that more research is needed to understand how to address environmental issues. For example, scientists are studying how species interact with their habitats. They are studying how to make farming less harmful to the environment. They are researching ways to restore damaged ecosystems. They are investigating how climate change is affecting the environment. Scientists provide important information to lawmakers so that they can make informed decisions.

Corporate Responsibility

More corporations are now taking action to include environmental protection in their practices. Many car companies are developing hybrid cars that get much better gas mileage. Chemical companies are looking for new ways to recycle toxic chemicals. Architects are looking at how to construct buildings using environmentally friendly products. Many grocery stores are selling organic produce.

Many corporations are taking these positive steps because the public is concerned about the environment. They know that many consumers are buying products with the environment in mind. Corporations are also making these changes because in many cases they save money. Recycling can save energy, water, and other resources. Using less water in production facilities saves water and energy. All of this helps increase their profits.

Another growing trend focuses on **corporate social responsibility.** Social responsibility means that businesses act in a way that is also good for society. This can mean that corporate profits are balanced with support to communities and the environment.

Citizen science project

A project in which volunteers work with scientists to answer real-world questions

Link to ➤➤➤

Home and Career

Consumer action groups have become much more organized by using the Internet. People who want to work toward similar goals now commonly create informal groups online. These groups can organize and act quickly.

Citizen Action

Many people feel that environmental problems are so big that individual actions do not really matter. Yet change happens at all levels. Individuals can create huge changes in the way society acts. A good example is Rachel Carson. Her book, *Silent Spring*, helped create awareness about the problems with pesticides. It also helped get legislation passed that regulated toxic chemicals.

There are many types of actions that people can take to make a difference. Here are some types of activities that can make a difference locally, nationally, and globally.

Taking Consumer Action. Every time you buy something, you are affecting the environment. Some purchases also affect the lives of people in other parts of the world. If you buy something with a lot of packaging, it increases the amount of solid waste. If you buy organic foods or shade-grown coffee, you encourage good environmental practices. As a consumer, you have the power to create change. By making more environmentally friendly consumer choices, you can have a positive impact.

Getting Involved in Ecological Restoration and Research. Throughout the country, there are opportunities to get involved in environmental activities. You can help plant trees, create trails, and get rid of nonnative plants. You can also get involved in projects with scientists to help conduct research. These **citizen science projects** provide scientists with data about local species and habitats.

❃ ❃

Technology and Society

The Internet allows people to communicate instantly. Digital cameras, Weblogs (or blogs), and e-mail provide means of communication between ordinary people in different countries. This means that each person has the ability to be a reporter. People can provide firsthand information about the environment in their countries.

Influencing Policy and Voting. As a citizen, you can influence policies by letting your voice be heard. You can visit your elected representatives and explain your views on different issues. You can also write letters, send e-mails, and make phone calls. These are all ways to let people in government and business know how you feel. Many people join nonprofit groups, such as the National Audubon Society or Defenders of Wildlife. These and many other groups are working to protect the environment.

One of the most important actions you can take to express your views is by voting. Elected representatives have the power to create major social changes. Your vote can help elect someone who shares your ideas about environmental and social issues. In a democracy, voting is an important right and responsibility. You can begin voting at age 18. Learning everything you can about a candidate is an important part of the voting process.

There are many other ways to get involved in environmental protection. You can educate others about all the issues you have learned about in this book. You can also choose a career that will help protect the environment directly. You can join international organizations working to create a more sustainable society. You can also donate time to organizations taking actions you believe are important. Whatever you decide to do, you can make a difference. Getting involved can help make the world a better place for current and future generations.

Science Myth

Myth: Political action groups must be allied with a political party.

Fact: Most political action groups work with all political parties. Groups of people who are concerned about issues try to communicate with as many officials as possible.

Word Bank

corporate social
  responsibility
policy
regulatory agency

On a sheet of paper, write the word or words from the Word Bank that complete each sentence correctly.

1. Lawmakers can create a law or a _____ to protect the environment.

2. The U.S. Environmental Protection Agency is a _____.

3. Businesses that practice _____ are concerned about environmental protection and social issues.

On a sheet of paper, write the letter of the answer that completes each sentence correctly.

4. In a democracy, _____ is a basic right and one of the most effective ways to create change.

A conducting research   **C** voting
B lobbying   **D** writing a book

5. Science helps protect the environment through _____.

A voting   **C** enforcement
B consumption   **D** research

6. Helping scientists track monarch butterflies is an example of _____.

A a citizen science project   **C** a policy
B corporate social responsibility   **D** a democracy

Critical Thinking

On a sheet of paper, write the answers to the following questions. Use complete sentences.

7. Give an example of a choice you can make that will help protect the environment.

8. Describe four things that you can do to help create a more sustainable society.

9. How does the U.S. government protect the environment?

10. What does it mean for a company to be concerned about corporate social responsibility?

Materials

- Internet and library reference materials
- pencil
- paper

Getting Involved

Protecting the environment and creating sustainable communities requires action from both the government of a country and its citizens. Citizens have a right and responsibility to learn about the policies and issues their community faces. Being informed allows people to vote and participate in important government decisions.

How can you become a better-informed citizen? In this lab, you will research the different citizen action groups and issues in your local area. You will learn and use the skills that will help you become an informed voter.

Procedure

1. Work in pairs or small groups to research local environmental issues. You may use the Internet or your local newspaper to find recent news about environmental issues.

2. Create a list of citizen action groups found in your state. Research which of your local issues each group might take an interest in.

3. Choose one issue and obtain materials about it from your state's citizen action groups.

4. Find out the opinions on both sides of the issue. Read editorials from major newspapers or other media concerning your issue.

5. Have your group agree upon a position about the issue. Write a paper explaining your group's position.

Continued on next page

6. Use your paper to prepare a letter to the editor of your local newspaper. Sign your letter as a group and send it in.

Cleanup/Disposal
Return any materials and make sure your area is clean.

Analysis
1. Which issue did your group choose for your research? Explain why.

2. What action was recommended by the citizen action group? Do you agree or disagree with this opinion?

Conclusions
1. How do citizen action groups, newspapers, and other types of participants play an important role in determining environmental policies?

2. How do you think citizen action groups can be helpful?

Explore Further
Find the outcome of an environmental issue that was voted on recently in your area. Then find out what the voter turnout was for that day. If possible, calculate the percentage of eligible voters that voted that day.

Supplying Vitamins to the World

One common problem around the world is a lack of vitamins and minerals. Many people do not get a variety of foods, or the food they get is of low quality. As a result, they often do not get the proper amount of vitamins and minerals. This can cause birth defects, problems with development, or problems with the immune system. A person's immune system helps them to fight off diseases. Fortunately, these problems can often be solved by fortifying food with vitamins. Fortifying foods involves adding vitamins and minerals to the foods that people already eat.

For example, folic acid is important for having healthy babies. Approximately 200,000 birth defects occur each year because the mother does not get enough folic acid before and during her pregnancy. Currently, 38 countries add folic acid to flour to help prevent these problems.

Vitamin A is usually found in foods like eggs, liver, fish, and spinach. About 40 percent of children under five in developing countries have problems with their immune systems. This is because they do not get enough Vitamin A. As a result, many countries fortify milk, oil, and margarine with Vitamin A.

Approximately 20 million children are born each year with developmental problems because of iodine deficiency. Iodine is regularly added to salt in many countries as a response to this threat.

Malnutrition is not only the result of people not getting enough to eat. It is also the result of people not getting the right things to eat. In a sustainable society, all people must have the means to remain healthy. Fortifying foods can help with this.

1. Why do people often suffer from vitamin deficiencies even if they get enough to eat?

2. Give two examples of foods that are enriched with nutrients. What health problems do they help prevent?

- Creating a more sustainable world means supporting ecological, economic, and social health all at once.

- Indicators can be used to measure advances or declines in sustainability.

- Economic growth is traditionally measured with the gross domestic product. The genuine progress indicator incorporates more varied social and environmental data.

- Environmental economists try to account for the value of natural resources in economics.

- A sustainable global economy recognizes the value of natural capital, encourages businesses that support human and environmental health, and strives for a more fair distribution of wealth.

- One aim of sustainable communities is to contain sprawl and encourage more efficient use of space and resources. Another is to encourage public transportation, walking, and biking.

- More sustainable uses of community resources include recycling programs, renewable energy use, and innovative wastewater treatment.

- Governments can help protect the environment through laws and policies enforced by regulatory agencies.

- Many businesses are working to develop more sustainable practices.

- Scientists conduct research that helps people better understand natural processes and what is needed to ensure resource conservation.

- Individuals can contribute to sustainability by becoming better informed, voting, buying more sustainable products, and supporting groups working on sustainability.

Vocabulary

citizen science
   project, 492
commuter train, 481
corporate social
   responsibility, 491
economist, 478
environmental
   economist, 478

financial capital, 478
genuine progress
   indicator, 477
gross domestic
   product, 476
indicator, 474
natural capital, 478
policy, 490

public transportation,
   482
quantify, 474
regulation, 490
regulatory agency,
   490
sprawl, 481

suburb, 481
sustainable
   community, 481
sustainable global
   economy, 479
urban growth
   boundary, 482

citizen science
    projects

corporate social
    responsibility

economists

environmental
    economists

financial capital

gross domestic
    product

indicators

natural capital

public
    transportation

quantify

regulatory agency

sprawl

suburbs

sustainable
    communities

sustainable global
    economy

urban growth
    boundary

Vocabulary Review

On a sheet of paper, write the word or words from the Word Bank that complete each sentence correctly.

1. People use _____ to measure and track changes over time.

2. A(n) _____ is run by the government to enforce regulations.

3. Indicators allow communities to _____ their progress toward sustainability.

4. No development can occur around a city past the _____.

5. Experts in the field of economics are known as _____.

6. Wealth that is used to generate more wealth is called _____.

7. The _____ has traditionally been used as an indicator of economic growth.

8. Experts called _____ work to account for the value of nature in economics.

9. Natural resources that produce a flow of goods and services are sometimes referred to as _____.

10. Businesses that contribute to a sustainable society practice _____.

11. Communities that surround cities are called _____.

12. Low-density, unplanned suburban growth is called _____.

13. Buses, subways, and commuter trains are examples of _____.

14. An economy that contributes to the sustainability of Earth is a(n) _____.

15. Places built around the idea of sustainability are _____.

16. Many volunteers take part in a(n) _____ that helps scientists learn more about the natural world.

Continued on next page

Chapter 13 R E V I E W - continued

Concept Review

On a sheet of paper, write the letter of the answer that completes each sentence correctly.

17. A(n) _____ is sometimes defined as an area and the people and other living things that interact within it.

   A island
   B community
   C indicator
   D economy

18. The Superfund Act is legislation that _____.

   A cleans up the environment
   B helps car companies
   C creates wildlife corridors
   D prevents sprawl

19. The people of Easter Island vanished because they _____.

   A were defeated in war
   B experienced a volcanic eruption
   C left the island for more resources
   D used up their natural resources

20. The annual value of Earth's ecosystem services is estimated to be _____ that of human-produced goods and services.

   A the same as
   B less than
   C more than
   D nothing, compared to

21. A sustainable aspect of cities is their efficient use of _____.

   A space
   B asphalt
   C pollution
   D restaurants

22. If you wanted to make sure the food you bought was pesticide-free, you would buy _____ produce.

   A leafy
   B green
   C organic
   D free range

Critical Thinking

On a sheet of paper, write the answers to the following questions. Use complete sentences.

23. What do you think would be a possible argument against putting a price tag on something like a wolf?

24. Describe the relationship between density of community development and transportation.

25. What are five actions you can take this week to create a more sustainable world? Explain how each will contribute to sustainability.

Test-Taking Tip Learn from your mistakes. Review corrected homework and tests to understand your errors.

Appendix A: Measurement Conversion Factors

Metric Measures

Length
1,000 meters (m) = 1 kilometer (km)
100 centimeters (cm) = 1 m
10 decimeters (dm) = 1 m
1,000 millimeters (mm) = 1 m
10 cm = 1 decimeter (dm)
10 mm = 1 cm

Area
100 square millimeters (mm^2) = 1 square centimeter (cm^2)
10,000 cm^2 = 1 square meter (m^2)
10,000 m^2 = 1 hectare (ha)

Volume
1,000 cubic millimeters (mm^3) = 1 cubic centimeter (cm^3)
1,000 cubic centimeters (cm^3) = 1 liter (L)
1 cubic centimeter (cm^3) = 1 milliliter (mL)
100 cm^3 = 1 cubic decimeter (dm^3)
1,000,000 cm^3 = 1 cubic meter (m^3)

Capacity
1,000 milliliters (mL) = 1 liter (L)
1,000 L = 1 kiloliter (kL)

Mass
100 centigrams (cg) = 1 gram (g)
1,000 kilograms (kg) = 1 metric ton (t)
1,000 grams (g) = 1 kg
1,000 milligrams (mg) = 1 g

Temperature Degrees Celsius (°C)
0°C = freezing point of water
37°C = normal body temperature
100°C = boiling point of water

Time
60 seconds (sec) = 1 minute (min)
60 min = 1 hour (hr)
24 hr = 1 day

Customary Measures

Length
12 inches (in.) = 1 foot (ft)
3 ft = 1 yard (yd)
36 in. = 1 yd
5,280 ft = 1 mile (mi)
1,760 yd = 1 mi
6,076 feet = 1 nautical mile

Area
144 square inches (sq in.) = 1 square foot (sq ft)
9 sq ft = 1 square yard (sq yd)
43,560 sq ft = 1 acre (A)

Volume
1,728 cubic inches (cu in.) = 1 cubic foot (cu ft)
27 cu ft = 1 cubic yard (cu yard)

Capacity
8 fluid ounces (fl oz) = 1 cup (c)
2 c = 1 pint (pt)
2 pt = 1 quart (qt)
4 qt = 1 gallon (gal)

Weight
16 ounces (oz) = 1 pound (lb)
2,000 lb = 1 ton (T)

Temperature Degrees Fahrenheit (°F)
32°F = freezing point of water
98.6°F = normal body temperature
212°F = boiling point of water

To change	To	Multiply by	To change	To	Multiply by
centimeters	inches	0.3937	meters	feet	3.2808
centimeters	feet	0.03281	meters	miles	0.0006214
cubic feet	cubic meters	0.0283	meters	yards	1.0936
cubic meters	cubic feet	35.3145	metric tons	tons (long)	0.9842
cubic meters	cubic yards	1.3079	metric tons	tons (short)	1.1023
cubic yards	cubic meters	0.7646	miles	kilometers	1.6093
feet	meters	0.3048	miles	feet	5,280
feet	miles (nautical)	0.0001645	miles (statute)	miles (nautical)	0.8684
feet	miles (statute)	0.0001894	miles/hour	feet/minute	88
feet/second	miles/hour	0.6818	millimeters	inches	0.0394
gallons (U.S.)	liters	3.7853	ounces avdp	grams	28.3495
grams	ounces avdp	0.0353	ounces	pounds	0.0625
grams	pounds	0.002205	pecks	liters	8.8096
hours	days	0.04167	pints (dry)	liters	0.5506
inches	millimeters	25.4000	pints (liquid)	liters	0.4732
inches	centimeters	2.5400	pounds avdp	kilograms	0.4536
kilograms	pounds avdp	2.2046	pounds	ounces	16
kilometers	miles	0.6214	quarts (dry)	liters	1.1012
liters	gallons (U.S.)	0.2642	quarts (liquid)	liters	0.9463
liters	pecks	0.1135	square feet	square meters	0.0929
liters	pints (dry)	1.8162	square meters	square feet	10.7639
liters	pints (liquid)	2.1134	square meters	square yards	1.1960
liters	quarts (dry)	0.9081	square yards	square meters	0.8361
liters	quarts (liquid)	1.0567	yards	meters	0.9144

Appendix B: The Periodic Table of Elements

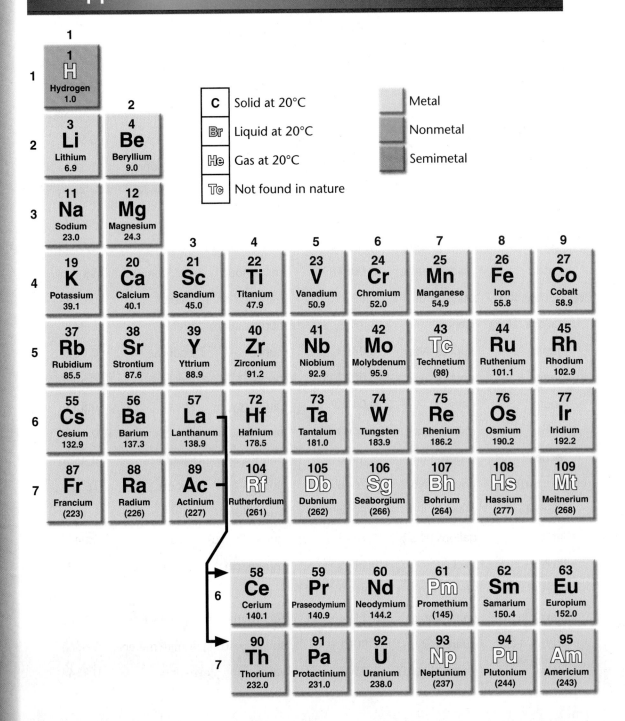

		C	Solid at 20°C		Metal
		Br	Liquid at 20°C		Nonmetal
		He	Gas at 20°C		Semimetal
		Tc	Not found in nature		

Group 1

1
H
Hydrogen
1.0

Group 2

3 **Li** Lithium 6.9

4 **Be** Beryllium 9.0

11 **Na** Sodium 23.0

12 **Mg** Magnesium 24.3

Group 3

21 **Sc** Scandium 45.0

39 **Y** Yttrium 88.9

57 **La** Lanthanum 138.9

89 **Ac** Actinium (227)

Group 4

22 **Ti** Titanium 47.9

40 **Zr** Zirconium 91.2

72 **Hf** Hafnium 178.5

104 **Rf** Rutherfordium (261)

Group 5

23 **V** Vanadium 50.9

41 **Nb** Niobium 92.9

73 **Ta** Tantalum 181.0

105 **Db** Dubnium (262)

Group 6

24 **Cr** Chromium 52.0

42 **Mo** Molybdenum 95.9

74 **W** Tungsten 183.9

106 **Sg** Seaborgium (266)

Group 7

25 **Mn** Manganese 54.9

43 **Tc** Technetium (98)

75 **Re** Rhenium 186.2

107 **Bh** Bohrium (264)

Group 8

26 **Fe** Iron 55.8

44 **Ru** Ruthenium 101.1

76 **Os** Osmium 190.2

108 **Hs** Hassium (277)

Group 9

27 **Co** Cobalt 58.9

45 **Rh** Rhodium 102.9

77 **Ir** Iridium 192.2

109 **Mt** Meitnerium (268)

Row 4: 19 **K** Potassium 39.1 — 20 **Ca** Calcium 40.1

Row 5: 37 **Rb** Rubidium 85.5 — 38 **Sr** Strontium 87.6

Row 6: 55 **Cs** Cesium 132.9 — 56 **Ba** Barium 137.3

Row 7: 87 **Fr** Francium (223) — 88 **Ra** Radium (226)

Period 6 (Lanthanides)

58 **Ce** Cerium 140.1

59 **Pr** Praseodymium 140.9

60 **Nd** Neodymium 144.2

61 **Pm** Promethium (145)

62 **Sm** Samarium 150.4

63 **Eu** Europium 152.0

Period 7 (Actinides)

90 **Th** Thorium 232.0

91 **Pa** Protactinium 231.0

92 **U** Uranium 238.0

93 **Np** Neptunium (237)

94 **Pu** Plutonium (244)

95 **Am** Americium (243)

2
He
Helium
4.0

Atomic number — **5**
Element symbol — **B**
Element name — Boron
Atomic mass — 10.8

13	14	15	16	17
5 **B** Boron 10.8	**6** **C** Carbon 12.0	**7** **N** Nitrogen 14.0	**8** **O** Oxygen 16.0	**9** **F** Fluorine 19.0	**10** **Ne** Neon 20.2

| **13** **Al** Aluminum 27.0 | **14** **Si** Silicon 28.1 | **15** **P** Phosphorus 31.0 | **16** **S** Sulfur 32.1 | **17** **Cl** Chlorine 35.5 | **18** **Ar** Argon 39.9 |

10	11	12
28 **Ni** Nickel 58.7	**29** **Cu** Copper 63.5	**30** **Zn** Zinc 65.4	**31** **Ga** Gallium 69.7	**32** **Ge** Germanium 72.6	**33** **As** Arsenic 74.9	**34** **Se** Selenium 79.0	**35** **Br** Bromine 79.9	**36** **Kr** Krypton 83.8
46 **Pd** Palladium 106.4	**47** **Ag** Silver 107.9	**48** **Cd** Cadmium 112.4	**49** **In** Indium 114.8	**50** **Sn** Tin 118.7	**51** **Sb** Antimony 121.8	**52** **Te** Tellurium 127.6	**53** **I** Iodine 126.9	**54** **Xe** Xenon 131.3
78 **Pt** Platinum 195.1	**79** **Au** Gold 197.0	**80** **Hg** Mercury 200.6	**81** **Tl** Thallium 204.4	**82** **Pb** Lead 207.2	**83** **Bi** Bismuth 209.0	**84** **Po** Polonium (209)	**85** **At** Astatine (210)	**86** **Rn** Radon (222)
110 **Ds** Darmstadtium (281)	**111** **Rg** Roentgenium (272)	**112** **Uub*** Ununbium (285)	**113** **Uut*** Ununtrium (284)	**114** **Uuq*** Ununquadium (289)	**115** **Uup*** Ununpentium (288)	**116** **Uuh*** Ununhexium		

*Official name and symbol have not been assigned.

64 **Gd** Gadolinium 157.3	**65** **Tb** Terbium 158.9	**66** **Dy** Dysprosium 162.5	**67** **Ho** Holmium 164.9	**68** **Er** Erbium 167.3	**69** **Tm** Thulium 168.9	**70** **Yb** Ytterbium 173.0	**71** **Lu** Lutetium 175.0
96 **Cm** Curium (247)	**97** **Bk** Berkelium (247)	**98** **Cf** Californium (251)	**99** **Es** Einsteinium (252)	**100** **Fm** Fermium (257)	**101** **Md** Mendelevium (258)	**102** **No** Nobelium (259)	**103** **Lr** Lawrencium (262)

Note: Atomic mass values are in atomic mass units (amu). Most atomic masses are averages based on the element's isotopes. They are rounded to the tenths place. An atomic mass in parentheses is the mass of the element's most stable isotope.

Appendix C: Weather and Weather Forecasting

As you read in Chapter 2, three atmospheric conditions come together to produce weather: air temperature, humidity, and air pressure. A meteorologist measures these conditions, looks for patterns, and uses this information to predict the weather.

Forecasting Tools

Air temperature is measured with a thermometer. Most thermometers are made of a thin tube filled with colored alcohol. Heat causes a liquid to expand, or take up more space. So when the air gets warmer, the liquid in the thermometer expands and moves up the tube. If the air gets cooler, the liquid contracts, or takes up less space. Then the liquid moves down the tube.

The unit of measure for temperature is the degree (°). Two scales for measuring temperature are shown in the diagram below. People in the United States usually use the Fahrenheit scale. People in most other countries, and all scientists, use the Celsius scale.

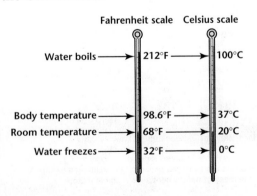

Air pressure is the pressure of the atmosphere pushing down on the earth. Air pressure is measured with an instrument called a barometer. In a mercury barometer, air pushes down on a dish of mercury, forcing mercury to rise in a tube. In an aneroid barometer, air pushes on a short metal can. A pointer connected to the can shows the amount of air pressure.

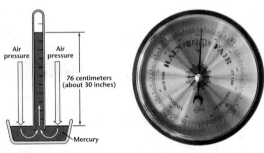

Mercury barometer   **Aneroid barometer**

Humidity is measured as relative humidity and calculated as a percent. A relative humidity of 50 percent means the air contains half of its water vapor capacity. When the air is completely filled with water vapor and cannot hold more, the relative humidity is 100 percent.

A psychrometer is an instrument used to measure relative humidity. It is actually made up of two thermometers. The bulb of one thermometer is covered with a damp cloth. As water evaporates from the cloth, it cools. The lower the humidity, the faster the water evaporates and the lower the temperature drops.

The relative humidity is then found by comparing the temperatures of the two thermometers to a special chart.

Weather information is collected in many ways. Weather stations are collections of instruments that measure temperature, air pressure, humidity, cloud cover and type, precipitation, and wind speed and direction. Weather balloons carry instruments high into the atmosphere. Weather satellites in orbit around the earth provide views of cloud patterns. Radar sends out radio waves that bounce off rain or snow. The returning waves make an image that shows where precipitation is occurring.

Air Masses

Weather data from a large area of the earth show meteorologists where air masses are located. An air mass is a huge body of the lower atmosphere that has similar temperature and humidity throughout. An air mass can be warm or cold. It can have a lot of water vapor or very little. Air masses are so large that two or three of them can cover the United States. As air masses move, they bring their weather to new places.

A front is a moving boundary line between two air masses. A warm front occurs where a warm air mass glides up over a cooler air mass. As the warm air rises, it cools and water vapor condenses into clouds. The air pressure drops, and a period of steady precipitation begins.

When the front passes, skies clear and the barometer rises. The temperature rises as warm air replaces the cooler air.

A cold front occurs where a cold air mass pushes out and wedges under a warmer air mass. The warm air mass rises quickly. If the warm air mass has a lot of water vapor, towering storm clouds form quickly. Heavy precipitation follows, but only for a short period of time. Several hours after the front passes, the weather becomes clear and cool.

Highs and Lows

Cold air is more dense than warm air. Therefore, cold air exerts more pressure on the earth's surface than does warm air. A cold air mass, then, is usually an area of high pressure, or a high. Highs often have fair weather. Air moves outward from an area of high pressure in a clockwise rotation. However, air moves into an area of low pressure, or a low. The air coming into a low is warm and rotates counterclockwise. Lows often have clouds and precipitation. As you read in Chapter 2, lines called isobars connect areas of equal pressure. Isobars form circular patterns around highs and lows.

In most of the United States and Canada, weather moves from west to east. Therefore, a high passing though Oklahoma will soon pass through Arkansas. The high will likely bring similar weather to both places.

Appendix D: Food Production, Preservation, and Transportation

Food Production

Farms are places where crops and farm animals are raised in large quantities. The trip from the farm to the dinner table has many steps. Even a simple snack, such as a slice of bread or glass of milk, goes through a lot of processes before reaching the consumer. Both foods start their journey on a farm.

Bread is made from flour, a wheat product. Wheat is grown and harvested on a farm then carried to a mill. There it is ground into flour. After packaging, flour is transported to a factory by truck or train. Other raw materials needed to make bread arrive at the factory by truck. Flour, water, sugar, salt, yeast, and other ingredients are mixed to make dough. The dough is shaped into loaves and then baked. Once cooled, the bread is sliced, wrapped, and tied. Individual packages of bread are put in large containers for shipment to distribution centers. From there the bread is sent to grocery stores.

Milk production begins on a dairy farm. Raw milk is collected from cows, then immediately cooled. Insulated trucks carry raw milk to a processing facility. Within 72 hours, the milk is pasteurized, heated to kill bacteria that can cause illness. Pasteurized milk is cooled, packaged, and shipped to distribution centers and grocery stores.

Global Food Market

Milk and bread may be produced within 160 kilometers of a grocery store. However, most of the food in a grocery store is not from local sources. In the United States, the average distance between farm and dinner plate ranges from 2,500 to 4,000 kilometers. To reach its destination, food may travel by train, airplane, or ship. For example, the tuna in a supermarket's seafood department may have been caught in the Atlantic Ocean. It traveled to a coastal processing plant in an insulated refrigeration tank on the ship. From the plant, refrigerated or frozen fish was sent to a distributor. The distributor then delivered the fish to the grocery store. The produce section may contain grapes from Chile, kiwi from Australia, and bananas from Jamaica. This fresh produce made its way to the grocery store in refrigeration tanks on ships, airplanes, trains, and trucks.

Food Preservation

Most food is packaged and preserved to keep it in good condition during shipment. Food preservation is not a new practice, however. An early food preservation technique was drying fresh meat or fish in the sun. Another was covering meat with salt. Canning has been in practice since the early 1800s. Many of these and other traditional methods are still in use.

The goal of all food preservation is to prevent food spoilage. Food spoilage is caused by the growth of microorganisms like bacteria and fungi. When food spoils, it takes on an unpleasant taste and may be dangerous to eat. Food spoilage can lead to food-borne illnesses. Symptoms may include nausea, diarrhea, and vomiting.

Types of modern food preservation include cold temperatures, drying, ionizing radiation, and preservatives. Cold storage is effective because bacteria grow very slowly in cold temperatures. Refrigeration protects food for several days or weeks. Freezing is an extension of refrigeration that gives food an even longer shelf life. A food's shelf life is how long it keeps from spoiling.

Drying is a technique that reduces the amount of water in food. The moisture content of dried food is less than 30 percent. Like refrigeration, drying slows the growth of microorganisms. Bacteria and fungi are living things, so they cannot survive without water. In freeze-drying, food is frozen, then placed in a vacuum chamber. In a vacuum, air pressure is reduced. At low pressure, the ice in frozen food changes directly to a vapor. Like drying, this process lowers the amount of moisture in the food. Unlike ordinary drying, food remains cold during the entire process.

One of the newest methods of preserving food is ionizing radiation. Because it has a lot of energy, ionizing radiation kills microorganisms that can spoil food. Chicken, fruits, and vegetables have been irradiated for some time. The United States Food and Drug Administration (FDA) only recently approved irradiation of beef.

Chemicals in Food

Some foods contain preservatives, chemicals that are added to prevent the growth of microorganisms. Acids, salt, and sugar are common preservatives. Other preservatives are benzoates, nitrites, sulfates, and sorbic acid. These chemicals either greatly slow bacterial growth or kill bacteria.

Preservatives are not the only chemicals added to food. Algin, which is made from seaweed, gives ice cream and other products a smoother texture. Citric acid and lactic acid add flavor and keep food at the proper acidity. Lecithin and methylcellulose prevent food products from separating into layers. Some manufacturers add dietary supplements, such as iron, folic acid, vitamin B2, and vitamin B3.

The FDA

The FDA watches over the quality of food and other consumer products. One of the FDA's biggest jobs is to make sure that food is safe to eat. The FDA has defined what a food product must be or contain to be labeled with its common name. The agency also sets standards of minimum quality for foods. In addition, the FDA requires that food labels be accurate so that consumers know what they are buying. It even regulates food packaging.

Food Packaging

Once food is preserved, it is packaged and sent to the consumer. Some of the earliest food packages were leaves and the skins of animals. Today, food packaging has many more forms and functions. All types of packaging protect food from spoilage and contamination. Food packaging also provides a way for the producer to communicate with the consumer. Packaging materials include paper, plastic, metal, glass, and edible films and coating. Most packages are made up of a combination of these materials. A milk carton is a good example. It may be made of paper with a plastic pour spout.

Glossary

A

A horizon (ā hə rī´ zn) the second layer of soil, made up of decaying organic material, living things, and inorganic particles; also called topsoil (p. 400)

Abiotic factor (ā bī ot´ ik fak´ tər) a nonliving part of the environment (p. 83)

Abyss (ə bis´) the deepest ocean zone (p. 199)

Acid (as´ id) a sour-tasting substance that reacts with metals to produce hydrogen (p. 342)

Acid deposition (as´ id dep ə zish´ ən) another term for acid rain (p. 342)

Acid rain (as´ id rān) precipitation with high levels of acidity (p. 342)

Acidic (ə sid´ ik) containing a higher level of acid (p. 180)

Acronym (ak´ rō nim) a word formed from the first letters of other words (p. 434)

Active solar system (ak´ tiv sō´ lər sis´ təm) a system that collects and delivers solar energy (p. 269)

Adaptation (ad ap tā´ shən) a trait that makes an organism better suited to its environment (p. 136)

Aerobic decomposition (âr ō´ bik dē kom pə zish´ ən) the natural breakdown of organic matter that requires water and oxygen (p. 366)

Aesthetics (es thet´ iks) visual appearance (p. 274)

Affluence (af´ lü əns) wealth (p. 235)

Agricultural Revolution (ag´ rə kul chər əl rev ə lü´ shən) a period in history when hunter-gatherers learned to farm and raise animals for food (p. 13)

Agricultural solid waste (ag´ rə kul chər əl sol´ id wāst) crop and animal waste (p. 363)

Agriculture (ag´ rə kul chər) another word for farming (p. 13)

Air pollutant (âr pə lüt´ nt) a material in the air that harms living things and nonliving materials (p. 328)

Air pollution (âr pə lü´ shən) pollution in the air (p. 328)

Air pressure (âr presh´ ər) pressure caused by the weight of the atmosphere (p. 64)

Algae (al´ jē) tiny organisms that make their own food (p. 24)

Alpine tundra (al´ pīn tun´ dra) tundra located above the tree line of high mountains (p. 191)

Altitude (al´ tə tüd´) the height above sea level (p. 166)

Ammonium (ə mō´ nē əm) a form of nitrogen that some plants can absorb (p. 58)

Amphibian (am fib´ ē ən) an animal that spends part of its life in water and part on land (p. 178)

Analysis (ə nal´ ə sis) the process of making sense of an experiment's results; also the fifth step of the scientific method (p. 27)

Anemia (ə nē´ mē ə) a blood condition that can result from lack of iron (p. 409)

Aphotic zone (ā fō´ tik zōn) the bottom zone of ocean life, where there is no light (p. 199)

Applied science (ə plīd´ sī əns) a field of study that uses scientific knowledge to solve practical problems (p. 3)

Aquaculture (ak´ wə kul chər) fish farming (p. 421)

Aquatic (ə kwat´ ik) living or growing in water (p. 164)

Aquifer (ak´ wə fər) underground layers of rock, sand, or gravel that trap, store, and transport water (p. 296)

Arctic tundra (ärk´ tik tun´ dra) tundra located north of the Arctic Circle (p. 191)

Asteroid (as´ tə roid) a rocky space object (p. 432)

Atmosphere (at´ mə sfir) the layer of air surrounding the earth (p. 49)

Atom (at´ əm) the basic building block of matter (p. 57)

Axis (ak´ sis) a straight line an object seems to rotate around (p. 62)

B

Bacteria (bak tir´ ē ə) the simplest organisms that carry out all basic life activities (p. 46)

Ban (ban) to forbid by law (p. 82)

Barrier reef (bar´ ē ər rēf) a long coral reef that acts as a barrier against tides and winds (p. 200)

Base (bās) a bitter, slippery substance that contains the hydroxyl radical (p. 343)

Bedrock (bed´ rok) the solid layer of rock beneath soil and other loose materials (p. 399)

Bias (bī´ əs) a personal belief that can affect an experiment's results (p. 24)

Bioaccumulation (bī´ ō ə kyü myə la´ shən) the process by which toxic chemical compounds accumulate through the food chain (p. 312)

Biodegradable (bi ō di grā´ də bəl) able to be broken down by organisms into simpler substances (p. 361)

a	hat	e	let	ī	ice	ȯ	order	u̇	put	sh	she	ə	a	in about
ā	age	ē	equal	o	hot	oi	oil	ü	rule	th	thin		e	in taken
ä	far	ėr	term	ō	open	ou	out	ch	child	ᴛʜ	then		i	in pencil
â	care	i	it	ȯ	saw	u	cup	ng	long	zh	measure		o	in lemon
													u	in circus

Biodiversity (bī ō di vėr′ sə tē) the variety of life on Earth; another name for nature (p. 21)

Biomass (bī′ ō mas) plant material that is burned for fuel (p. 276)

Biome (bī′ ōm) a group of ecosystems with similar temperature and rainfall, or salinity and water depth (p. 164)

Biosphere (bī′ ə sfir) the parts of the earth where living things are found (p. 49)

Biotic factor (bī ot′ ik fak′ tər) a living part of the environment (p. 83)

Birth rate (bėrth′ rāt) the number of births per 1,000 people in a given year (p. 219)

Bog (bog) an area of wet, spongy ground full of decomposing plant matter (p. 192)

Boom-bust cycle (büm bust sī′ kəl) a cycle in which predators increase as prey increases, and predators decrease as prey decreases (p. 107)

Built environment (bilt en vī′ rən mənt) what humans have made, such as roads and buildings (p. 3)

Buttress (but′ ris) special root structures that support a tree and make it more stable (p. 174)

Bycatch (bī′ kach) unwanted fish and other animals (p. 420)

Calcium (kal′ sē əm) a mineral important for teeth, muscles, and bone growth (p. 407)

Calorie (kal′ ər ē) the unit of heat needed to raise one gram of water one degree Celsius (p. 407)

Camouflage (kam′ ə fläzh) colors, patterns, or behaviors that help organisms hide in their surroundings (p. 107)

Canopy (kan′ ə pē) the layer formed by the leaves and branches of the forest's tallest trees (p. 174)

Captive breeding (kap′ tiv brē′ ding) the practice of raising plants or animals in zoos, botanical gardens, and aquariums (p. 461)

Carbohydrate (kär bō hī′ drāt) a sugar or starch that living things use for energy (p. 407)

Carbon sequestration (kär bən sē kwə strā′ shən) the long-term storage of carbon in forests, soils, oceans, and underground (p. 351)

Carbon sink (kär bən singk) a place where carbon builds up and is stored (p. 351)

Carnivore (kär′ nə vôr) an animal that eats other animals (p. 92)

Carpooling (kär′ pül ing) sharing car rides with others to reduce energy use (p. 281)

Carrion (kar′ ē ən) a dead animal or rotten meat (p. 93)

Carrying capacity (kar′ ē ing kə pas′ ə tē) the largest number of living things an area can support (p. 219)

Catalytic converter (kat l it′ ik kən vėr′ tər) a device designed to reduce emissions of air pollutants from vehicle exhaust (p. 337)

Category (kat′ ə gôr ē) a group (p. 20)

Cell (sel) the basic unit of life (p. 8)

Cellular respiration (sel′ yə lər res pə rā′ shən) the process cells use to release energy from food (p. 89)

Chain reaction (chān rē ak′ shən) a reaction that causes itself to continue (p. 262)

Channel (chan′ l) the bed of a river or stream that directs flowing water (p. 205)

Chaparral (shap ə ral′) dry grasslands found in coastal areas (p. 186)

Chemical reaction (kem′ ə kəl rē ak′ shən) a chemical change (p. 51)

Chemosynthesis (kem ō sin′ thə sis) a process bacteria and other forms of life use to create energy from chemicals (p. 92)

Chlorophyll (klôr′ ə fil) a green pigment in plants that absorbs sunlight (p. 91)

Chloroplast (klôr′ ə plast) a structure in a cell that harvests energy from the sun (p. 91)

Cholera (kol′ ər ə) an intestinal infection caused by contaminated water or food (p. 310)

Citizen science project (sit′ ə zən sī′ əns proj′ ekt) a project in which volunteers work with scientists to answer real-world questions (p. 492)

Clear-cutting (klir kut′ ing) harvesting all trees in a large area (p. 421)

Climate (klī′ mit) the average weather in a particular area (p. 62)

Climate change (klī′ mit chānj) a change in Earth's climate associated with global warming (p. 347)

Climax community (klī′ maks kə myü′ nə tē) the last step in the succession of an ecosystem (p. 114)

Coal (kōl) a solid fossil fuel made up of almost pure carbon (p. 257)

Coastal wetland (kō′ stl wet′ land) a wetland washed by tides, always under salt water or under a mix of freshwater and salt water (p. 200)

Coexist (kō eg zist′) to exist at the same time, in the same place (p. 106)

Cold desert (kōld dez′ ərt) a desert where temperatures can drop below 0°C (p. 194)

Colony (kol′ ə nē) a group of the same kind of organisms growing and living together (p. 200)

Comet (kom′ it) a ball of ice, rock, frozen gases, and dust that orbits the sun (p. 45)

Commensalism (kə men′ sə liz əm) a relationship between two species where one benefits and the other is not affected (p. 145)

Community (kə myü´ nə tē) a group of different species that live in the same area (p. 88)

Community-supported agriculture (kə myü´ nə tē sə pôr tid´ ag´ rə kul chər) a system where members pay a farm for weekly deliveries of fresh produce (p. 415)

Commuter train (kə myü´ tər trān) a train that provides transportation from suburbs or other locations to business areas (p. 481)

Compact fluorescents (kəm pakt´ flü res´ ntz) energy-efficient lightbulbs (p. 281)

Competition (kom pə tish´ ən) a relationship in which different individuals or populations try to use the same limited resources (p. 105)

Compost (kom´ pōst) decomposed organic waste that is high in nutrients (p. 239)

Compound (kom´ pound) a combination of two or more elements (p. 151)

Condensation (kon´ den sā´ shən) the process of changing from a gas to a liquid (p. 56)

Conifer (kon´ ə fər) a cone-bearing tree that has needles instead of leaves and stays green all year (p. 179)

Coniferous forest (kō nif´ ər əs fôr´ ist) a forest in northern latitudes dominated by conifers (p. 179)

Consequence (kon´ sə kwens) the effect of an action (p. 34)

Conservation (kon sər vā´ shən) protecting natural resources (p. 127)

Conservationist (kon sər vā´ shə nist) someone interested in protecting species and ecosystems (p. 127)

Conserve (kən sėrv´) to save or preserve (p. 186)

Consumer (kən sü´ mər) an organism that feeds on other organisms (p. 92)

Consumption (kən sump´ shən) the process of using resources and producing waste (p. 227)

Contaminate (kən tam´ ə nāt) to pollute (p. 256)

Continental crust (kon tə nen´ tl krust) the lighter crust that makes up the continents (p. 45)

Continental drift (kon tə nen´ tl drift) the theory of how continents move over time (p. 49)

Contour farming (kon´ tür fär´ ming) planting crops around the contours of the land rather than in straight rows (p. 402)

Control group (kən trōl grüp) the group in an experiment that has no variable changed (p. 26)

Control rod (kən trōl rod) a nonradioactive rod used to control the fission process (p. 262)

Coral bleaching (kôr´ əl blēch´ ing) a process in which a coral dies and turns white (p. 24)

Coral reef (kôr´ əl rēf) a marine ecosystem formed by the skeletons of corals (p. 200)

Core (kôr) the hot center of the earth (p. 45); the center of a nuclear reactor, where fuel rods and control rods are inserted (p. 264)

Coriolis effect (kôr ē ō´ lis ə fekt´) the effect of Earth's spinning on the movement of air from the equator to the poles and back (p. 63)

Corporate social responsibility (kôr´ pər it sō´ shəl ri spon sə bil´ ə tē) the role of business in contributing to a better society and a cleaner environment (p. 491)

Corrosive waste (kə rō´ siv wāst) waste that eats or wears away material by chemical action (p. 374)

Crop yield (krop yēld) the size of the harvest from a particular crop (p. 395)

Crude oil (krüd oil) a thick, liquid fossil fuel found underground (p. 255)

Crust (krust) the outer layer of the earth (p. 45)

Culture (kul´ chər) the languages, religions, customs, arts, and dress of a people (p. 4)

Cyanobacteria (sī ə nō bak tir´ ē ə) the first organisms on Earth to use sunlight to make their own food; also known as blue-green algae (p. 47)

Cycle (sī´ kəl) a repeating pattern (p. 13)

D

Dam (dam) a barrier built across a river to control the flow of water (p. 273)

Data (dā´ tə) information collected during experiments (p. 27)

Daylighting (dā´ lī ting) using sunlight to replace or supplement artificial light (p. 267)

Dead zone (ded zōn) an area in the ocean where most marine organisms cannot survive (p. 396)

Death rate (deth rāt) the number of deaths per 1,000 people in a given year (p. 219)

Debris (də brē´) the remains of something that was destroyed (p. 44)

Deciduous tree (di sij´ ü əs trē) a tree that sheds its leaves at the end of the growing season (p. 177)

Decomposer (dē kəm pō´ zər) an organism that breaks down dead organisms and other organic waste (p. 93)

Deep-well injection (dēp wel in jek´ shən) a process where toxic liquids are pumped into cracks in underground rock layers (p. 382)

Deforestation (dē fôr ist ā´ shən) the removal of forest ecosystems for land development (p. 175)

a	hat	e	let	ī	ice	ô	order	ù	put	sh	she	ə	a in about
ā	age	ē	equal	o	hot	oi	oil	ü	rule	th	thin		e in taken
ä	far	ėr	term	ō	open	ou	out	ch	child	ᴛʜ	then		i in pencil
â	care	i	it	ȯ	saw	u	cup	ng	long	zh	measure		o in lemon
													u in circus

Demographer (di mog´ rə fər) a scientist who studies population (p. 221)

Depleted (di plēt´ id) used up (p. 297)

Deposit (di poz´ it) a layer of material laid down naturally (p. 255)

Desert (dez´ ərt) an area with a high rate of evaporation that receives very little precipitation; can be hot or cold (p. 194)

Detritus (di trī´ təs) dead, decaying plant and animal material (p. 199)

Developing nation (di vel´ ə ping nā´ shən) a nation that has not yet become industrialized (p. 223)

Diatom (dī´ ə tom) a tiny alga found in the ocean millions of years ago (p. 255)

Disphotic zone (dis fō´ tik zōn) the middle zone of ocean life, which gets little or no light (p. 199)

Dissolve (di zolv´) to break apart (p. 8)

Distinct (dis tingkt´) separate; not the same (p. 138)

Distribution (dis trə byü´ shen) the location of species in a community (p. 114)

Diverse (də vėrs´) varied (p. 115)

Diversity (də vėr´ sə tē) variety (p. 19)

Divert (də vėrt´) to turn from one course to another (p. 302)

Domain (dō mān´) the highest level of classification of living things (p. 83)

Domesticated (də mes´ tə kā tid) bred for human use (p. 395)

Dormant (dôr´ mənt) inactive (p. 178)

Downstream (doun´ strēm) the direction a river or stream flows, away from its source (p. 273)

Draft animal (draft an´ ə məl) a horse or other large animal that pulls farm equipment (p. 394)

Drift net (drift net) a net that floats freely through the ocean (p. 419)

Drip irrigation (drip ir ə gā´ shən) irrigation in which water is delivered in drops directly to the plants' roots (p. 317)

Drought (drout) an unusually long period of little rainfall (p. 300)

Dry deposition (drī dep ə zish´ ən) acid pollutants that settle on the earth as solids (p. 342)

Dysentery (dis´ n ter ē) an intestinal infection marked by severe diarrhea (p. 310)

E

Ecological restoration (ē kə loj´ ə kəl res tə rā´ shən) the process of returning a damaged ecosystem to its original condition (p. 460)

Ecological view (ē kə loj´ ə kəl vyü) the opinion that it is important to protect biodiversity to preserve ecosystems and the services they provide (p. 456)

Ecologist (ē kol´ ə jist) a scientist who studies ecology (p. 82)

Ecology (ē kōl´ ə jē) the interactions among living things and the nonliving things in their environment (p. 82)

Economic (ē kə nom´ ik) having to do with money or finances (p. 152)

Economist (i kon´ ə mist) an expert in the field of economics (p. 478)

Economy (i kon´ ə mē) a system of production, distribution, and consumption (p. 152)

Ecosystem (e´ kō sis təm) all of the living and nonliving things found in an area (p. 19)

Ecosystem diversity (e´ kō sis təm də vėr´ sə tē) the diversity of ecosystems on Earth (p. 126)

Ecosystem service (e´ kō sis təm sėr´ vis) a benefit provided by Earth's ecosystems (p. 149)

Edible (ed´ ə bəl) able to be safely eaten (p. 406)

Electromagnetic radiation (i lek trō mag net´ ik rā dē ā´ shən) radiation that is made up of electric and magnetic waves (p. 9)

Electron (i lek´ tron) a tiny particle with a negative charge that moves around the nucleus of an atom (p. 261)

Element (el´ ə mənt) matter that has only one kind of atom (p. 57)

Emergent (i mėr´ jənt) a tree that grows taller than the canopy trees around it (p. 174)

Emission (i mish´ ən) a release of a substance into the environment (p. 330)

Endangered (en dān´ jərd) at risk of extinction (p. 131)

Endemic (en dem´ ik) found in one part of the planet and nowhere else (p. 132)

Energy (en´ ər jē) the ability to do work; found in many different forms (p. 9)

Energy conservation (en´ ər jē kon sər vā´ shən) using less energy and wasting less energy (p. 281)

Energy efficiency (en´ ər jē ə fish´ ən sē) the percentage of useful work from an input of energy (p. 281)

Energy efficient (en´ ər jē ə fish´ ənt) wastes less energy (p. 281)

Energy pyramid (en´ ər jē pir´ ə mid) a diagram comparing the amounts of energy available to populations at different tropic levels (p. 98)

Environment (en vī´ rən mənt) an organism's natural and human-made surroundings (p. 2)

Environmental economist (en vī rən mən´ təl i kon´ ə mist) an economist who works to account for nature's value in economics (p. 478)

Environmental justice (en vī rən mən´ təl jus´ tis) dealing with environmental problems in a way that treats people equally (p. 35)

Environmental science (en vī rən mən´ təl sī´ əns) the study of how living things, including humans, interact with their environment (p. 2)

Environmentally intelligent design (en vī rən mən´ tə lē in tel´ ə jənt di zīn´) an approach that tries to change production so no harmful waste is created (p. 238)

Equator (i kwā´ tər) the imaginary line halfway between the North and South Poles (p. 62)

Equity (ek´ wə tē) fairness (p. 236)

Erode (i rōd´) to break apart or wear away (p. 113)

Eruption (i rup´ shən) an explosion from beneath the earth's surface (p. 45)

Estuary (es´ chü ər ē) a marine ecosystem where freshwater and salt water meet (p. 200)

Ethanol (eth´ ə nol) a fuel made from corn or sugar cane (p. 276)

Ethics (eth´ iks) a set of moral principles (p. 33)

Eutrophication (yü trə fə kā´ shən) the process by which plant nutrients increase plant growth and decrease available oxygen (p. 311)

Evaporation (i vap ər ā´ shən) the process of water changing from liquid to vapor (p. 55)

Evergreen (ev´ ər grēn) a tree that keeps its leaves or needles all year (p. 179)

Evolution (ev ə lü´ shən) the process of genetic change in a population over time (p. 136)

Evolve (i volv´) to develop and change genetically over time (p. 135)

Experimental group (ek sper ə men´ tl grüp) similar to the control group, except for the variable being tested (p. 26)

Exponential growth (ek spo nen´ shəl grōth) growth that increases by larger and larger amounts (p. 217)

Extinct (ek stingkt´) when no members of a species remain (p. 21)

Extinction (ek stingk´ shən) the loss of all members of a species (p. 131)

Extract (ek strakt´) to take out or harvest (p. 193)

Extremophile (ik strē´ mə fil) a tiny organism that lives in one of Earth's harshest environments (p. 46)

F

Family planning (fam´ ə lē plan´ ing) deciding when to have children and how many to have (p. 225)

Famine (fam´ ən) when large numbers of people in an area are hungry due to a natural disaster or war (p. 409)

Farmers market (fär´ mərs mär´ kit) a place where local farmers can sell their produce (p. 415)

Fat (fat) a chemical that stores large amounts of energy (p. 407)

Feedlot (fēd´ lot) a small area where large numbers of livestock are raised together (p. 397)

Fertility rate (fər til´ ə tē rāt) the average number of births per woman (p. 225)

Fertilizer (fèr´ tl ī zər) an organic or inorganic plant nutrient (p. 311)

Field study (fēld stud´ ē) a study conducted in a natural environment (p. 26)

Financial capital (fə nan´ shəl kap´ ə təl) wealth that is used to generate more wealth (p. 478)

Finite (fī´ nīt) having an end, limited (p. 203)

First law of energy (fèrst lȯ ov en´ ər jē) energy is neither created nor destroyed (p. 251)

Fish ladder (fish lad´ ər) a series of pools that allow fish to move upstream over a dam (p. 273)

Fishery (fish´ ər ē) an industry that catches and sells fish (p. 230)

Flowing-water ecosystem (flō´ ing wȯ´ tər e´ kō sis təm) a freshwater ecosystem that has flowing water, such as a river or stream (p. 203)

Fly ash (flī ash) waste ash from coal-burning electrical power plants (p. 363)

Food chain (füd chān) the feeding order of organisms in a community (p. 96)

Food web (füd web) all the food chains in a community that are linked together (p. 97)

Forest floor (fȯr´ ist flȯr) the layer of decomposing material that covers the forest soil (p. 175)

Fossil (fos´ əl) the remains of animals and plants found in rocks (p. 70)

Fossil fuel (fos´ əl fyü´ əl) oil, coal, or another source of energy that comes from fossilized plants and animals (p. 228)

Freshwater (fresh´ wȯt ər) water with very low amounts of dissolved salt (p. 167)

Fuel cell (fyü´ əl sel) a device for converting chemicals to electricity (p. 283)

Fuel rod (fyü´ əl rod) a radioactive rod used in nuclear fission (p. 262)

G

Gene (jēn) the information about a trait passed from parent to offspring (p. 125)

Generate (jen´ ə rāt) to create by physical process (p. 206)

Generator (jen´ ə rā tər) a machine that generates electricity (p. 255)

Genetic diversity (jə net´ ik də vèr´ sə tē) the diversity of genes among individuals and species (p. 125)

a	hat	e	let	ī	ice	ô	order	ů	put	sh	she	ə	a	in about
ā	age	ē	equal	o	hot	oi	oil	ü	rule	th	thin		e	in taken
ä	far	ėr	term	ō	open	ou	out	ch	child	ㅝH	then		i	in pencil
à	care	i	it	ȯ	saw	u	cup	ng	long	zh	measure		o	in lemon
													u	in circus

Genuine progress indicator (GPI) (jen´ yü ən prog´ res in´ də kā tər) a measure of progress that includes economic, social, and environmental factors (p. 477)

Geothermal (jē ō ther´ məl) heat from inside the earth (p. 275)

Geyser (gī´ zər) a jet of hot liquid or steam that shoots out of a crack in Earth's crust (p. 275)

Gill net (gil net) a net that traps a fish's head and gill covers (p. 419)

Glacier (glā´ shər) a thick mass of ice that covers a large area (p. 69)

Global (glō´ bəl) affecting the entire world (p. 19)

Global warming (glō´ bəl wôrm´ ing) an increase in Earth's average surface temperature (p. 20)

Grassland (gras´ land) a large, grassy biome with few shrubs or trees (p. 183)

Gray water (grā wô´ tər) wastewater that does not contain animal waste and can be used to water crops (p. 318)

Green Revolution (grēn revə lü´ shən) a large increase in crop yields achieved by developing new varieties of plants (p. 406)

Greenhouse effect (grēn´ hous ə fekt´) the warming of the atmosphere because of trapped heat energy from the sun (p. 348)

Greenhouse gas (grēn´ hous gas) a gas in the atmosphere that helps trap heat around the earth (p. 348)

Gross domestic product (GDP) (grōs də mes´ tik prod´ əkt) the total value of all goods and services produced in a country in a given period of time (p. 476)

Groundwater (ground´ wô´ tər) water found underground (p. 51)

Growth rate (grōth rāt) the rate at which a population is increasing or decreasing (p. 216)

H

Habitat (hab´ ə tat) the place where an organism lives (p. 14)

Habitat fragmentation (hab´ ə tat frag mən tā´ shən) breaking up large areas of habitat into smaller pieces (p. 434)

Hatchery (hach´ ər ē) a place where the eggs of fish are hatched (p. 445)

Hazardous waste (haz´ ər dəs wāst) waste that is very dangerous to living things and the environment (p. 360)

Headwaters (hed´ wô tərz) the upper part of a river or stream, near its source (p. 205)

Heavy metal (hev´ ē met´ l) a metallic element that can damage living things, such as mercury, arsenic, or lead (p. 366)

Hepatitis (hep ə tī´ tis) a disease that damages the liver (p. 310)

Herbicide (hėr´ bə sīd) a chemical used to kill weeds (p. 311)

Herbivore (hėr´ bə vôr) an animal that eats only plants (p. 92)

Hibernate (hī´ bər nāt) to pass the winter in a sleeplike condition (p. 178)

HIPPO (hip´ ō) an acronym that stands for the five major reasons for biodiversity loss (p. 434)

Homo sapiens (hō´ mō sā´ pē enz) the scientific name for modern humans (p. 12)

Horizon (hə rī´ zn) a layer of soil (p. 400)

Horizontal zone (hôr ə zon´ tl zōn) an ocean zone classified by the distance from shore (p. 198)

Host (hōst) an organism that provides food for a parasite (p. 146)

Hot desert (hot dez´ ərt) a desert where temperatures are hot all year (p. 194)

Hot spring (hot spring) a natural flow of groundwater heated inside the earth (p. 275)

Household hazardous waste (hous´ hōld haz´ ər dəs wāst) harmful wastes, such as batteries, bleach, and paint, that are generated by households (p. 362)

Humidity (hyü mid´ ə tē) the amount of moisture in the air (p. 64)

Humus (hyü´ məs) decomposed plant and animal matter that is part of fertile soil (p. 178)

Hunter-gatherer (hun´ tər gath´ ər ər) a person who hunts, gathers food, and moves from place to place to survive (p. 12)

Hybrid vehicle (hī´ brid vē´ ə kəl) a vehicle that runs on both a gasoline engine and an electric motor (p. 282)

Hydropower (hī´ drō pou´ ər) energy that comes from moving water (p. 273)

Hydrosphere (hī´ drə sfir) the water layer of the earth (p. 49)

Hypothesis (hī poth´ ə sis) an educated guess; also the third step of the scientific method (plural: hypotheses) (p. 26)

I

Ice age (īs āj) a period of global cooling (p. 69)

Ignitable waste (ig nīt´ ə bəl wāst) waste that catches on fire easily (p. 374)

Immature (im ə chúr´) too young to reproduce (p. 421)

Impermeable (im pėr´ mē ə bəl) not allowing water to flow through (p. 297)

Impurity (im pyúr´ ə tē) pollution or contamination (p. 259)

Inbreeding (in´ brēd ing) the mating of relating individuals (p. 441)

Incinerator (in sin´ ə rā tər) a facility where trash is burned instead of being buried in a landfill (p. 368)

Indicator (in´ də kā tər) a measure of change (p. 474)

Indigenous (in dij´ ə nəs) native to a place (p. 175)

Indoor air pollution (in´ dôr âr pə lü´ shən) pollution that is found and measured indoors (p. 329)

Industrial Revolution (in dus´ trē əl rev ə lü´ shən) a period in history when humans started using machines to produce food and other products (p. 14)

Industrial smog (in dus´ trē əl smog) a form of smog produced by burning coal and oil (p. 335)

Industrial solid waste (in dus´ trē əl sol´ id wāst) waste from manufacturing and other industrial processes (p. 363)

Industrialized agriculture (in dus´ trē ə līzd ag´ rə kul chər) large-scale agriculture (p. 395)

Industrialized nation (in dus´ trē ə līzd nā´ shən) a nation with well-developed industries and economies (p. 222)

Industry (in´ d ə strē) the making and selling of a particular good or service (p. 300)

Inefficient (in ə fish´ ənt) wasteful (p. 252)

Infectious waste (in fek´ shəs wāst) waste that can cause diseases (p. 375)

Inorganic (in ôr gan´ ik) not containing carbon (p. 92)

Insulation (in sə lā´ shən) a material that prevents heat or cold from escaping into or out of a space (p. 268)

Integrated waste management (in tə grā´ tid wāst man´ ij mənt) controlling solid waste using a combination of approaches, including source reduction and recycling (p. 378)

Interbreed (in tər brēd´) to breed together (p. 138)

Internet (in´ tər net) a worldwide network of computers (p. 27)

Intertidal zone (in tər tī´ dl zōn) the zone between the high and low tide marks (p. 198)

Introduced species (in´ trə düsd spē´ shēz) an organism brought into an area where it is not found naturally (p. 434)

Invertebrate (in vėr´ tə brit) an insect or another species without a backbone (p. 130)

Iron (ī´ ərn) a mineral that helps move oxygen through the bloodstream (p. 407)

Irrigate (ir´ ə gāt) to artificially supply land with water for agriculture or landscaping (p. 302)

Isotopes (ī´ sə tōps) atoms of the same element that have different numbers of neutrons (p. 261)

J

J-curve (jā kėrv) a J-shaped curve (p. 217)

Jet stream (jet strēm) a strong air current high in the atmosphere (p. 64)

K

Keystone species (kē´ stōn spē´ shēz) a species whose presence contributes to the diversity of its ecosystem (p. 146)

Kilocalorie (kil´ ə kal ər ē) 1,000 calories; referred to as a calorie in everyday usage (p. 407)

Kinetic energy (ki net´ ik en ər jē) the energy of motion (p. 250)

Kingdom (king´ dəm) the second level of classification of living things (p. 83)

Krill (kril) tiny, shrimplike animals that provide food for marine creatures (p. 198)

L

Lake (lāk) an inland body of freshwater, larger than a pond and too deep for plants to grow on the bottom (p. 204)

Landscape (land´ skāp) the characteristics of the land (p. 13)

Landscaping (land´ skāp ing) improving the natural beauty of a piece of land (p. 302)

Latitude (lat´ ə tüd) the distance north or south of the equator, measured in degrees (p. 166)

Law (lò) a principle (p. 251)

Leachate (lēch´ āt) contaminated water that leaks from a dump or landfill (p. 366)

Leukemia (lü kē´ mē ə) a cancer of the blood cells (p. 263)

Lichen (lī´ kən) an organism made up of a fungus, a green alga, and a cyanobacterium (p. 113)

Life expectancy (līf ek spek´ tən sē) the total number of years a person is expected to live (p. 223)

Life-support system (līf sə pôrt´ sis´ təm) a system that provides everything needed to stay alive (p. 44)

Light pollution (līt pə lü´ shən) bothersome brightness or glare caused by human-made lights (p. 338)

Lithosphere (lith´ ə sfir) the solid surface and interior of the earth (p. 49)

Loam (lōm) a soil made up of clay, silt, and sand; considered best for growing crops (p. 400)

Local (lō´ kəl) affecting a certain place (p. 19)

Log (lòg) to harvest trees (p. 175)

Longline (lòng´ līn) a long cable with baited hooks every few meters (p. 420)

Low-flow (lō´ flō) designed to use less water (p. 318)

M

Malaria (mə ler´ ē ə) a disease that causes chills, fever, and even death (p. 455)

a	hat	e	let	ī	ice	ò	order	ù	put	sh	she	ə	a in about
ā	age	ē	equal	o	hot	oi	oil	ü	rule	th	thin		e in taken
ä	far	ėr	term	ō	open	ou	out	ch	child	ᴛʜ	then		i in pencil
â	care	i	it	ò	saw	u	cup	ng	long	zh	measure		o in lemon
													u in circus

Malnutrition (mal nü trish´ ən) not getting enough calories or nutrients from one's food (p. 236)

Mandated (man´ dā tid) enforced by law (p. 282)

Mangrove swamp (mang´ grōv swämp) a saltwater swamp dominated by mangrove trees (p. 201)

Mantle (man´tl) the layer of the earth that surrounds the core (p. 45)

Marine biome (mə rēn´ bī´ ōm) an ocean or other saltwater ecosystem (p. 197)

Mass extinction (mas ek stingk´ shən) a period of time when high numbers of species are becoming extinct (p. 131)

Mass-produce (mas prə düs´) to produce in large quantities using machines (p. 14)

Matter (mat´ ər) anything that has mass and takes up space (p. 88)

Meltdown (melt´ doun) complete melting of a nuclear reactor's core (p. 264)

Mesosphere (mes´ ə sfir) the layer of the atmosphere between the stratosphere and the thermosphere (p. 52)

Meteorite (mē´ tē ə rīt´) a piece of rock that hits the surface of a planet or moon after traveling through space (p. 45)

Methane (meth´ ān) a gas released by decaying organisms (p. 258)

Microorganism (mī krō ôr´ gə niz əm) an organism too small to be seen without being magnified (p. 83)

Migrate (mī´ grāt) to move from one region, climate, or environment to another (p. 178)

Migration (mī´ grā shən) a large movement of people from one place to another (p. 216)

Mimicry (mim´ i krē) a method of defense in which a species looks, sounds, or acts like a more dangerous species (p. 108)

Mine (mīn) to extract minerals from the earth (p. 230)

Mineral (min´ ər əl) an element or combination of elements found in the earth (p. 84)

Molecule (mol´ ə kyül) the smallest part of a substance that has the same properties of the substance (p. 89)

Mollusk (mol´ əsk) a soft-bodied animal that lives inside a hard shell (p. 129)

Molten (mōlt´ n) melted into a liquid (p. 44)

Moral (môr´ əl) helping to decide between right or wrong (p. 33)

Mountaintop removal (moun´ tan top ri mü´ vəl) a form of coal mining in which the entire top of a mountain is removed (p. 257)

Mouth (mouth) the place where a stream or river enters another, larger body of water (p. 205)

Municipal solid waste (myü nis´ ə pəl sol´ id wāst) garbage generated by homes, businesses, and institutions (p. 362)

Mutation (myü tā´ shən) a sudden change in an organism's genes (p. 136)

Mutualism (myü´ chü ə liz əm) a relationship between two species where both species benefit (p. 145)

N

Natural capital (nach´ ər əl kap´ ə təl) natural resources that produce a flow of goods and services (p. 478)

Natural environment (nach´ ər əl en vī´ rən mənt) all living and nonliving things founding nature (p. 3)

Natural gas (nach´ ər əl gas) underground deposits of gas, mostly methane (p. 258)

Natural resource (nach´ ər əl ri sôrs´) a material found in nature that his useful to humans (p. 3)

Natural selection (nach´ ər əl si lek´ shən) the process by which organisms best suited to their environment pass on their genes to their offspring (p. 136)

Nectar (nek´ tər) a sweet liquid produced by many flowers (p. 143)

Neritic zone (nə ri´ tik zōn) the zone between the intertidal zone and the edge of the continental shelf (p. 198)

Neutral (nü´ trəl) neither an acid nor a base; having a pH of 7 (p. 343)

Neutron (nü´ tron) a tiny particle in the nucleus of an atom with no electrical charge (p. 261)

Niche (nich) the role an organism plays in an ecosystem; an organism's way of life (p. 104)

Nitrate (nī´ trāt) a form of nitrogen that most plants can absorb (p. 58)

Nitrogen oxide (nī trə jən ok´ sīd) a pollutant produced by burning fossil fuels (p. 256)

Noise pollution (noiz pə lü´ shən) noise that interrupts daily life (p. 338)

Nonbiodegradable (non bi ō di grā´ də bəl) not able to be broken down by organisms (p. 361)

Nonpoint-source pollution (non´ point sôrs pə lü´ shən) pollution that cannot be traced back to a specific source (p. 309)

Nonrenewable (non ri nü´ ə bəl) available in limited supply (p. 253)

Nontoxic (non tok´ sik) not poisonous to the environment (p. 237)

Northern Hemisphere (nôr´ thərn hem´ ə sfir) the parts of the world north of the equator (p. 63)

No-till farming (nō til fär´ ming) leaving the soil undisturbed as a new crop is planted (p. 402)

Nourishment (nėr´ ish mənt) food (p. 106)

Nuclear fission (nü´ klē ər fish´ ən) a process of producing energy by splitting atoms (p. 262)

Nuclear power plant (nü´ klē ər pou´ ər plant) a facility where nuclear energy is converted into electricity (p. 262)

Nuclear reactor (nü´ klē ər rē ak´ tər) a device in which nuclear fission takes place (p. 262)

Nucleus (nü´ klē əs) the center of an atom (p. 261)

Nursery (nèr´ sər ē) a place where marine organisms hatch and grow (p. 201)

Nutrient (nü´ trē ənt) a chemical organisms need to grow (p. 9)

O

O horizon (ō hə rī´ zn) the topmost layer of soil; also called humus (p. 400)

Obesity (ō bē´ sə tē) the state of being significantly overweight (p. 236)

Objective (əb jek´ tiv) not influenced by personal feelings or opinions (p. 33)

Oceanic crust (ō shē an´ ik krust) the heavier crust that makes up the ocean floor (p. 45)

Oceanic zone (ō shē an´ ik zōn) the open ocean (p. 199)

Old-growth forest (ōld grōth fòr´ ist) a forest containing trees that can be hundreds or thousands of years old (p. 115)

Omnivore (om´ nə vôr) an animal that eats both plants and animals (p. 93)

Open dump (ō´ pən dump) a place where garbage is dumped without environmental controls (p. 365)

Ore (òr) a mineral that contains metal (p. 362)

Organic (ôr gan´ ik) living or once-living material containing carbon (p. 93)

Organic farming (ôr gan´ ik fär´ ming) growing produce without the use of chemicals (p. 414)

Organic waste (ôr gan´ ik wāst) waste from living organisms (p. 311)

Organism (ôr´ gə niz əm) a living thing; one of many different forms of life (p. 2)

Origin (ôr´ ə jin) the source or beginning (p. 70)

Outdoor air pollution (out´ dôr âr pə lü´ shən) pollution that is found and measured in outdoor air (p. 329)

Overconsumption (ō vər kən sump´ shən) using more resources than can be replaced (p. 20)

Overfishing (ō vər fish´ ing) catching fish faster than they can reproduce (p. 421)

Overgrazing (ō vər grāz ing) allowing animals to eat more vegetation than is healthy for the soil (p. 185)

Overnutrition (ō vər nü trish´ ən) eating too many calories, especially fats and sugars (p. 409)

Overpopulation (ō vər pop yə lā´ shən) when a population is too large to be supported by local resources (p. 221)

Ozone (ō´ zōn) a harmful gas found in photochemical smog (p. 336)

Ozone layer (ō´ zōn lā ər) the layer of the atmosphere that protects Earth from harmful solar radiation (p. 53)

P

Pangaea (pan jē´ ə) the single landmass on Earth that began to break up 200 million years ago (p. 68)

Parasite (par´ ə sīt) an organism that absorbs food from a host and harms it (p. 146)

Parasitism (par´ ə sī tiz əm) a relationship between two species where one species benefits and the other is harmed (p. 146)

Parent material (pâr´ənt mə tir´ ē əl) the material from which soil first forms (p. 399)

Particle (pär´ tə kəl) a tiny piece (p. 57)

Particulate matter (pär tik´ yə lit mat´ ər) liquid or solid particles in the air (p. 328)

Passive solar cooling (pas´ iv sō´ lər kül´ ing) cooling by blocking sunlight from a building (p. 267)

Passive solar energy (pas´ iv sō´ lər en´ ər jē) energy produced directly by sunlight, without extra machinery (p. 267)

Passive solar heating (pas´ iv sō´ lər hēt´ ing) heating a building directly by sunlight (p. 267)

Pasture (pas´ chər) land used for livestock grazing (p. 395)

Pathogen (path´ ə jən) an organism that can cause disease (p. 301)

PCBs (pē sē bēz) a group of toxic industrial chemicals that were once used in making paint, electrical equipment, and other products (p. 374)

Peat (pēt) partly decomposed plant material found in wetlands (p. 276)

Permafrost (pèr´ mə frôst) permanently frozen ground at high latitude and high elevation (p. 192)

Permeable (pèr´ mē ə bəl) allowing water to flow through (p. 297)

Pesticide (pes´ tə sīd) any chemical used to kill or control pests (p. 10)

Petroleum (pə trō´ lē əm) another word for crude oil (p. 255)

pH (pē āch) a number tells whether a substance is an acid or a base (p. 343)

Photic zone (fō´ tik zōn) the top zone of ocean life, which gets sunlight all year (p. 198)

Photochemical smog (fō tō kem´ ə kəl smog) a mixture of pollutants produced primarily by burning gasoline (p. 336)

Photosynthesis (fō tō sin´ thə sis) a process plants use to change energy from the sun into stored sugars (p. 91)

Photovoltaics (fō tō vol tā ikz) devices that convert solar energy into electricity; also called solar cells (p. 269)

a	hat	e	let	ī	ice	ô	order	ù	put	sh	she	ə	a in about
ā	age	ē	equal	o	hot	oi	oil	ü	rule	th	thin		e in taken
ä	far	èr	term	ō	open	ou	out	ch	child	ᴛʜ	then		i in pencil
â	care	i	it	ò	saw	u	cup	ng	long	zh	measure		o in lemon
													u in circus

Phytoplankton (fī tō plangk´tən) a microscopic plant that forms the base of the marine food chain (p. 198)

Pigment (pig´ mənt) a chemical that absorbs certain kinds of light energy (p. 91)

Pioneer species (pī ə nir´ spē´ shēz) the first species to arrive in an area (p. 113)

Plantation agriculture (plan tā´ shən ag´ rə kul chər) large-scale farms that grow single crops; usually located in tropical areas (p. 396)

Plate tectonics (plāt tek ton´ iks) the study of plates and how they move (p. 49)

Poacher (pōch´ er) a person who hunts wildlife illegally (p. 454)

Point-source pollution (point sôrs pə lü´ shən) pollution that comes from a particular source (p. 308)

Polar ice cap (pō´ lər īs kap) an enormous mass of ice located at both the North and South Poles (p. 56)

Policy (pol´ ə sē) a plan of action for political issues (p. 490)

Pollen (pol´ ən) the male reproductive cells of plants (p. 143)

Pollination (pol ə nā´ shən) the transfer of pollen between plants for reproduction (p. 143)

Pollution (pə lü´ shən) anything added to the environment that is harmful to living things (p. 14)

Pond (pond) an inland body of freshwater, smaller than a lake and shallow enough for plants to grow on the bottom (p. 204)

Population (pop yə lā´ shən) a group of organisms of the same species that live in the same area (p. 87)

Population trend (pop yə lā´ shən trend) a change in population over time (p. 221)

Porosity (pô ros´ ə tē) the percentage of a volume of soil that is empty space (p. 400)

Potential energy (pə ten´ shəl en´ ər jē) the energy stored in an object (p. 250)

Poverty level (pov´ ər tē lev´ əl) the amount one must earn to afford what is needed to live (p. 223)

Power grid (pou´ ər grid) a network of power lines used to distribute electricity to a region (p. 270)

Prairie (prâ´ rē) a temperate grassland with very fertile soil (p. 184)

Precipitation (pri sip ə tā´ shən) the moisture that falls to the earth from the atmosphere (p. 56)

Predation (prē dā´ shən) a relationship in which one species eats another species (p. 106)

Predator (pred´ ə tər) an organism that hunts and feeds on other consumers (p. 106)

Prevailing winds (pri vā´ ling winds) the three major wind belts on Earth (p. 64)

Prey (prā) a consumer that is eaten by another organism (p. 106)

Primary air pollutant (prī´ mer ē âr pə lüt´ nt) a harmful chemical that enters the air directly (p. 329)

Primary consumer (prī´ mer ē kən sü´ mər) an herbivore that feeds on plants (p. 98)

Primary succession (prī mer´ ē sək sesh´ ən) succession in a lifeless environment that creates a community (p. 113)

Principle (prin´ sə pəl) a basic law or truth (p. 32)

Producer (prə dü´ sər) an organism that makes its own food (p. 91)

Protein (prō´ tēn) a chemical used by cells to grow and work (p. 407)

Protein-calorie malnutrition (prō´ tēn kal´ ər ē mal nü trish´ ən) not consuming enough fats, carbohydrates, or protein (p. 408)

Proton (prō´ ton) a tiny particle in the nucleus of an atom with a positive electrical charge (p. 261)

Proxy data (prok´ sē dā´ tə) fossilized evidence that helps scientists understand past climate conditions (p. 70)

Public transportation (pub´ lik tran spər tā´ shən) buses, subways, and other forms of transportation shared by the public (p. 482)

Purification (pyur ə fi kā´ shən) cleaning by separating out pollutants or impurities (p. 303)

Q

Quantify (kwän´ tə fī) to express something as a number (p. 474)

R

Radical (rad´ ə kəl) a group of two or more atoms that act like one atom (p. 343)

Radioactive (rā dē ō ak´ tiv) giving off energy while changing into another substance (p. 262)

Radioactive waste (rā dē ō ak´ tiv wāst) waste that contains or is contaminated by radioactive materials (p. 312)

Radioisotope (rā dē ō ī´ sə tōp) a radioactive element that helps scientists determine a rock's age (p. 70)

Rangeland (rānj´ land) grass-covered land that animals can graze on (p. 397)

Rapid assessment (rap´ id ə ses´ mənt) a brief, high-speed survey of an area's biological diversity (p. 132)

Recharge (rē chärj´) to refill an aquifer (p. 297)

Recharge zone (rē chärj´ zōn) an area in which water travels downward to become part of an aquifer (p. 297)

Recreation (rek rē ā´ shən) play or amusement (p. 294)

Recreational view (rek rē ā´ shə nal vyü) the opinion that it is important to protect biodiversity because natural areas provide opportunities for outdoor activities (p. 456)

Recycle (rē sī´ kəl) to reuse the same matter in different forms (p. 89)

Refinery (ri fī nər ē) a place where crude oil is turned into usable forms of oil (p. 255)

Regional (rē′ jə nəl) affecting part of the world, such as a country (p. 19)

Regulation (reg yə lā′ shən) a rule enforced by a government agency (p. 490)

Regulatory agency (reg′ yə lə tôr ē ā′ jen sē) a government agency that enforces laws and regulations (p. 490)

Renewable (ri nü′ ə bəl) able to be renewed by natural processes (p. 230)

Reproduce (rē prə düs′) to breed and produce offspring (p. 9)

Reproduction (rē prə duk′ shən) the process by which living things produce offspring (p. 88)

Reproductive age (rē prə duk′ tiv āj) neither too old nor too young to have children (p. 222)

Reptile (rep′ tīl) a scaly, egg-laying animal that breathes with lungs (p. 178)

Reserve (ri zėrv′) an amount of a natural resource known to be available (p. 257)

Reservoir (rez′ ər vwär) a pond or lake, either natural or artificial, for the storage of water (p. 304)

Respiratory (res′ pər ə tōr ē) related to breathing (p. 330)

Revolve (ri volv′) to move in a circle around a point (p. 63)

Rotate (rō′ tāt) to turn in a circle (p. 62)

Runoff (run′ óf) rain or melted snow that flows over land to streams, rivers, lakes, and the ocean (p. 309)

Rural (rür′ əl) away from the city (p. 152)

S

Salinity (sə lin′ə tē) the amount of salt dissolved in sea water (p. 167)

Salt marsh (sȯlt märsh) a marsh periodically flooded by marine water (p. 201)

Salt water (sȯlt wȯ′ tər) water with high amounts of dissolved salts (p. 167)

Sample (sam′ pəl) a small part of a larger unit (p. 133)

Sanitary landfill (san′ ə ter ē land′ fil) a site for disposing of solid waste on land (p. 365)

Sanitation (san ə tā′ shən) disposal of waste (p. 223)

Saturated (sach′ ə rāt id) unable to hold more liquid (p. 200)

Savanna (sə van′ ə) a tropical grassland with scattered trees or clumps of trees (p. 184)

Scarcity (skâr′ sə tē) not having enough of something (p. 298)

Scavenger (skav′ ən jər) an animal that feeds on dead animals (p. 93)

Scientific journal (sī ən tif′ ik jėr′ nl) a science magazine (p. 27)

Scientific method (sī ən tif′ ik meth′ əd) a series of steps used to test possible answers to scientific questions (p. 24)

Scrubber (skrub′ ər) a device that removes sulfur from industrial smokestack emissions (p. 345)

Seasonal (sē′ zn əl) existing only at certain times during the year (p. 204)

Second law of energy (sek′ ənd lȯ ov en′ ər jē) energy always changes from higher-quality to lower-quality forms (p. 252)

Secondary air pollutant (sek′ ən der ē âr pə lüt′ nt) a harmful chemical that forms as a reaction between other chemicals in the air (p. 329)

Secondary consumer (sek′ ən der ē kən sü′ mər) a carnivore or omnivore that feeds on herbivores (p. 98)

Secondary succession (sek′ ən der ē sək sesh′ ən) succession in an environment that was disturbed by humans or natural causes (p. 114)

Secure chemical landfill (si kyür′ kem′ ə kəl land′ fil) a dump designed specifically for hazardous waste (p. 382)

Sedimentary rock (sed ə men′ tə rē rok) a layered rock formed of sand, gravel, and mud (p. 70)

Seed bank (sēd bangk) a place where seeds of endangered and threatened plant species are stored (p. 461)

Seed dispersal (sēd dis pėr′ səl) scattering seeds away from a parent plant (p. 144)

Seep (sēp) to soak into something (p. 296)

Sewage (sü′ ij) human-generated liquid pollution that flows from homes, businesses, and industries; also called wastewater (p. 310)

Sewage treatment plant (sü′ ij trēt′ mənt plant) a place where sewage is cleaned before returning to surface water (p. 310)

Shade-grown coffee (shād grōn kȯ′ fē) coffee grown in the shade of tropical trees (p. 415)

Shelterbelt (shel′ tər belt) a row of trees planted to help block wind (p. 402)

Siltation (sil tā′ shən) the buildup of soil in aquatic ecosystems (p. 402)

Skeptical (skep′ tə kəl) questioning or doubting (p. 33)

Slag (slag) the waste leftover from smelting (p. 362)

Sludge (sluj) the semisolid leftovers from sewage treatment processes (p. 363)

Smelting (smel′ ting) the process of removing metals from rocks through melting (p. 362)

Smog (smog) a haze that forms as a result of vehicle and industry emissions (p. 335)

a	hat	e	let	ī	ice	ȯ	order	ú	put	sh	she	ə	a in about
ā	age	ē	equal	o	hot	oi	oil	ü	rule	th	thin		e in taken
ä	far	ėr	term	ō	open	ou	out	ch	child	ᴛʜ	then		i in pencil
â	care	i	it	ȯ	saw	u	cup	ng	long	zh	measure		o in lemon
													u in circus

Soil erosion (soil i rō′ zhən) the movement of soil from one place to another (p. 397)

Solar collector (sō′ lər kə lek′ tər) a device that captures solar energy and converts it to heat (p. 269)

Solar energy (sō′ lər en′ ər jē) energy from the sun (p. 267)

Solid waste (sol′ id wāst) solid materials, such as paper, metals, and yard waste, that are thrown away (p. 360)

Solvent (sol′ vənt) a liquid that can dissolve other substances (p. 381)

Source reduction (sôrs ri duk′ shən) generating less waste (p. 379)

Southern Hemisphere (suth′ ərn hem′ ə sfir) the parts of the world south of the equator (p. 63)

Speciation (spē shē ā′ shən) the evolution of a new species (p. 138)

Species (spē′ shēz) a group of organisms that can breed with each other (p. 9)

Species diversity (spē′ shēz də vėr′ sə tē) the diversity of species on Earth (p. 124)

Specimen (spes′ ə mən) an example of a species (p. 129)

Spiritual (spir′ ə chü əl) having to do with religion or the soul (p. 152)

Spiritual view (spir′ ə chü əl vyü) the opinion that it is important to protect biodiversity because all species have a purpose for living (p. 456)

Sprawl (sprôl) low-density, unplanned suburban development (p. 481)

Sprinkler system (spring′ klər sis′ təm) a device used to spray water, usually in a circular pattern (p. 302)

Stabilize (stā′ bə līz) to remain the same (p. 222)

Standard of living (stan′ dərd ov liv′ ing) the way of living that is usual for a person, community, or country (p. 222)

Standing-water ecosystem (stan′ ding wó′ tər e′ kō sis təm) a body of freshwater surrounded by land that does not have flowing water (p. 203)

Staple crop (stā′ pəl krop) a crop that is a basic part of many people's diets (p. 150)

Starve (stärv) to die because of hunger (p. 224)

Stratosphere (strat′ ə sfir) the layer of the atmosphere above the troposphere (p. 52)

Strip mining (strip mīn′ ing) a form of mining in which the surface layer of rock is removed (p. 257)

Subatomic particle (sub e tom′ ik pär′ tə kəl) a proton, neutron, or electron (p. 261)

Subjective (səb jek′ tiv) influenced by personal feelings or opinions (p. 33)

Subsistence agriculture (səb sis′ təns ag′ rə kul chər) growing just enough food to meet immediate local needs (p. 223)

Suburb (sub′ ėrb) a community that surrounds a city (p. 481)

Succession (sək sesh′ ən) the process of ecological change in a community over time (p. 112)

Sulfur oxide (sul′ fər ok′ sīd) a pollutant produced by burning fossil fuels (p. 256)

Surface water (sėr′ fis wó′ tər) water that is visible on the surface of the earth (p. 294)

Sustainable agriculture (sə stān′ ə ble ag′ rə kul chər) ways of producing food for current generations that do not deprive future generations (p. 413)

Sustainable community (sə stān′ ə ble kə myü′ nə tē) a community built around the idea of sustainability (p. 481)

Sustainable global economy (sə stān′ ə ble glō′ bəl i kon′ ə mē) an economy that contributes to the sustainability of the earth (p. 479)

Sustainable society (sə stān′ ə ble sə sī′ ə tē) a society where current needs are met while preserving natural resources and systems for future generations (p. 19)

Sustainably harvested (sə stān′ ə blē här′ vist id) harvested in a way that does not damage an ecosystem (p. 238)

Symbiosis (sim bē ō sis) a close relationship between two species (p. 145)

Synthetic (sin′ thet ik) human-made; not natural (p. 361)

T

Taiga (tī ga) another name for a coniferous forest (p. 179)

Tailings (tā′ lingz) debris produced by mining (p. 263)

Taxonomy (tak son′ ə mē) a branch of science that deals with classifying species (p. 129)

Temperate deciduous forest (tem′ pər it di sij′ ü əs fôr′ ist) a deciduous forest that grows in temperate regions of the world (p. 177)

Temperate grassland (tem′ pər it gras′ land) a grassland biome found in temperate areas of the world; also called steppes, pampas, veldts, and prairies (p. 184)

Temperate rain forest (tem′ pər it rān fôr′ ist) a forest found in a temperate zone that receives large amounts of rain (p. 173)

Tentacle (ten′ tə kəl) an armlike body part used to capture food (p. 145)

Terrestrial (tə res′ trē əl) living or growing on land (p. 164)

Tertiary consumer (tėr′ shē er ē kən sü′ mər) a carnivore or omnivore that feeds on other consumers (p. 98)

Theory (thē′ ə rē) a well-tested hypothesis that explains many scientific observations (p. 32)

Thermal pollution (thėr′ məl pə lü′ shən) heat added to water by humans that causes ecological changes (p. 312)

Thermosphere (thėr′ mə sfir) the layer of the atmosphere above the mesosphere (p. 52)

Tide (tīd) the regular rise and fall of the ocean's surface due to the gravity of the sun and moon (p. 274)

Till (til) to plow up the soil (p. 402)

Topsoil (top′ soil) the top, fertile layer of soil (p. 185)

Toxic (tok′ sik) poisonous (p. 45)

Toxic waste (tok′ sik wāst) waste that is poisonous to living things (p. 228)

Trait (trāt) an inherited characteristic of an organism (p. 125)

Transform (tran sfòrm′) to change from one form to another (p. 251)

Transpiration (tran spi′ rā shən) the movement of water from inside a plant through its pores and into the atmosphere (p. 56)

Transport (tran spôrt′) to move from one place to another (p. 253)

Trawl net (trôl net) a net dragged through the ocean (p. 420)

Trophic level (trō fik lev′ əl) a link in a food chain (p. 98)

Tropical rain forest (trop′ ə kəl rān fòr′ ist) a forest that grows in tropical regions and receives a large amount of rain (p. 173)

Tropics (trop′ iks) areas of land near the equator (p. 62)

Troposphere (trop′ ə sfir) the layer of the atmosphere people live and breathe in (p. 52)

Tundra (tun′ drə) a treeless plain that stays frozen most of the year and receives very little precipitation (p. 191)

Tunnel mining (tun′ l mīn′ ing) a form of coal mining in which "rooms" of coal are extracted; also called pit mining (p. 257)

Turbine (tėr′ bən) a device with blades that can be turned by steam, water, or wind (p. 255)

U

Ultraviolet radiation (ul trə vī′ ə lit rā dē ā′ shən) high-energy radiation from the sun (p. 53)

Understory (un′ dər stòr ē) the forest layer beneath the canopy (p. 175)

Upstream (up′ strēm) in the opposite direction of the way that water is flowing in a stream or river (p. 273)

Uranium (yü rā′ nē əm) a radioactive element used in nuclear fission (p. 262)

Uranium mill (yü rā′ nē əm mil) a place where uranium is processed for use in nuclear fission (p. 263)

Urban (er′ bən) inside a city (p. 152)

Urban growth boundary (er′ bən grōth boun′ dər ē) a line around a city past which new development cannot occur (p. 482)

Urban heat island effect (er′ bən hēt ī′ lənd ə fekt′) increased temperatures in urban areas caused by human development and activity (p. 337)

Utilitarian view (yü til ə târ′ ē ən vyü) the opinion that it is important to protect biodiversity for the products it provides (p. 456)

Utility (yü til′ ət ē) a company that performs a public service (p. 253)

V

Value (val′ yü) what is important to a person (p. 21)

Vapor (vā′ pər) water or other materials in the form of a gas (p. 51)

Variable (ver′ ē ə bəl) what is tested in an experiment (p. 26)

Vegetation (vej ə tā′ shən) the plant life found in an area (p. 166)

Vent (vent) an opening in the earth that lets out gases and other materials (p. 45)

Ventilation (ven tl ā′ shən) a means of supplying fresh air (p. 263)

Vertical zone (vėr′ tə kəl zōn) an ocean zone classified by water depth (p. 198)

Vibration (vī brā′ shən) movement back and forth (p. 251)

Virus (vī′ rəs) a nonliving microorganism that can infect cells and cause disease (p. 310)

Vitamin C (vī′ tə mən sē) a vitamin that supports health and growth (p. 407)

W

Warning coloration (wôr′ ning kul ə rā′ shən) the bright colors or patterns on animals that scare off predators (p. 108)

Waste stream (wāst strēm) the creation, collection, and disposal of waste (p. 360)

Water cycle (wȯ′ tər sī′ kəl) the movement of water between the atmosphere and the earth's surface (p. 55)

Water table (wȯ′ tər tā′ bəl) the top of the groundwater layer (p. 296)

Water treatment (wȯ′ tər trēt′ mənt) the process of removing contaminants from water to make it safe for humans (p. 301)

Waterlogged (wȯ′ tər lògd) saturated with water (p. 206)

Watershed (wȯ′ tər shed) an area of land from which precipitation drains into a particular river, stream, or lake (p. 295)

Weather (weᴛʜ′ ər) the moment-by-moment conditions in the atmosphere (p. 62)

Weathering (weᴛʜ′ ər ing) the process by which bedrock is broken down into small particles (p. 399)

a	hat	e	let	ī	ice	ȯ	order	u̇	put	sh	she	ə	a	in about
ā	age	ē	equal	o	hot	oi	oil	ü	rule	th	thin		e	in taken
ä	far	èr	term	ō	open	ou	out	ch	child	ᴛʜ	then		i	in pencil
â	care	i	it	ȯ	saw	u	cup	ng	long	zh	measure		o	in lemon
													u	in circus

Well (wel) a hole that is dug or drilled to get water from the earth (p. 297)

Wet deposition (wet dep ə zish´ ən) acid pollutants that reach the earth in precipitation (p. 342)

Wetland (wet´ land) a low area that is saturated with water (p. 200)

Wildlife corridor (wīld´ līf kôr´ ə dər) an area of trees, shrubs, and other vegetation that provides cover and habitat for wildlife between isolated patches of habitat (p. 441)

Wildlife trade (wīld´ līf trād) the buying or selling of wildlife or wildlife products (p. 435)

Wind farm (wind färm) an area with many connected groups of wind turbines (p. 274)

Wind turbine (wind tėr´ bən) a tower with moving blades that converts wind movement into energy (p. 274)

World food supply (wėrld füd sə plī´) the amount of food available for the world's population (p. 406)

World population (wėrld pop yə lā´ shən) the total number of people on Earth (p. 216)

X

Xeriscaping (zēr´ i skāp ing) a type of landscaping that uses native and drought-tolerant plants (p. 318)

Z

Zooplankton (zō ō plangk´ tən) microscopic animals that float freely in the water (p. 198)

Index

Uranium
  defined, 262
  mill defined, 263
  mining, 263
  and radon gas, 330
Urban defined, 152
Urban growth boundary
  defined, 482
Urban heat island effect,
  337
Utilitarian view defined,
  456
Utility
  companies in waste
    conversion, 287
  defined, 253

Photo and Illustration Credits

Cover photos: first/top layer, © Royalty-free/Photodisc/Getty Images; second layer, © Royalty-free/Hans Wolf/Photodisc Green/Getty Images; third layer, © Royalty-free/Photodisc/Getty Images; fourth layer, © Royalty-free/Photodisc/Getty Images; fifth layer, © Royalty-free/Russell Illig/Photodisc Green/Getty Images; p. iii, © Royalty-free/Shutterstock; p. vii, © Royalty-free/Shutterstock; p. viii: upper left image, © Royalty-free/Shutterstock; upper right image, © Royalty-free/Shutterstock; lower left image, © Royalty-free/Shutterstock; lower right image, © Royalty-free/Shutterstock; center image, © Royalty-free/Shutterstock; p. xxii, © Royalty-free/Shutterstock; p. 5: top, © Eric Feferberg/AFP/Getty Images; bottom, © WWF; p. 28, © Royalty-free/Shutterstock; p. 34, © Royalty-free/Shutterstock; p. 37, © Gabe Palmer/Corbis; p. 42, © Royalty-free/Shutterstock; p. 46, © B. Murton/Southampton Oceanography Centre/Photo Researchers, Inc.; p. 66, © Royalty-free/Shutterstock; p. 71, © Corbis; p. 75, © Jeremy Woodhouse/Masterfile; p. 80, © Royalty-free/Shutterstock; p. 94, © Joe Sohm/The Image Works, Inc.; p. 100, © Robert Brenner/PhotoEdit; p. 107, © Bill Beatty/Visuals Unlimited; p. 117, © John Lamb/Stone/Getty Images; p. 122, © Royalty-free/Shutterstock; p. 130, © Bruce Rasner/Rotman/Nature Picture Library; p. 131, © Pascal Goetgheluck/Science Photo Library/Photo Researchers, Inc.; p. 132, © Royalty-free/Shutterstock; p. 137, © Reuters/Corbis; p. 145, © C & M Denis-Huot/Peter Arnold, Inc.; p. 157, © Kevin Schafer/Photographer's Choice/Getty Images; p. 162, © Royalty-free/Shutterstock; p. 179, © Jeff Greenberg/The Image Works, Inc.; p. 181, © Syracuse Newspapers/The Image Works, Inc.; p. 193, © Wolfgang Kaehler/Corbis; p. 209, © Aldo Brando/Stone/Getty Images; p. 214, © Royalty-free/Shutterstock; p. 217, © Royalty-free/PhotoDisc; p. 224, © Richard Levine/Alamy Images; p. 230, © Dr. William J. Weber/Visuals Unlimited; p. 238, © Royalty-free/Shutterstock; p. 243, © Royalty-free/PhotoDisc; p. 248, © Royalty-free/Shutterstock; p. 250, © Royalty-free/Shutterstock; p. 258, © Phototake Inc./Alamy Images; p. 262, © Hoa Qui/Index Stock Imagery; p. 287, © AP/Wide World Photos; p. 292, © Royalty-free/Shutterstock; p. 303, © John Burke/Index Stock Imagery; p. 310, © Royalty-free/Shutterstock; p. 317, © Jack Clark/AgStock U.S.A.; p. 319, © Royalty-free/Shutterstock; p. 321, © Steve Allen/Brand X Pictures/JupiterImages; p. 326, © Royalty-free/Shutterstock; p. 330, © Blair Seitz/Science Photo Library/Photo Researchers, Inc.; p. 344, © Royalty-free/Shutterstock; p. 347, © Richard H Smith/Taxi/Getty Images; p. 350, © Royalty-free/Shutterstock; p. 351, © Jim Reed/Photo Researchers, Inc.; p. 358, © Royalty-free/Shutterstock; p. 373, © Royalty-free/Shutterstock; p. 376, © Galen Rowell/Corbis; p. 381, © Frank Pedrick/The Image Works, Inc.; p. 383, © Royalty-free/Shutterstock; p. 387, © Inga Spence/Visuals Unlimited; p. 392, © Royalty-free/Shutterstock; p. 408, © Maximilian Stock Ltd/Anthony Blake Photo Library; p. 416, © Anthony Boccaccio/The Image Bank/Getty Images; p. 419, © Royalty-free/Shutterstock; p. 422, © Royalty-free/Shutterstock; p. 425, © Vanessa Vick/Photo Researchers, Inc.; p. 430, © Royalty-free/Shutterstock; p. 440, © Topham/The Image Works, Inc.; p. 446, © Royalty-free/Shutterstock; p. 447, © Royalty-free/Shutterstock; p. 454, © Royalty-free/Shutterstock; p. 457, © Jeff Greenberg/PhotoEdit; p. 460, © Royalty-free/Shutterstock; p. 465, © AP/Wide World Photos p. 470, © Royalty-free/Shutterstock; p. 472, © Royalty-free/Shutterstock; p. 478, © Royalty-free/Shutterstock; p. 483, © Royalty-free/Shutterstock; p. 484, © Jeff Haynes/AFP/Getty Images; p. 485, © image100/Alamy Images; p. 489, © Royalty-free/Shutterstock; p. 497, © Royalty-free/Shutterstock; p. 506, © Royalty-free/Shutterstock; p. 508, © Royalty-free/Shutterstock; p. 509, © Royalty-free/Shutterstock; p. 510, © Royalty-free/Shutterstock; illustrations: John Edwards Illustration